A Quarter Century of Post-Communism Assessed

M. Steven Fish • Graeme Gill • Milenko Petrovic
Editors

A Quarter Century of Post-Communism Assessed

palgrave
macmillan

Editors
M. Steven Fish
University of California
Berkeley, CA, USA

Graeme Gill
University of Sydney
Sydney, Australia

Milenko Petrovic
University of Canterbury
Christchurch, New Zealand

ISBN 978-3-319-82824-4 ISBN 978-3-319-43437-7 (eBook)
DOI 10.1007/978-3-319-43437-7

Printed on acid-free paper

This Palgrave Macmillan imprint is published by Springer Nature
The registered company is Springer International Publishing AG
The registered company address is: Gewerbestrasse 11, 6330 Cham, Switzerland

Contents

Introduction 1
M. Steven Fish, Graeme Gill and Milenko Petrovic

Part I General Trends and Regional Patterns

Chapter 1: What Has a Quarter Century of Post-Communism Taught Us About the Correlates of Democracy? 11
M. Steven Fish

Chapter 2: Post-Communist Transition Under the Umbrella of Uneven EUropeanisation: East Central Europe, the Baltic States and the Balkans 41
Milenko Petrovic

Chapter 3: Trajectories of Political Development in the Post-Soviet States 75
Graeme Gill

Chapter 4: Curbing Post-Communist Corruption: External Pressure vs. Domestic Commitment 99
Leslie Holmes

Part II Central and Eastern Europe

Chapter 5: The V4 Countries and the EU: A Comparative Perspective 129
Vladimir Baláž, Katarina Karasová and Allan M. Williams

Chapter 6: Constitutional Identity? The Hungarian Model of Illiberal Democracy 161
András L. Pap

Chapter 7: Establishing the Rule of Law in Kosovo and Bosnia and Herzegovina: The Contribution of the EU Civilian Missions 187
Efstathios T. Fakiolas and Nikolaos Tzifakis

Chapter 8: Old Paradigms of Ethnicity and Post-Soviet Transition in the Baltic States 217
Šarūnas Liekis

Part III Ukraine, Russia and Kazakhstan

Chapter 9: Ukraine's Democratisation Path Post-Orange Revolution: Examining the Internal and External Impediments to Successful Democratic Reform in Ukraine 247
Nicholas Ross Smith

Chapter 10: Post-Communist Russia and the West: From Crisis to Crisis? 271
James Headley

Chapter 11: Russia's Security-Related Decision-Making: The Case of Crimea 295
Stephen Fortescue

Chapter 12: Kazakhstan and the Eurasian Economic Union: The Dilemmas of Alliance-Making in the Post-Soviet Period 319
Kirill Nourzhanov

Index 345

List of Figures

Fig. 1.1	Economic development and democracy, aggregate for 1992–2012	17
Fig. 1.2	Economic development and democracy, 2012	18
Fig. 1.3	Fuel income and democracy, 1992–2012	20
Fig. 1.4	Geographical location and democracy, 2012	25
Fig. 1.5	Proportion of population adhering to Western Christianity and democracy, 2012	27
Fig. 1.6	Proportion of the population adhering to Islam and democracy, 2012	28
Fig. 1.7	Proportion of the population adhering to Orthodox Christianity and democracy, 2012	28
Fig. 5.1	Exports of goods and services in the V4 countries and southern EU member Countries, as % GDP. *Source*: UNCTAD (2015b): *Goods and services (BPM5): Trade openness indicators, annual, 1980–2014, International Trade in Goods and Services, online database*	132
Fig. 5.2	The share of the EU15 in exports of goods and services from the V4 countries and southern EU Member Countries, in %. *Source*: UNCTAD (2015b): *International Trade in Goods and Service in 1995–2014, online database*	134
Fig. 5.3	Outflows over 4000 nationals from each country in 1997–2004 (left) and 2005–2013 (right). Country size reflects stocks of the foreign born population from the top partner countries. *Sources*: Eurostat (2015d): *International Migration* and authors' own computations	151
Fig. 9.1	Ukraine's nations in transit ratings 2003–2015	250
Fig. 9.2	Ukraine's Transformation Index ratings 2003–2014	251

List of Tables

Table 1.1	Regressions of extent of regime outcomes on hypothesized determinants	15
Table 1.2	Observed and predicted democracy scores by country, 2008	33
Table 2.1	Growth in real GDP and foreign direct investment (FDI) inflow in East European states	46
Table 2.2	Indicators of post-communist democratisation and marketisation and foreign direct investment inflow in East European states, 1999–2014	51
Table 2.3	Progress in EU accession	54
Table 3.1	Political trajectories of former Soviet republics	76
Table 4.1	CPI (perceptions-based) corruption scores 1997–2015	102
Table 4.2	GCB (bribery experience) percentages 2004–2013	103
Table 4.3	The most problematic factors for doing business: ranking of corruption	104
Table 4.4	Diversion of public funds	105
Table 4.5	Irregular payments and bribes	106
Table 4.6	Favouritism in decisions of government officials	107
Table 4.7	Enterprise perceptions and experiences of corruption	108
Table 4.8	Type of political system	117
Table 4.9	CPI (perceptions-based) scores in other post-communist EU member-states 1997–2015	118
Table 5.1	Economic development in the V4 countries and southern EU members in 1980–2014	131
Table 5.2	Domestic and foreign industry value added: share in gross exports in 2011 (%)	137

Table 5.3 Population by educational attainment level, sex and age (%) for the age group 24–35, in 2004 and 2014 140
Table 5.4 Average annual net FDI flows in the V4 countries and southern EU members in 1993–2013 143
Table 5.5 Selected indicators of the V4 and southern EU member countries in research and innovation 147
Table 5.6 Stock of foreign nationals in selected EU countries (period averages) 150
Table 8.1 Ethnic composition of the Baltic States (in thousands) 223
Table 11.1 Permanent members of the Russian Security Council at the time of the events in Crimea 303
Table 12.1 Public attitude towards the common market (CU + SES) in Belarus, Kazakhstan and Russia 328

Introduction

M. Steven Fish, Graeme Gill and Milenko Petrovic

During the quarter century following the collapse of communist regimes in Eastern Europe and Eurasia, the successor states have followed a wide diversity of development paths. While some countries have largely fulfilled the hopes that accompanied the communist demise, other countries have fallen far short. Some have become full-blown democracies, while others are still struggling to implement transitional reforms or have merely exchanged the Soviet-type dictatorship for another form of harsh authoritarianism. Some countries have followed dramatically different paths of economic reform as well. Some have embraced rapid, thoroughgoing reform, while policy change in others has been halting and uncertain. Patterns of economic development have varied as well. Some countries have traveled a long way toward convergence with their Western neighbors, experiencing substantial and steady growth of output and marked improvement in infrastructure. Other countries have posted less impressive gains.

Without attempting to provide a unique explanation for cross-national and cross-regional post-communist trajectories, the authors contributing to

G. Gill (✉)
Department of Government and International Relations,
University of Sydney, Sydney, Australia
e-mail: graeme.gill@sydney.edu.au

Fish, Gill, Petrovic (eds.), *A Quarter Century of Post-Communism Assessed*, DOI 10.1007/978-3-319-43437-7_1

this volume discuss the circumstances and factors that have led to the democratization and robust marketization of some post-communist states and not others. Apart from a continuous increase of authoritarianism in most non-Baltic post-Soviet states since the mid-1990s (which in recent years appears also to have spread to some European post-communist states that have for long been considered well-consolidated democracies),[1] the only common pattern identified has been that those post-communist states that were able to tie their reforms to the EU's conditional offer of membership were transformed more successfully than those that could not.

Bunce et al. (2010)[2] identified "three waves of democratic change" in this enormously heterogeneous region[3]: The first wave encompasses the initial democratization of all the ex-communist states during 1989–1992, and the second wave refers to democratization (of some of these states) "associated with accession to the European Union" (Bunce et al. 2010, p. viii). It is more difficult to see the specific outcomes of the third wave (unless they are again "associated with accession" to the EU). The third wave is meant to refer to the "second democratisation" of most of the post-communist Balkan states, which occurred between November 1996 and October 2000: Slovakia's parliamentary election held in September 1998 and the "colour revolutions" in Georgia of November 2003, in Ukraine of November 2004–January 2005, and in Kyrgyzstan of February–April 2005, all of which removed from power post-communist authoritarian leaders. While there were some positive developments in Ukraine and Georgia in the first few years after their revolutions and even some significant lasting improvements regarding the fight against corruption in Georgia (see Leslie Holmes' chapter in this volume), democracy in both of these countries is still very "shaky" (see Graeme Gill's and Nicolas Smith's contributions in this volume), and Kyrgyzstan remains closer to autocracy than to democracy.[4] As was the case after the initial democratization in the early 1990s (after the "first wave"), the lasting gains and significant improvements from the "third wave" of democratization of post-communist states have only been felt by those countries that were able to tie their reforms to accession to the EU, and these were the Balkan states – first Bulgaria and Romania – and then the so-called Western Balkan countries, particularly Croatia, Serbia, and Montenegro (see Chap. 2 in this volume for more detail).

The above-defined commonalities and differences among the countries of post-communist Eastern Europe and Eurasia are reflected in the organizational structure of this book. The book is divided into three parts. In the first part, the authors of Chaps. 1–4 provide analyses and a general assessment of the achievements of post-communist transition(s) in the post-communist world and in particular groups of countries, and offer both agent-driven and structure-driven explanations of the trajectory of regime change. In the latter two parts, the chapters take up particular aspects of the transition process, including institution building and foreign policy making, rather than surveying the general path of development adopted by particular states.

Part I begins with Steven Fish's quantitative analysis of the role of structural factors in shaping different regime outcomes in thirty post-communist Eurasian states. Fish finds that the structural conditions have powerfully shaped regime outcomes in the region. Still, he concludes that "structure is not fate. Factors other than the big background conditions examined here might shape outcomes" (p. 37). Milenko Petrovic and Graeme Gill then focus on the role of other factors in Chaps. 2 and 3 respectively. In their respective examinations of the different pathways of the East European and Baltic states and the non-Baltic post-Soviet states, they do not deny the importance of some historical legacies (particularly those related to the link between pre-communist socioeconomic backwardness and the effects of communist industrialization and urbanization) in setting the general and sometimes different conditions in which the initial replacement of the communist regimes occurred. However, Petrovic and Gill primarily look for the reasons behind the different post-communist trajectories in the different constellations and work of political agents. Among these are the balance of power between reformers (or "democrats") and anti-reformers (or "authoritarians") on the domestic political scene, as well as the role of external actors in providing (or discouraging) foreign support and assistance for democratization and economic reform. Petrovic explains the less successful post-communist transition in the Balkan states (when compared to the countries in East Central Europe and the Baltics) as primarily the result of political decisions made by the non-reformist Balkan political elites in the early 1990s and EU leaders in the mid-2000s, both of which resulted in a much smaller amount of EU support and assistance for reform to these states. Gill explains the survival and subsequent increase in authoritarianism in most of the non-Baltic post-Soviet states as an outcome of the political forces that structured the regime change in the first place, with a democratic outcome being more likely when civil society forces played a major role in shaping the shift from authoritarian rule.

A similar conclusion about the role of agent-driven actions for the success of post-communist transition can be drawn from Leslie Holmes' chapter, which concludes the first part of this book by comparing general and specific types of corruption in four post-communist states. These states are in different regions, and have different structural predispositions and levels of democratization. When compared to Russia as well as Bulgaria and Romania, which were both admitted to the EU in 2007 and are generally acknowledged as having more/better consolidated democracies with better general democracy scores, Holmes finds Georgia to be the least corrupt by far. Owing to the strong commitment of President Saakashvili and his radical policies, Georgia has not only achieved a better result than countries, such as Russia, Bulgaria, and Romania, but also by 2015 had reached a score of 52 in Transparency International's Corruption Perception Index, which placed it close to or even better than many other EU member states in that year. In 2015 Spain had a score of 58; Latvia a score of 55; and Hungary, Slovakia, and Croatia a score of 51. Greece, Romania, Italy, and Bulgaria had significantly worse scores of 46, 46, 44, and 41, respectively.

Part II comprises four chapters that look at the experience with various aspects of post-communist political and economic transition of particular countries, which were able to tie their transition to accession to the EU. In Chap. 5 Vladimir Baláž, Katarina Karasová, and Allan Williams compare challenges and achievements of the economic integration of the four Visegrad group (V4) countries (Poland, Hungary, the Czech Republic, and Slovakia) into the EU with the experiences of Greece, Spain, and Portugal two decades earlier. They conclude that although the V4 countries started their convergence with the incumbent EU members from considerably lower levels of GDP per capita than the three southern entrants, the V4 countries have achieved higher growth rates than those southern countries; their integration is generally considered a success story in the history of EU enlargement. In Chap. 6, András Pap discusses the characteristics of the emerging model of "Hungarian illiberal democracy" and explains how it happened: the country that once led the post-communist world in liberal-democratic reforms democratically opted for Orban's authoritarianism 25 years later. In Chap. 7, Efstathios T. Fakiolas and Nikolaos Tzifakis examine the efforts and mixed results of the EU civilian missions deployed in Bosnia and Herzegovina (European Union Policy Mission (EUPM)) and Kosovo (European Union Rule of Law (EULEX)) to advance the consolidation of state-building and the establishment of the rule of law. They argue that despite serious problems and obstacles, the two missions have proven able to smoothly work to the benefit of their operational objectives whenever they have stayed in tune with local interests and coordinated their practices with other EU policies active in the region. Part II concludes with Sarunas Laikis' discussion of the peculiarities of the post-communist transition in the Baltic states. He focuses on the similarities and differences between interethnic relations and government ethnic policies, and argues that while these did not affect successful post-communist transition, they did affect their relations with their powerful neighbor Russia.

Part III focuses on three countries whose paths of development have not been tied to EU accession, although one of them (Ukraine) does harbor such aspirations. In Chap. 9, Nicholas Smith examines the internal and external impediments to democracy experienced by Ukraine following the Orange Revolution. He focuses particularly upon one internal and one external impediment. The internal obstacle is the oligarchization of power. The external problem is Ukraine's geopolitical location, which leaves it cross-pressured by the EU, which urges democratization, and Russia, which encourages autocracy. Smith concludes that were the EU to offer Ukraine a clear path to membership, Europe's democracy promotion efforts in that country would be strengthened. In Chap. 10, James Headley charts the way in which Russia's relations with the West have lurched from crisis to crisis, beginning with Bosnia in 1994 and going through to Syria in 2013. He argues that in this trajectory, Russian policy has been fairly consistent. Russia has become more assertive, but this is partly due to the way Western states have consistently sought to downplay and ignore Russia's role in international affairs. In Chap. 11, Stephen Fortescue analyzes the process of decision-making in Russia as revealed by the decision to annex Crimea. Although the evidence for understanding governmental decision-making in any system is usually difficult to get and often contradictory in what it suggests, Fortescue makes a strong case that the decision to take Crimea was taken by a small group around Putin. This conclusion is important not only for what it tells us about the specific decision on Crimea, but also for what it implies for the institutional development of the Russian political system. In Chap. 12, Kirill Nourzhanov charts Kazakhstan's attitude to the Eurasian Economic Union (EEU). He argues that the country's accession to the EEU does not represent a divergence from an independent foreign policy, but is a pragmatic response to its understanding of its place in the world. And far from losing the capacity for independent action, it remains an active, independent middle power.

The chapters in this book highlight the diversity that now characterizes the countries of former communist Eastern Europe and Eurasia. The region constitutes an ideal laboratory for social science research. Given the similarities in the starting points of each of these countries at the time of the collapse of communism, explaining the diversity of outcomes should keep scholars busy for some time to come.

Notes

1. This is particularly the case for Hungary (which is also discussed in Chap. 6 of this volume) and to a lesser extent for Slovakia and some Western Balkan states. It coincides with a recently increasing impression that authoritarianism is increasing globally. Hence, the *Journal of Democracy* has devoted two of its issues in 2015 to this topic: *The Authoritarian Resurgence* (vol. 26, No. 2, April 2015) and *Authoritarianism Goes Globally* (Vol. 26, No. 4, October 2015) while the last issue of Freedom House's Nations in Transit of June 2015 is entitled *Democracy on the Defensive in Europe and Eurasia.*
2. Bunce, V., McFaul, M., Stoner-Weiss, K. (Eds.) (2010). *Democracy and authoritarianism in the post-communist world.* Cambridge: Cambridge University Press.
3. Whose "countries are united by their common recent history of a particular form of authoritarian regime and little else," Steven Fish, in this volume, p. 36)
4. See data in Tables 1.2 and 3.1 in this volume as well as Freedom House Nation in Transit's 2015 democracy scores, according to which this country is considered a "semi-consolidated authoritarian regime."

M. Steven Fish is Professor of Political Science at the University of California-Berkeley. He has published six authored or co-authored books and numerous journal articles and book chapters on democracy and regime change in developing and post-communist countries, religion and politics, and constitutional systems and national legislatures. His book *Are Muslims Distinctive? A Look at the Evidence* (Oxford, 2011) was selected for *Choice*'s Outstanding Academic Titles, 2012: Top 25 Books.

Graeme Gill is Professor Emeritus of Government and Public Administration at the University of Sydney and a Fellow of the Academy of Social Sciences in Australia. He has been President of the International Council for Central and East European Studies (ICCEES) from 2010 to 2015. In addition to several co-authored and edited volumes, he has published twelve authored books on various aspects of Soviet and Russian politics. The most recent is *Building an Authoritarian Polity. Russia in Post-Soviet Times* (Cambridge, 2016)

Dr Milenko Petrovic is Senior Lecturer Above the Bar at the National Centre for Research on Europe and at the Department of Global, Cultural and Language Studies, University of Canterbury, New Zealand. He is the author of *The Democratic Transition of Post-Communist Europe – in the Shadow of Communist Differences and an Uneven Europeanisation* (Palgrave Macmillan, 2013) and the author/co-editor of two other volumes and numerous journal articles and shorter contributions on comparative politics, post-communist transition and EU enlargement.

PART I

General Trends and Regional Patterns

Chapter 1: What Has a Quarter Century of Post-Communism Taught Us About the Correlates of Democracy?

M. Steven Fish

The post-communist region furnishes students of democratization with a fertile field for investigation. Countries of the region span almost the entire spectrum of possible outcomes in terms of political regimes. Three decades ago, all of Eurasia and Eastern Europe slumbered in a hyperauthoritarian deep freeze. Now the region includes some of the world's most open polities (e.g. Estonia) and some of its most closed (e.g. Uzbekistan), as well as everything in between.

The region's countries also differ widely in terms of conditions that might influence trajectories of regime change. While post-communist space is geographically contiguous, creating the appearance of a real region, the only thing that unifies it is a recent history of a particular type of authoritarian regime. Only the nature of the antecedent authoritarian regime and the timing of its collapse are "controlled for"; everything else varies. Deeper historical and cultural commonalities are largely absent. Latin Americanists who wish to study the effects of religion on paths of regime change (or anything else) must foray outside their area, since Catholicism predominates in every major country in Latin America. The same may be said about Islam in the Middle

M.S. Fish (✉)
University of California, Berkeley, CA, USA
e-mail: sfish@berkeley.edu

Fish, Gill, Petrovic (eds.), *A Quarter Century of Post-Communism Assessed*, DOI 10.1007/978-3-319-43437-7_2

East and North Africa (MENA). The post-communist region is different. Not only do countries diverge in terms of religion, but also on other potential causal variables that might influence political regime type, such as level of economic development and geographical proximity to democracies outside the region.

Thus, countries in post-communist space exhibit variation in both outcomes and predictors of political regime, which facilitates fruitful cross-national, within-region analysis aimed at uncovering the correlates of democratization.

Numerous studies have investigated regime outcomes in the region. There is no consensus on the formula for success or failure of transition; scholars differ over even whether structural variables or more proximate factors that are the product of human design and action serve as the main drivers of regime outcomes (e.g. Møller 2009; Petrovic 2013; Pop-Eleches 2007).

The available data do not allow us to make strong statements about causation. I aim only to offer observations and raise questions about how the first quarter century of post-communism might help inform our thinking about democratization.

Structural Explanations for Regime Outcomes

Data

What does the post-communist experience tell us about the conditions that promote or inhibit democratization? Here I examine four of the structural conditions that have long been at the center of analyses on the determinants of political regime around the world: level of economic development, economic dependence on hydrocarbons, geographical location, and religious tradition. Countries in the region exhibit wide variation on each of these variables.

The observations in the analysis are country years for all 30 post-communist countries. The years covered are 1992 to 2012, which is the last year for which the data are available. Countries are added to the dataset as they become independent. Thus, data begin for Slovakia in 1993, for Montenegro in 2006, and for Kosovo in 2008.

The dependent variable is level of democracy. It is measured using the "Electoral Democracy Index" recently released by the Varieties of Democracy (V-Dem) project, which furnishes data on a multitude of political variables for most countries in the world on a yearly basis between 1900 and 2012 (V-Dem 2016). The values of the dependent variable range from 0 to 1.

The first independent variable is gross domestic product (GDP) per capita, which indicates level of economic development. Data for this variable are drawn from the V-Dem dataset. We would expect greater wealth to create more propitious conditions for open politics. Over the five decades since Seymour Martin Lipset offered his now-celebrated theory linking wealth to democracy, a host of studies have addressed the matter. Many of them have refined Lipset's formulation and some have qualified it, but the bulk of studies find that countries that enjoy higher levels of economic development have better chances for having democracy (Lipset 1981; Diamond 1992).

The second independent variable is petroleum, natural gas, and coal production per capita, which indicates countries' economic reliance on fuels. Data for this variable are also drawn from the V-Dem dataset. Numerous works in political science and economics have found a negative correlation between oil and open politics, suggesting that countries with economies based on fossil fuels face special challenges in democratization (Ross 2013; Fish 2005).

The third independent variable is the distance between a country's capital city and Vienna, which represents countries' proximity to the West. The literature on regime change includes works that present strong evidence for neighborhood diffusion effects in the realm of political regime. Geographical proximity to democracies may provide advantages for democratization, while location in a neighborhood full of authoritarian regimes might make democratization harder (Brinks and Coppedge 2006). In the post-communist region, nearness to what might be regarded as the world region that is friendliest to democracy, Western Europe, may be of particular importance (Kopstein and Reilly 2000). Distance from Vienna is as good a measure as any of proximity to Western Europe.

The fourth independent variable is the proportion of a country's population made up of adherents of the major religions. These data are taken from the Association of Religion Data Archives. Many analysts have regarded certain religious traditions as more likely than others to produce cultural and social norms that are conducive to democracy. Generally speaking, Western Christian traditions, meaning Catholicism and Protestantism, are seen as holding advantages, while Christian Orthodoxy is regarded as less favorable to democracy (Huntington 1991; Hofmann 2011). Islam is sometimes regarded as posing particularly difficult challenges, and some studies based on global cross-national data have shown that predominantly Muslim societies lag on democratization (Fish 2011). Adherents of all of these traditions are present in large numbers in the post-communist region. A fourth tradition, Buddhism, predominates in Mongolia.

Analysis of Data

What do the data from the post-communist region show about the possible effects of these structural variables on regime outcomes? Table 1.1 presents the results of ordinary least squares regressions of political regime scores on the four independent variables of interest, with robust standard errors and independent variables lagged by 2 years.

Many more specifications than the seven presented here are of course possible. With statistical analyses of this type, one must always be cautious about the dangers of presenting those models that conform to some preestablished notions held by the analyst. That is to say, we have to be wary of presenting findings that we "expect" or "want" and ignoring others. The findings presented in the seven models here are representative of the findings that we could present showing all specifications produced by alternative combinations of two or three independent variables per model (e.g. a model including only fuel income per capita and distance to Vienna); I strive to engage in no "cherry-picking."

Each of the independent variables may exert an effect. The signs are all in the expected directions; there are no counterintuitive findings. Wealth and fuels production are both statistically significant at a demanding level in all specifications and the signs are in the expected directions. Higher levels of wealth are associated with higher democracy scores; more fuels production with lower scores. Distance from Vienna is statistically significant in three of the five specifications in which it is included, including the fully specified model (model 7). The sign is negative, indicating that greater distance from the West is associated with lower democracy scores. Religious tradition appears to exert effects as well. The variables for Orthodox Christianity and Islam are statistically significant at a demanding level. The signs on the coefficients are negative, indicating that higher proportions of Orthodox Christians and higher proportions of Muslims are both correlated with lower democracy scores. While Western Christian has an expected positive coefficient and is significant in model 5, it fails to reach significance in the fully specified model.

We may be reasonably confident in the effects of level of economic development, fuels production, proportion Orthodox Christian, and proportion Muslim. Proximity to the West may exert effects, but since it is not

Table 1.1 Regressions of extent of regime outcomes on hypothesized determinants

	V-Dem index of electoral democracy						
	(1)	*(2)*	*(3)*	*(4)*	*(5)*	*(6)*	*(7)*
Constant	–0.92***	–1.05***	–0.76***	–0.46***	–0.37**	–0.15	0.58***
	(0.13)	(0.14)	(0.13)	(0.15)	(0.15)	(0.13)	(0.13)
GDP per capita (ln)	0.18***	0.20***	0.17***	0.14***	0.11***	0.10***	0.03**
	(0.01)	(0.02)	(0.02)	(0.02)	(0.02)	(0.01)	(0.01)
Fuel income per capita		–0.15***	–0.14***	–0.14***	–0.11***	–0.07***	–0.05***
		(0.01)	(0.02)	(0.01)	(0.01)	(0.01)	(0.01)
Distance to Vienna			–0.02*	–0.03***	–0.01	0.004	–0.02**
			(0.01)	(0.01)	(0.01)	(0.01)	(0.01)
Orthodox (%)				–0.15***			–0.30***
				(0.02)			(0.03)
Western Christian (%)					0.30***		–0.02
					(0.03)		(0.04)
Muslim (%)						–0.40***	–0.52***
						(0.03)	(0.03)
Observations	583	437	437	437	437	437	437
Adjusted R^2	0.25	0.41	0.42	0.46	0.51	0.59	0.72

$^{*}p < 0.1$, $^{**}p < 0.05$, $^{***}p < 0.01$

robust to all specifications, we must be more guarded about reporting its influence on regime type. Because Western Christian does not retain significance in the fully specified model, we have evidence that any influence it has on regime type is superseded by the other included variables.

The results suggest that conjecture based on conventional assumptions about the influence of economic development, oil dependence, geographical location, and predominant religious tradition would not have misled the observer. Wealthier countries have fared better than poorer ones and less fuel-dependent economies better than more fuel-dependent ones. Those that are closer to the West appear to have done better than those that are farther away. And, even according to the fully specified model, Catholic countries have done better than Orthodox countries, which have done better than Muslim countries.

The Structural Correlates of Democracy: A Closer Look

Let us take a closer look at each of the independent variables in a bivariate context. Here we are dealing only with descriptive statistics. The multivariate analyses presented above suggest that each of the structural variables under discussion might matter for regime outcomes, and also show that the magnitude of the variables' effects change with the inclusion of other variables. Taking a step back and examining the bivariate relationships in the data, however, enables us to consider more carefully what the post-communist experience might contribute to thinking about the correlates of political regime type. It also sheds light on the performance of a number of post-communist polities, highlights the possible limitations of the four independent variables of interest for understanding trajectories of post-communist regime change, and raises questions for future research on the post-communist region.

Wealth and Democracy

The post-communist experience lends weight to economic theories of democracy, but perhaps less weight than one might expect. At 0.50, the correlation is positive and substantial but not overwhelming. Development matters but does not determine outcomes alone. Figure 1.1 presents the aggregate scatter plot with all observations. The figure illustrates the positive relationship. The cluster in the upper left portion of the figure poses a particularly obvious set of outliers. Those points represent

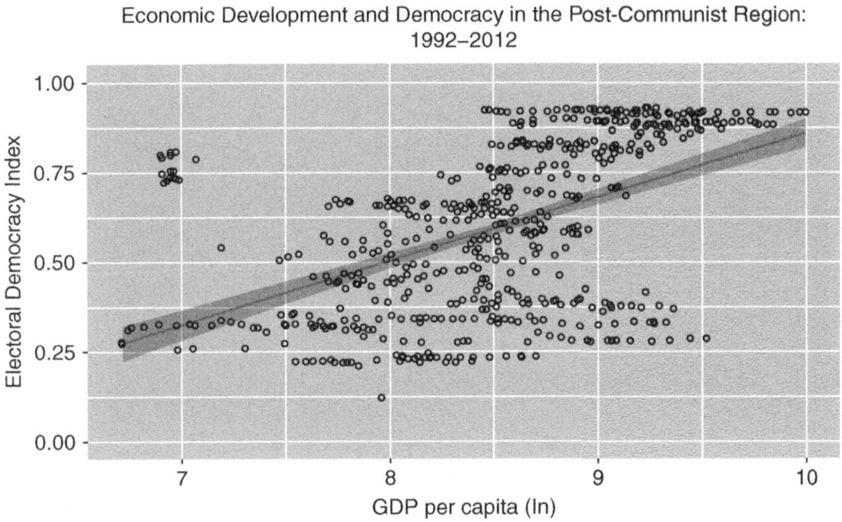

Fig. 1.1 Economic development and democracy, aggregate for 1992–2012

Mongolia's scores. Mongolia is one of the poorest countries in the region, but has nevertheless undergone dramatic, robust democratization.

In order to better identify cases, we may have a look at a scatter plot that presents data for a single year. Figure 1.2 shows data for 2012 alone, using country abbreviations to mark points. Data are missing in this year for Kosovo and Mongolia.

The underachievers are noteworthy. Many observers have been surprised to see how far Russia has gone in its reversion to autocracy. Russia was a partly open polity during the late 1980s and the 1990s, and there were good reasons to expect it to have avoided tumbling backwards. It is the home of a highly educated, largely urban population. Moscow and St. Petersburg are world-class cities. Even at its economic low in the early and mid-1990s, Russia was a middle-income country, and it has become an upper-middle income country since then. It was never naïve to think that some form of democracy could have worked in Russia after the demise of the Soviet system. If economic development were political fate, Russia would have done much better. Instead, democratization failed spectacularly despite a fairly high level of economic modernity. As its GDP per capita has risen during the current century, moreover, Russia's democracy scores have actually fallen.

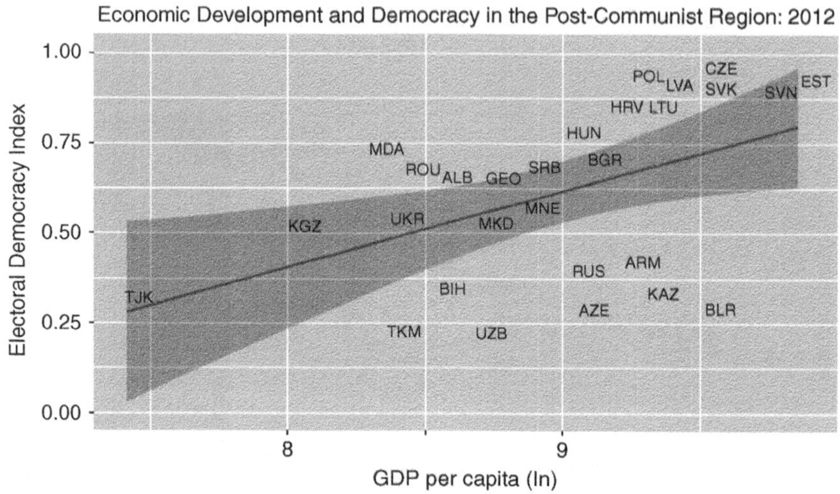

Fig. 1.2 Economic development and democracy, 2012

Russia is not alone. In the lower-right portions of the scatter plots we find several Eurasian countries. Observations that exceed a value of 9 on the independent variable in Fig. 1.1 consist of Armenia 2007–2012, Azerbaijan 2011–2012, Belarus 2006–2012, Kazakhstan 2006–2012, and Russia 2009–2012. Figure 1.2, which is based on data for 2012 alone, makes for a better visual, and each country is also found in the lower-right portion of that scatter plot. Each of these countries has done worse in terms of democratization than one would have predicted given its level of development.

If we move away from our data and go outside the post-communist region, we find many other exceptions to the rule about development and democracy. The post-communist region is not exceptional in having outliers that defy expectations. Ghana and Indonesia, like Mongolia, over-achieve in democracy for their level of development. How have they managed to achieve and sustain open politics at relatively low levels of income? Singapore and Saudi Arabia, like Russia, underachieve. Why have they failed to democratize despite prosperity? The post-communist region provides a broad spectrum of values on both the dependent variable (political regime) and the independent variable (here, level of development), and there are numerous important outliers. As such, the region's experience might help scholars plumb an important research question: When is a low level of development not an insuperable obstacle to democratization (as it has not been in Mongolia), and when is it clearly insufficient to promote democratization (as in Russia)?

Despite the richness of the literature on regime change, we still do not have good answers to that question. We might note that the realm of civil society in Mongolia is unusually rich and dense, and has been such since the early 1990s, while the opposite obtains in Russia (Fish 1995, 1998). Perhaps a muscular civil society that is capable of constraining state power and organizing and articulating popular demands may abet robust democratization. Countries that manage to generate strong civil societies even prior to thoroughgoing industrialization may sometimes be able to overcome the disadvantages of economic underdevelopment for democracy (Lussier 2016; Lussier and Fish 2012). Measuring the strength of civil society and analyzing it in a broad cross-national framework is challenging, but consideration of the possible link between the strength of civil society and democratization in poor countries is worthy of close consideration, and the post-communist experience adds a host of useful data to the global mix.

Fuels Dependence

While the correlation between economic development and democracy is positive, the association between fuels dependence and democracy is negative. The correlation of –0.31 indicates a substantial but not overpowering relationship.

The scatter plot is shown in Fig. 1.3. In the upper-left portion of the graph, we find cases of high democratization/low fuels production; in the lower-left portion of the graph, cases of low democratization/low fuels production. The large number of points stretching from top to bottom on the far left side of the graph makes for a messy visual, but indicates that at a low level of resource endowment there are many cases of full-blown democracy and full-blown autocracy, as well as everything in between.

Perhaps the most interesting part of the figure is the void in the upper-right portion. There are no instances of any country in any year with over $1500 per capita of resource income scoring as high as 0.4 on democracy. The post-communist experience would seem to lend credence to the argument found in the political science literature that oil can spoil democracy's chances. The severe underperformance in democratization of the hydrocarbon-reliant countries, Russia, Azerbaijan, Kazakhstan, and

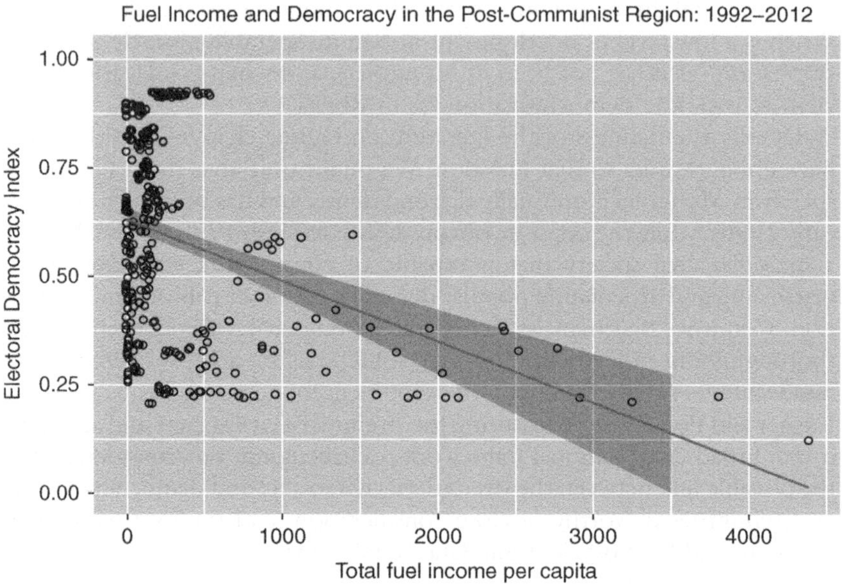

Fig. 1.3 Fuel income and democracy, 1992–2012

Turkmenistan, as well as the strong performance of so many countries that are not oil exporters, including relatively poor countries such as Albania to Mongolia, adds to the evidence that oil vexes democracy.

The argument is controversial. Some scholars, including specialists on the post-communist region, argue that oil dependence per se does not compromise democracy's chances. They claim that oil becomes a liability only under certain circumstances. For example, it is possible that patterns of ownership in the oil sector affect whether or not oil curses democracy (Jones Luong and Weinthal 2010). The argument is noteworthy, and Russia's democracy scores did fall as the oil sector was being renationalized under Putin. Still, a clear causal relationship remains to be shown. It is possible that restatizing previously privatized assets and restoring authoritarian rule were both parts of Putin's program but were not causally related. Furthermore, the other big hydrocarbon exporters in the region have known nothing but authoritarianism since the demise of the Soviet system.

In broader global context, oil and democracy do not mix comfortably. Not all major oil producers perform as badly on democracy as do the post-communist oil states or, for that matter, the oil-soaked monarchies of the Persian Gulf. Yet they have failed to reach and maintain status as fully open polities, and some analysts point to oil as a possible culprit. Venezuela, Ecuador, Nigeria, and some other oil-reliant countries have avoided full-blown autocracy, but they have not established a recent record of continuous open politics. As of this writing, the only country in the world with a heavily hydrocarbon-reliant economy that also enjoys robust democracy is Norway. Unlike so many other countries, Norway had decades of experience with stable open politics before it became a large hydrocarbon producer in the 1970s. If a country's people already firmly control the state through an array of strong institutions before striking oil, they may well be able to sustain democracy after the strike. Most developing countries, however, do not find themselves in such an enviable position. In the resource-rich countries of Africa, the MENA, and the post-communist region, fuels began to flow before the possibility of democratization arose, and oil abundance may well contribute to the enduring nonemergence of open politics in these countries.

Yet Mongolia presents a potentially crucial case on this score. It underwent democratization at the time of the demise of its Communist Party regime at the beginning of the 1990s and never looked back. But immense quantities of new energy sources have recently been located in Mongolian soil, and the past half-decade has witnessed the beginning of development of those sources and blistering rates of economic growth as a result. The riches discovered to date are mostly metals and high-quality coal; oil and natural gas have not (yet) been discovered in massive quantity.

A similar story is unfolding in West Africa. The post-communist region and portions of Africa experienced their waves of regime change simultaneously, in the early 1990s. In Africa, like in the post-communist region, the movement to democracy proved to be lasting in some countries and ephemeral in others. In both regions, resource-reliant countries figured prominently among those that underwent abortive transitions or no real transitions at all (Radelet 2010). While democratization continued (and continues) to flounder in Nigeria and never happened at all in oil-reliant Gabon, Congo-Brazzaville, Angola, and Equatorial Guinea, in other countries democracy stuck. It has already persisted for a quarter century in Ghana and Benin, neither of which were major energy producers when they underwent regime change. Since undergoing democratization, however, Ghana has discovered substantial oil reserves, and in recent years has emerged as an energy exporter.

Will Mongolia's rapid shift to status as a major energy resources producer jeopardize its fledging democratic institutions? How will the process unfold in Ghana? Each country had roughly two decades of democracy under its belt before its resource riches suddenly transformed its economy, much less experience with open politics than Norway had before becoming a major hydrocarbons exporter. Whether, and if so, how, resource abundance will affect the fate of democratization in Mongolia and Ghana poses a fascinating question for research on the relationship between natural resource wealth and political regime.

To summarize the findings from the post-communist region: Not being energy-reliant is consistent with any outcome in terms of political regime, while being energy-reliant is inconsistent with democracy. In the data on the post-communist region, oil is a sufficient but not necessary condition for nondemocratic outcomes. Perhaps the most arresting evidence of an oil curse is the fact that not a single case of successful democratization in the region has occurred in a country that has a hydrocarbon-based economy.

The post-communist experience not only lends weight to the argument that oil curses democracy. It also enriches our understanding of how it curses it.

In their explanations for how oil undermines popular rule, comparative social scientists have emphasized the rentier effect, the truncated modernization effect, and the repression effect. The rentier effect refers to the state's ability to contain demands for political change by buying off the population. In rentier states such as Qatar, the government can afford to shower the people with social services without taxing them. Under such conditions, according to the argument, people are likely to be too satisfied to rebel against autocracy. The truncated modernization effect refers to how oil production can make a country rich in terms of per capita GDP without necessarily inducing the ensemble of social changes, such as the universalization of literacy and dramatic improvements in public health, that normally accompany modernization driven by rapid improvements in agriculture- and manufacturing-based industrialization. The repression effect refers to the ability of governments to use the superprofits from energy resources to finance powerful militaries and police apparatuses that would be unaffordable in the absence of black gold. Those agencies of coercion can be deployed to shore up authoritarian regimes.

But we do not see these dynamics at work in the post-communist world, at least not as clearly as in many countries outside the region.

The rentier effect is, at best, only weakly present. While oil revenue can swell state coffers in the likes of Russia, there still is not enough oil wealth per capita to buy off the population and thereby preempt any popular dissatisfaction with the regime. The governments of the hydrocarbon economies in the region can afford to provide social services at a somewhat higher level than would be possible in the absence of hydrocarbon rents, but they still must tax their populations. The region has no Kuwaits.

We do not see the truncated modernization effect at work in the region, either. Russia and Kazakhstan and, to a lesser extent, Azerbaijan and Turkmenistan are industrialized countries that do not bear the economic peculiarities, such as a high per capita GDP combined with the persistence of illiteracy, found in oil states such as Libya and Saudi Arabia. The distinctiveness and distortions found in hydrocarbon-rich post-communist economies are due less to resource abundance than to the legacy of the Soviet economic model. These idiosyncrasies, which include underdeveloped agricultural and service sectors and a surfeit of inefficient large-scale manufacturing industry, are common to all Soviet-type command economies, not just the energy producers.

A repression effect cannot be ruled out, and hydrocarbon rents undoubtedly help rulers finance their security apparatuses. Russia's military modernization has depended in part on a long run of high oil prices. But we have little reason to think that the sprawling police apparatuses that rulers command in Russia, Kazakhstan, Azerbaijan, and Turkmenistan would be much weaker in the absence of oil rents. Nor has oil wealth been necessary to maintain a powerful police state apparatus, as Serbia under Slobodan Milosevic, Belarus under Aleksandr Lukashenko, and Uzbekistan under Islam Karimov show.

But the post-communist experience suggests that oil can poison democracy's prospects in ways other than by creating a rentier state, truncating modernization, or funding a powerful coercive apparatus. One way that oil has undermined democracy in the region is by what we might call a corruption effect. It elevates the risk of massive official corruption because there is so much to steal and because officials can filch wealth from a stream of resource revenues more furtively than they can from taxes.

Russia shows how rampant corruption can derail regime change in fledgling democracies by denting enthusiasm for open politics at both the elite and mass levels (Fish 2005). This dynamic was amply evident during the 1990s. Leading liberals who assumed high posts in Boris

Yeltsin's government in the early 1990s were, by the end of the decade, noticeably less enthusiastic about democracy than they had been earlier. Officials had stolen so much and had so much to hide that democracy, with its inquisitive free media and nosey citizens' groups, did not look so good anymore. At the mass level, many people came to identify democracy with the conversion of the public treasury into a feeding trough for top officials. The spectacle understandably produced popular disillusionment. It bolstered the appeal of Vladimir Putin, a figure who did not pretend to cherish democratic ideals but who promised to deliver justice by putting the state's house in order and humbling the state-appointed billionaires who pillaged the country's wealth. During his early years in power, Putin did just that – though he also established his own oligarchy and endowed his favorites with largesse that Yeltsin's oligarchs could only dream of.

In sum, the post-communist experience provides support for the notion that an abundance of hydrocarbon wealth may countervail democratization. It further shows how it does so. The Russian case, in particular, illustrates how factors other than rentier, truncated modernization, and repression effects may dim democracy's prospects.

Proximity to the West

The literature on democratization includes numerous works that investigate the influence of "neighborhood effects." While distance from Vienna is not statistically significant in all specifications in the multivariate analysis, when it is significant the sign is in the expected direction. The post-communist experience may support arguments that geographical location can influence regime outcomes. The bivariate correlation of 0.50 between distance from Vienna and democracy scores shows that proximity to the West might pose advantages for democratization. Generally speaking, countries that are closer to the "good neighborhood" of Western Europe do better than those in the less-good neighborhood of Inner Asia, abutting the Middle East and China.

Democratic neighbors are usually friendly to nearby democratic experiments. The dark spots in the United States' checkered history of relations with Latin America notwithstanding, since the 1980s the US government has backed democratization in the hemisphere. It supported fledgling democratic regimes and reacted sternly to President Alberto Fujimori's attack on Peru's constitutional order in 1992.

In contrast, leaders of authoritarian regimes often feel threatened by people who show that popular rule can work next door. Autocrats always want their people to believe that democracy is unsuitable or unworkable. Thus, when Filipinos revolted against the dictatorship of Ferdinand Marcos in 1986 and showed that democracy born of popular protest was possible in Asia, South Korea's military rulers cracked down on opposition at home. Their ham-handed move only intensified calls for their departure, which happened the following year. In the post-communist region, we can understand Putin's strenuous efforts to thwart democratization in Ukraine in terms of his anxiety about diffusion effects. A thriving open polity there would show Russians that democracy can work in a society that is a lot like their own.

Figure 1.4 shows the relationship between geographical location and regime outcomes. Given that the independent variable does not change over time, I present a scatter plot for a single year, 2012, to illustrate the point.

A strong correlation between westward location and performance on democracy is evident, but the outliers suggest that geography is not fate. Mongolia is again a dramatic overachiever. Sandwiched between democracy-despising behemoths, it is hard to imagine a country doing better in a worse neighborhood.

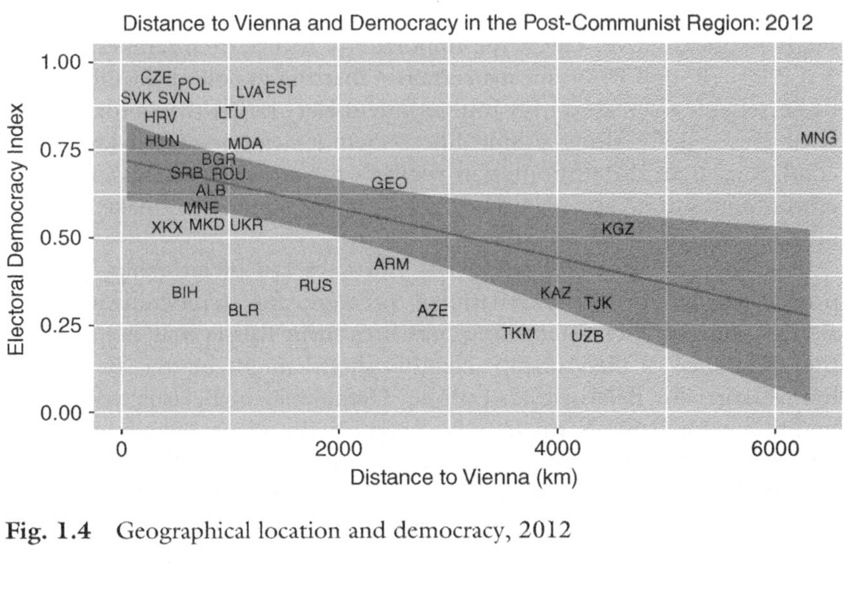

Fig. 1.4 Geographical location and democracy, 2012

Post-communist countries in Eastern Europe, on the other hand, enjoyed advantages of being in the "good neighborhood" of Western Europe. Especially important was the promise of membership in the European Union (EU). Elites and mass publics alike longed to join Europe and reap the economic benefits of EU membership. Since the EU requires that new entrants be democracies, the countries that had a shot at meeting the economic criteria for accession also had an incentive to hold free elections and uphold civil rights. The countries of the former USSR (plus Mongolia), excluding the Baltic states, did not have a good chance of meeting the economic criteria for membership, and therefore did not have the same incentives to meet the EU's political standards (Dimitrova and Pridham 2004).

On the other end of the spectrum, in the lower-left portion of the scatter plot, we find Bosnia and Belarus, which have remained resistant to democracy despite their European location and, in the Bosnian case, despite being an EU "potential candidate" since 2003. The civil war in Bosnia and enduring intercommunal tensions may well have disfavored democracy. That said, the war ended in 1995, and Croatia and Serbia, which were also the sites of vicious ethnic conflict, evolved toward open politics once hostilities ceased. It is also possible to argue that non-democratization has been as much of a cause as an effect of the persistence of intercommunal tensions. Bosnian politics and administration are structured by ethnicity and take place under the watchful eye of the High Representative. Given the opportunity to live in a democracy, it is possible – though by no means certain – that the people of Bosnia would be better able to create a truly multiethnic society rather than a society that is divided rigidly along ethnic lines. Democracies may provide better conditions than do authoritarian regimes for squarely addressing inter-ethnic contention and hammering out agreements that make durable intercommunal comity possible.

Belarus, sometimes referred to as Europe's last dictatorship, has also proven impervious to international pressure for democratization. In Belarus, however, countervailing pressures from Russia may help explain the endurance of dictatorship. Neighborhood might matter, but Russia looms larger for Belarus than Europe. Democracy in Belarus would be a nightmare for Russia's rulers, who prop up President Lukashenko with colossal energy subsidies that amount to about 15 percent of Belarus's GDP (Alachonvič 2015). What is more, Belarus never had a chance at EU membership, keeping an important inducement to democracy off the table.

Religion

Authors have long recognized the centrality of religion in culture. Religion is not just about whether people attend services on Friday afternoon, Saturday evening, or Sunday morning; nor does religion influence only practicing adherents. Even in relatively secular societies, religious traditions suffuse the values, attitudes, and beliefs that make up the stuff of political culture.

Figures 1.5–1.7 show the scatter plots for proportion of the population made up of adherents of Western Christian traditions (meaning Catholicism and Protestantism together), Islam, and Orthodox Christianity, respectively. Religious composition of societies does not change markedly from year to year, so data for a single year (2012) are shown for the purpose of clarity.

What might appear to be peculiarities in the data arise from cross-national differences in the proportion of the population that declares adherence to no religion. In most countries even nominal adherents claim affiliation with the tradition of their ancestors. For example, even though most Romanians and Georgians are not practicing Orthodox Christians, the vast majority associate themselves with their country's Orthodox Christian Church. In these countries, affiliation with the church

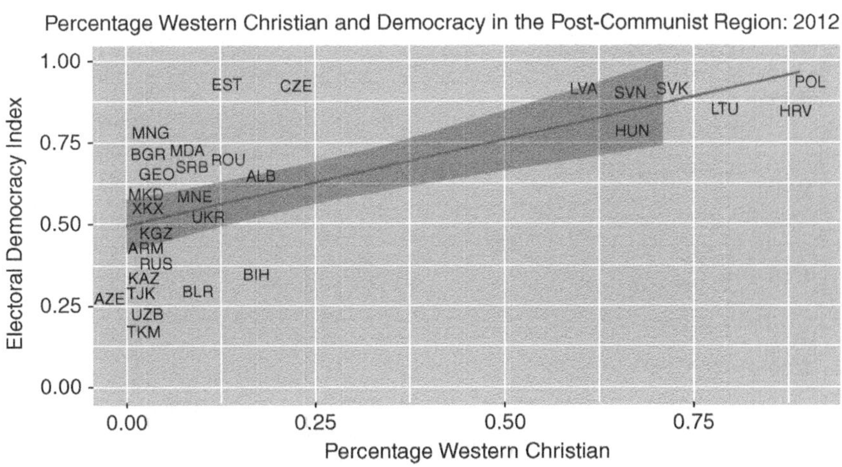

Fig. 1.5 Proportion of the population adhering to Western Christianity and democracy, 2012

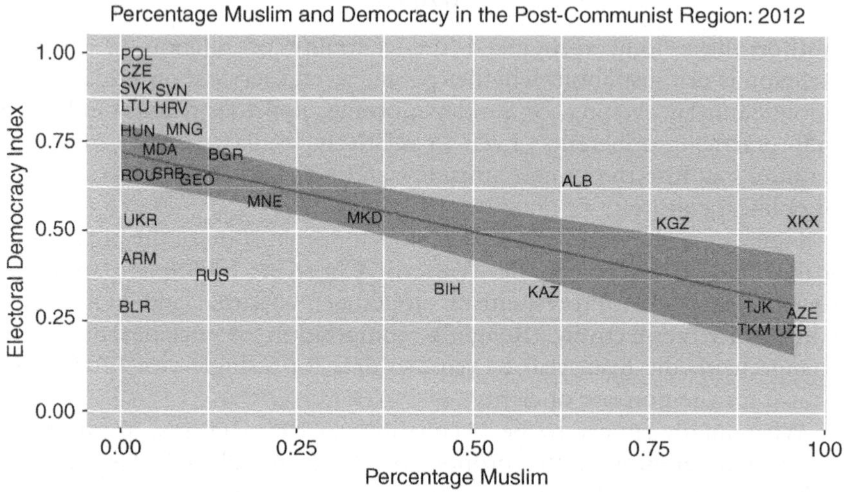

Fig. 1.6 Proportion of the population adhering to Islam and democracy, 2012

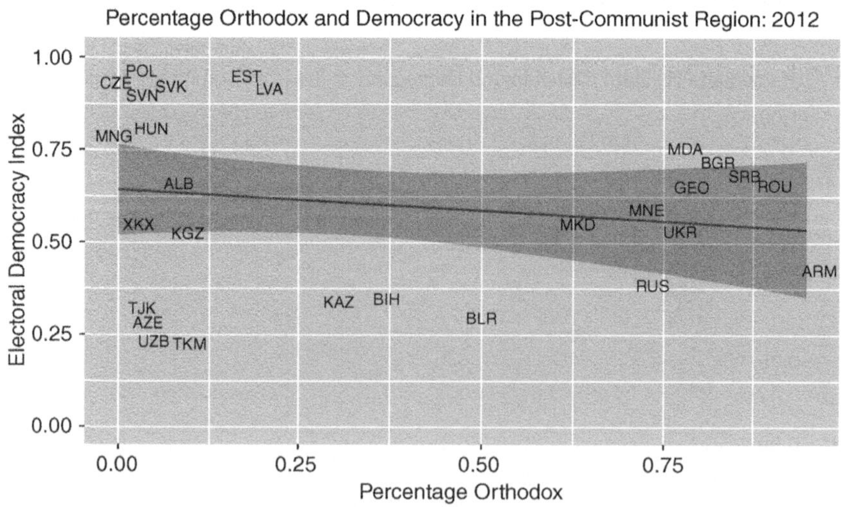

Fig. 1.7 Proportion of the population adhering to Orthodox Christianity and democracy, 2012

is often considered a proper part of allegiance to the nation, whether or not one is theistic or lives by the tenants of the faith. In a handful of countries in the region, however, majorities or large pluralities tell researchers that they are affiliated with no religious tradition. Thus, while Estonians have traditionally identified as Lutherans and Czechs as Catholics, both countries have low scores on percentage Western Christian (as well as on identification with other religious traditions).

Figure 1.5 illustrates the relationship between the proportion of the population that identifies as Catholic or Protestant (both together called Western Christian here) and the democracy index. At 0.68, the correlation is high. Again we can make no inferences about causation from these descriptive statistics, but we may note that no country in which half or more of the population identifies as Catholic or Protestant scores below 0.75 on democracy. The lower right-hand portion of the figure is empty. The data provide a bit of evidence that countries in which Western Christian traditions predominate enjoy relatively propitious conditions for democratization.

The data countervail the once widely held notion that Catholicism is inconsistent with democracy. Here I add proportion Catholic and Protestant together, so the proportion Catholic alone is not evident, but the vast majority of Western Christians in the region are Catholics; only Estonia, Latvia, and Hungary have substantial Protestant minorities. Catholicism clearly does not prevent democratization in the post-communist region.

In the early decades after World War II, some scholars claimed that Catholicism was antithetical to democracy. According to these arguments, the Catholic Church inculcated acceptance of rigid hierarchy and unquestioning acceptance of authority, leaving Catholics amenable to authoritarian rule (Lipset 1981, 1994; Huntington 1991). By the end of the previous century, that theory was largely discredited. Indeed, predominantly Catholic societies figured prominently in what is sometimes called the Third Wave of democratization that started in the mid-1970s in Spain, Portugal, and Greece and culminated in Mexico and Indonesia at the turn of the century. Predominantly Southern Europe, Latin America, the Philippines, and finally Eastern Europe accounted for the bulk of the successful cases of transition. The evidence adduced here adds another nail in a coffin that is already safely sealed.

While predominately Catholic countries do well on democratization in the region, the opposite is true for countries in which Islamic tradition predominates. As Fig. 1.6 shows, a higher proportion of Muslims is associated with worse performance on democratization. Proportion Muslim and the democracy index are correlated at –0.69. Among countries with Muslim-majority populations, Albania, Kyrgyzstan, and Kosovo are overachievers. Other countries with large Muslim populations do not fall far from the regression line, with the exception of Bosnia, which is an underachiever in democracy.

The post-communist evidence supports findings in the broader literature showing that Muslim societies may face special challenges in democratization. Studies based on global data have found a robust correlation between Islam and authoritarianism. A host of explanations has been adduced, including supposedly greater gender inequality among Muslims and Muslims' purported tendency to reject the separation of the secular and the sacred.

The post-communist region provides potentially valuable terrain for investigating such ideas. The strong, negative correlation raises the possibility that there may be something about Islam that disfavors democracy in the region. Yet the region also is unusual in the extent to which politics was secularized and gender equality enforced by antecedent authoritarian regimes. In the 1930s and 1940s, the Soviet regime literally stripped Central Asian women of their burkas and hijabs, and regimes throughout the region banished the sacred from politics and established the world's most aggressively secular political orders. Still, it is possible that even long decades of Sovietism did not eradicate the influence of religion on popular attitudes and social practices. Even if Muslims in the post-communist region are more liberal than their coreligionists in, say, the MENA, they might still hold more conservative attitudes on gender and be less amenable to purely secular politics than are non-Muslims in the region. Perhaps attitudes on gender and secularism have little to do with the link between Islam and authoritarianism in the region; it is possible that other factors are at work. Comparative within-region, cross-national research on the relationship between religion, on the one hand, and political attitudes and social practices, on the other, may provide some answers. It may enrich our understanding of the link – if there is in fact a link – between Islam and authoritarianism in the world more broadly.

Perhaps the most interesting correlation on religion and democracy that emerges from the analysis is found in the data on Orthodox Christianity, shown in the scatter plot in Fig. 1.7. The correlation, at –0.17, is not high, and countries with substantial Orthodox populations exhibit a wide range of scores on democracy. Among countries in which Orthodox traditions predominate, Russia and Belarus have moved from Soviet-type authoritarianism to a new, post-Soviet brand of autocracy. Armenia (whose Armenian-Rite Church is here classified as Orthodox) has also done poorly, albeit better than Russia or Belarus. Yet Bulgaria, Serbia, Georgia, Moldova, and Romania have made substantial strides toward democracy. In the middle of the Orthodox pack are Ukraine, Montenegro, and Macedonia.

At the time that Samuel Huntington penned his foundational works on democratization (1991) at the beginning of the 1990s and then the *Clash of Civilizations* (1996) shortly after that, Greece and predominantly Greek Cyprus were the only predominantly Christian Orthodox societies that had extensive experience with democracy. Romania, Bulgaria, and Serbia had some experience with open politics in the late nineteenth and early twentieth centuries, and their Orthodox churches at times demonstrated bravery in resisting Communist Party regimes after World War II (Petrovic 2013). Still, Orthodoxy was regarded by some scholars, including Huntington, as an impediment to democratization. The national and statist character of most Orthodox churches meant that church and state were yoked together in Orthodox societies. Even if the sacred and the secular were not tightly joined in people's mindsets, as some argue they are among Muslims, the state's organizational dominion over the church meant that the creative tension between temporal and religious authorities evident in countries with Western Christian traditions could not emerge. Since Polish Catholics take their religious instructions from Rome and not Warsaw, and since Rome and not Warsaw presides over the appointment of the church's Polish priests, the church could play a creative – and oppositional – role in Poland. One would not expect the predominant religious organization to play such an autonomous part in Orthodox Russia or Romania, where temporal authorities traditionally enjoy sway over matters affecting their national churches' financing, doctrine, and personnel.

But the post-communist experience reveals that Christian Orthodoxy is not inconsistent with democracy. Romania and Bulgaria scored above 0.6 on democracy in every year of the two decades covered by the data. The Orthodox Church has not necessarily played a progressive role in either country since the demise of communism. But neither has it prevented democratization, and people whose religious allegiance is to Orthodox Christianity have proven inclined and able to forge open polities. The post-communist experience may relegate theories on the incompatibility of Orthodoxy with democracy to the same trash bin that contains such ideas about Catholicism and democracy (see Papanikolaou 2012).

Taking Stock of the Strengths and Limitations of Structural Explanations

The post-communist experience appears to provide evidence that big background conditions strongly influence outcomes in political regime. As shown in the multivariate regressions presented above, economic development, economic reliance on energy resources, geographical location, and religious affiliation, taken together, explain the bulk of cross-national variation in political regimes over the first two post-communist decades. Investigating the bivariate relationships in the data sheds light on how each structural variable correlates with regime outcomes and how certain countries' scores differ from what one might have expected given their values on particular independent variables.

Table 1.2 is based on the results of the multivariate regression presented in model 7 of Table 1.1. It shows the observed and predicted scores on the democracy index for each country for the year 2008. I pick this year because it is relatively late in the period under examination and has less missing data than previous or subsequent years, though scores are missing for Kosovo, Montenegro, and Serbia. Because Serbia has data for 2007 (while neither Kosovo nor Montenegro have such data), I use its score in that year. The table sums up how each country did on its democracy score in that year given the expectations of the model.

As we would expect given the discussion above, the basic model provides a strong basis for making predictions about regime outcomes in specific countries. Croatia's score was exactly what we would have expected it to be, knowing the country's level of economic development, hydrocarbon production, distance from Vienna, and religious composition. The same is true for Hungary. Observed and predicted scores on the democracy index are within 0.05 points for Kazakhstan, Kyrgyzstan, Lithuania, Slovakia, and Slovenia, and for Azerbaijan, the Czech Republic, Latvia, and Moldova they are within 0.1.

But structure is not destiny. Some countries' scores differ substantially from what the model would predict. Albania, Mongolia, Poland, and Romania score significantly higher than the model would predict. Serbia, which was torn by war in the late 1980s and early 1990s, recovered rapidly

Table 1.2 Observed and predicted democracy scores by country, 2008*

Country	*Observed electoral democracy score*	*Predicted electoral democracy score*	*Residual value*
Albania	0.61	0.45	0.16
Armenia	0.37	0.54	–0.17
Azerbaijan	0.27	0.18	0.09
Belarus	0.28	0.71	–0.43
BiH	0.34	0.49	–0.15
Bulgaria	0.73	0.51	0.22
Croatia	0.80	0.80	0
Czech Republic	0.91	0.84	0.07
Estonia	0.91	0.78	0.13
Georgia	0.60	0.49	0.11
Hungary	0.82	0.82	0
Kazakhstan	0.33	0.28	0.05
Kosovo	0.51	N/A	N/A
Kyrgyzstan	0.31	0.28	0.03
Latvia	0.87	0.79	0.08
Lithuania	0.83	0.81	0.02
Macedonia	0.65	0.45	0.20
Moldova	0.49	0.55	–0.06
Mongolia	0.75	0.64	0.11
Montenegro	0.58	N/A	N/A
Poland	0.92	0.81	0.11
Romania	0.66	0.53	0.13
Russia	0.37	0.41	–0.04
Serbia (2007)*	0.70	0.55	0.15
Slovakia	0.88	0.83	0.05
Slovenia	0.89	0.83	0.06
Tajikistan	0.33	0.21	0.12
Turkmenistan	0.22	0.07	0.15
Ukraine	0.65	0.60	0.05
Uzbekistan	0.23	0.23	0

*Data for Serbia are for 2007. Kosovo and Montenegro are missing.

after the ouster of Slobodan Milosevic in 2000 and subsequently posted democracy scores that exceed what we could have expected. In our analyses above, we did not account for civil or international conflict, which we might have expected to correlate with lower scores on democracy. While Bosnia's and Armenia's underperformance on democratization suggests that war and intercommunal division might diminish democracy's prospects, Serbia shows that they do not necessarily do so.

The most dramatic divergences between observed and predicted scores are for Bulgaria and Belarus. Bulgaria does very well and Belarus very poorly.

Alternatives to Structural Explanations

Accounting for outcomes in places such as Belarus and Bulgaria requires us to look beyond the structural variables we examined earlier. A host of nonstructural variables, as well as structural variables that we did not consider, might also shape regime outcomes. Here we will have a brief look at two nonstructural factors that might influence regime outcomes.

Constitutional Arrangements

One potentially weighty nonstructural factor is the distribution of power between the executive and legislative branches of government. Over the past several decades, a vigorous debate has raged in political science over whether presidentialism or parliamentarism provides the firmer institutional basis for robust democratization. Some scholars tout the advantages of parliamentarism, which are said to include stronger checks on executive power, government that better represents voters' traits and preferences, and flexibility in governments' terms in office (Linz and Valenzuela 1994; Stepan and Skach 1993). Other analysts prefer presidentialism. They argue that the stability of new democracies is enhanced by having a powerful elected executive who can stand above partisan and communal divisions and represent the nation as a whole. Presidents are also sometimes seen as being more decisive and capable of carrying out unpopular but needed decisions (Horowitz 1996; Mainwaring and Shugart 1997).

While it would be an exaggeration to say that the field has reached consensus, a preponderance of evidence seems to favor pro-parliamentary arguments (Bunce 2000). Countries in which executive power is constituted on the basis of the outcome of parliamentary elections and in which governments are accountable to parliament often do well in democratization. Spain and South Africa furnish examples. Democracy has succeeded in many countries with powerful presidents and relatively weak legislatures, including Mexico and Argentina. Yet the evidence suggests that presidential systems are more likely to succeed where the chief executive, while wielding formidable clout, nevertheless must contend with a legislature that is also vested with substantial powers. Presidential systems that also feature strong legislatures include Indonesia, Chile, and the United States. Some countries with semipresidential systems that vest substantial power in the legislature, most notably Taiwan, have also performed well in democratization. Countries whose constitutions place the bulk of power in executive presidencies generally fare worse. Backsliding toward authoritarianism following antiauthoritarian breakthroughs in countries such as Kenya, Mali, and the Philippines illustrate the problem.

The post-communist experience boosts pro-parliamentary arguments (Fish 2006). With the exception of Moldova, every country in the region that adopted a parliamentary system has performed better than the expectations of the structural model would predict. Albania, Bulgaria, Serbia, and Macedonia are the most striking examples. Countries that embraced parliament-heavy semipresidential systems, namely Mongolia, Poland, and Romania, have also done well. Polities that opted for strong presidents and weak parliaments, notably Russia, Armenia, and Belarus, have been distinct underperformers. Georgia, with its presidential system, has done better than expected, but like Chile, the United States, and Indonesia, Georgia also has a legislature that enjoys substantial authority. What is more, the powers of Georgia's parliament have actually expanded as a result of recent constitutional reforms (Babeck et al. 2012). Turkmenistan, with its presidential dictatorship, beat the model's predictions, but the model predicted such a dismal outcome that it would be difficult for Turkmenistan not to have exceeded expectations. The post-communist experience, when added to the record of other world regions, suggests that executive presidents may have become a stauncher foe of democratic consolidation than have assertive militaries, anti-democratic grassroots movements, or ethnonational separatists.

Leadership

The post-communist experience also raises the possibility that leadership is of great importance in regime outcomes. The notion that leadership can influence trajectories of regime change, or for that matter outcomes in any other realm, has been déclassé in Anglophone social science for decades. Leadership cannot be quantified and is not readily tractable to cross-national analysis, but it is not less significant for that reason (Samuels 2003). While the influence of Boris Yeltsin's occupation of the Russian presidency at the time of the Soviet collapse cannot be calculated, it may have been substantial. The effect of Yeltsin's successor on regime outcomes has probably been even greater. Had Yeltsin chosen someone other than Putin as his intended successor at the end of the previous century, Russia might look different today. Democracy was already on the ropes at the end of the Yeltsin era, but the reversion to hard autocracy in the current century might not have happened at all, or might have taken a different form. The role of the individual leader in retreat from democracy is evident in neighboring Belarus as well. The country's turn away from open politics in the mid-1990s and subsequent drop into a neo-Soviet deep freeze is tied closely to the personality of Aleksandr Lukashenko. Hungary's retreat from full-blown democracy over the past several years is hard to imagine without reference to the toxic talents of Prime Minister Viktor Orban.

The significance of leadership is evident in economic as well as political reform and change. Estonia's emergence as the region's leader in economic-institutional development owes a great deal to the extraordinary leadership of Mart Laar, who first took charge as prime minister in 1992, at the age of 32. Laar's unyielding ideological commitment to imposing hard budget constraints on enterprises across the board had the effect of cutting off budding political capitalists and opening Estonia's economic arena to genuine entrepreneurs. Most countries in the post-communist region have experienced the emergence of political capitalism, a system in which fortunes are built on access to state coffers and privileges bestowed by political authorities rather than on business acumen *per se*. Laar, who pursued his policies even when they were unpopular and even at the cost of losing power 2 years later, helped make Estonia the post-communist region's greatest economic success story and least corrupt polity (Abrams and Fish 2015).

Conclusion

The post-communist region is an artificial entity. Its countries are united by their common recent history of a particular form of authoritarian regime and little else. This peculiarity of the region, however, makes it favorable terrain for investigating questions that interest social scientists.

One of those questions is which factors condition whether or not countries get popular rule. As Eurasia and Eastern Europe neared the end of the 1980s, all countries were ruled by hegemonic Communist Party organizations. There were shades of difference in the degree of political closure among countries, but all were hardcore autocracies. Over the next several decades, however, the region witnessed the emergence of virtually the entire spectrum of regimes, from full-blown democracy (as in Poland and Estonia) to harshest autocracy (as in Uzbekistan and Turkmenistan). For the scholar interested in what shapes prospects for democracy, the region presents a relatively uniform starting point followed by the emergence of extraordinary variation on the outcome of interest. The independent variables of interest differ widely within the region as well.

Investigation of data on democracy and its correlates in the post-communist region provides substantial support for structural theories of political regime. Four big background conditions, none of which are the products of human volition and all of which undergo within-country change very slowly or not at all, explain the bulk of variation in outcomes on political regime. Economic development, income from oil production, geographical location, and religious tradition do a good job of predicting cross-national differences.

Still, structure is not fate. Factors other than the big background conditions examined here might shape outcomes. Constitutional arrangements and leadership, each of which is the product of human design and neither of which may be considered a background condition, might have mattered as well.

The investigation presented in this chapter has many limitations. As always, the quality of cross-national, observational data cannot be regarded as high. The statistical operations presented here are rudimentary and aimed at highlighting big correlations; they do not enable us confidently to make causal inferences. What is more, large-N analysis such as that offered here cannot substitute for in-depth studies of a single case or a small number of cases.

What the analyses presented here can do is clear some brush and highlight potentially productive areas and questions for inquiry. The cases that deviate strongly from expectations might be especially useful. They might serve as "crucial deviant cases," which some scholars regard as particularly helpful for generating novel theories. How has poor, geographically isolated Mongolia fared so well in democratization? Mongolia is the only predominantly Buddhist society in the region, so we cannot assess the effect of its religious tradition with any confidence, but moving out of region and examining how aspects of Buddhist culture might affect political regime could present a fruitful avenue for research. Perhaps factors that have little to do with economic, geographical, or cultural conditions have safeguarded Mongolia's democratization and will continue to do so.

Is Mongolia's parliament-heavy semipresidential system key to its success? Is extraordinary leadership to credit? Or perhaps a lot of luck? If Mongolia has been running mostly on luck, it is possible that structural limitations will catch up with it. As the country's reliance on energy resources extracted from the ground grows, will Mongolians be able to maintain open politics? Might they experience something like the spiral of corruption and consequent disillusionment with democracy that afflicted Russia in the 1990s, with similar results for political regime? Or can Mongolia continue to beat the odds?

Bulgaria's much-better-than-predicted performance raises similar questions. How has Bulgaria overcome its relative economic underdevelopment, location at some distance from the West, and Orthodox Christian tradition? Is its constitutional system, with its muscular parliament and relatively underpowered presidency, to credit? Is just not having oil, combined with its institutions that confine the executive, enough? Or is something else at work? In-depth country studies might turn up chains of causation that could generate insights that would be relevant outside the region.

Including such cases in small-N, multiregional designs could be especially fruitful. Once the analyst has a handle on how Mongolia or Bulgaria has done it, extending the analysis to other relatively poor democracies could be a productive next step. Mongolia, Ghana, Indonesia, and El Salvador, for example, each rank in the bottom half of the world's countries in terms of economic development; GDP per capita does not exceed about $4000 in any of them. What enables democracy to thrive on ten dollars a day in these places but not in most other less developed countries?

Bibliography

Abrams, N. A., & Fish, M. S. (2015). Policies first, institutions second: Lessons from Estonia's economic reforms. *Post-Soviet Affairs*, 31(6), 491–513.

Alachonvič, A. (2015, August 26). How Russia's subsidies save the Belarusian economy. *Belarus Digest*. http://belarusdigest.com/story/how-russias-subsidies-save-belarusian-economy-23118. Retrieved February 2016.

Babeck, W., Fish, S., Reichenbecher, Z. (2012). *Rewriting a constitution: Georgia's shift toward Europe*. Baden-Baden, Germany: Nomos Verlagsgesellschaft.

Brinks, D., & Coppedge, M. (2006). Diffusion is no illusion: neighbor emulation in the third wave of democracy. *Comparative Political Studies*, 39(4), 463–489.

Bunce, V. (2000). Comparative democratization: big and bounded generalizations. *Comparative Political Studies*, 33(6–7), 703–734.

Diamond, L. (1992). Economic development and democracy reconsidered. *American Behavioral Scientist*, 35(4–5), 450–499.

Dimitrova, A., & Pridham, G. (2004). International actors and democracy promotion in Eastern Europe: the integration model and its limits. *Democratization*, 11(5), 91–112.

Fish, M. S. (1995). *Democracy from scratch: opposition and regime in the new Russian revolution*. Princeton, NJ: Princeton University Press.

Fish, M. S. (1998). Mongolia: democracy without prerequisites. *Journal of Democracy*, 9(3), 127–141.

Fish, M. S. (2005). *Democracy derailed in Russia: the failure of open politics*. New York: Cambridge University Press.

Fish, M. S. (2006). Stronger legislatures, stronger democracies. *Journal of Democracy*, 17(1), 5–20.

Fish, M. S. (2011). *Are Muslims distinctive? A look at the evidence*. New York: Oxford University Press.

Fish, M. S., & Wittenberg, J. (2009). Failed democratization. In C. W. Haerpfer, P. Bernhagen, R. F. Inglehart, C. Welzel (Eds.), *Democratization* (pp. 249–265). New York: Oxford University Press.

Hofmann, E. T. (2011, July 7). *Reflections on Orthodoxy and the Construction of Civil Society and Democracy in Russia*. Washington, DC: The Kennan Institute of the Woodrow Wilson Center. https://www.wilsoncenter.org/publication/reflections-orthodoxy-and-the-construction-civil-society-and-democracyrussia. Retrieved January 2016.

Horowitz, D. L. (1996). Comparing democratic systems. In L. Diamond & M. F. Plattner (Eds.), *The global resurgence of democracy* (2nd ed., pp. 143–149). Baltimore: Johns Hopkins University Press.

Huntington, S. P. (1991). *The third wave: democratization in the late twentieth century*. Norman, OK: University of Oklahoma Press.

Huntington, S. P. (1996). *The clash of civilizations and the remaking of world order*. New York: Simon and Schuster.

Jones Luong, P., & Weinthal, E. (2010). *Oil is not a curse: ownership structure and institutions in Soviet successor states*. New York: Cambridge University Press.

Kopstein, J., & Reilly, D. A. (2000). Geographic diffusion and the transformation of the post-communist world. *World Politics*, 53(1), 1–37.

Linz, J. J., & Valenzuela, A. (Eds.) (1994). *The failure of presidential democracy in Latin America*. Baltimore: Johns Hopkins University Press.

Lipset, S. M. (1981). *Political man: the social bases of politics* (Exp. ed.). Baltimore: Johns Hopkins University Press.

Lipset, S. M. (1994). The social requisites of democracy revisited: 1993 presidential address. *American Sociological Review*, 59(1), 1–22.

Lussier, D. N. (2016). *Constraining Elites in Russia and Indonesia: Political Participation and Regime Survival*. New York: Cambridge University Press

Lussier, D. N., & Fish, M. S. (2012). Indonesia: the benefits of civic engagement. *Journal of Democracy*, 23(1), 70–84.
Mainwaring, S., & Shugart, M. S. (Eds.) (1997). *Presidential democracy in Latin America*. New York: Cambridge University Press.
Møller, J. (2009). *Post-communist regime change: a comparative study*. New York: Routledge.
Papanikolaou, A. (2012). *The mystical as political: democracy and non-radical orthodoxy*. Notre Dame, IN: University of Notre Dame Press.
Petrovic, M. (2013). *The democratic transition of post-communist Europe: in the shadow of post-communist differences and uneven Europeanization*. New York: Palgrave Macmillan.
Pop-Eleches, G. (2007). Historical legacies and post-communist regime change. *Journal of Politics*, 69(4), 908–926.
Radelet, S. (2010). *Emerging Africa: how seventeen countries are leading the way*. Washington, DC: Center for Global Development.
Ross, M. L. (2013). *The oil curse: how petroleum wealth shapes the development of nations*. Princeton, NJ: Princeton University Press.
Samuels, R. J. (2003) *Machiavelli's children: leaders and their legacies in Italy and Japan*. Ithaca, NY: Cornell University Press.
Stepan, A., & Skach, C. (1993). Constitutional frameworks and democratic consolidation: parliamentarism versus presidentialism. *World Politics*, 46(1), 1–22.
Varieties of Democracy. (2016). V-Dem data version 6. https://v-dem.net/en/data/data-version-6/. Retrieved February 2016.

M. Steven Fish is Professor of Political Science at the University of California-Berkeley. He has published six authored or co-authored books and numerous journal articles and book chapters on democracy and regime change in developing and post-communist countries, religion and politics, and constitutional systems and national legislatures. His book *Are Muslims Distinctive? A Look at the Evidence* (Oxford, 2011) was selected for *Choice*'s Outstanding Academic Titles, 2012: Top 25 Books.

Chapter 2: Post-Communist Transition Under the Umbrella of Uneven EUropeanisation: East Central Europe, the Baltic States and the Balkans

Milenko Petrovic

A quarter century after the collapse of East European communism, there is little doubt that the simultaneous transitions from communist dictatorship to multiparty democracy, and from a command economy to a market economy, have been successful (or relatively successful) almost exclusively in those states which were able to tie their post-communist reforms to the European Union (EU)'s conditional offer of membership. A clearly established and remarkably strong correlation between the levels of progress in accession into the EU on one side, and success in post-communist political and economic transition on the other, has become a historical fact that has been recognised in a large body of literature for some time (see e.g. Bideleux 2001; Grabbe 2006; Pridham, 2001, 2005; Schimmelfennig 2008; Schimmelfennig et al. 2006; Vachudova 2005). However, while Mongolia is the only post-communist country to date which, due to a specific constellation of

M. Petrovic (✉)
University of Canterbury, Canterbury, New Zealand
e-mail: milenko.petrovic@canterbury.ac.nz

Fish, Gill, Petrovic (eds.), *A Quarter Century of Post-Communism Assessed*, DOI 10.1007/978-3-319-43437-7_3

domestic and external factors,[1] has been able to substantially democratise and marketise itself without relying on the EU's accession opportunity; the reasons why this opportunity has not been used with the same effectiveness in all three regions of post-communist Europe, to whom it was initially offered in the early 1990s, remain far less obvious. While many scholars (particularly those from the 'structuralist camp'),[2] EU officials and political analysts tend to explain the Balkan states' slower progress with post-communist reform and EU accession in comparison to the countries of East Central Europe (ECE) and the Baltics as being more or less an 'expected outcome' of the different structural capacities of these groups of states to adopt EU (i.e. 'Western') values and norms, and consequently meet the EU accession conditions, this chapter focuses on the importance of 'practical policy' measures and agent-driven actions for causing these post-communist regional differences. Not denying the relevance of some historical factors, particularly the importance of some specifics of their communist legacies linked to their pre-communist structural socio-economic (dis)advantages, this chapter argues that the main reason for the different post-communist trajectories of the Balkan states, when compared to those of the ECE and Baltic states, lies primarily in the politically determined different levels of assistance and support received from the EU for conducting post-communist reforms.

While the lack of EU and Western assistance in the Balkan states during the early stages of post-communist transition in the 1990s was primarily caused by poor decisions made by domestic political elites who at the time did not express a strong desire for reform or closer relations with the EU, external factors bear a large amount of responsibility for the insufficient level of EU support for reforms that the so-called Western Balkan states have received since the mid-2000s. This chapter identifies the negative impact of the changed EU approach towards further enlargement after it began feeling 'enlargement fatigue' in the aftermath of its 2004/2007 enlargement, which led to the adoption of tougher accession conditions for the new candidates from the Western Balkans, as being particularly important in this regard. These tougher conditions will be investigated in greater detail in the third section of this chapter, which follows an assessment provided in the first two sections of the importance and the main forms of the received foreign assistance for post-communist reform by the three groups of countries which were perceived as potential EU members from the very beginning of their post-communist transition.

A Different Desire for Post-Communist Reform, But a Similar Need for Foreign Assistance

When the communist regimes started to collapse in four ECE states – Poland, Hungary, Czechoslovakia and East Germany – and the three Baltic Soviet republics in the late 1980s, the level of desire for regime change among the peoples and their political leaders in other Soviet republics and in the Balkan communist states was much lower for a variety of reasons, the least important of which were structural ones. While some structural predispositions, primarily those related to the uneven level of pre-communist socio-economic development and, to some extent, a different historical experience with the institutions of liberal democracy (particularly with regard to its complete lack in almost all the non-Baltic post-Soviet states), were of some importance for setting the general preconditions for transition, the existence or lack of a strong desire for regime change in particular states at the end of the period of communist rule was primarily the result of some specific aspects of their communist political and socio-economic systems.

As defined and argued by this author in greater detail in his 2013 monograph (Petrovic 2013), some weaknesses in the nature of rule of domestic communist elites, combined with a history of violent (Soviet or Soviet-driven) suppression of major protests and incentives for change or reform (as was the case in Czechoslovakia), in the three ECE communist states (Ekiert 1996, 2003) and the existence of enormously strong anti-Russian and anti-Soviet sentiment (particularly in the Baltic states, Poland and Hungary), played a key role in the creation of important anti-communist national(ist) or liberal democratic political alternatives in these states. In some of them – as was the case with the movement led by Solidarity and the Catholic Church in Poland, and to a lesser level with the activities of Charter 77 and other dissident groups in Czechoslovakia – these political alternatives were articulated outside of the ruling communist elite, whereas in Hungary and to some extent (during and after 1988) in the Baltic states they were promoted by and within the ruling communist parties themselves (Crampton 1997, Chapter 22; Ekiert 1996, 2003; Petrovic 2013, Chapters 3 and 4). On the other hand, the relatively strong grip on power of domestic communist dictators, who thoroughly eliminated any traces of anti-communist and anti-regime opposition within and outside the ruling party, coupled with the generally positive popular perception and positive socio-political effects of the initially successful economic industrialisation and urbanisation of the Balkan states and (most) non-Baltic Soviet republics during the 1950s and early 1960s (Lavigne 1999, Chapter 4; Turnock 1989), simply did not allow for any wider articulation, let alone coordination, of anti-regime and anti-communist sentiment in these states.

Nevertheless, after the gradual erosion of the communist party's monopoly in Poland and Hungary during the 1980s was further supported by Gorbachev's decision not to interfere in the internal affairs of 'other socialist states' (Crampton 1997, Chapter 22), and following the eruption of mass protests and mass movements in the Baltic states during 1988 and 1989 and in East Germany and Czechoslovakia in October and November 1989, the communist regimes quickly collapsed, not only in these states, but also in all the remaining countries of the Soviet Bloc (including in two non-Bloc members—Yugoslavia and Albania). By the end of 1991, all the states in the region of formerly communist Eastern Europe officially adopted legislation that began the process of their post-communist political democratisation and economic marketisation. However, the existence of the above-discussed different levels of anti-communist opposition and the desire for regime change, which had been developed during communist rule in particular groups of states, more or less directly led to the selection of different and contrasting political options (and their protagonists) in the first multiparty elections in the newly formed post-communist states (see also McFaul 2002; Ekiert 2003). While the first post-communist elections in the ECE and Baltic states witnessed landslide victories for anti-communist and liberal democratic political parties, the winners of the first multiparty elections organised at about the same time in 1990 in all the Balkan and almost all the post-Soviet non-Baltic states (for the latter, see Gill's chapter in this volume) were either (cosmetically) 'reformed' ex-communists or national populist parties (Petrovic 2013, Chapter 1).

An immediate consequence of these different political choices in the different countries and regions of post-communist Europe was a quick start with reforms and closer relations with the West and the EU in ECE and Baltic states (Lavigne 1999; Mayhew 1998) and slow reform and establishment of the systems of imperfect or 'illiberal' democracy in the remaining post-communist states (Petrovic 2013; Vachudova 2005; Graeme Gill and Nicholas Smith in this volume). Furthermore, the selection of the non-reformist pathway, coupled with strong nationalism (i.e. unresolved or inadequately resolved ethnic relations during communist rule; see Petrovic 2013 and Roeder 2004) in many countries of the second group led to the eruption of inter-ethnic animosities and conflicts. The most serious of them resulted in the eruption of armed conflicts such as the civil wars in Croatia and Bosnia and Herzegovina (B–H), the Armenia–Azerbaijan war over Nagorno–Karabakh, and armed clashes between national armies and rebel ethnic groups in Georgia, Moldova and Chechnya.

However, if the desire for (real) regime change and political and economic reform was different across post-communist Europe, the socio-economic circumstances in which the states of the former communist bloc fell after the collapse of the old regime were extraordinarily similar. A deep economic, so-called transitional, crisis characterised by enormously high inflation, everyday shortages of basic life necessities, rapidly declining living standards for the vast majority of people and a lack of domestic resources, including elementary knowledge of how to profile and introduce necessary (particularly market-economic) reforms, were phenomena which no post-communist state in Eastern Europe and Eurasia could have escaped in the early 1990s (for more details and country examples see Berend 2001; Gros and Steinherr 2004; Svejnar 2002). The reliance on foreign assistance of all forms, including rudimentary items such as food and medicine, was also universally present in all post-communist states. As seen in Table 2.1, by the late 1990s of all the countries of the post-communist world, only three countries from ECE were able to regain the level of their real GDP per capita in 1989.

As soon as they got rid of communist rule, the newly emerged democracies in ECE and the Baltics did not need to wait too long for necessary (Western) assistance. However, from the very beginning, this assistance was very unevenly allocated among the particular (groups) of post-communist states. This was a result of the above-discussed different political choices and reform pathways these states had chosen at the initial stage of their post-communist transformation.

The Different Level of Foreign Assistance as a Consequence of the Different Choices Made at the Beginning of Post-Communist Transition

The necessary assistance for overcoming the transitional economic crisis and conducting post-communist (foremost economic) reform in the countries of the former communist bloc in Eastern Europe was expected to come primarily from Western states and the international organisations which were founded and largely financed by these states: that is from those

Table 2.1 Growth in real GDP and foreign direct investment (FDI) inflow in East European states

	GDP growth – annual rates							*Cumulative FDI (mil. US $)*		*Estimated real GDP (1989 = 100)*
	1989	*1990*	*1991*	*1992*	*1993*	*1994*	*1995*	*1989–1993*	*1994–1997*	*1998*
The Czech Republic	1.4	-1.2	-11.6	- 0.5	0.1	2.2	5.9	1,546	5,826	95
Hungary	0.7	-3.5	-11.9	-3.1	-0.6	2.9	1.5	5,756	9,527	95
Poland	0.2	-11.6	-7.0	2.6	3.8	5.2	7.0	981	7,458	117
Slovakia	1.4	-2.5	-14.6	-6.5	-3.7	5.2	6.5	374	713	100
Slovenia	-1.8	-4.7	-8.9	-5.5	2.8	5.8	4.9	167	760	104
Estonia	8.1	-6.5	-13.6	-14.2	-8.8	-2.0	4.3	236	652	76
Latvia	6.8	2.9	-10.4	-34.9	-14.9	2.2	-0.9	50	1,418	59
Lithuania	1.5	-5.0	-5.7	-21.3	-16.2	-9.8	3.3	30	583	65
Croatia	-1.6	-7.1	-21.1	-11.7	-8.0	5.9	6.8	115	1,052	78
Macedonia	0.9	-9.9	-7.0	-8.0	-9.1	-1.8	-1.2	–	66	72
Romania	-5.8	-5.6	-12.9	-8.8	1.5	3.9	7.1	179	2,440	76
FR Yugoslavia*	1.3	-7.9	-11.6	-27.9	-30.8	2.5	6.1	–	740	47**
Bulgaria	0.5	-9.1	-11.7	-7.3	-1.5	1.8	2.9	101	848	66
Albania	9.8	-10.0	-28.0	-7.2	9.6	8.3	13.3	65	293	86
Bosnia–Herzegovina	na	-23.2	-12.1	-80.1	-10.0	0.0	20.8	–	–	na
Armenia	14.2	-7.4	-11.7	-41.8	-8.8	5.4	6.9	–	103	41
Azerbaijan	-4.4	-11.7	-0.7	-22.6	-23.1	-19.7	-11.8	–	2,094	44
Belarus	8.0	-3.0	-1.2	-9.6	-7.6	-12.6	-10.4	18	481	78
Georgia	-4.8	-12.4	-20.6	-44.8	-25.4	-11.4	2.4	–	304	33
Moldova	8.5	-2.4	-17.5	-29.1	-1.2	-30.9	-1.4	–	192	32
Russia	na	-4.0	-5.0	-14.8	-8.7	-12.7	-4.0	–	5,205	55
Ukraine	4.0	-3.4	-10.6	-9.7	-14.2	-22.9	-12.2	–	1,505	37

*Serbia and Montenegro; **GDP in 2000

Source: EBRD Transition Report, 1999 and 2001.

whose values and norms served as the basic inspiration for regime change across communist East Central and Eastern Europe during the 1980s (Crampton 1997). Political requirements, including a basic insistence on political democratisation and respect for human and minority rights and freedoms that came along with Western economic advice and financial support (Janos 2001), were less of an additional burden and more of a form of additional assistance and a guide for the recipient countries in securing the long-term consolidation of their newly established institutions of democracy. Although the importance of the bilateral arrangements (particularly those made with leading world economies such as the United States, Japan and Germany) should not be underestimated, the role of international organisations and financial institutions has been crucial in defining both the level of provided assistance and the content of additional (or conditional) requirements which came along with this assistance. This becomes particularly relevant when examining the roles of the IMF, the World Bank, the EU, and the European Bank for Reconstruction and Development (EBRD – Lavigne 1999; Stiglitz 2002).

While more coordinated assistance and aid in fighting the challenges of the economic crisis and in economic system reconstruction started to come to the ex-communist countries of Eastern Europe as early as 1989, especially with the foundation of the PHARE programme of economic assistance to Poland and Hungary, the EU's predecessor, the European Community (EC),[3] soon afterwards offered a broader level of economic cooperation through beneficial association agreements, the so-called Europe Agreements (EA) to effectively all the European countries of the former Soviet bloc. By December 1991 it had already signed such agreements with three ECE post-communist states (Poland, Hungary and the still united Czechoslovakia), and by March and February 1993 it had done the same with Romania and Bulgaria, respectively (for more details see Lavigne 1999, pp. 218–228). However, the most valuable assistance for the long-term process of conducting and consolidating economic reforms and democratic institutions in post-communist states came in the form of the EU's offer for membership, which was accompanied by a set of accession conditions and followed by substantial EU financial support (so-called pre-accession assistance). As discussed and shown in the above-mentioned EU enlargement literature (see page 41), the membership promise that the leaders of the 12 EU member states at the time decided to give at their 1993 Copenhagen meeting to those post-communist European states which had expressed an interest and displayed an ability to meet the conditions for accession defined at that same meeting (see European Council 1993) served as both a very strong motivation for undertaking the process of reforms and as a source of necessary resources for making those reforms in the interested countries.

While valuable, the financial and economic assistance, which the official candidates for EU membership received from the EU in the form of trade concessions, donations and specially created funds for supporting development and transitional reforms (see endnote 3), was far less important than assistance which the candidate countries received from the EU in the form of provided guidelines and expertise throughout the process of accession negotiations for modelling and implementing necessary reforms. The obligation of the applicants to fully comply with the required accession conditions – starting with a general 'achieved stability of institutions guaranteeing democracy, the rule of law, human rights and respect for and protection of minorities, [and] the existence of a functioning market economy' (European Council 1993, 7.A. iii) and finishing with the more specific 31 or 35 acquis communautaire[4], which were the focus of accession negotiations – was crucially important assistance for applicant countries to successfully accomplish their post-communist transition. As the acquis communautaire factually represent the body of EU laws and regulations and effectively cover the complete legal and institutional framework for the functioning of a country's economic and socio-political system, the candidates for EU membership from former communist Europe did not have to 'worry' about the right design, content and proper introduction of post-communist reforms. They got them all in the form of the 31 or 35 acquis chapters, whose content has steadily increased over the years to reach the current number (for the more recent candidates) of '160,000 pages' (Gateva 2015, p. 21), which have to be negotiated (i.e. adopted and implemented) before a country can become an EU member. Although sometimes criticised for being too detailed, bureaucratic and patronizing (Dimitrova 2002; Raik 2004), the EU's accession requirement for the fulfilment of the acquis criteria was an enormously important form of assistance. It enabled the candidate for EU membership from post-communist Europe to secure a relatively swift and effective process of building democratic and market economy institutions, as none of them had any previous experience or the necessary resources for constructing and setting these up on their own.

However, the advantage of the countries who were able to get the status of EU accession states before their less successful post-communist counterparts was not limited in that respect to the much higher amount of technical and financial assistance which they received from the EU alone (as accession states). As discussed above, the much stronger desire for a change and to 'go West' was expressed in the countries of ECE and the Baltic states at a very early stage of their post-communist transition, leading them to become the first post-communist countries to apply for EU membership and open accession negotiations with the EU either in March 1998 or in February 2000 (see Table 2.3). This enabled these countries to gain an international reputation as politically stable and economically prosperous societies (both guaranteed by the EU and its member states), which granted them easier access to other types of foreign assistance for reforms. Among these, in addition to the above-mentioned various forms of multilateral and bilateral assistance, including beneficial financial arrangements and the so-called soft loans granted by the IMF, the World Bank or the EBRD, the higher inflow of foreign direct investment (FDI) was particularly important.

Although FDI could have not been considered a 'poor' form of foreign assistance in a technical sense, the inflow of FDI, which brought the necessary (private) capital and modern technology as well as a managerial culture and entrepreneurship skills, was an enormous support for the successful privatisation and restructuring of the command-type economies of the former communist states (see, e.g. Lavigne 1999, pp. 254–261; Bevan and Estrin 2004). In this respect, it could be argued that the received amount of FDI was a critical factor for securing the long-term sustainability of the introduced economic reforms and stable economic growth in the post-communist states. Needless to say, the highly positive economic effects of FDI inflow had strong positive impacts on the further acceleration of post-communist reform (both socio-economic and political) and the EU integration of the countries in question.[5] Hence, despite the fact that neither the country's accession negotiations with the EU nor the received amount of FDI can be considered 'poor' forms of foreign assistance, even less so a form of aid as such, these were by far the best possible form of assistance that a post-communist country could have received for conducting its transitional reforms.[6] This confirms a remarkably strong correlation among the levels of progress in accession into the EU, the received amount of FDI, and success in post-communist political and economic transition, which was clearly established by the time of the completion of the 2004/2007 EU enlargement.

As shown in Table 2.2, eight countries of ECE and the Baltics (EU-8), which opened accession negotiations with the EU already in March 1998 or (Latvia, Lithuania and Slovakia) in February 2000, had the best average scores in both success in post-communist political and economic transition (as measured by Freedom House's Nations in Transit (NIT) Democracy Score, the Transparency International Corruption Perception Index (TICPI) and EBRD indicators of economic transition)[7] and the highest received amount of FDI of all four groups of countries presented in Table 2.2. The second best results regarding both criteria were achieved by Bulgaria and Romania, which also opened accession negotiations with the EU in February 2000, but which as late starters with reforms (for reasons explained in the first section) were not able to complete accession negotiations together with the first group of states; they did so 2 years later and became EU members on 1 January 2007, only 2 years and 8 months after the first group, despite their serious problems with corruption and organised crime (see European Commission 2006, Phinnemore 2010; L. Holmes, Chap. 4 in this volume). The Western Balkan states, which started with reforms after Bulgaria and Romania but which were included in the EU's Stabilization and Association Process (SAP) from 1999 to 2000 and got the status of 'potential candidates' for EU membership a few years later (see the third section of this chapter), significantly improved their transition indicators and increased the amount of FDI received during the first half of the 2000s. However, the fourth group of countries in the table are seven European post-Soviet states which have never been considered as potential EU members and have never received any official offer or promise in this respect.[8] They had the lowest scores among all four groups of states in both political and economic transition indicators and started to have significantly worse democratisation scores after the late 1990s. Although the combined population of these seven post-Soviet states is over 200 million people, the total cumulative inflow of FDI in all seven of them from 1989 to 2006 was only slightly above the total FDI received by the small Western Balkan states and about the same as the combined amount of FDI received in the same period by the two late reformers Bulgaria and Romania (whose total population at present does not exceed 27 million).

As developments in this group of post-Soviet states, and generally in all non-Baltic post-Soviet states, is not within the scope of this chapter – but rather of Chaps. 3 and 4 of this volume as well as the chapters presented in Part III – the discussion in the following section

Table 2.2 Indicators of post-communist democratisation and marketisation and foreign direct investment inflow in East European states, 1999–2014[a]

	*Democracy score**			*Economic transition***			*TICPI****		*Cumulative FDI (mil. US $)*	
	1999	*2006*	*2014*	*1999*	*2006*	*2014*	*2006*	*2014*	*1989–2006*	*2007–2012*
EU-8 (2004)	***2.12***	***2.03***	***2.32***	***3.4***	***3.7***	***3.9x***	***51***	***57***	***224,585 T***	***97,462 Tx***
Hungary	***1.88***	***2.14***	***3.18***	***3.7***	***3.9***	***4.0***	***52***	***54***	***45,738***	***8,844***
Poland	***1.58***	***2.36***	***2.21***	***3.5***	***3.7***	***4.0***	***37***	***61***	***81,665***	***60,415***
Romania	*3.54*	*3.29*	*3.46*	*2.8*	*3.3*	*3.7*	*31*	*43*	*35,550*	*35,255*
Bulgaria	*3.58*	*2.89*	*3.29*	*2.8*	*3.5*	*3.7*	*40*	*43*	*19,225*	*27,812*
Croatia	*4.46*	*3.75*	*3.68*	*3.0*	*3.5*	*3.8*	*34*	*48*	*13,623*	*14,635*
Maced FYR	3.83	3.82	4.07	2.7	3.1	3.6	27	45	1,628	2,402
Albania	4.75	3.82	4.14	2.6	2.9	3.5	26	33	2,098	5,364
Bosnia–Herzegovina	5.42	4.04	4.46	2.0	2.6	3.0	29	39	2,680	4,193
Montenegro	5.50	3.93	3.89	1.6	2.5	3.3	na	42	1,326	4,755
Serbia	5.50	3.68	3.68	1.4	2.7	3.2	30	41	9,837	11,441
Ex-USSR 7	4.92	5.46	5.64	2.3	2.6	3.0	27	34	55,723 *T*	65,164 *Ty*

T – total; *x* – seven countries only (from 2008 the EBRD no longer provides data for the Czech Republic); *y* – six countries only (excluding Russia).
Ex-USSR 7: Armenia, Azerbaijan, Belarus, Georgia, Moldova, Russia and Ukraine.
*Freedom House NIT "democracy score" (1 being the highest: full democracy; 7 being the lowest: complete dictatorship) are published annually in June and show the state of play in the respective countries during the previous year. The scores given in this table for particular years (e.g. 2014) are actually published in the NIT publication for the following year (2015 in this case).
**EBRD economic transition indicators (4.33 = standards of advanced industrial [market] economies; 1 = standards of a centrally planned economy) are published annually in October in the *Transition Report* and refer to the state of play in the previous 12 months.
***Transparency International's Corruption Perception Index (TICPI) is published annually in December and gives information about the corruption level for that particular year. Since 2012, the TICPI has ranged from 100 (very clean) to 0 (highly corrupt), while in the period until 2011 it ranged from 10 (very clean) to 0 (highly corrupt). For simplicity's sake, it has been converted to a 100–0 scale for all years shown in the table.
[a]Data for Kososvo are not included as they are not available for most years before its declaration of independence in 2008. EU member states are given in italics; EU members from 2004: EU-8 (2004) are given in bold and italics.
Sources: Freedom House Nations in Transit, various years; EBRD Transition Report, various years.

focuses on explaining the reasons which prevented the Western Balkan states from continuing to improve all three indicators presented in Table 2.2 at the same rapid pace as they did during the first half of the previous decade.

The Slow Progress of the Western Balkans After the Completion of the 2004/2007 Enlargement: Domestic Problems, or a Lack of EU Assistance and Interest?

While the slow post-communist democratisation and marketisation of the Western Balkan states during the 1990s, together with their effectively non-existent cooperation (let alone association) with the EU, which were expected and logical outcomes of the wrong political choices which were made by their peoples and political leaders at the very beginning of their post-communist transition,[9] the deceleration of reforms, and particularly the very slow progress in EU accession of all these states after reforms and EU accession process were successfully initiated in the early 2000s, can hardly be considered as expected or logical. On the contrary, after the wars in B–H and Croatia ended in 1995, and after their Balkan neighbours – Bulgaria and Romania – elected reformist and pro-EU governments in 1996 and 1997, respectively, and were able to catch up with (some of) the countries of ECE and the Baltics in opening accession negotiations with the EU by 2000, there were heightened expectations that the other Balkan states, the states of the 'Western Balkans',[10] would also be able to quickly follow the positive example of their eastern neighbours. These expectations were further strengthened when the EU soon afterwards offered these countries the 'coherent strategy' of 'conditionality' and '[a] gradual approach' in offering EU cooperation and assistance for 'peace and stability, economic renewal, democracy…and [mutual] cooperation' (EU General Affairs Council 1997, Annex III; see also Pippan 2004).

The positive impact of this new EU strategy, which by 1999 was transformed into the above-mentioned SAP for the Western Balkan states, on post-communist democratisation and the introduction of necessary economic and institutional reforms in the related countries, rapidly became obvious. Not only did the two largest countries in the region, Serbia (then with Montenegro) and Croatia, almost simultaneously replace their post-communist authoritarian regimes with strongly pro-reformist and pro-EU governments during a 10-month period in 1999/2000,[11] but also all the countries in the region (with the only exception of Macedonia) succeeded in significantly accelerating their post-communist political and economic transformation in the first half of the 2000s (see Table 2.2).

Although these positive trends were strongly supported and further boosted by the conclusions of several EU Council and European Council meetings on the bright prospects of all the Western Balkan states for an 'EU future',[12] the progress of these countries in developing contractual relations with the EU was comparatively much slower than those achieved by the aspiring accession states during the 2004/2007 enlargement round (Table 2.3).

Twenty years after the end of civil wars in Croatia and B–H, and 15 years after the 'second democratisation' of Serbia and Croatia (which is a longer period than that from the collapse of communism in late 1989 to the accession to the EU of the first eight post-communist states on 1 May 2004), Croatia is the only Western Balkan state to have succeeded in joining the EU, doing so on 1 July 2013. Of the remaining candidates and potential candidates for EU membership from the Western Balkans, which have all signed association treaties with the EU[13] and (with the exception of Kosovo) have submitted their application for EU membership, only Montenegro and as of very recently (December 2015) Serbia have opened accession negotiations with the EU (Table 2.3).

Relations between the EU and the Western Balkan states started to slow down a couple of years before the 2008 Global Financial Crisis, when the EU, under the pressure of emerging *enlargement fatigue* and fears for the EU's 'absorption/enlargement capacity' in its key 'old' member states (Phinnemore 2006; Petrovic 2009; Petrovic and Smith 2013), decided to 'renew [the] consensus on enlargement' (European Council 2006, point 4), that is tighten accession conditions for new applicants. The key points of this tightening of the general accession conditions were an increase in the total number of acquis chapters from 31 to 35, a tightening of requirements for the closure of each chapter, and the introduction of a clause which defines the accession negotiations as an 'open-ended process whose outcome cannot be guaranteed beforehand' (European Commission 2005). In the following years the EU also began to prioritise the importance (and early opening) of the 'key chapters' on the rule of law, institution building and economic governance (European Commission 2014; Grabbe 2014), and to further tighten criteria for their successful completion. However, in addition to these conditions, which comprised a general set of additional accession conditions for the new candidates, the changed approach for the new

Table 2.3 Progress in EU accession[a]

	Signed EA/SAA	*Entered into force*	*Membership application*	*Accession negotiations opened*	*Accession negotiations closed*
Poland	16.12.1991	1.2.1994	1.4.1994	31.3.1998	12.12.2002
Hungary	16.12.1991	1.2.1994	8.4.1994	31.3.1998	12.12.2002
The Czech Republic*	4.10.1993	1.2.1995	17.1.1995	31.3.1998	12.12.2002
Slovakia*	4.10.1993	1.2.1995	27.6.1995	15.2.2000	12.12.2002
Slovenia	10.6.1996	1.2.1999	10.6.1996	31.3.1998	12.12.2002
Estonia	12.6.1995	1.2.1998	24.11.1995	31.3.1998	12.12.2002
Latvia	12.6.1995	1.2.1998	27.10.1995	15.2.2000	12.12.2002
Lithuania	12.6.1995	1.2.1998	8.12.1995	15.2.2000	12.12.2002
Bulgaria	8.3.1993	1.2.1995	14.12.1996	15.2.2000	16.12.2004
Romania	1.2.1993	1.2.1995	22.6.1995	15.2.2000	16.12.2004
Albania	12.6.2006	1.4.2009	28.4.2009	No	No
Bosnia–Herzegovina	16.6.2008	1.6.2015	15.2.2016	No	No
Croatia	9.4.2001	1.2.2005	20.2.2003	5.10.2005	30.6.2011
Macedonia FYR	9.4.2001	1.04.2004	22.03.2004	No	No
Montenegro	15.10.2007	1.05.2010	15.12.2008	16.6.2012	No
Serbia	29.4.2008	1.09.2013	22.12.2009	21.1.2014provis.**	No
Kosovo	27.10.2015	1.04.2016	No	No	No

*Czechoslovakia – 16.12.1991.

**The first chapters (35 and 32) were opened on 14 December 2015.

[a]EU-8 (2004), Bulgaria and Romania are given in bold

Source: European Commission Archive on Past Enlargements and other documents.

candidates for EU membership after 2006 also included the identification of '(additional) specific' conditions for some of the candidates. As will be shown in the following two subsections, these constitute an even bigger and more serious burden which the Western Balkan countries have had to face on their way to EU accession.

Socio-political Conditions and Open Issues in the Western Balkan States

Stagnation and the worsening of the levels of democratisation – which is a visible aspect in all of the countries of post-communist East-Central and Eastern Europe after the mid-2000s (Table 2.2) and particularly after the emergence of the Global Financial Crisis in 2008 – and their very slow recovery in the following years have been reflected in the socio-political developments of the Western Balkan states. Due to the negative impact of this and some other factors which will be discussed in the ensuing sections, none of these states has been able to significantly improve its level of democratisation since the mid-2000s. While there have been some important improvements in the fight against corruption, particularly in the three most advanced (or democratised) countries in the region (e.g. Croatia, Montenegro and Serbia) which were also able to keep the same (or even slightly improve their) NIT democracy scores, all the other states in the region have worsened their performance in this area over the last 10 years (see Table 2.2).

However, in comparison to negative trends in other post-communist states, particularly in the Eurasian post-Soviet states, as well as in countries such as Hungary and Slovakia, which were declared 'consolidated democracies' even before they became full EU members in 2004, the worsening of the NIT 'democracy scores' in the Western Balkan states has been relatively moderate. Furthermore, when compared to the achieved democracy (and economic transition) scores in other EU members from ex-communist Europe (particularly the most recent entrants – Croatia, Bulgaria and Romania) from the years before they joined the EU, or more accurately before they started accession negotiations (see the data in Tables 2.2 and 2.3), the current conditions in the most advanced Western Balkan states – Montenegro, Serbia and until recently Macedonia – are not all that different (for more details in this regard, see Petrovic and Smith 2013). Nevertheless, the EU leaders did not try to speed up the accession of these states after the 2004/2007 enlargement, but rather decided to try to avoid 'mistakes' from the previous enlargement rounds, particularly those related to the 'premature accession' of Romania and Bulgaria (Vachudova 2014; Grabbe 2014).[14] Fearing for the future and 'absorption capacity' of EU institutions they instead decided, as mentioned earlier, to tighten the general (Copenhagen 1993) conditions and then to 'develop new', specific accession conditions for particular Western Balkan states that were almost exclusively related to the unsolved or contested statehood status of some of them.

As is more or less regularly repeated in EU Commission and Freedom House annual reports on the state of conditions in the individual countries of the Western Balkan region, the functioning of recently established democratic institutions in these countries is heavily burdened by administrative inefficiency and especially by weak judicial systems which are not able to eliminate the involvement of criminal activities and corruption in the work of these institutions. The destabilising impact of these political system weaknesses, which are by no means specific to the Western Balkans,[15] has been enormously strengthened and prolonged by the continuing existence of inter-ethnic problems and conflicts in and among the Western Balkan states. Leaving aside Albania, which continues to struggle with a very weak level of consolidation of democratic institutions and enormously high corruption, a major source of political instability in all three Western Balkan states with the worst state of democracy (B–H, Macedonia, and Kosovo – the NIT democracy score for Kosovo was 5.14 and TICPI score 33 in 2014) remains the problematic and conflicting internal ethnic relations regarding the very constitutional definition of these countries.

In addition to the problems in relation between Serbia and Kosovo regarding Kosovo's contested statehood status[16] and the ever-present high level of tensions between Kosovo's Albanian majority and Serbian ethnic minority, a very serious lack of inter-ethnic trust in B–H and Macedonia continues to politically destabilise these countries as well as to threaten regional stability. While in Kosovo the ethnic animosities are linked to corruption, which is like in Albania of endemic proportions (Bogdani 2015) and very similar in scale to the levels of corruption experienced in the semi-authoritarian and authoritarian regimes of the Eurasian states (see Table 2.2), ethnic mistrust in Macedonia, coupled with increased animosity between the evermore authoritarian government of Prime Minister Gruevski and the largest opposition party, has in recent years paralysed political life and the chance for further improvements in the functioning of democratic institutions in this country. Similarly in B–H, when discussing the poor state of the national economy and the political standstill, the political representatives of all three ethnic groups continue to firstly blame the 'obstructions' made by the political leadership of other ethnic groups and then international factors (particularly the EU and the United States) for 'not doing enough' to prevent this obstruction. While the leaders of the Bosniak/Croat Federation, and particularly the ethnic Bosniaks, continue to excuse their poor governing performance by claiming that the 'non-functioning' of federal institutions is due to the 'Dayton approach' being 'too confederative', the Bosnian Serbs' political leaders are preoccupied with defending their 'Dayton autonomy' from such 'attacks'.[17] In this regard, almost nothing has changed since the mid-2000s when Knaus and Cox (2004) identified these tendencies in the behaviour of the political leaders of the three core ethnic groups in B–H.

The EU Response

Somewhat paradoxically, two decades after the signing of the Dayton Peace Agreement on B–H and 16 years after the Kumanovo Agreement and UN resolution 1244 on Kosovo,[18] these two democratically unstable countries continue to have a semi-protectorate status (initially and officially by the UN, nowadays effectively by the EU in coordination with the United States and NATO), while political life in Macedonia remains exposed to the less direct but strong supervision of the EU and United States. While the presence of various international civilian and military missions for more than 20 years in B–H and for over 16 years in Kosovo have provided a significant amount of support in securing peace and building state institutions (particularly an independent judicial sector and professional police force – see Chap. 7 in this volume) in these two former federal units of former Yugoslavia, neither of them can yet be defined as a viable or functional state.

Although the EU, which has gradually taken on the effective supervision of this country in place of the UN,[19] had begun very early on to condition its assistance to B–H with political requirements regarding the building of more efficient government apparatus, many of these requirements never had a real chance to be adopted, let alone the implementation by the B–H political parties. This is particularly related to EU demands for changes to the national legislature that would grant greater executive powers to the institutions of central government on the account of the governments of two entities that required (as stated in the Dayton Agreement and in the national constitution based on that agreement) a consensual majority of political representatives of all three major ethnic groups. Not only have such demands been continuously and strongly opposed by Bosnian Serb (and to a large extent by Bosnian Croat) politicians, they have also (as stated earlier) been continuously used by the political representatives of all three ethnic groups as an excuse for their not doing or incorrectly doing things which they objectively could have accomplished (Knaus and Cox 2004). In this way, this conditioned assistance, which was offered under the formula of 'progress in association and integration with the EU for progress in the political centralisation of the country',[20] was more of an additional hindrance than a form of constructive assistance that would help the state as a whole consolidate democratic institutions and cope with economic challenges and necessary reforms.

As in B–H, the relatively large presence of the international (particularly EU) factor in Kosovo since 1999 has not yet resulted in transforming this former Serbian province into a functioning state, while the level of its democratisation is by far the worst in the region. However, some progress in relations with Serbia achieved in the last couple of years within the so-called Belgrade–Pristina dialogue for the normalisation of relations between the two parties, held under EU supervision (see European Union 2016) gives at least a modest hope for Kosovo's better future. This hope can hardly be expected with current political developments in either B–H or Macedonia, despite much better achieved levels of democratisation (see Table 2.2) and current socio-economic development of the latter two.

Although it is not so intensively exposed to EU monitoring and control as B–H and Kosovo, Macedonia is another former Yugoslav republic with a contested statehood status. It continues to be hampered by the demands of its quite large Albanian ethnic minority (making up one quarter of the country's total population) for further territorial (i.e. ethnic) decentralisation and the possible (con)federalisation of governmental power as well as problematic relations with neighbouring Greece and Bulgaria regarding the interpretation of the country's history and the use of its very name and language. Moreover, the relations with these two neighbouring countries, who are also members of the EU, remain the only 'official' reason (or excuse) that has blocked any progress in this country's accession to the EU for more than 10 years.

While not hesitating to send its missions and experts to assist the troubled Western Balkan states in building state institutions, or, as was the case with Macedonia, to send its highest representatives to assist in (temporarily) resolving the political unrest that has resulted from the long-standing imbalances which Macedonia has been living with more or less from the time of the declaration of its independent statehood,[21] the EU has resisted providing an option of a quicker accession pathway that could have helped these states to 'clean their mess' while progressing with the accession process (Grabbe et al. 2010). Instead of this, and in accordance with its tougher approach adopted in 2006, EU leaders have expected these troubled states in the meantime to follow the EU's instructions (i.e. the additional Copenhagen-plus-plus-plus or SAP-plus-plus conditions – see the following sections) and solve their long-standing problems alone. The problem is that these long-standing problems have been primarily related to the very constitutional order of these states, on which interested Western Balkan nations and ethnic groups have sharply divided opinions. Therefore, the EU incentives for the (final) settlement should be properly balanced while being effective in order to please all the interested parties. However, this has often not been the case. With regard to the EU 'incentive' for the solution of the Greek–Macedonian dispute over Macedonia's name, it can simply be said that there was no such incentive at all. Nevertheless, the EU did not hesitate in punishing the incompliance of the West Balkan parties with its (dis)incentives and de facto additional accession conditions by preventing the countries in question from advancing to the next step in the accession process.

When, for instance, the European Council rejected the recommendation of the Commission (based on its positive assessment of the country's preparedness) to grant official candidate status to Serbia in December 2011, the reason for this was neither Serbia's failure to meet any of the (tightened) Copenhagen accession conditions nor the SAP conditions (which were de facto the Copenhagen-plus conditions for the Western Balkan states) regarding cooperation on regional peace and stability defined in the late 1990s. Rather, the reason was Serbia's unsatisfactory progress 'in the Belgrade-Pristina dialogue' on issues which arose after the declaration of Kosovo's independence in 2008 and Serbia's rejection to recognise it (European Council 2011, point 13). Similarly, when the European Council decided to grant Serbia official candidate status 3 months later, the only reason for the change of the Council's previous opinion was a positive report received in the meantime from the EU Council which stated that 'Serbia has continued to show credible commitment and achieved further progress in moving forward with the implementation in good faith of agreements reached in the Belgrade-

Pristina dialogue' (EU General Affairs Council 2012, p. 1). Hence, the above-elaborated slow progress of Serbia in opening accession negotiations once it got the status of an official candidate for EU membership in March 2012, and even after the negotiations were officially launched in January 2014, has not been determined by Serbia's (weak) progress in post-communist reform (which by 2014 had definitely reached or even slightly overcome the level of Romania, Bulgaria and Croatia at the time they opened their accession negotiations in 2000 or 2005, respectively, see Table 2.2 and Petrovic and Smith 2013 for more details), but was exclusively a result of its progress 'in the Belgrade-Pristina dialogue' (see also Poznatov 2015).

The main reason for the slow progress of Macedonia in the EU accession process is even more 'external' than Serbia's and is almost bizarre, particularly after the Commission had recommended to the Council to open accession negotiations with Macedonia already in 2009. This reason has nothing to do with either Macedonia's ability to meet the original or tightened Copenhagen accession conditions or the later defined SAP conditions. The main and, in fact, the only official reason Macedonia has now been waiting for more than a decade to open accession negotiations after it was recognised as an official candidate for EU membership in December 2005 [which is an absolute record in the history of all EU/EC/EEC enlargements since the foundation of the European Economic Community (EEC) in 1957] is much more trivial and has been entirely determined by the Greek veto in the Council imposed due to concerns regarding Macedonia's official name.[22] Taking into account the deepness of the economic and financial crises which Greece has now been in for years and its dependence on international aid and assistance, it is hard to believe that serious engagement by the EU and its leading member states (possibly with the United States) in persuading these two parties to find a compromise could not have solved this 'problem' many years ago and opened a pathway for Macedonia's much quicker EU accession. However, the EU's inaction in this regard and its waiting for the Macedonian political leadership to find a way to meet these specific accession conditions more or less alone, by reaching a compromise solution with Greece,[23] as well as the continuous postponement of the opening accession negotiations, have started to have serious negative repercussions on the socio-political stability of Macedonia. Years spent in limbo – neither here nor there regarding the country's EU accession bid – have not only 'encouraged' Bulgaria to join Greece in opposing the Commission recommendation for opening accession negotiations with Macedonia since 2012[24] and negatively impacted the general enthusiasm in the country regarding its possible integration into the EU (and also NATO, as this attempt has also been vetoed by Greece). They have also contributed to the backsliding of some of the previous achieved reforms. As is partially visible through the worsening of the country's democracy score (Table 2.2) it was also recognised in the latest Commission report on Macedonia (European Commission 2015b), that 'the last decade's reforms are being undermined by real and potential political interference in the work of the judiciary' (p. 12). However, although the Commission is aware of such damaging effects of the continuous postponement of the opening of accession negotiations with Macedonia, it obviously cannot do much about it by itself. Hence, while it states in this report that '[t]he "name issue" with Greece needs to be resolved as a matter of urgency' (p. 5), several pages later in the same document it also states that there have not been any formal talks held on the name issue between the two parties in the last year (p. 24).

While Kosovo's progress in its relations with the EU could be assessed as satisfactory (although it has only very recently completed the first step on its long road to the EU membership by signing the SAA, see Table 2.3) taking into account its late start and very weak level of democratisation (and even more so the fact that its statehood status is still contested by five EU member states), according to the European Commission, the case of B–H is at a 'standstill' (European Commission 2015a). As shown in Table 2.3, after this country had signed its SAA with the EU in 2008, the EU member states needed 7 years to ratify it (which is another negative record in the history of all EU/EC/EEC enlargements held by one Western Balkan country). Moreover, during this period the EU leaders effectively did not until very recently 'allow' the Bosnian and Herzegovinian government to submit an official application for membership (subjecting it to the prior successful accomplishment of certain conditions) despite an existing consensus about this among the political leaders of all three core ethnic groups in the country.

While the official explanation of the Commission for such slow progress in EU accession of B–H is that this 'country remains at a standstill in the European integration process ... [due to] a lack of collective political will on the part of the political leaders to address the reforms necessary for progress on the EU path' (European Commission 2014, p. 24), the reasons for this 'standstill' can also be found in the very content of these reforms. As discussed earlier, most of these 'necessary reforms' are related to the proposed or demanded changes by the European Commission to the national legislature, including the constitution that should grant greater executive powers to the central/federal government in order to overcome 'a complex institutional architecture [established by the Dayton Peace Treaty and the country's constitution] that remains inefficient and which is subject to different interpretations' (European Commission 2015a, p. 7). However, the basic problem is that the political elites of the Bosnian Serbs, and to a large extent of the Bosnian Croats, who are supported by a significant majority of their respective populations, consider this 'complex and inefficient institutional architecture' as the basic guarantor of their wellbeing and even survival as an ethnicity in B–H, and they are not ready to voluntarily accept any rebuilding of this 'architecture' (i.e. the centralisation of the country's legislature), even if the price for it is the country's very accession to the EU (Inserbia.info 2015; Balkaninside 2014).

Nevertheless, the European Commission and EU leaders have continued to insist on the necessity of these types of reforms to B–H's legal and political institutions and repeatedly copy such demands in its documents, instead of trying to find some compromise formula which would enable the country to go ahead with the existing constitution and legislative order (possibly with some minor changes that could have been consensually agreed),[25] as suggested by some scholars years ago (Grabbe et al. 2010; Petrovic 2009). While the official excuses for such a continuing status quo or 'standstill' in B–H's (non)progress in EU accession, similarly as in the above-discussed 'naming issue' of Macedonia, are that compromise formulas either do not exist or are extremely difficult to be found, the above-discussed positive steps in Serbia's and Kosovo's accession process convincingly confirm that compromises can be reached even in areas where they initially seem to be genuinely impossible. Finding a formula which will encourage the Serbian and Kosovan governments to take part together in the Brussels talks,[26] and even more so find a way to open the process of Kosovo's accession to the EU despite the fact that five EU member states still do not recognise its statehood, seems to be a much greater challenge than finding acceptable compromises which would overcome current obstacles to B–H's and Macedonia's accession to the EU. The slightly changed focus of EU actions towards B–H, and the EU demands made of that country since 2014 towards addressing instead the 'outstanding socio-economic challenges it faces' (European

Commission 2015a, p. 4; see also EU Foreign Affairs Council 2014), which firstly led to the entering into force of B–H's SAA with the EU on 1 June 2015 and then 'allowed' EU leaders to finally officially 'allow' B–H to submit its application for EU membership on 15 February 2016, is definitely a step (although a quite late one) forward. Only time will tell whether this will be followed by other similar EU actions that may help drag B–H, together with its Western Balkan neighbours, out of the 'stalled accession' in which it has stayed for some years.

Conclusion

While the fact that Montenegro has until very recently been the only EU candidate country from the Western Balkans able to open some of the 35 acquis negotiating chapters may look a bit surprising, this perfectly well reflects the shortages of the changed EU approach to the accession of the Western Balkan states after 2006. The reasons for this are not only related to the longer or similarly long official EU candidate status of the other two candidates Macedonia (which got this status half a decade before Montenegro) and Serbia (which became an official EU candidate 14 months after Montenegro on 1 March 2012). They are also related to Montenegro's not very convincing democratic record[27] and its less successful economic transition compared to Macedonia and similarly successful economic transition compared to Serbia (see the indicators given in Table 2.2). However, the surprise is even bigger when one looks at the number of negotiating chapters which Montenegro has succeeded in opening since the launch of its accession negotiations in June 2012. While Macedonia is still waiting to officially launch its accession negotiations due to the reasons discussed above, and Serbia opened its first chapters only in December 2015, despite its accession negotiations being officially 'launched' almost 2 years before and only 16 months after Montenegro (Table 2.3), the latter opened 20 negotiating chapters by the end of 2015, two of which have already been provisionally closed.

The current state of play of progress in the accession process of the candidates for EU membership from the Western Balkans is a result of the different capacities of individual Western Balkan states to meet the EU accession conditions, but even more so a result of the changed EU approach towards further enlargement after the emergence of enlargement fatigue in the mid-2000s. This changed approach has not only included the establishment of a general set of additional accession conditions for the new candidates for EU membership but also the identification of some specific (additional) conditions for some of the candidates. While their post-communist counterparts which joined the EU within the 2004/2007 enlargement round had to meet a relatively clearly defined set of accession conditions (defined in June 1993) that did not change by the time they concluded their accession negotiations, the EU candidates from the Western Balkans have had to cope with a tougher set of continuously increasing requirements from the very beginning of their EU aspirations. While in this regard the SAP conditions related to the post-war reconciliation and peace-building in the region were just and necessarily imposed (as the 'Copenhagen-plus' criteria) on these states due to developments during the 1990s, the same can hardly be said for the conditions that the EU imposed on these states after it began feeling 'enlargement fatigue' in the mid-2000s. The problem was not so much in the additional conditions which were set equally for all the new candidates (the Copenhagen-plus-plus conditions for the Western Balkan states) after the European Council's decision to 'renew [the] consensus on enlargement' in 2006, but rather in specific conditions which were additionally imposed on the individual Western Balkan states (the Copenhagen-plus-plus-plus conditions), primarily with regard to protracted disputes about their own or their neighbours' statehood status.

While Montenegro and Albania (and earlier Croatia) were spared EU requirements to comply with these specific conditions related to statehood status, progress in the accession process of the other four candidates or potential candidates for EU membership from the Western Balkans in recent years has been almost exclusively determined by the EU's assessments of their compliance with these (additional) specific conditions. This is particularly true when considering the progress in EU accessions of Serbia, Macedonia and B–H. Their additional problems with these 'extra' post-2006 conditions were not only related to the additional 'costs of compliance' (Schimmelfennig 2008), that is, the fact that they needed to (additionally) deal with these additional conditions as such. A greater factor which made this additional engagement largely fruitless was that, as shown earlier, these specific conditions (or EU incentives) were often inappropriately formulated, with very little respect for a country's specifics and realistic chances to meet them. In this way, and in sharp contrast to the experience of the countries of the 2004/2007 EU enlargement, the Western Balkan candidates and potential candidates for EU membership (with the partial exception of Croatia, Albania and Montenegro) since 2006 have been largely denied the most important form of EU assistance for post-communist reform – the possibility to link their political and economic reforms to the EU accession negotiation process. This has ultimately led to the more difficult access of these countries to other types of foreign assistance (including the inflow of FDI) and in the most drastic cases of Macedonia and B–H, it has actually resulted in the backsliding of some of the previously achieved reforms.

Notes

1. Among these, the determination of its political elite seemed to be particularly important (for more details see Fish 1998, 2001).
2. Samuel Huntington (1993, 1996) is the best known, but definitely not the only important author in this group (see e.g. Janos 2000, 2001; Kitschelt 2003; Darden and Grzymała-Busse 2006; Seroka 2008; Cirtautas and Schimmelfennig 2010).
3. The PHARE (Poland, Hungary, Assistance to the Restructuring of the Economy) programme was launched in 1990, and soon after it became the main programme of pre-accession financial assistance for the countries included in the 2004/2007 enlargement round. The programme primarily focused on development of the necessary institutions and administrative structures to implement the acquis accession requirements (see below). Through PHARE as well as The Instrument for Structural Policies for Pre-Accession (ISPA) and Special Accession Programme for Agriculture and Rural Development (SAPARD) programmes launched in 2000 for supporting projects in infrastructure, agriculture and rural development, the EU distributed nearly 23.5 billion euro (EUROPEAID 2015, pp. 25, 68) to 10 beneficiary post-communist states during the period from 1990 to 2006 (when these programmes ceased to exist).
4. There were 31 acquis chapters for the candidates which opened their accession negotiations with the EU in 1998/2000. For the candidates who opened their accession negotiations after 2005, the number of chapters increased to 35 (see the discussion in the ensuing sections).
5. On the other hand, the increasing FDI inflow did not come about all that automatically as soon as particular countries had acquired the status of an EU accessory state; it resulted from the introduced economic reforms (particularly those related to the large-scale privatization) and specific actions these countries had made, often under the pressure of the EU during the accession negotiations (see Bandelj 2008, 2010).
6. Why the inflow of FDI was more important than the other forms of financial assistance for post-communist reform can be easily seen when comparing the

total amount which the countries of the 2004/2007 enlargement received as pre-accession assistance from the EU during the period 1990–2006 (see note 3) with the figures given in Table 2.2. This comparison clearly shows that the former was three times less than the amount of FDI which was received solely by Bulgaria and Romania in the same period.

7. Similar comparative results can be obtained from other international organizations or projects specializing in monitoring and assessing democratisation, marketisation and human rights and political and civil liberties protection around the world (such as the Global Ranking Association, the Varieties of Democracy project etc.). In this chapter, we will stick with the above three organizations as the widely recognised and most often used. Although it is already included in the NIT's democracy score (which looks at the state of play of political rights, civil liberties, corruption, the rule of law, media, civil society and the electoral process), the level of corruption in the respective countries as measured by the TICPI is also given here as a separate indicator – in order to address the importance of this factor of democratisation, which is often used as an expression of not only the existing level of corruption in the public sector but also of the general stability of democratic institutions and the rule of law in the respective countries.
8. This is despite the fact that six of these states have been included in the EU's European Neighbourhood Policy, since 2003 and in the so-called "Eastern Partnership" since 2009 (see e.g. Petrovic and Klatt 2015).
9. With the exception of Albania in 1991, the first multiparty post-communist elections in which non-reformist ex-communist or national populist parties were elected in all of these states were held during the course of 1990 (see Petrovic 2013, Chap. 1).
10. Albania, Bosnia and Herzegovina, Croatia, Macedonia, Montenegro, Serbia and Kosovo, since 2008.
11. After the death of Croatia's authoritarian president Tudjman in December 1999 and the overthrow of Serbia's post-communist dictator Milosevic in October the following year.
12. These culminated in the adoption of the *Thessaloníki Agenda* in 2003 which declared that all the Western Balkan states "will [ultimately] be an integral part of united Europe" (EU General Affairs and External Relations Council 2003, Art. 41).
13. The so-called Stabilisation and Association Agreements (SAA), which were basically similar to the Europe Agreements on primarily asymmetrical economic/trade concessions signed with the countries of the 2004/2007 enlargement in the early 1990s (see Table 2.3). However, the SAA contained additional requirements regarding stabilisation, reconciliation and mutual cooperation among the post-Yugoslav states in accordance with the SAP, launched in 1999.

14. The more thorough analyses actually show that there is no real evidence that the post-accession trajectories of these two countries have significantly differed from those of their post-communist counterparts who joined the EU in 2004 (Pop-Eleches and Levitz 2010; Sedelmeier 2014).
15. They remain a serious problem in many post-communist countries of the 2004/2007 EU enlargements, particularly in Romania, Bulgaria and some countries which worsened their democracy scores and corruption indexes in recent years (see Table 2.2 and Chap. 4 by L. Holmes in this volume).
16. Kosovo's independence (declared in February 2008) is still not officially recognised by Serbia, the United Nations and many other states (including five EU member states), but it is recognised by over 100 members of the UN and most other international organisations, such as the IMF, World Bank and (de facto) the EU itself.
17. The civil/ethnic war in Bosnia and Herzegovina which broke out in April 1992 was terminated by the Dayton Peace Accords, which were initiated and agreed to in November and formally signed as "The General Framework Agreement for Peace in Bosnia and Herzegovina" by the leaders of Bosnia–Herzegovina, Serbia and Croatia in Paris on 14 December 1995. This Agreement established Bosnia and Herzegovina as a de facto confederative state consisting of two semi-independent entities – the "Republika Srpska" and "the Federation of Bosnia and Herzegovina" (i.e. the Bosniak-Croat entity) – with a feeble federal Bosnian-Herzegovinian government (the agreement is available in full at http://peacemaker.un.org/sites/peacemaker.un.org/files/BA_951121_DaytonAgreement.pdf).
18. The Kumanovo Agreement is a document signed between the International Security Force "KFOR" (initially NATO) and the governments of the Federal Republic of Yugoslavia (i.e. Serbia and Montenegro) and of the Republic of Serbia which ended the NATO intervention (bombing) of Serbia and Montenegro and prohibited the presence of "any Forces of the FRY and the Republic of Serbia" in the territory of Kosovo (art. 4). The agreement (available at: http://www.nato.int/kosovo/docu/a990609a.htm) was authorised by the UN Security Council's Resolution 1244 of 10 June 1999 which de facto placed Kosovo under the UN protectorate.
19. The Office of the High Representative (OHR) for B–H was established by the UN Security Council "[to] oversee implementation of civilian aspects of the Peace Agreement ending the war in Bosnia and Herzegovina" and "to ensure that Bosnia and Herzegovina evolves into a peaceful and viable democracy on course for integration in Euro-Atlantic institutions" (OHR website), but all High Representatives were from EU countries and the EU is the main donor of the Office. Furthermore, the UN legislative and police mission in B–H (UNBIH) established after the adoption of the Dayton

Peace agreement has been replaced by the European Union Police Mission (EUPM) from 1 January 2003 (ceased to exist by 2012 – see Chap. 7 in this volume for more details) and the UN (de facto NATO) military mission "Stabilization Force" (SFOR) was replaced by presently still active (with some 600 military personnel) EU military mission EUFOR ALTHEA on 2 December 2004 (for more details see: www.euforbih.org).

20. Since the late 2000s, the EU requirements have defined the necessity of the country's constitutional change in the above direction as the *sine qua non* for its progress in the SAP process and towards EU accession (see e.g., European Commission, *Annual Progress Reports on Bosnia-Herzegovina* for all years in the period 2007–2015 available from the Commission's website).
21. After an open armed rebellion by the Albanian minority in early 2001, internal ethnic peace was re-established in Macedonia by the Ohrid Agreement of August 2001 along with many difficulties and the strong involvement of EU Commissioner and High Representative for Foreign Affairs Javier Solana. On several occasions, Macedonia received EU envoys who brokered peace deals between the disputing ethnic and political parties. The latest such a visit occurred in July 2015 when EU Commissioner Hahn came to stop everyday street protests and break an agreement about the "tender truce" and the early elections in 2016 between the Gruevski government and the major opposition party Social Democrats (SDSM), who have been boycotting parliament for almost a year since alleging fraud in the last parliamentary election of April 2014 (see e.g. Bechev 2015).
22. Due to its potential expansionistic connotation regarding the northern Greek province with the same name, Greece strongly opposes the use of the domestically preferred term "Macedonia" as this country's name. As a result, the country was admitted to the UN in 1992 under the "provisional" name (the Former Yugoslav Republic of Macedonia), which is still in official use by the UN, international organisations and those states which accept Greek argument, and will remain so until the two parties find a mutually acceptable solution. It is solely for reasons of simplicity, and without any attempt to interfere in the ongoing "name debate" that this country is referred to as "Macedonia" in this chapter.
23. Macedonia and Greece had agreed already in 1995, when they formalised bilateral relations to negotiate this problem under the auspices of the United Nations; however, these negotiations are very occasional and informal and are without any resolute political incentive which could have moved them forward.
24. Because of "stealing from Bulgaria's history and badmouthing [it]" (EurActiv 2012).

25. As stated in note 20, all the Commission's annual progress reports on B–H in recent years have insisted on the changes to (i.e. centralisation of) the constitution, particularly after the so-called *Sejdić-Finci* ruling of the European Court of Human Rights on the (non-)electability of representatives of national minorities to the Bosnian and Herzegovinian collective presidency. While there seems to exist consensus among the representatives of all three major ethnic groups about the necessity of amending the constitution in this respect (see European Commission 2015a, p. 21), the demanded changes are more problematic for the Bosnian politicians in the area of the current (mainly consensual) decision-making process in the federal parliament and the jurisdiction of the federal institutions over the regional levels of government, particularly over the Serbian entity and the so-called Croatian Cantons in the Bosniak-Croat entity.
26. While the Serbian officials explain their participation in the Brussels talks as participation in talks with the government of the "autonomous province of Kosovo" (hence the name "Belgrade-Pristina Dialogue" instead of "Serbia-Kosovo Dialogue"), Kosovo's officials have defined the same talks as "intergovernmental" and as Serbia's de facto acknowledgment of Kosovo's independence.
27. Montenegro, which has been an official candidate for EU membership since 17 December 2012, is the only post-communist state in Europe which has never experienced an electoral change of ruling party or leader. Prime Minister Milo Djukanović and his Democratic Party of Montenegrin Socialists (formerly the League of Montenegrin Communists) have been in power throughout the whole period of post-communist (and even the last few years of communist) history of the country. Djukanović himself has served six terms as prime minister and one as president of the country during this period. In several occasions (last time in October and November 2015) there have been organised large street protests led by the opposition against the alleged government corruption and mafia style rule of "the thief" Milo (see e.g. BBC 2015; Hopkins 2012; Vachudova 2014).

Bibliography

Balkaninside. (2014, April 15). Milorad Dodik: lack of consensus – obstacle to EU accession. *Balkaninside*. http://www.balkaninside.com/milorad-dodik-lack-of-consensus-obstacle-to-eu-accession. Accessed February 2016.

Bandelj, N. (2008). *From communists to foreign capitalists: the social foundations of foreign direct investment*. Princeton, NJ: Princeton University Press.

Bandelj, N. (2010). How EU integration and legacies mattered for foreign direct investment into central and eastern Europe. *Europe-Asia Studies, 62* (3), 481–501.

BBC. (2015, October 25). Protesters call for Montenegro PM to step down. *BBCNews.* http://www.bbc.com/news/world-europe-34630358. Accessed February 2016.

Bechev, D. (2015, May 8) Breaking Macedonia's vicious circle. *EU Observer*, https://euobserver.com/opinion/128635

Berend, T. (2001). The "crisis zone" revisited: Central and Eastern Europe in the 1990s. *East European Politics and Societies, 15*(2), 250–268.

Bevan, A., & Estrin, S. (2004). The determinants of foreign direct investment into European transition economies. *Journal of Comparative Economics, 32*(4), 775–787.

Bideleux, R. (2001). Europeanisation and the limits to democratisation in East Central Europe. In: G. Pridham and A. Ágh (Eds.), *Prospects for democratic consolidation in East-Central Europe*. Manchester and New York: Manchester University Press.

Bogdani, A. (2015, June 9). Albanian justice system slammed as totally corrupt. *BalkanInsight.* http://www.balkaninsight.com/en/article/judges-in-albania-pays-up-to-300-000-for-their-positions-report-says. Accessed February 2016.

Cirtautas, A. M., & Schimmelfennig, F. (2010). Europeanisation before and after accession: conditionality, legacies and compliance. *Europe-Asia Studies, 62*(3), 421–441.

Crampton, R. J. (1997 [1994]). *Eastern Europe in the twentieth century and after* (2nd ed.). London and New York: Routledge.

Darden, K., & Grzymała-Busse, A. (2006). The great divide: literacy, nationalism, and the communist collapse. *World Politics, 59*(1), 83–115.

Dimitrova, A. (2002). Enlargement, institution-building and the EU's administrative capacity requirement. *West European Politics, 25*(4), 171–190.

Ekiert, G. (1996). *The state against society. Political crises and their aftermath in East Central Europe*. Princeton, NJ: Princeton University Press.

Ekiert, G. (2003). Patterns of postcommunist transformation in Central and Eastern Europe. In: E. Grzegorz & S. E. Hanson (Eds.), *Capitalism and democracy in Central and Eastern Europe. Assessing the legacy of communist rule* (pp. 89–119). Cambridge: Cambridge University Press.

EU General Affairs Council. (1997). Council conclusions on the application of conditionality with a view to developing a coherent EU-strategy for the relations with the countries in the region, 29–30 April, Annex III.

EU Foreign Affairs Council. (2014, April 14). *Council conclusions on Bosnia and Herzegovina*. Luxembourg.

EU General Affairs and External Relations Council. (2003, June 16). *The Thessaloniki agenda for the Western Balkans: moving towards European integration*. Luxembourg: Council Conclusions, Annex A.

EU General Affairs Council. (2012, February 28). *Council conclusions on enlargement and the stabilisation and association process*. Brussels.

EurActiv. (2012, November 2). Bulgaria vetoes Macedonia's EU accession talks. *EurActiv.com*. http://www.euractiv.com/enlargement/bulgaria-vetoes-macedonia-eu-acc-news-515809. Accessed February 2016.

EUROPEAID. (2015). *Evaluation of PHARE financial assistance to Bulgaria (BG), Cyprus (CY), Czech Republic (CZ), Estonia (EE), Hungary (HU), Latvia (LV), Lithuania (LT), Malta (MT), Poland (PL), Romania (RO), Slovakia (SK), Slovenia (SI), Final Report*. Brussels: European Commission.

European Bank for Reconstruction and Development. (various years). *Transition report*. London: EBRD.

European Commission. (2005, October 3). *Negotiation framework* [with Croatia], Luxemburg. http://ec.europa.eu/enlargement/pdf/st20004_05_HR_framedoc_en.pdf. Accessed February 2016.

European Commission. (2006, September 26). *Monitoring report on the state on preparedness for EU membership – Bulgaria and Romania*, COM (2006) 549 final. Brussels.

European Commission. (2014, October 8). *Enlargement strategy and main challenges* 2014–15, COM (2014) 700 final. Brussels.

European Commission. (2015a, November 10). *Bosnia and Herzegovina report*. Commission Staff Working Document, SWD (2015) 214 Final, Brussels.

European Commission. (2015b, November 10). *The former Yugoslav Republic of Macedonia Report*. Commission Staff Working Document, SWD (2015) 214 Final, Brussels.

European Council. (1993, June 21–22). *Presidency conclusions*. Copenhagen.

European Council. (2002, December 12–13). *Presidency conclusions*. Copenhagen.

European Council. (2006, December 14–15). *Presidency conclusions*. Brussels.

European Council. (2011, December 9). *Presidency conclusions*. Brussels.

European Union. (2016). External action service website. Brussels. http://www.eeas.europa.eu/dialogue-pristina-belgrade/index_en.htm. Accessed February 2016.

Fish, M. S. (1998). Mongolia: democracy without prerequisites. *Journal of Democracy, 9*(3), 127–141.

Fish, M. S. (2001). The inner Asian anomaly: Mongolia's democratization in comparative perspective. *Communist and Post-Communist Studies, 34*, 323–338.

Freedom House. (various years). *Nations in transit*. http://www.freedomhouse.org. Accessed February 2016.

Gateva, E. (2015). *European union enlargement conditionality*. Palgrave Studies in European Union Politics, Houndmills, Basingstoke: Palgrave Macmillan.

Grabbe, H. (2006). *The EU's transformative power: Europeanization through conditionality in Central and Eastern Europe*. Houndmills, Basingstoke, Hampshire and New York: Palgrave Macmillan.

Grabbe, H. (2014). Six lessons of enlargement ten years on: the EU's transformative power in retrospect and prospect. *Journal of Common Market Studies, 52*, 40–56.

Grabbe, H., Gerald, K., & Korski, D. (2010, May). Beyond wait-and-see: the way forward for EU Balkan policy. *Policy Brief*, European Council on Foreign Relations.

Gros, D., & Steinherr, A. (2004). *Economic transition in Central and Eastern Europe* (2nd updated ed.). New York: Cambridge University Press.

Hopkins, V. (2012, July 5) Montenegro: mafia state in the EU neighbourhood. *Open Democracy*. http://www.opendemocracy.net/valerie-hopkins/montenegro-mafia-state-in-euneighbourhood. Accessed February 2016.

Huntington, S. P. (1993). The clash of civilizations. *Foreign Affairs, 72*(3), 22–49.

Huntington, S. P. (1996). *The clash of civilizations and the remaking of world order*. New York: Simon & Schuster,

Inserbia.info. (2015, November). Dodik: EU membership might not be the best path for BiH. *Inserbia.info*. http://inserbia.info/today/2015/11/dodik-eu-membership-might-not-be-the-best-path-for-bih/. Accessed February 2016.

Janos, A. C. (2000). *East Central Europe in the modern world. The politics of the borderlands from pre-to postcommunism*. Stanford: Stanford University Press.

Janos, A. C. (2001). From eastern empire to western hegemony: East Central Europe under two international regimes. *East European Politics and Societies, 15*(2), 221–249.

Kitschelt, H. (2003). Accounting for post communist regime diversity: what counts as a good cause? In: E. Grzegorz & S. E. Hanson (Eds.), *Capitalism and democracy in Central and Eastern Europe. Assessing the legacy of communist rule* (pp. 49–86). Cambridge: Cambridge University Press.

Knaus, G., & Cox, M. (2004). Bosnia and Herzegovina: Europeanisation by decree. In: J. Batt (Ed.), *The Western Balkans: moving on* (pp. 55–68), Chaillot Paper, No. 70. Paris: Institute for Security Studies.

Lavigne, M. (1999 [1995]). *The economics of transition: From socialist economy to market economy* (2nd ed.). Houndmills, Basingstoke and New York: Palgrave.

Mayhew, A. (1998). *Recreating Europe. The European union's policy towards Central and Eastern Europe*. Cambridge: Cambridge University Press.

McFaul, M. (2002). The fourth wave of democracy and dictatorship. Noncooperative transitions in the postcommunist world. *World Politics, 54*(2), 212–244.

Petrovic, M. (2009). (What about) the further enlargement of the EU? In between European enlargement fatigue and Balkan instability challenges. *Australian and New Zealand Journal of European Studies, 1*(2), 39–58.

Petrovic, M. (2013). *The democratic transition of post-communist Europe – in the shadow of communist differences and an uneven Europeanisation.* Houndmills, Basingstoke: Palgrave Macmillan.

Petrovic, M., & Klatt, G. (2015). The European union and its post-communist neighbours: EU enlargement and the European neighbourhood policy. In: N. Witzleb, A. M. Arranz & P. Winand (Eds.), *The European union and global engagement: institutions, policies and challenges* (197–215). Cheltenham: Edward Elgar.

Petrovic, M., & Smith, N. (2013). In Croatia's slipstream or on an alternative road? Assessing the objective case for the remaining Western Balkan states acceding into the EU. *Southeast European and Black Sea Studies, 13*(4), 553–573.

Phinnemore, D. (2006). Beyond 25 – the changing face of EU enlargement: commitment, conditionality and the constitutional treaty. *Journal of Southern Europe and the Balkans, 8*(1), 7–26.

Phinnemore, D. (2010). And we'd like to thank . . . Romania's integration into the European union. *European Integration, 32*(3), 291–308.

Pippan, C. (2004). The rocky road to Europe: The EU's stabilisation and association process for the Western Balkans and the principle of conditionality. *European Foreign Affairs Review, 9*(2), 219–245.

Pop-Eleches, G., & Levitz, P. (2010). Monitoring, money and migrants: countering post-accession backsliding in Bulgaria and Romania. *Europe-Asia Studies, 62*(3), 461–479.

Poznatov, M. (2015, July 10). Merkel reassures Serbia during Belgrade vist. *Euroactive.com.* http://www.euractiv.com/sections/enlargement/merkel-reassures-serbia-during-belgrade-visit-316220. Accessed February 2016.

Pridham, G. (2001). Rethinking regime change theory and international dimension of democratisation: ten years after in East-Central Europe. In: G. Pridham & A. Ágh (Eds.), *Prospects for democratic consolidation in East-Central Europe.* Manchester and New York: Manchester University Press.

Pridham, G. (2005). *Designing democracy. EU enlargement and regime change in post-communist Europe.* New York: Palgrave Macmillan.

Raik, K. (2004). EU accession of Central and Eastern European countries: democracy and integration as conflicting logic. *East European Politics and Societies, 18*(4), 567–594.

Roeder, P. G. (2004). The triumph of nation-states: lessons from the collapse of the Soviet Union, Yugoslavia and Czechoslovakia. In: M. Michael & K. Stoner-Weiss (Eds.), *After the collapse of communism. Comparative lessons of transition* (pp. 21–57). Cambridge: Cambridge University Press.

Schimmelfennig, F. (2008). EU political accession conditionality after enlargement: consistency and effectiveness. *Journal of European Public Policy, 15*(6), 918–937.

Schimmelfennig, F., Engert, S., Knobel, H. (2006). *International socialization in Europe: European organizations, political conditionality and democratic change*. London: Palgrave.
Sedelmeier, U. (2014). Anchoring democracy from above: The European union and democratic backsliding in Hungary and Romania after accession. *Journal of Common Market Studies, 52*(1), 105–121.
Seroka, J. (2008). Issues with regional reintegration of the Western Balkans. *Journal of Southern Europe and the Balkans, 10*(1), 15–29.
Stiglitz, J. (2002). *Globalization and its discontents*. London: Penguin.
Svejnar, J. (2002). Transition economies: performance and challenges. *Journal of Economic Perspectives, 16*(1), 3–28.
Transparency International. (various years). *Corruption perceptions index*. Berlin: Transparency International.
Turnock, D. (1989). *Eastern Europe: an economic and political geography*. London and New York: Rutledge.
Vachudova, M. A. (2005). *Europe undivided. Democracy, leverage, and integration after communism*. Oxford, New York: Oxford University Press.
Vachudova, M. A. (2014). EU leverage and national interests in the Balkans: the puzzles of enlargement ten years on. *Journal of Common Market Studies, 52*, 122–138.

Dr Milenko Petrovic is Senior Lecturer Above the Bar at the National Centre for Research on Europe and at the Department of Global, Cultural and Language Studies, University of Canterbury, New Zealand. He is the author of *The Democratic Transition of Post-Communist Europe – in the Shadow of Communist Differences and an Uneven Europeanisation* (Palgrave Macmillan, 2013) and the author/co-editor of two other volumes and numerous journal articles and shorter contributions on comparative politics, post-communist transition and EU enlargement.

Chapter 3: Trajectories of Political Development in the Post-Soviet States

Graeme Gill

When the Soviet Union fell in 1991, there were widespread hopes that democratic regimes would emerge in the countries that were the former republics of the USSR. Such hopes have been dashed in all but a few cases. Although there is some dispute regarding the methodology and accuracy of the ratings given by various agencies including Freedom House, assuming consistency of judgement/measurement over time, they do give a sense of a country's political trajectory. Table 3.1 shows the ratings and designations of the 15 former Soviet republics in the first year of independence, a decade later, and in 2015 (https://freedomhouse.org).

The designations in Table 3.1 are not, in Freedom House's view, synonymous with particular regime types. They reflect a judgement about the state of political rights and civil liberties in each country, and are therefore a mark of the degree of openness or closure of the political system. The lower the score, the more open the system is, and conversely, the higher the score, the more closed it is. Generally, systems with high levels of respect for and observance of political rights and civil liberties tend to be democracies. Accordingly, we will interpret the designation

G. Gill (✉)
Department of Government and International Relations,
University of Sydney, Sydney, Australia
e-mail: graeme.gill@sydney.edu.au

Fish, Gill, Petrovic (eds.), *A Quarter Century of Post-Communism Assessed*, DOI 10.1007/978-3-319-43437-7_4

Table 3.1 Political trajectories of former Soviet republics

	1992	*2001*	*2015*
Armenia	Partly free 3.5	Partly free 4.0	Partly free 4.5
Azerbaijan	Partly free 5	Not free 5.5	Not free 6.0
Belarus	Partly free 3.5	Not free 6.0	Not free 6.5
Estonia	Partly free 3.0	Free 1.5	Free 1.0
Georgia	Partly free 4.5	Partly free 4.0	Partly free 3.0
Kazakhstan	Partly free 5.0	Not free 5.5	Not free 5.5
Kyrgyzstan	Partly free 3.0	Not free 5.5	Partly free 5.0
Latvia	Partly free 3.0	Free 1.5	Free 2.0
Lithuania	Free 2.5	Free 1.5	Free 1.0
Moldova	Partly free 5.0	Partly free 3.0	Partly free 3.0
Russia	Partly free 3.5	Partly free 5.0	Not free 6.0
Tajikistan	Not free 6.5	Not free 6.0	Not free 6.0
Turkmenistan	Not free 6.5	Not free 7.0	Not free 7.0
Ukraine	Partly free 3.0	Partly free 4.0	Partly free 3.0
Uzbekistan	Not free 6.0	Not free 6.5	Not free 7.0

The rating scale is from 1 the best to 7 the worst.

'free' as equating to democratic, 'not free' to authoritarian, and 'partly free' to 'hybrid' (on hybrid regimes, see Diamond 2002; Levitsky & Way 2010). Increased confidence in the rankings is given by the fact that where each country falls is broadly consistent with scholarly opinion. One further qualification is required: in the years intervening between these three points, the annual scores for individual countries may have varied but, except for cases noted later in this chapter, not sufficiently to shift the country from one category to another, and in any case such variation does not gainsay the overall trends.

Of the 15 states,[1] only Estonia, Latvia and Lithuania would be classified as fully fledged democracies at any of these times in the two-and-a-half decades since independence, and generally they have retained this status throughout; both Estonia and Latvia were not classed thus at the outset, but both had achieved scores of 2.5 by 1994. All of the other states fall short of being fully fledged democracies. Of the remaining 12 states, in 2015 only Georgia, Moldova and Tajikistan had improved their rating compared with 1992, while Ukraine was at the same level after having deteriorated significantly in the years in between. All of the other states – Armenia, Azerbaijan, Belarus, Kazakhstan, Kyrgyzstan (although here there was improvement from 2001 to 2015), Russia, Turkmenistan and

Uzbekistan – slipped in their rankings, meaning they were less democratic in 2015 than they had been in the first flush of independence in 1992. How are we to explain the failure of democracy to take root in most of the newly independent states of the former Soviet Union (FSU)?

Explanations for regime[2] trajectory have generally fallen into two categories—legacy or path dependent arguments and explanations focused upon the role of particular agents. This has been evident in some of the literature on political outcomes in the post-Soviet space as well as in other parts of the world.

Culture and Regime Forms

One of the principal ways in which a legacy argument has been mounted has been in terms of values viz. a particular country follows an authoritarian path because the culture is suffused with authoritarian values that provide an inhospitable environment for democracy to take root (Gill 2015, pp. 2–5). In this view, a country will have an authoritarian political system because it has an authoritarian culture. This has been a particularly prominent line of argument with regard to Russia. Some have sought to argue along psychological lines, that Russia has a particular 'national character' reflected in popular attitudes or that the Russian people have particular psychological traits (e.g. Dicks 1960; Gorer & Rickman 1949; Mead 1955). Others have eschewed psychology while still arguing that Russian culture was dominated by authoritarian values (e.g. Szamuely 1974; Billington 1966; Berdyaev 1948). Yet others have argued that Russian history and its perceived patterns reflect authoritarian popular attitudes towards authority (e.g. Pipes 1974; White 1979). This approach underpinned much of the 'political culture' literature of the 1970s.

The basic approach here was to see Russian history and culture as being characterized by a model of authority in which supreme power was vested in an autocratic leader, that that power was legitimated by a higher authority, and that the populace owed total loyalty and obedience to the authority figure. No opposition was possible, although there was some room here in the traditional notion of the right to rebel against a false tsar. Nevertheless, the basic model saw initiative and innovation coming from the top with the people as the passive receptors of direction from the authority figure. The people were not seen as active participants in political life, but as the passive receivers of wisdom from above. This was clearly an authoritarian conception of power that was deeply unsympathetic to democracy. This conception of authority was seen as underpinning tsarist autocracy, being carried forward into the Soviet era and, because of the dominance of Russia and the Russians in the Soviet period, of leaching through into the non-Russian parts of the USSR as well. Furthermore, those non-Slavic parts of the Union were also seen to have indigenous political cultures sympathetic to such a conception of authority.

The explanation here seemed simple: an authoritarian political system was underpinned by and consistent with an authoritarian political culture. The dominance of authoritarian values constituted a buffer to non-democratic rule because it portrayed such rule as the norm. In this sense, an authoritarian regime would gain a sense of legitimacy through the popular value system. Such legitimacy would have been absent had authoritarian political forms faced a political culture where ideas of democratic accountability and popular control were dominant because the modus operandi of the system would have seemed so at odds with the cultural values. This logic seems simple and compelling, but it does obscure some important qualifying factors (e.g. McAuley 1984).

One is the question of causality. The assumption behind much of the literature is that Russia has an authoritarian political culture and that this has shaped the political system. The problem is that this assumes that causality runs only one way, the political institutions are determined by cultural values. However, the culture itself is partly shaped by the state and what it does. One need only think of the way in which state-directed socio-economic change in the USSR, especially collectivization and industrialization, reshaped society, including in particular driving the process of urbanization that transformed much of the populace from village-based peasants into city-living workers, with the accompanying changes in social values. This means that values and structures interact in an important way, each shaping the other in a dynamic relationship. Accordingly, models that posit values determining structures is too simplistic and misunderstands the complex ways in which they interact. But once we accept that they interact rather than one being caused by the other, the danger is that the argument could become circular: institutions shape values which shape institutions.[3]

Much of the political culture literature also makes questionable assumptions about the nature of the values in a particular culture. One assumption is that a culture remains largely unchanging and is standard across the society. Clearly values change over time, and a political culture rarely remains in the form in which it originally emerged. Furthermore, it can change at different speeds and in different ways in different parts of the society; attitudinal differences between city and country is a common distinction observers have drawn consistently across cultures. Once it is acknowledged that values can both change and be differentially distributed across the society, it is difficult to argue for a direct causal relationship between a society's values and its political structure. In addition, when scholars seek to identify the dominant values in a particular culture, they are selective in the choice of what they see as being important. This means that some potentially contradictory elements in a culture may be downplayed. For example, the model of authority assuming popular passivity outlined above and said to belong to Russian culture is sharply at odds with the history of rural revolts and revolutions in Russia, while the presumed absence of democratic principles jars with the dominance of democratic rhetoric in many of the official pronouncements of the Soviet regime. This is not to say that the authoritarian elements in Russian culture were not there; but there were contradictory elements as well. The culture was not homogenous, and therefore it is difficult to draw a direct and unambiguous link between values and structure.

This does not mean that values did not influence political institutions and the way they developed, nor that they had no relevance to questions of regime legitimacy. If there is a discrepancy between popular values and regime form, the buffer of popular support enjoyed by the regime is likely to be thin and the credit the regime enjoys with the people is limited. If values and the regime form align, the popular basis of the regime is likely to be stronger. But given the points made above, the precise relationship between values and regime is more complex than it may at first appear. Probably the most that can be said is that while values may help to shape regime outcomes, they do not determine them.

Applying this logic to the different regime trajectories evident in Table 3.1, it is striking that democracy has appeared most consolidated in the three Baltic republics which because of the date of their incorporation into the USSR (1940/1945), were exposed to Soviet values for a significantly shorter period than most of the rest of the country. A similar point can be made with regard to one of the only three countries whose democratic credentials have strengthened over the last 25 years, Moldova. This clearly does not prove that culture was decisive in shaping regime outcomes, but it is suggestive that it may have had a role to play. But it is really to elsewhere than culture that we have to turn to explain regime trajectories.

Another legacy/path dependent explanation relates to the circumstances of the collapse of the old regime in each state. This will be analysed after reviewing arguments about the importance of agency.

The Role of Agency

A number of scholars have sought to explain authoritarian regime outcomes and survival through the actions of political actors (Gill 2015, pp. 9–16). While such actions can contribute to the development of longer term structural factors (see the ensuing sections), in the short term they can have important effects on regime development. Attempts to explain authoritarian regime survival usually involve a combination of at least two of the following three elements:

- regime strength and capacity, or how regime elites go about building the regime;
- opposition strength and capacity, or how opposition forces seek to develop a viable opposition to the regime; and
- international influences, or how international actors attempt to affect domestic political development.

These three elements – what regimes do, what oppositions do, and what international actors do – interact with each other to shape regime-building. Different explanations deploy these elements to different degrees to explain authoritarian regime survival. The three examples discussed later in this chapter show how these different elements can be combined to produce theoretically robust explanations of political change and its absence.

Valerie Bunce and Sharon Wolchik (2011) have sought to explain under what conditions post-communist authoritarian leaders have been thrown out of office at the ballot box. The main focus of their argument is the role of the opposition and of international influences. They reject the view that the strength of the regime, the position of civil society, economic performance, recent political developments like a crackdown on opposition or US government support for the opposition can give any real insight into regime change or survival. Their focus is on the independent role of elections in bringing about regime change. The key, in their view, is the electoral strategy adopted by the opposition. They are, therefore, not interested in either the strength or structural position of the opposition, but only in the electoral strategy it brings to the election.

For Bunce and Wolchik (2011), the components of a successful electoral strategy include opposition unity, measures to improve the quality and transparency of electoral procedures, a well-organized campaign that offers policy alternatives and aims to increase voter turnout, and the conviction that real change is possible. This electoral model is said to have travelled from the Philippines in 1986 through Latin America into eastern Europe and then the FSU. International diffusion is therefore central to the argument and to regime change. They argue that central to the adoption of this model by opposition forces in the respective countries was not just a modelling of their actions on the earlier success of others, but the role played by democratic activists from the successful cases in the later ones. Transnational networks of pro-democracy activists gave practical advice and sometimes material assistance to domestic oppositions, and thereby helped them to develop successful campaigns. Bunce and Wolchik argue that where this model was applied – Slovakia, Croatia, Serbia, Georgia, Ukraine and Kyrgyzstan – authoritarian leaders were removed, and where it was not – Armenia, Azerbaijan and Belarus – those leaders retained power. Certainly in terms of the political trajectories reflected in Table 3.1, the three successes in the FSU improved their democratic credentials immediately after the respective colour revolutions and the three failures worsened theirs.

This is an attractive argument because it emphasizes the capacity of the opposition to bring about change, seemingly regardless of the strength of the regime. It is also credible because there is a logic to the argument that the better the election campaign mounted by the opposition, the more likely it is to enjoy success. However, as it stands, the argument is incomplete because it ignores the role played in this by the regime. The authors argue (Bunce & Wolchik 2011, pp. 226–227) that 'the regimes where challenges to authoritarian rule did not succeed tend to be stronger on the whole than the other regimes', but because there was significant variation in regime capacity (data for this is on p. 225) they saw no consistent link between regime strength and electoral outcome. It is not clear why differences in capacity should negate the basic picture that emerges: that stronger regimes tended to survive. Furthermore, Bunce and Wolchik focus upon electoral authoritarian regimes where a democratic process is used to stabilize a non-democratic regime. This means that the regime creates the rules that structure the electoral process, including measures that will tilt that process to the disadvantage of opposition forces. In those cases where there was electoral turnover as a result of the electoral model identified by Bunce and Wolchik, the ability of the opposition to carry out that model was a direct result of the regime effectively allowing them to do so. Rather than cracking down on the opposition, or tightening electoral controls even more, the regime had enabled the opposition to implement its electoral strategy and thereby mount an effective challenge to the regime. It may not have been a conscious decision by the regime to allow this to happen, but by enabling it to occur, the regime was central to the whole process. This basic point is reflected in the fact that the figures cited by Bunce and Wolchik (2011, p. 217) seem to suggest that generally the more 'democratic' the countries were, the more likely they were to experience successful electoral challenge and regime change. The fact that this was not universal reflects the fact that the nature of the regime was not the only influential factor. Thus, while the focus on electoral strategy does help to explain electoral outcomes, neglect of the way in which the capacity to implement this strategy was dependent upon the regime and the attitude it took to the structuring of the electoral process, makes this explanation for regime change only partial.

A different approach is to be found in the work of Steven Levitsky and Lucan Way (2010). They emphasize the importance of international influence with regime strength and capacity a contingent factor. Rather than seeing elections as independent mechanisms of regime change, the key factor in their view was international influence. There are two types of such influence, leverage and linkage. Leverage was defined as a government's vulnerability to external pressure to democratize, something that was affected by the political and economic strength of the state, competing Western foreign policy objectives, and the influence of countries that sought to negate such Western influence. But in their view, leverage alone was rarely sufficient to bring about regime change principally because this focused overwhelmingly on electoral matters. Linkage was more complex, involving the density of ties and cross-border flows among competitive authoritarian countries on the one hand, and the US, pre-2004 European Union (EU) and the Western-dominated multilateral institutions on the other. Levitsky and Way identified six types of linkage: economic, intergovernmental, technocratic, social, informational and civil society. Linkage was seen as a mechanism that could increase the costs to regimes of abusing democratic principles and strengthen domestic pro-democracy constituencies, and thereby weaken authoritarian regimes. Both leverage and linkage were therefore about reducing the room for authoritarian regimes to function, and thereby to hamstring them so much that they would fall.

They argued further that where levels of linkage were low, the domestic organization of power by the regime was crucial. In their view, the role of the weakness or internal decay of states was often unrecognized in the literature, and that a coherent and well-organized state or party structure could assist autocrats to defeat democrats. Effective state and party organizations could enhance an authoritarian elite's capacity to prevent defection, co-opt or suppress opponents, blunt protests and win elections. Where state and party were strong, powerful opposition could be overcome; where they were weak, relatively weak opposition could prevail. Central to this dynamic was coercive power, and the regime's ability to use force to strengthen its position and overcome any challenges. They saw such coercive capacity as having two dimensions: scope, meaning the effective reach of the apparatus, and cohesion, meaning the level of compliance within the state apparatus. Broad scope and a high level of cohesion in the state (and party) apparatus was the key to regime survival. Coercion was where these two dimensions came together. A regime had to be able to wield the degree of coercion necessary to retain control, yet it was precisely high-intensity coercion that could most strain the unity upon which cohesion was built. While Levitsky and Way (2010) acknowledge that opposition capacity can be a factor, this is clearly seen as subordinate to the organizational power of the regime.

The essence of their argument is that where high levels of linkage to the West existed, competitive authoritarian regimes democratized. Where such linkage was low, regime outcomes depended upon the incumbents' organizational power. Where state and ruling party structures were well organized and cohesive, a regime was able to remain stable and authoritarian; where these underdeveloped or lacked cohesion, regimes were unstable, but they were rarely democratized (Levitsky & Way 2010, p. 5).

Like that of Bunce and Wolchik (2011), this is a persuasive argument. However, the primacy accorded to international influence and the relegation of state strength to contingency status risks underestimating the role of the state and regime. Vulnerability to international influence in either its linkage or leverage form in part depends upon the strength of the state and the skill with which state elites handle those international connections. A strong state (in terms of scope and cohesion) will be much better able to fend off or to moderate international influences than a weaker state. Geographical location can be important here too, with close proximity to larger powers seeking to exercise democratizing influence (like the US or the EU) potentially increasing the impact that leverage or linkage may have. Lack of proximity may even compensate for greater weakness in the state. The role of the state is particularly important given the nature of authoritarian regimes. Because of the capacity of this type of regime to limit the autonomy and power of social forces in the society, the capacity of these to independently link up with external sources of influence (governments, NGOs), and thereby enhance the potency of leverage and linkage, will be more limited when the regime is strong than when it is weak. In this sense, external influences will be moderated through the authoritarian regime structures. This means that rather than the state's organizational strength coming into play only when international linkages are weak, the nature of state organization will help to shape the role that international influences play domestically. The regime/state is not contingent; it is central. Nevertheless, it is striking that democracy is strongest among those states in Table 3.1 that are closest to the EU, both geographically (except Belarus) and ideologically.

The centrality of the state is recognized in the third type of approach, which emphasizes regime strength and capacity. An example of this is work by Way (Way 2005, 2010; Way & Levitsky 2006), who seeks to explain why authoritarian regimes in Armenia, Belarus, Moldova and Russia survived in the 1990s–2000s while Georgia, Kyrgyzstan and Ukraine succumbed. He argues that autocrats were more likely to survive when they had at least one of what he calls 'pillars of incumbent strength'. These were a single, highly institutionalized and coherent ruling party; an extensive, well-funded and cohesive coercive apparatus; and the state's discretionary control over the economy. In Way's view, ruling parties helped to discourage elite defection by institutionalizing the distribution of patronage[4] and they helped pro-government deputies ride the coat-tails of more popular incumbents and thereby establish a dominant place in the legislature. He believed that non-material sources of cohesion, such as an ideology or revolutionary tradition, strengthened a regime by making it less vulnerable to economic crisis or perceived swings in its popularity, both of which could affect patronage considerations based upon access to material resources. But it was a powerful coercive apparatus that was key to maintaining control because this strengthened state capacity. However, such an apparatus had to be well-resourced; its effectiveness could be undermined by significant under-funding and by large wage arrears. And finally, discretionary control over the economy gave a regime the capacity to consolidate support by giving it access to material resources, to buy off the opposition, and to deny the opposition resources (e.g. McMann 2006). For Way, each of these three pillars strengthened the regime against potential oppositional activity. Way also recognized the role that state organizational power plays in the shaping of opposition mobilization.

Way's focus on the characteristics of the regime acknowledges a key element in the durability and sustainability of authoritarian regimes. However, the argument that only one of the three pillars is sufficient to guarantee survival is problematic. It is unlikely that a regime could survive for long on the basis of only one of these pillars. In particular, discretionary control over the economy seems particularly weak; it is difficult to see how such control could be maintained without an effective state structure, including a coercive apparatus. This may not have to be developed to the extent envisaged in Way's three pillars, but there would need to be at least some form of organizational control outside the economic sphere if such economic control were to be maintained.

None of these approaches, alone, are sufficient to explain post-1991 regime trajectories. In seeking to do this, we need to take into account as the two primary factors regime strength and opposition strength, with international influence being subordinate to these two. It is the relationship between these three, but especially the first two, that is at the heart of the explanation that follows.

The Nature of Regime Change

Crucial in the structuring of regime development was the constellation of forces at work in the process of the fall of the USSR (for longer treatments see Bremmer & Taras 1997; Dawisha & Parrott 1997a, b; Gill 2002; Smith 1999). While this has been called a 'revolution from above' (Hahn 2002), the situation was actually much more complex, with different models of regime change occurring in different of the constituent Soviet republics. There were four such models:

1. Popular forces drive regime change, establishing a dominant position in the legislature and consolidate their rule. This occurred in Estonia, Latvia and Lithuania.
2. Popular forces drive regime change, but are unable to consolidate their power and are displaced or forced to share power, or succumb to caesarist proclivities of the leader. This was evident in Moldova, Georgia and Armenia.

3. Elite domination, with power shared by a mixture of old regime elites and new people, and popular forces do not play a big part in the process. Cases of this are Russia, Ukraine and Kyrgyzstan.
4. Old regime forces retain power largely because of the suppression of autonomous political forces in the years of perestroika. In Uzbekistan, Turkmenistan and Kazakhstan, such control was largely unchallenged, but a significant challenge had to be overcome in Tajikistan, Belarus and Azerbaijan.

The three countries in Model 1 were those classified as democracies as per Table 3.1 while the six countries in Model 4 were classed as non-democracies ('not free') either all or most of the time covered by the table. The countries in Model 2 are classed as partly free throughout along with Ukraine in Model 3, while the others in Model 3 (Russia and Kyrgyzstan) are mainly partly free but with one entry under not free. Models 1 and 4 countries are clear in the matching of path of regime change with subsequent regime trajectory, while those in models 2 and 3 are more mixed and ambiguous. How do we explain these different patterns?

Model 1

In the Baltic states, the course of regime change was driven directly by the Popular Front movements that had emerged in 1988. These were the best organized and ideologically most focused of the popular front movements to emerge in the USSR at this time. In both Latvia and Lithuania, they gained parliamentary majorities in the 1990 republican elections while in Estonia they had a majority with the support of reformist communists. The strength of these movements provoked a split within the ruling republican communist parties with reformist elements going over to the nationalist side, with the result that when the coup occurred in Moscow in 1991, the local political scene was dominated by those favouring the replacement of Soviet power and rooted primarily in the social movements and the parliaments they controlled. They then went about creating a multiparty democracy, with limited opposition from old regime elements.

The drive to consolidate democracy was fuelled by the desire of these elites to integrate with 'Europe', seen in terms of gaining entry to the EU. This aspiration was in turn fuelled by the encouragement and support they were given from within the EU, where the incorporation of the Baltic states into the USSR in 1940 had been seen as a grievous historical injustice (reflected in the refusal of many Western states formally to acknowledge that these countries were part of the USSR) that needed to be set right. The desire to gain EU entry was behind the subsequent moderation of the initial discriminatory citizenship policies in Estonia and Latvia that had clearly discriminated against the local ethnic Russian populations and that was the chief reason these countries had been marked as only partly free in 1992.

The decisive factor in the trajectories of the Baltic states is that the political process was dominated by elites who were closely linked to the Popular Front social movements and were committed to relatively open, democratic politics, even if this was combined with a tendency to place barriers in the way of full-scale participation by the ethnic Russian population. Entry to the EU provided further buffers for the sustenance of a democratic system, while those who might have wanted a more authoritarian set of arrangements (and may have looked to Russia for support) were weak and clearly outnumbered in the respective political systems. This was a direct result of the way perestroika (1985–1991) unfolded in these countries.

Model 4

These were the polar opposites of the countries in Model 1. In the six countries in this model, the sorts of popular forces that had been so strong in the Baltic states during perestroika were very weak. Not only had there been little organized mobilization from below during perestroika, but in each of these countries the authorities had set out consciously to hamper such a development. Organizers were harassed, meetings broken up, publications seized or prevented from appearing, organizations refused registration and elections rigged, such that opposition forces could mount little real challenge to the existing authorities. In Uzbekistan, Turkmenistan and Kazakhstan, the ruling party did not split and either simply changed its name or continued to operate as the leader's personal machine, and the party first secretary became president of the new republic. In Tajikistan, the party leader at the time of the 1991 coup (Kahar Makhkamov) was removed from office because of his support for that coup and was replaced by the person who had been party leader until removed in 1985 (Rakhmon Nabiev). Nabiev immediately cracked down on his opponents. However, Nabiev was forced to resign in 1994 in the face of civil disturbances and was ultimately replaced by former communist leader Emomali Rakhmon (originally his name was Rakhmonov) who sought to consolidate his position based on a communist successor party and exclusionary policies. The country continued to be wracked by civil war until late in the decade when Rakhmon was able to consolidate his position. The important point about this is that despite the threats to the rule of successive leaders, the civil conflict did not lead to the destruction of the old ruling apparatus which was able to survive and continue to sustain Rakhmon in power, nor did it generate effective civil society organizations.

In Belarus during perestroika, the communist authorities had kept a tight rein on the development of autonomous social forces, with the result that the most important of these, the Popular Front of Belarus (PFB), won only about 7% of the seats in the legislature in the 1990 election. The communist party hierarchy was split between reform and old-style communists, and this enabled the PFB leader Stanislau Shushkevich to effectively become the leader of the republic. However, he could do little in the face of conservative elements within the parliament and bureaucracy, and in early 1994 he lost office. In what was seen as a free and fair election, in the middle of 1994, Aleksandr Lukashenka was elected president and proceeded to consolidate authoritarian rule. Thus, in Belarus, popular forces had had some success only because of a temporary split in the ranks of their conservative opponents, and when this was repaired, those elements were able to shut out the effect of those seeking a more democratic form of rule. In Azerbaijan too opposition forces were too weak to be able to challenge the old regime forces whose aggressive use of the advantages of incumbency and the instruments of the state ensured their dominance. The communist party and its leader, Ayaz Mutalibov, appeared secure in power at the end of 1991, but the outbreak of fighting with Armenia over the outstanding issue of Nagorno–Karabakh destabilized elite politics, leading to the fall of old regime representatives and the temporary emergence into political prominence of the leader of the Azeri Popular Front (Abulfez Elchibey). However, Elchibey was overthrown in a coup in mid-1993, and former member of the Soviet party's Politburo, Heidar Aliev became the leader of the republic. He then cracked down on all opposition and consolidated authoritarian rule.

In all of these countries, the strength of old regime forces was sufficient to enable them to consolidate themselves in power, even if in three cases this was after a struggle. In all cases, popular forces were much weaker than those of the old regime, and were excluded from power. The result was authoritarian regimes which, in the eyes of many, were comparable to the Soviet forebear from which they had sprung. The key element was the closure of politics early in the new state's life. Furthermore, this could not be offset by democratizing influences from the West. Geography was part of this, with most of these countries not situated close to the West like the Baltics were, although this was less true of Belarus, and the US was able to project its power into the region through the establishment of an airbase in Central Asia to help prosecute the war against Al Qaida. But more important was the fact that these regimes consciously worked to ensure that such influence did not seep over their borders. These regimes took steps to keep civil society under strict control, and thereby stifled the principal channel through which potential democratizing influence could flow. The drive of regime elites to build an authoritarian polity allied to the weakness of domestic opposition and the authorities' ability to limit Western influence combined to consolidate authoritarian rule in these countries.

Model 2

If in Model 4, popular, anti-regime forces played little role in the transfer of power, in the countries in Model 2 they were central to this process. However, they were unable to build and consolidate a democratic regime. In Moldova, the Moldovan Popular Front (MPF) won a majority in the 1990 republican election; sidelined the old-style communist party; and supported a reformist communist, Mircea Snegur, as chair of the Supreme Soviet. The developing pro-independence stance of the government generated irredentist sentiments among the ethnic Russian population of the Transdnistr region, which, with the declaration of Moldovan independence and along with the Gagauz region, rejected the authority of the Moldovan government, leading to armed conflict. The basis of that government was also less secure because of the split between those who supported full Moldovan independence and those wishing reunification with Rumania. Following Snegur's election as president in December 1991, the ruling authorities split as Snegur and the MPF parted ways over a variety of policy questions, including the future trajectory of Moldova—independence/Rumania and presidential/parliamentary system. Snegur now turned for support to the old-regime communists, and leading members from the former ruling Politburo joined him in the leading offices of state. The elections in early 1994 placed the successor party to the former communist party in power. Thus, the initial oppositionist elite fragmented, leaving the way open for the successor party to gain power, but without excluding opposition forces from the political scene. This correlation of forces is reflected in Moldova's consistent rating as much more democratic than most of its former Soviet neighbours.

In Georgia, the opposition forces that had come together under the Round Table banner won about 60% of the parliamentary seats in the October–November 1990 election and its representative, Zviad Gamsakhurdia, won the presidency in May 1991. However, Gamsakhurdia's increasingly authoritarian behaviour and his attempt to consolidate power in his hands personally led to a split in the new government. Armed clashes at the end of 1991 to early 1992 forced Gamsakhurdia to flee and led to the creation of a provisional government from among the opposition forces. However, their ability to consolidate power was hindered by the continuation of armed conflict with pro-Gamsakhurdia forces and independence movements in South Ossetia and Abkhazia. At the centre, a struggle between the parliament and the new president, former Soviet foreign minister Eduard Shevardnadze, broke out, but over time Shevardnadze was able to strengthen the presidency and his own personal power. Thus, the initial oppositionist regime fractured and opened the way for the return to power of a former member of the communist power structure.

Armenian politics, like that of Georgia, was overshadowed by armed conflict, in this case with Azerbaijan over Nagorno–Karabakh. The initial government was led by the popular front Pan-Armenian National Movement (PANM), whose representative Levon Ter-Petrossian was elected president in October 1991. Despite some tensions between parliament and president in 1992, the situation remained stable until 1993–1994 when popular unrest developed in the capital over economic policy and the performance of the government. The PANM split and Ter-Petrossian suspended the main opposition party. When elections were held in 1995, against a background of complaints about Ter-Petrossian's increasingly authoritarian behaviour – including the banning of a number of opposition parties – the president's party won, but in an election that was deemed to be not fair. When Ter-Petrossian won the presidential election in 1996, widespread opposition demonstrations were suppressed by force. Ter-Petrossian held on to power until a split among his supporters led him to resign in February 1998. So although the popular movement that gained power at the time of the Soviet collapse remained in control, it became dominated by its leader who took on authoritarian powers.

So unlike in Model 1 where popular movements gained power and were able to consolidate a democratic structure, in Model 2 states the popular movements split and, in the cases of Moldova and Georgia, this opened the way for elements of the old regime to return to power, while in Armenia it facilitated the personal dominance of the leader. In all three cases, at this stage, the countries remained resistant to attempts from the West to influence the course of developments. Indeed, in all three cases, influences from Russia that were not supportive of democratization may have been more significant.

Model 3

If popular forces were central to regime change in Model 2 countries, they were of little importance in Model 3 countries, where the principal dynamic of political development emanated from within the elites. In Russia at the time of the fall of the USSR, both the parliament and the presidency were occupied mainly by figures from the old regime structures, although in the case of the presidency (and part of the parliament) these had forsaken their old regime affiliations and adopted a reformist stance. However, conflict soon broke out between the president and parliament, with the former resolving this in 1993 through the use of force. Boris Yeltsin then used the electoral process in an attempt to consolidate himself in power, something that failed because although he won the subsequent presidential election, opposition forces effectively won the parliamentary polls of 1993 and 1996. The stand-off between the president and parliament, combined with Yeltsin's attempt to gather power into his own hands, meant that during the initial decade, he sought successfully to marginalize the parliament and the popular forces that should have been able to use this institution to play a significant role in public life. Elite politics remained strained throughout the 1990s, and was only consolidated following Vladimir Putin's accession to the presidency in 2000, after which the authoritarian trends evident under Yeltsin gathered pace (Gill 2015).

In Ukraine, the emergence of a popular movement, Rukh, which was able to gain over a quarter of the seats in the parliament in the March 1990 election, led to a split within the ruling communist party between those sympathetic to opposition calls for independence and those wishing to remain part of the USSR. With the collapse of the coup in Moscow in August 1991, the reformist Leonid Kravchuk left the communist party, declared Ukrainian independence, and in December he was elected president. Kravchuk rested upon an alliance of reformed ex-communists (attracted in part by his refusal to follow Russia down the path of economic shock therapy) and nationalist democrats from Rukh, attracted by his support for independence and tough line with Russia on a series of issues. Despite tension between the president and parliament, elite politics was relatively stable. However, party development, and therefore the channel through which popular forces would be expected to exert themselves, remained retarded; in the parliamentary election in 1994, the overwhelming majority of candidates returned were independents, while the ethnic divide that was to dominate subsequent Ukrainian electoral politics was already evident and significantly hindered national party development. At the presidential election in 1994, Kravchuk was defeated by another former communist official Leonid Kuchma, whose election brought on a dispute with the parliament over whether the regime should be presidential or parliamentary. Kuchma won this struggle and a new more presidential constitution was introduced. The precedent of the replacement of the president through the electoral process was now set and continued to operate in Ukrainian politics, but so too did the fact of party weakness. So in Ukraine, the main drive of political development in the first decade of independence emanated from an alliance of former communists and nationalists, with the former the more influential, while civil society forces remained fragmented.

In Kyrgyzstan, there were no social movements that could have a significant effect upon the course of politics at the time of the collapse of the USSR. In the February 1990 election, nearly all seats were filled by communists associated with the ruling party. The presidency was filled by Askar Akaev, who was a former head of the Academy of Sciences. A dispute between the president and parliament over the distribution of power was initially resolved peacefully, but the two bodies were soon in conflict over the course of reform. The conservative parliament acted as a break on the president in his quest to introduce economic and political change. Akaev sought to go over the head of the parliament, making a series of appeals to the people for support, and ultimately he was able to bring about a new parliamentary election in February 1995. In the election, most seats were won by government officials, clan leaders and intellectuals, with political parties playing almost no role. This did not bring about a reconciliation between Akaev and the parliament, and the former proceeded to take a series of steps designed to strengthen the presidency and consolidate his grip on it. Thus in Kyrgyzstan, the weakness of opposition forces enabled successor elements of the old regime to maintain powerful positions within the political structure and shape the course of development.

Each of these countries in Model 3 remained relatively open to Western influences, although these seem to have had few effects. However, as the colour revolutions in Ukraine in 2004 and Kyrgyzstan in 2005 show, such influence had greater effect after the initial period of independence.

Regime Change and Political Trajectory

How were these different patterns of regime change significant in shaping the subsequent course of regime development? Essentially the patterns established at the outset set the broad course for subsequent developments: generally democracy was more likely where popular forces had an important part to play in establishing the initial outlines of rule; where those forces were weaker, the greater the likelihood of authoritarian rule; and where they were practically non-existent, a stronger form of authoritarianism appeared. The mechanism whereby this worked is that, in most cases, ruling political elites have little incentive to adopt a democratic form of government which will cast their tenure into doubt unless they are pressured to do so by popular forces from below. Such popular forces are likely to press for democratic reform to open the system up for their own participation; where they are weak or non-existent, elites have little reason to introduce a structure that would place their positions in jeopardy. This is particularly the case in a context like the FSU where elites had little practical experience of effective democratic practices and procedures and little real commitment to these. This process is clearly reflected in the experience of the states in the FSU.

In the countries in Model 1, the Baltic republics where popular forces drove regime change and dominated in the immediate post-fall conditions, reformist political elites and emergent parties generally cooperated to sideline representatives of the old regime and to build a democratic system. They established parliamentary systems with regular free and fair elections, and welcomed the influence and advice that the EU countries in particular were all too willing to give. Thus, from the outset, the system was open to popular forces.

In the countries in Model 4 (Azerbaijan, Belarus, Kazakhstan, Tajikistan, Turkmenistan and Uzbekistan) where popular forces were particularly weak at the time of the fall of the USSR, old regime elites were able to consolidate themselves in power, close off the system to the entry of new political forces, and generally institute an authoritarian style of rule. This involved the harassment and repression of opposition forces, the exertion of pressure on civil society and the hampering of its development, and the closing out of potential democratizing influences from the West. This was not always achieved without incident; the civil war in Tajikistan and the so-called Andijan massacre in Uzbekistan in 2005 are the two most important cases of opposition to the rulers occurring under these regimes, but generally the authorities have been able to keep popular mobilization under control. The willingness to use force in the face of such action has been an important factor underpinning this sort of regime development. In the absence of popular constraint, political elites built authoritarian polities.

For the countries in the other two models, the situation was more complex. In the countries in Model 2 (Armenia, Georgia and Moldova), the popular movements that were instrumental in regime change split, but not in a way that generated viable political parties. The split in each case was between the president and much of the popular movement, with presidential aspirations for enhanced powers being instrumental (but not alone) in this. The consequent struggle was not resolved through the electoral process, although both sides at times sought to mobilize popular support for their positions, with the result that these conflicts did not contribute to the building of viable political parties or a vibrant civil society. Furthermore, the presence of armed irredentist conflicts (plus the civil war in Georgia) created a context for the development of public politics that was not conducive to the emergence of democracy. The strongly authoritarian elements that were evident in these polities retained a prominent position, in the case of Georgia notwithstanding the colour revolution of 2003. That such authoritarian trends did not become all-powerful and drive democratic elements completely from the scene simply reflects the fact that no elite was in a position to be able to establish hard authoritarian rule had they wished to do so, with the result that these countries were hybrids of the democratic and authoritarian.

In the countries in Model 3 (Kyrgyzstan, Russia and Ukraine), where popular forces were so weak that they played little part in the regime change, the political elite that inherited power was itself split between old regime elements and reformist forces, with many people ranged between. The weakness of popular pressure on the elites meant that it was largely within the hands of those elites to determine the sort of political system that would exist in the country. The balance of forces in each case was sufficient to ensure that, in the first decade of independence at least, neither side could gain the complete ascendancy, with the result that the regimes that emerged had a combination of democratic and authoritarian elements, although as Table 3.1 suggests (except for Ukraine) the weight of the authoritarian was heavier than in the countries in Model 2.

The continuing importance of the circumstances of regime change is reflected in the data in Table 3.1. In 8 of the 15 countries, the designation that country had in 1992 was repeated in 2001 and 2015, meaning that although there may have been changes to the way the system worked (perhaps reflected in different numerical scores in some of the intervening years not shown here), these were essentially changes within the same regime type. Three countries that began as 'not free' remained 'not free'—Tajikistan, Turkmenistan and Uzbekistan. Four remained as 'partly free' – Armenia, Georgia, Moldova and Ukraine – while Lithuania retained the 'free' epithet throughout. In the other seven countries, there was a subsequent change in regime type. In five of these, the designation as at 2001 was repeated in 2015, meaning that there was no change of regime type in that time; 'not free' on both occasions were Azerbaijan, Belarus and Kazakhstan, while Estonia and Latvia were 'free' at both times. In two cases, there was a change in regime type from 2001 to 2015: Kyrgyzstan went from 'not free' to 'partly free', following the overthrow of Akaev by the colour revolution, and Russia moved from 'partly free' to 'not free', reflecting the coming to power of Putin. This shows a significant level of broad continuity, particularly if the 1992 designation is considered the default given that it is the first year after the collapse of the USSR and real trends had not yet emerged. This pattern is clearly consistent with the argument that the circumstances of the fall of the Soviet Union, and in particular the shape of the constellation of forces that came into power at that time, was crucial in shaping subsequent regime trajectories. The elites in power built the sort of political system that best served their interests, democratic where those elites were connected with and thereby influenced by the mass of the populace through social movements and political parties, authoritarian systems where they were not thus connected.

This is not a determinist argument. Had, for example, Gamsakhurdia or Ter-Petrossian been different types of personalities, the dominance of the social movements they headed may have been the pathway to a more democratic polity. Had Yeltsin called immediate elections, the dispute with the parliament may not have eventuated and the basis for a more democratic polity may have emerged. Had Vytautus Landsbergis in Lithuania been more autocratically inclined, the smooth path in that country may have been disrupted. Had irredentist conflicts not existed in Armenia, Azerbaijan, Georgia and Moldova, the path of political development may have been different. But these contingent factors did not exist, and in their absence the structuring effects of the circumstances of regime change seem undeniable.

A recent study by Henry Hale (2015) is consistent with this thesis. Hale argues that, with the exception of the Baltic states, all of the states of the FSU developed as 'patronal polities' where the currency of politics was personal association rather than formal institutions or ideologies. His argument is that, with the fall of the USSR, leading politicians (including in parliamentary Moldova) (Hale 2015, chapter 10) set up pyramids of power shadowing and overlapping with the official power structure through which they ran the country.[5] He posited a particular cycle of development whereby if the leader was perceived as a 'lame duck' and/or suffered a significant drop in popular support, he became vulnerable to challenge and overthrow, including from within his machine. Hale argues this sort of situation existed in all cases of presidential overthrow during the period: Ter-Petrossian in Armenia (1998), Shevardnadze in Georgia (2003), Kuchma-Viktor Yanukovych in Ukraine (2004), Akaev in Kyrgyzstan (2005), Kurmanbek Bakiev in Kyrgyzstan (2010), Mikheil Saakashvili in Georgia (2013), and Yanukovych in Ukraine (2014) (Hale 2015, pp. 181–278). Although this meant the overthrow of the political 'boss', it did not mean either a change in regime type or the destruction of the way in which politics was structured. Despite some apparent opening up of the regime after such leadership changes, these were temporary and the structures of patronal politics reasserted themselves (although it may be too early for a definitive judgement about the second Ukrainian case). Those who gained power at the outset, used that power to build the sort of systems that they wanted.

We do not have to accept all of Hale's elegant framework to recognize that there has been significant continuity in the authoritarian structures of post-Soviet government throughout much of the FSU and that this continuity is a result of the way political elites have structured post-Soviet political life. Crucial in this has been the forces at work at the time of the fall of the USSR. Where mass-based forces were active and powerful, the outcome has tended to be more democratic; where those forces were weak or non-existent, the result has been authoritarian. This pattern applies regardless of differences in levels of economic reform and privatization. The primary driving force in the construction of the various types of polities has thus been the correlation of forces at the time of independence, and the consequent level of restraint that could prevent authoritarian elites from building and maintaining non-democratic regimes. This may be seen as a continuing legacy of the USSR into the present and future.

Notes

1. This chapter is only concerned with the 15 former union republics of the USSR and does not include those statelets that have emerged as a result of frozen conflicts, North Ossetia, Abkhazia or Transdnistr.
2. A regime is defined as the set of rules that govern access to power in the political system.
3. The danger of circularity also exists when scholars shift from an understanding of political culture as subjective values to a wider one including institutions and patterns of action (Lukin 2000, pp. 28–31; McAuley 1984).
4. This is a more general argument about the effect of authoritarian parties in mitigating elite conflict and bringing about unity. For an extended analysis, see Brownlee (2007).
5. Although, he does acknowledge some failures in this initially: Gamsakhurdia in Georgia, Elchibey in Azerbaijan, Nabiev in Tajikistan and Kravchuk in Ukraine (Hale 2015, pp. 127–133).

Bibliography

Berdyaev, N. (1948). *The Russian idea*. New York: Palgrave Macmillan.

Billington, J. H. (1966). *The icon and the axe. An interpretive history of Russian culture*. New York: Alfred A. Knopf.

Bremmer, I., & Taras, R. (Eds.) (1997). *New politics. Building the post-Soviet nations*. Cambridge: Cambridge University Press.

Brownlee, J. (2007). *Authoritarianism in an age of democratization*. Cambridge: Cambridge University Press.

Bunce, V. J., & Wolchik, S. L. (2011), *Defeating authoritarian leaders in post-communist countries*. Cambridge: Cambridge University Press.

Dawisha, K., & Parrott, B. (Eds.) (1997a). *Conflict, cleavage and change in Central Asia and the Caucasus*. Cambridge: Cambridge University Press.

Dawisha, K., & Parrott, B. (Eds.) (1997b). *Democratic changes and authoritarian reactions in Russia, Ukraine, Belarus and Moldova*. Cambridge: Cambridge University Press.

Diamond, L. J. (2002). Thinking about hybrid regimes. *Journal of Democracy, 13*(2), 21–35.

Dicks, H. V. (1960). Some notes on the Russian national character. In: C. E. Black (Ed.), *The transformation of Russian society* (pp. 558–573). Cambridge, MA: Harvard University Press.

Gill, G. (2002). *Democracy and post-communism. Political change in the post-communist world*. London: Routledge.

Gill, G. (2015). *Building an authoritarian polity. Russia in post-Soviet times.* Cambridge: Cambridge University Press.

Gorer, G., & Rickman, J. (1949). *The people of Great Russia. A psychological study*. London: The Cresset Press.

Hahn, G. (2002). *Russia's revolution from above. Reform, transition and revolution in the fall of the Soviet communist regime 1985–2000*. New Brunswick: Transaction Publishers.

Hale, H. E. (2015). *Patronal politics. Eurasian regime dynamics in comparative perspective*. Cambridge: Cambridge University Press.

https://freedomhouse.org (accessed 27 October 2015).

Levitsky, S., & Way, L. A. (2010). *Comparative authoritarianism. Hybrid regimes after the cold war*. Cambridge: Cambridge University Press.

Lukin, A. (2000). *Political culture of Russian democrats*. Oxford: Oxford University Press.

McAuley, M. (1984). Political culture and communist studies: one step forward, two steps back. In: A. Brown (Ed.), *Political culture and communist studies* (pp. 13–39). Basingstoke: Macmillan.

McMann, K. M. (2006). *Economic autonomy and democracy. Hybrid regimes in Russia and Kyrgyzstan*. Cambridge: Cambridge University Press.

Mead, M. (1955). *Soviet attitudes toward authority. An introductory approach to problems of Soviet character*. New York: William Morrow.

Pipes, R. (1974). *Russia under the old regime*. London: Weidenfeld & Nicolson.

Smith, G. (1999). *The post-Soviet states. Mapping the politics of transition*. London: Arnold.

Szamuely, T. (1974). *The Russian tradition*. London: Secker & Warburg.

Way, L. A. (2005) Authoritarian state building and the sources of regime competitiveness in the fourth wave. The cases of Belarus, Moldova, Russia, and Ukraine. *World Politics, 57*(2), 231–261.

Way, L. (2010). Resistance to contagion: Sources of authoritarian stability in the former Soviet Union. In: V. Bunce, M. McFaul, K. Stoner-Weiss (Eds.), *Democracy and authoritarianism in the post-communist world* (pp. 229–252). Cambridge: Cambridge University Press.

Way, L. A., & Levitsky, S. (2006). The dynamics of autocratic coercion after the cold war. *Communist and Post-Communist Studies, 39*(3), 387–410.

White, S. (1979). *Political culture and Soviet politics*. London: Palgrave Macmillan.

Graeme Gill is Professor Emeritus of Government and Public Administration at the University of Sydney and a Fellow of the Academy of Social Sciences in Australia. He has been President of the International Council for Central and East European Studies (ICCEES) from 2010 to 2015. In addition to several co-authored and edited volumes, he has published twelve authored books on various aspects of Soviet and Russian politics. The most recent is *Building an Authoritarian Polity. Russia in Post-Soviet Times* (Cambridge, 2016).

Chapter 4: Curbing Post-Communist Corruption: External Pressure vs. Domestic Commitment

Leslie Holmes

Introduction

At the end of the 1990s, based on businesspeople's perceptions, the World Bank rated the Commonwealth of Independent States the most corrupt region in the world, while Central and Eastern Europe and the Baltics, though not as bad, were not far behind (Pradhan et al. 2000, pp. xiii–xiv; see too Kaufmann et al. 1999a, b).[1] Since that assessment, the situation has improved in much of the post-communist world, and other regions have assumed the dubious honour of being perceived to be the most corrupt on the planet. Many analysts cite inter alia the communist legacy in explaining the existence and persistence of corruption in post-communist states such as Russia. However, some have also pointed to the potential influence of the EU in curbing corruption and countering the communist legacy in those post-communist states admitted to it, arguing that conditionality in the run-up to admission can play a very positive role and that, once

L. Holmes (✉)
School of Social and Political Sciences,
University of Melbourne, Melbourne, Australia
e-mail: leslieth@unimelb.edu.au

Fish, Gill, Petrovic (eds.), *A Quarter Century of Post-Communism Assessed*, DOI 10.1007/978-3-319-43437-7_5

admitted, Brussels can continue to exert pressure. But is this the case? Are post-communist states admitted to the EU better able to reduce corruption than other post-communist states?

This chapter addresses this issue by focusing on the perceived and experienced corruption in four post-communist states—Russia, two countries admitted to the EU in 2007 (Bulgaria and Romania), and one non-EU country that has been the star performer in terms of reducing corruption, Georgia. Bulgaria and Romania have been selected as examples of 'crucial' or 'critical' case studies – similar to negative case-testing, in that they are used to test an hypothesis or theory under least favourable conditions (i.e. we already know that both countries are perceived to have a serious problem of corruption).[2] It is demonstrated that, while there is evidence to suggest that corruption levels did improve somewhat in Bulgaria and Romania in the years immediately preceding their admission to the EU and have since more or less stabilised or even become somewhat better, the situation has not improved as much as could be hoped for, at least in the case of Bulgaria (Romania fares better). On the basis of these four case studies, it is argued that the EU can and does exert pressure on both applicant states and member-states to reduce corruption, and that it appears that this may have a positive effect – bearing in mind that correlation does not prove causation. In our conclusions, we remind the reader that Bulgaria and Romania were selected as 'crucial' case studies, and we then consider how other post-communist EU member-states have been performing in terms of reducing corruption. This again suggests that, in general, membership of the EU has a positive effect on corruption levels. However, it is also argued there that domestic political will and capacity are ultimately crucial to success.

The Corruption Situation

Corruption is notoriously difficult to measure. One reason is that what people understand by the term varies somewhat not only across cultures but even among individuals and groups within the same culture. However, there are other factors. Most crimes have victims who can and often do report illegal actions to the authorities. Corruption is different. Some forms, notably so-called social corruption – such as various forms of favouritism (nepotism, cronyism, etc.) and arguably gift-giving – are not illegal in most jurisdictions. Indeed, in some Asian countries, such as Indonesia and Laos, nepotism is not necessarily illicit; within the dominant culture, someone promoted to high office who did not then promote members of his or her family would be seen by many citizens, at least in the past, as disloyal and behaving improperly. Other forms, mainly of economic corruption, either do not involve anyone other than the corrupt official (e.g. embezzlement) or involve bilateral collusion. In the former case, corrupt officials do not generally report themselves, whereas in the latter, someone who has paid a bribe to avoid a fine or improperly secure a building permit is unlikely to report the fact that they paid a corrupt official, since they might then have to pay the fine or lose their permit.

Given this, official legal statistics on corruption – the number of cases reported; the number investigated; the number of prosecutions; the number of convictions; sentences meted out – have limited value. While they can tell us, for instance, that the ratio of convictions to prosecutions is higher in country A than in country B, or that sentences for similar crimes appear to be much harsher in country B than in country A, they tell us little about the actual scale of corruption in either state.

Because of this problem with official legal statistics, analysts have devised various alternative methods for assessing the scale of corruption in any given state. The first and still most popular is to mount perceptual and attitudinal surveys, of which the best known is Transparency International's (TI's) Corruption Perceptions Index (CPI); this has appeared annually since 1995. The methodology changed somewhat in 2012, since when, according to TI itself, it is legitimate to compare one year's findings with another's.[3] Unfortunately, TI warns against comparing one year's results with another's for pre-2012 CPIs. However, here, in line with the practice of many analysts, pre-2012 data are cited as well as the most recent results, faute de mieux; those uneasy about reading the results as time-series data can at least compare country scores in any given year.

Since 2012, the CPI has been scaled 0–100, whereby the lower the score, the more corrupt a country is perceived to be; the CPIs through 2011 were scaled 0–10, with the directionality being the same (i.e. less corrupt countries had higher scores). In Table 4.1, pre-2012 scores have been presented according to the new scaling to make comparison easier. Moreover, the scores in the earliest CPIs were given to two decimal places; again for the sake of easy comparability, these have been rounded here to one decimal place before removing the decimal point.

Table 4.1 reveals that, with the exceptions of 2003, when it was significantly better than Georgia, and 2005, when it was just marginally better than Georgia, Russia has consistently been seen as the most corrupt

Table 4.1 CPI (perceptions-based) corruption scores 1997–2015

	1997	*2000*	*2003*	*2005*	*2006*	*2010*	*2012*	*2013*	*2014*	*2015*
Bulgaria		35	39	40	40	36	41	41	43	41
Georgia			18	23	28	38	52	49	52	52
Romania	34	29	28	30	31	37	44	43	43	46
Russia	23	21	27	24	25	21	28	28	27	29

Note: Empty cells = no data.
Source: Transparency International website, http://www.transparency.org/research/cpi/overview. Accessed 28 November 2015 and 20 March 2016.

of the four countries analysed here, and by quite a margin. Second, Russia does appear to have improved significantly towards the end of President Medvedev's term (in office 2008–2012), and has apparently been essentially in a steady state since Putin returned to the presidency in 2012. A third point is that Georgia has improved *significantly* since 2003, a point explored later in this chapter. Finally, while Bulgaria had improved just 2 years before its admission to the EU in comparison with the year 2000, Romania had not; its score in both years was almost identical. On the other hand, Bulgaria was perceived to have actually become *more* corrupt within three years of joining the EU, though it has since improved somewhat; this said, it has been treading water in recent years. Romania appears to have steadily improved (the drop between 2012 and 2014 is marginal), and has pulled away from Bulgaria in the most recent (2015) CPI.

It must be acknowledged that perceptions may not reflect the actual corruption situation, although it is impossible to determine exactly what the latter is in any country. Moreover, perceptions are a form of reality anyway, since we all make decisions based on them. Nevertheless, partly in response to criticisms of its perceptions indices, TI has since 2003 also published a Global Corruption Barometer (GCB) that includes responses to a question designed to measure citizens' actual experiences of corruption. Table 4.2 shows the responses to the question 'In the past 12 months, have you or has anyone living in your household paid a bribe in any form?' (in more recent GCBs, this has become more precise, by specifying eight to nine agencies, though an aggregate figure for each country is still available).

A number of observations can be made on the basis of Table 4.2. First, Bulgaria appears to be considerably less prone to bribery than Romania, even though they are often treated as basically very similar, including by

Table 4.2 GCB (bribery experience) percentages 2004–2013

	2004	*2007*	*2009*	*2010–2011*	*2013*
Bulgaria	6	7	5	8	8
Georgia	6		2	4	4
Romania	25	33	14	29	17
Russia	21	17	31	26	

Notes:
1. Empty cells = no data.
2. Percentages are only of those respondents who have come into contact with the various bodies over the previous year.
Source: Transparency International website, http://www.transparency.org/research/gcb/overview. Accessed 28 November 2015 (the latest GCB results are to be released region by region late-2015 to mid-2016, but were still unavailable for Central and Eastern Europe as of mid-March 2016).

the EU, in terms of the overall corruption situation. Second, there is no clear pattern for Bulgaria in terms of pre-accession or post-accession to the EU; an apparent improvement in the first 2 years of membership was seemingly followed by an increase in bribe paying. In the case of Romania, it appears that the situation may have significantly improved shortly after the country joined the EU, but to have been volatile since then. Third, while Russia's scores are also volatile, they are invariably high. Finally, the 'star performer' among our four selected countries is again Georgia.

While some maintain that experiential responses, such as those included in the GCB, are more useful than perceptual ones, they have at least one major drawback, viz. that experiential questions of the general public are very unlikely to detect high-level (grand) corruption. In addition to the CPI, one of the few methods that can help us to gauge the latter is state capture assessment. According to one recent analysis, which is based partly on World Bank governance indicators, Bulgaria and Romania are both examples of states with a high degree of 'corporate state capture' in which 'public power is exercised primarily for private gain' (Innes 2014, p. 88).[4]

Another potential indicator of the corruption situation is the business community's direct perceptions of the situation as reflected in the World Economic Forum's annual (since 2004) Global Competitiveness Report (GCR). This provides results of four questions of direct relevance here. The first asks businesspeople to rank-order 15[5] variables (e.g. access to financing; inflation; tax rates; inefficient government bureaucracy;

Table 4.3 The most problematic factors for doing business: ranking of corruption

	2006	*2008*	*2009*	*2011*	*2014*	*2015*
Bulgaria	3	1	2	1	1	2
Georgia	2	10	10	12	14	14
Romania	2	7	6	5	4	5
Russia	1	1	1	1	1	1

Sources: Schwab and Porter (2006, 2008); Schwab (2009, 2011, 2014, 2015).

corruption) in terms of how problematic these factors are for doing business. The results of this are shown in Table 4.3.

Table 4.3 demonstrates clearly that corruption is and has long been a very significant problem for businesspeople in Bulgaria – where it actually became worse shortly after joining the EU – and Russia; that it became much less of a problem in Romania between 2006 and 2008 (i.e. from just before to just after accession to the EU), then gradually became more of a problem, but has very recently become slightly less of one relative to other factors; and that it is considered ever less of an issue, and a relatively marginal one, for Georgian businesspeople.

The second GCR response of relevance here relates to the business community's perception of the seriousness of the problem of the diversion of public funds to private interests because of corruption. This is scaled 1 (very common) to 7 (never occurs), so that the lower the figure, the more significant the problem is perceived to be.

In Table 4.4, the score is in many ways more revealing than the rank, since it provides a picture of the situation within a given country, rather than one of how that country is faring relative to other countries. Bulgaria's scores since 2008 suggest that this form of corruption did reduce somewhat for several years after the country became an EU member-state, but that this Balkan state may now be backsliding. Moreover, with the exception of 2011 (when Russia was the worst), Bulgaria is perceived to have been the worst country of our four in terms of this particular form of corruption, though Russia joined it in this questionable position in 2015. Romania's situation appears to have deteriorated significantly between 2009 and 2011, but then to have more or less stabilised, though it is still not as good as it was in 2008 and 2009. Contrary to what might be expected given both President Medvedev's anti-corruption campaign and President Putin's lukewarm approach to

Table 4.4 Diversion of public funds[6]

	2006 Score	*2006 Rank*	*2008 Score*	*2008 Rank*	*2009 Score*	*2009 Rank*	*2011 Score*	*2011 Rank*	*2014 Score*	*2014 Rank*	*2015 Score*	*2015 Rank*
Bulgaria	2.6	108	2.5	116	2.6	113	2.9	88	2.5	118	2.7	110
Georgia	3.6	59	4.3	45	4.2	43	4.5	39	4.5	32	4.5	33
Romania	3.2	82	3.3	80	3.3	75	2.8	96	3.0	83	2.9	97
Russia	3.0	88	2.9	102	2.7	106	2.4	120	2.7	102	2.7	110

Notes: Ranks are global – 2006 N = 125; 2008 N = 134; 2009 N = 133; 2011 N = 142; 2014 N = 144; 2015 N = 140.

Sources: Schwab and Porter (2006, p. 405, 2008, p. 366); Schwab (2009, p 348, 2011, p. 392, 2014, p. 408, 2015, pp. 125, 177, 305 and 307).

Table 4.5 Irregular payments and bribes[7]

	2011 Score	*2011 Rank*	*2014 Score*	*2014 Rank*	*2015 Score*	*2015 Rank*
Bulgaria	3.6	92	4.2	55	3.8	76
Georgia	5.3	33	5.6	23	5.7	23
Romania	4.0	67	3.9	68	3.6	90
Russia	3.1	115	3.4	102	3.4	98

Notes: Ranks are global – 2011 $N = 142$; 2014 $N = 144$; 2015 $N = 140$.
Sources: Schwab (2011, p. 394, 2014, p. 410, 2015, pp. 125, 177, 305, 307).

corruption (see ensuing sections), the situation in Russia apparently worsened between 2008 and 2011, but then seems to have marginally improved again. Finally, this type of corruption is apparently much less of a problem in Georgia than in any of the other three states.

The third set of responses from the GCR (Table 4.5) concerns bribe payments to state officials by the private sector; once again the scaling is between 1 (very common) and 7 (never occurs).

Unfortunately, this question was not asked until the 2010–2011 GCR, so that we have a less comprehensive picture than for the previous question. However, this time, Russia emerges as the worst of our four countries – and Georgia as once again easily the best performer (i.e. where bribery seems to be less of a problem). On this variable, Bulgaria appears to have improved quite significantly between 2011 and 2014, whereas Romania headed in the opposite direction, albeit only marginally so. Sadly, both countries' scores declined again in 2015.

The final GCR question cited here may relate to economic (bribery) *and* social corruption, since the motives for favouritism can be both economic incentive and 'mateship' (i.e. privileging people one knows) or nepotism. Yet again, the scaling for Table 4.6 is 1 (always shows favouritism) to 7 (never shows favouritism).

This time, the Bulgarian results are broadly in line with the trend identified in Table 4.4, but somewhat at odds with those in Table 4.5. There has apparently been little change in Romania since joining the EU, though its scores are marginally better than in the year before accession. The Russian situation seems to have deteriorated between 2008 and 2011, but – as with the results in Tables 4.4 and 4.5 – to have begun to improve again lately. As by now would be expected, Georgia again consistently comes 'top of the class'.

Table 4.6 Favouritism in decisions of government officials[8]

	2006 Score	*2006 Rank*	*2008 Score*	*2008 Rank*	*2009 Score*	*2009 Rank*	*2011 Score*	*2011 Rank*	*2014 Score*	*2014 Rank*	*2015 Score*	*2015 Rank*
Bulgaria	2.2[9]	112	2.4	111	2.5	110	2.5	111	2.1	134	2.3	122
Georgia	2.7	88	3.4	51	3.2	60	3.2	54	3.4	48	3.4	48
Romania	2.2	110	2.4	113	2.3	117	2.5	115	2.5	114	2.4	111
Russia	2.2	114	2.8	88	2.7	96	2.5	117	2.8	87	2.8	90

Notes: Ranks are global – 2006 $N = 125$; 2008 $N = 134$; 2009 $N = 133$; 2011 $N = 142$; 2014 $N = 144$; 2015 $N = 140$.

Sources: Schwab and Porter (2006, p. 408, 2008, p. 369); Schwab (2009, p. 351, 2011, p. 396, 2014, p. 412, 2015, pp. 125, 177, 305, 307).

Table 4.7 Enterprise perceptions and experiences of corruption

	2002 (A)	*2002 (B)*	*2005 (A)*	*2005 (B)*	*2008 (A)*	*2008 (B)*	*2011 (A)*[10]	*2011 (B)*
Bulgaria	53	51	65	43	71	10		13.6
Georgia	60	66	70	12	42	4		2.5
Romania	56	55	80	33	83	8		5.7
Russia	29	65	64	62	80	31	60	16.1

Notes:
A = Percentage of firms identifying corruption as a problem of doing business.
B = Percentage of firms reporting unofficial payments ('bribe tax', 'graft index' in 2011); unfortunately, the methodology used in BEEPS 2008 was slightly different from that in 2005 on this variable, and then again in 2011, so that the figures are not directly comparable over time (Knack and Kisunko 2011, p. 23); however, the methodology was the same in any given year across states, so that cross-polity comparison for any given year in the above table is valid.
Empty cells = no data.
Sources: 2002—Fries et al. (2003, p. 25); Holmes (2010, pp. 37–38).
2005, 2008—EBRD and World Bank (2010a, pp. 6, 19, 20, 2010b, pp. 6, 19, 20, 2010c, pp. 6, 19, 20, 2010d, pp. 6, 19, 20); see also Knack and Kisunko (2011, pp. xii, 5, 8–13, 76, 77).
2011—For Russia, column A—EBRD and World Bank (2013, pp. 4, 6); for column B—World Bank and International Finance Corporation (2012, pp. 9, 13, 2013, pp. 9, 13, 2014a, pp. 9, 13, 2014b, pp. 9, 13).

One final business-related survey source that can throw more light on the corruption situation in our four countries are the European Bank for Reconstruction and Development (EBRD)–World Bank Business Environment and Enterprise Performance Surveys (BEEPS) that have been conducted in 2002, 2005, 2008 and 2011. Table 4.7 summarises some key findings of relevance to us.

According to BEEPS data (B) in Table 4.7, the number of firms paying bribes substantially declined in all four countries between 2002 and 2008, and then again in Georgia, Romania and Russia in 2011; the percentage increased in Bulgaria in 2011 compared with 2008, but was still considerably lower than in 2002 and 2005. However, most of these data are at odds with the perceptual data (A), which suggested that, in 2008, a higher percentage of firms identified corruption as a problem of doing business than had done so in 2005 in three of our four states; Georgia was the only exception to this. Such a mismatch may simply endorse the notion that there are 'lies, damned lies, and statistics'. Alternatively, it may be in line with the findings of researchers who have compared perceptual and experiential data on corruption and discovered that they are often at odds with each other for various reasons (e.g. Treisman 2007, p. 212; Mishler and Rose 2008; Rose and Mishler 2010; Donchev and Ujhelyi 2014).[11]

Let us now delve a little deeper into the corruption situation in the two EU member-states selected for particular attention in this chapter.

Bulgaria and Romania: Some Comparisons and Contrasts

As already noted, many outsiders, including the EU, tend to treat Bulgaria and Romania as essentially Tweedledum and Tweedledee when it comes to corruption. However, it was demonstrated earlier that, at least according to our imperfect measurement techniques, the picture is not so clear. While their scores in terms of perceptions have often been either identical or else similar, with Bulgaria sometimes appearing to be a little worse and at other times a little better than Romania, in terms of the general public's direct experience of bribery, Bulgaria appears to be less corrupt than its neighbour.

Yet corruption is regularly identified by Bulgarian businesspeople as the number one problem in conducting business, whereas, while still a problem in Romania, it is not considered as big a hindrance as other factors. It is possible that the significant discrepancy between the general public's experience of bribery and the business community's assessment of the significance of corruption in Bulgaria is best explained in terms of ordinary citizens' fear of honestly reporting their direct involvement. However, this explanation is unconvincing. The main reason is that Bulgarian freedom of speech is considerably greater than that of many other countries in which the incidence of reported direct experience of bribery, according to many GCBs, is much higher. The more likely explanation for the apparent mismatch is that corrupt officials both target and collude with the business community far more than with the general public; this point gels with the argument that there is a high degree of corporate state capture in Bulgaria.

The fact that Bulgaria and Romania were admitted to the EU more than two and a half years later than eight other post-communist states that had sought admission has been explained primarily in terms of the EU's concerns about the two countries' high levels of corruption and organised crime (Watt 2006). Corruption – in all the post-communist applicant states – had long been an issue for the EU. Thus, when it produced its individual country analyses relating to *Agenda 2000*, combating corruption was the *only* political variable the EU emphasised in all 10 studies (for the comments on Bulgarian and Romanian corruption see European Commission 1997a, p. 20, 1997b, p. 17). However, concerns about the corruption situations in Bulgaria and Romania were more serious than those for other states. For example, Brussels had been strongly criticising the corruption situation for years before Romania was admitted to the EU (Pridham 2007, passim), and eyebrows were raised in early-2006, when the Romanian parliament proved unwilling to pass anti-corruption legislation (Pridham 2007, p. 249). Yet despite severe reservations that neither Bulgaria nor Romania had adequately addressed these concerns, both were admitted in January 2007.

It is sometimes claimed that the EU loses its potential leverage over individual states once they have been admitted to its ranks; this argument has certainly been made about the post-communist states, including Bulgaria and Romania (Mungiu-Pippidi 2007, p. 16). However, in fact, the EU continued to monitor the corruption situation in the two states following their accession, and set new precedents in the way it addressed what it perceived to be a continuing problem. Thus, a Cooperation and Verification Mechanism (CVM) was established in January 2007 to monitor Bulgaria's and Romania's anti-corruption measures and judicial reform (as well as measures against organised crime in the case of Bulgaria) and report on these every 6 months. As Gateva (2013, p. 421) notes, this mechanism constituted 'a new feature, that of post-accession conditionality' (also see Gateva 2015). In July 2008, the EU released what Deutsche Welle (2008) described as a 'scathing' report on Bulgaria's corruption and announced that it would be suspending certain payments to Sofia because of the latter's inefficiency and corruption, including in the distribution and use of EU funds such as the Special Accession Programme for Agriculture and Rural Development. The suspended funds have been estimated at between 'at least' €500 mn (Frankfurter Allgemeine 2008; BBC 2008) and more than more than €800 mn (Deutsche Welle 2008).[12] Then in November 2008, the European Commission announced that it would *permanently* cut €220mn of funds originally allocated to Bulgaria (Spiegel Online 2008; for a brief but insightful analysis of all this see Freeman 2008). This move was described in the mass media as unprecedented (e.g. Hope and Troev 2008). However, in 2009, the delayed funds were unfrozen, for reasons that were later described in a leading German newspaper in somewhat sensationalist and possibly misleading terms as Bulgarian and Romanian 'blackmail' (*Erpressung*); the EU, it was argued, is ultimately unable to impose ongoing sanctions, since so many important decisions in the EU require unanimous decisions, which disgruntled member-states can threaten to vote against (Schiltz 2013).

The situation in Bulgaria has not really improved in recent years. A January 2015 report on Bulgaria's progress since joining the EU made it clear that Brussels still considered corruption – particularly high-level – to be a serious problem in this Balkan country, and Sofia's anti-corruption efforts to be quite inadequate (European Commission 2015a, pp. 2, 7–8, 9–11; Rettman 2015). Although the January 2016 CVM report praised Bulgaria for at last adopting a national anti-corruption strategy (European Commission 2016a, p. 8), Bulgarian commentators noted the EU's continuing frustration with their country's lacklustre efforts to address its corruption problem (Cheresheva 2016). Thus, the Bulgarian National Assembly (parliament) failed in September 2015 to pass a much needed law against corruption that was drafted by Bulgaria's former EU Commissioner (now Deputy Prime Minister) and that would have permitted anonymous whistle-blowing as well as the establishment of a powerful Anti-Corruption Bureau similar to the well-regarded one in Romania (Zhelev 2015).

While the EU's 2015 assessment of the anti-corruption drive in Romania was markedly more positive than that of Bulgaria, it is clear that Brussels believed that more could still be done there too, particularly concerning high-level corruption, and that the progress made to date had not necessarily been consolidated in all areas (European Commission 2015b, pp. 9–13). Although the January 2016 CVM report was more upbeat, and noted a number of improvements in Romania, it still identified aspects of anti-corruption in Romania that needed to be addressed (European Commission 2016b, pp. 10-12, 2016c). Nevertheless, the fact that a former Romanian prime minister, Adrian Năstase, was sentenced and imprisoned in July 2012 and then again in January 2014 for corruption, while the man who was prime minister from May 2012 to November 2015, Victor Ponta, was indicted for corruption in August 2015, has been noted favourably by Brussels.

One final aspect of the impact of their high corruption levels on Bulgaria and Romania's attempts to be admitted to European 'clubs' is their ongoing and so far unsuccessful attempts to join the Schengen Area. As Vachudova and Spendzharova (2012) argue, admission to the Schengen Area 'free movement' zone may in recent years have acted as an incentive to Bulgarian and Romanian elites to curb corruption, even if the EU's CVM has proved to be less effective than originally hoped for.[13] In order to be admitted to this zone, the interior ministers of the existing 26 Schengen Area member-states must agree unanimously; the Netherlands, with some support from Finland, France and Germany, has been resisting admission for years, primarily on the grounds that too little has been done to combat high-level and judicial corruption in both Bulgaria and Romania. In fact, the reputation for (low-level) corruption among border guards and customs officers, especially in Bulgaria, is another reason for the resistance. If border officials can easily be bribed to collude with organised crime gangs involved with the smuggling and trafficking of drugs, arms and people into the Schengen Area, this significantly increases security problems for the existing members.

In September 2015, as the problem of refugees into Europe was growing almost exponentially, the Bulgarian and Romanian prime ministers Boiko Borisov and Victor Ponta indicated that their countries would be willing to accept migrant intake quotas if admitted to the Schengen Area (Zhelev and Bird 2015). However, by October, the Romanians appear to have given up hope of being admitted, at least for now (Chiriac 2015), whereas the Bulgarians were still anxious to join (Gotev 2015). In the light of both the Syrian refugee influx in 2015 and the terrorist attacks in Paris and Brussels in November 2015 and March 2016, it remains to be seen how long the Schengen Area will remain in its current form, if at all, anyway, so that there might be one less carrot outsiders can dangle in front of Bulgaria and Romania in the formers' endeavours to curb corruption in the latter.

The Russian Conundrum

In his last public speech before stepping down at the end of his second term as Russian president, Putin declared that the fight against corruption had been the most intractable problem of his 8 years in office (Putin 2008), while in the same month, soon-to-be president Dmitry Medvedev stated publicly that corruption constituted 'the most serious disease affecting our society' (Medvedev, 2008). Moreover, despite his extraordinary popularity among Russians, an August 2015 survey of Russians revealed that ordinary citizens continue to see Putin's anti-corruption measures as his biggest failure, replicating findings of nine earlier surveys going back to 2004 (Levada-Tsentr 2015; see also RT 2008; Kim 2010). According to many analysts, and based primarily on Russia's scores in the CPI, Russia is the most corrupt country in the world relative to its level of economic development. Clearly, there is a problem.

Almost as soon as he assumed the presidency in 2008, Medvedev declared war on corruption. However, towards the end of his presidency, in his final address as president to the Federal Assembly in December 2011, Medvedev had to acknowledge the widespread allegations of fraud, a form of corruption, in the December parliamentary elections; he did this even while claiming that his anti-corruption efforts constituted the eighth of his top ten achievements (Medvedev 2011).

But the various measurement techniques available make it clear that Medvedev's anti-corruption crusade had at most limited impact. While the level of petty corruption in some parts of the police may have declined in recent years,[14] the overall situation remains very disappointing. Much of this relates to Putin's weak commitment. While he 'talks the talk' of anti-corruption, he does not seriously 'walk the walk', almost certainly in part because he fears alienating his state bureaucracy and security agencies.

Putin continues to tinker with the anti-corruption legislation and to acknowledge that corruption is undermining the legitimacy of the system. In the case of the former, for instance, he signed into law a 'Federal Law on Amendments to Certain Legislative Acts of the Russian Federation to Improve Measures to Fight Corruption' (mainly regarding offshore money laundering) at the end of November 2015. Regarding the latter, in his address to the Federal Assembly in December 2015, Putin noted that corruption would be a major topic during the 2016 parliamentary election campaigns, and implicitly linked it to legitimacy:

> The election campaign must be honest and transparent, conducted within the framework of the law and with respect for the electorate. Moreover, we need to gain unconditional public trust in the election results and their full legitimacy.
>
> Respected colleagues! I believe that a lot of attention will be devoted in the parliamentary candidates' election programmes to questions concerning the fight against corruption. These questions are really a major concern for society. Corruption is hindering Russia's development. (Putin 2015)

This is all very well, but if it is accepted that Putin has been the de facto leader of Russia since 2000 (and de jure 2000–2008 and since 2012), the fact that he still had to make such statements in late-2015 supports the argument that his anti-corruption declarations and actions are little more than lip service.[15]

Georgia's Success

According to every technique available for measuring corruption levels, Georgia has dramatically improved since 2003; this shows up clearly in most of our tables. Unfortunately, we can only be certain that this point applies to low-level (petty) corruption, as experienced by ordinary citizens and smaller businesses; there is much evidence that high-level (grand) corruption has not declined by anything like the same extent, if at all.

This is one of the reasons that Georgia still does not figure among what are perceived to be the world's least corrupt countries (Nordic states, Singapore and New Zealand), its marked improvement since 2003 notwithstanding.

This is not the place to elaborate the details of Georgia's anti-corruption policy. However, two of its salient features that need noting here were that it was radical and that it reflected the strong commitment of President Saakashvili. It was not without problems, however, not least of which was a high level of arbitrariness. While this approach was for some years welcomed by many Georgians, it eventually led more and more citizens to become apprehensive about what they perceived to be the increasingly authoritarian tendencies of their president. This saw his party (the United National Movement) lose office in the October 2012 parliamentary elections.[16]

Georgia's anti-corruption reforms are sometimes seen in terms of a two-stage process. The first ran throughout 2004, during which time Saakashvili's new government prosecuted a number of high-ranking officials from the former government; streamlined licensing procedures; and introduced a new and dramatically reformed police force. However, these measures were basically taken 'on the run', seemingly with little planning, and were designed to show the Georgian population that the new government was serious about clamping down on the corruption that had been so rife during the Shevardnadze post-communist era (Shevardnadze was informally then formally president of Georgia 1992–2003). The second stage can be seen to have begun in January 2005, when a working group was established to devise a National Anti-Corruption Strategy and Action Plan. A Strategy was adopted in June 2005, followed by the first version of an Action Plan in September of that year; the latter was subsequently refined in March 2006 and April 2007 (for a critical overview of the Strategy and Action Plans see Karosanidze 2007). While many mistakes were subsequently made in the Georgian anti-corruption drive, and despite resistance to it from parts of the state bureaucracy, the overall story is one of success.[17]

Conclusions

Since both Bulgaria and Romania continue to suffer from high levels of corruption – at least by European standards – it could be argued that the EU's role in curbing malfeasance in these two relatively new members has been at best marginal. However, this would be to overstate and arguably misrepresent the case. The EU has certainly exerted pressure on both countries, not only in the pre-accession period but also since accession. This can be seen in the financial penalties imposed on Bulgaria, as well as in the resistance by a number of EU member-states to the two Balkan states' applications to join the Schengen Area; while this zone does not completely duplicate EU membership (it includes non-EU states, such as Norway and Switzerland, and does not include certain long-standing EU member-states, notably the UK), there is considerable overlap between the two units. Another point, emphasised by Dimitrova and Buzogány (2014), is that a comprehensive appreciation of the EU's role requires consideration of its indirect forms of influence, such as the use NGOs can and do make of EU policies, reports, etc. in attempting to influence Bulgarian and Romanian authorities. The EU could be argued to be exerting influence in this indirect manner as well as in the more obvious and overt ways. Finally, it is quite possible that the scale of corruption in both Bulgaria and Romania would be even larger were it not for external pressure.

But there is a limit to the extent to which either the EU or any other democratic external agent can or could legitimately be expected to influence individual member-states anyway. Ultimately, as analysts such as Noutcheva and Bechev (2008) and Ivanov (2010) correctly argue, domestic factors are more important. This point requires elaboration.

Jon Quah is among those who emphasise that the single most important factor in reducing corruption is political will (e.g. Quah 2015). In fact, as I have argued elsewhere (e.g. Holmes 2006, pp. 265-7, 2015, p. 125), this point needs unpacking and expansion. In terms of unpacking, we need to consider *whose* political will matters. The usual assumption is that this refers to the very top leadership. This is a sensible and justifiable inference: the will of the supreme leader (e.g. the president in a presidential system; the prime minister in a parliamentary system) *is* all-important. Perhaps the most significant reason why Georgia significantly reduced its corruption levels from 2003 was that President Saakashvili was wholeheartedly committed to anti-corruption, at least at the lower levels of the state. Conversely, while former law professor President Medvedev in Russia does appear to have been genuinely and seriously committed to reducing corruption, former KGB officer Putin has never been more than lukewarm in his commitment, his public declarations notwithstanding. Bulgarian leaders of various political hues have declared themselves to be committed to combating corruption, but none has had the real will of either Saakashvili or Medvedev. The Romanian case leads us to our second caveat, the need to expand on – here meaning add to – the concept of political will.

Before he was elected president in 1996, former professor of geology and university pro-rector Emil Constantinescu declared that the fight against corruption in Romania would be one of his top priorities if elected. Once in office, he did indeed mount a major campaign against corruption – so much so that both the mass media and other politicians criticised him for being too extreme. Thus, Transport Minister (and subsequently Romanian president) Traian Băsescu claimed that Constantinescu's anti-corruption drive had 'spun out of control' (cited in Gabanyi 2004, p. 366). In 2000, Constantinescu could have run again for president, but did not. In explaining his decision, he expressed his disappointment at not having made much progress in combating corruption in his country, and claimed that this was primarily because he had not had the support he needed from others in combating corruption. Indeed, there had been several corruption scandals in his own government.

The Constantinescu case leads us to the point that political will is a necessary but insufficient condition. In addition, political leaders need to have political *capacity*; if they cannot secure the support of their own administrations, their own commitment will not in itself suffice to make much impression on the corruption situation. Expressed another way, the political will of the leader is not the only will that matters; that of the government and the state bureaucracy is also crucial. Thus, Anderson and Gray (2006, p. 19) are correct when, in assessing Saakashvili's early successes and the significant role of 'strong leadership', they nevertheless conclude that 'Committed leadership is important, but transparent, accountable, and well-functioning institutions are the key to good governance over the long term'.

These institutions must include another component of political will that needs to be added to the equation, namely civil society. Since there is no adequate comparative measure of the salience of civil society, we here use a proxy measure, the Economist Intelligence Unit's *Democracy Index*. This index, based on 60 indicators, adopts a 'thicker' version of democracy than the approach of Freedom House and includes composite scores for civil liberties and political culture. Unfortunately, the *Democracy Index* dates only from 2007 (when the 2006 situation was assessed, see Table 4.8).

Citing Anderson and Gray (2006, p. 19) once again:

Table 4.8 Type of political system

	2006 Score	*2006 Type*	*2008 Score*	*2008 Type*	*2010 Score*	*2010 Type*	*2012 Score*	*2012 Type*	*2014 Score*	*2014 Type*
Bulgaria	7.10	FD	7.02	FD	6.84	FD	6.72	FD	6.73	FD
Georgia	4.90	H	4.62	H	4.59	H	5.53	H	5.82	H
Romania	7.06	FD	7.06	FD	6.60	FD	6.54	FD	6.68	FD
Russia	5.02	H	4.48	H	4.26	H	3.74	A	3.39	A

Notes: FD—Flawed Democracy; H—Hybrid; A—Authoritarian; Scaling—0–10 (the higher the score, the more democratic).

Sources: 2006—EIU (2007, pp. 3–4); 2008—EIU (2009, pp. 5–6); 2010—EIU (2010, pp. 4–6); 2012—EIU (2013, pp. 5–7); 2014—EIU (2015, pp. 5–7).

> Equally important is supporting the development of robust mechanisms for feedback from civil society. In the long term an informed public and civil society, an independent media, and tolerance of constructive criticism of the leadership are essential to sustaining the gains from reform.

A similar argument has been made more recently and at length by one of the best-regarded and most influential analysts of corruption, Michael Johnston (2014). This is where Georgia's achievements may still prove to be fragile. Since its political system is rated as 'hybrid' (i.e. between authoritarianism and flawed democracy), the roles of ordinary citizens, the mass media, etc. are still not substantial or robust enough to ensure sustained success.[18] In this sense, any future progress in reducing corruption in Russia would also be fragile, until and unless the country becomes markedly more democratic.

On the other hand, Bulgaria and Romania have better long-term prospects, since their institutions are more democratic – to no small extent because of EU influence. Even if the impact of targeted EU anti-corruption measures have only limited success, Brussels' more diffuse influence on democratisation will have indirect knock-on effects, including on corruption levels. Thus, if Bulgaria or Romania should in the future have leaders genuinely committed to combating corruption, there is a good chance that a sustained reduction in corruption levels will be achieved. The EU certainly can and should maintain the pressure on Sofia and Bucharest to take both anti-corruption and deeper democratisation seriously.

It was explained in the introduction to this chapter that Bulgaria and Romania had been selected as 'crucial' case studies for testing the

Table 4.9 CPI (perceptions-based) scores in other post-communist EU member-states 1997–2015

	1997	*2000*	*2003*	*2005*	*2006*	*2010*	*2012*	*2013*	*2014*	*2015*
Croatia		37	37	34	34	41	46	48	48	51
Czechia	52	43	39	43	48	46	49	48	51	56
Estonia		57	55	64	67	65	64	68	69	70
Hungary	52	52	48	50	52	47	55	54	54	51
Latvia		34	38	42	47	43	49	53	55	55
Lithuania		41	47	48	48	50	54	57	58	61
Poland	51	41	36	34	37	53	58	60	61	62
Slovakia		35	37	43	47	43	46	47	50	51
Slovenia		55	59	61	64	64	61	57	58	60

Note: Empty cells = no data.
Source: Transparency International website, http://www.transparency.org/research/cpi/overview. Accessed 28 November 2015 and 20 March 2016.

hypothesis that the EU can and does exert a positive influence on potential and actual member-states in terms of corruption levels. It has been demonstrated that, even in these difficult cases, the EU has certainly sought to exert influence on both states, and that it may have had some limited success. If we now focus on the other post-communist EU member-states, it transpires that most have experienced a reduction – often considerable – in perceived corruption levels in comparison with the years just before accession. This point emerges clearly from Table 4.9.

Table 4.9 reveals that in seven formerly communist states – Croatia, Czechia, Estonia, Latvia, Lithuania, Poland and Slovakia – the 2015 CPI score is a marked improvement on their score in the 3–4 years preceding their admission to the EU. The only exceptions are Hungary and Slovenia, both of which are perceived to have had rather similar levels of corruption in 2015 as in the early-2000s. This is not the place to examine the specific reasons for these exceptions; but it can be noted that both countries are still above the 50 mark that TI considers the cut-off point for unacceptable levels of corruption, with Slovenia being well above it. It is important here to repeat the 'Statistics 101' caveat made early in this analysis that correlation does not prove causation. The improvements in most states might be just as well explained in terms of a more stable political situation (though anyone familiar with the domestic politics of several of these countries in recent years would question this), a more stable economy (again, this is debatable in several states), or other factors. Nevertheless, it is legitimate to note that most post-communist states that have joined the EU appear to have less of a problem with corruption than they did before membership. Conversely, Georgia demonstrates that post-communist states in which the leadership has sufficient political will and capacity can make major inroads in the fight against corruption without EU assistance or pressure;[19] the durability of such improvements unless accompanied by deeper democratisation is unclear, however.

Notes

1. This chapter is based in part on research generously funded by the Australian Research Council (Grants DP0558453 and DP110102854).
2. These concepts overlap with Arend Lijphart's notion of 'theory-infirming' and 'deviant' case studies, though the distinction between these two in Lijphart's analysis is opaque (Lijphart 1971, pp. 691–693).
3. Nowadays, the country experts that assess countries for the CPI use both business perception data and other sources in evaluating the standard of governance; for details of the 12 sources used for the 2015 CPI see Transparency International (2015).
4. For earlier assessments of the level and nature of state capture in both these states plus Georgia and Russia, based on the EBRD and World Bank's Business Environment and Economic Performance Surveys (BEEPS), see Pradhan et al. (2000, pp. 13, 35); Gray et al. (2004, pp. 25, 28); Anderson and Gray (2006, pp. 18, 29). Martini (2014) provides a straightforward and up-to-date analysis of the concept of state capture.
5. Only 14 in 2006.
6. The GCR question was 'In your country, how common is diversion of public funds to companies, individuals, or groups due to corruption?' (weighted average).
7. The GCR score is the mean average across the five components of the following Executive Opinion Survey question: 'In your country, how common is it for firms to make undocumented extra payments or bribes connected with (a) imports and exports; (b) public utilities; (c) annual tax payments; (d) awarding of public contracts and licenses; (e) obtaining favourable judicial decisions?' (weighted average).
8. The GCR question was 'To what extent do government officials in your country show favouritism to well-connected firms and individuals when deciding upon policies and contracts?' (weighted average).
9. In this table, two or more countries may have the same score but be ranked differently because of rounding to one decimal place.

10. Unfortunately, the World Bank presented the data for three of our four countries (all except Russia) in a different format in the reports on BEEPS 2011; instead of providing the percentage of firms that identified corruption as a problem of doing business, they provided data on the percentage of firms that identified corruption as the main obstacle to doing business.
11. The mismatch may be less pronounced than it appears, since some analysts maintain that many respondents may not admit to having had direct experience of bribery even when they have; but see the following text concerning Bulgaria.
12. Unfortunately, the EU itself did not publicly reveal the figure. For its press release see European Commission (2008a), and for the report (which contains several Euro figures, but does not specify how much of each fund will be subject to delayed payment) see European Commission (2008b).
13. This said, in March 2016 the RAND Corporation recommended extending the CVM concept to other EU member-states (RAND 2016; Novinite 2016).
14. This is particularly true of the traffic police. However, it is not clear that this is a result of the police reforms that have been introduced since 2011. Rather, it seems that citizens' increasing use of mobile 'phone and dash-mounted cameras when stopped by the traffic police may be the principal explanation.
15. For a detailed analysis of the corruption and anti-corruption situation in Russia from the collapse of Communist power through most of the Medvedev presidency see Holmes (2012).
16. Saakashvili's second term as president ended in November 2013; under the Georgian Constitution, no individual may run for more than two consecutive terms. Saakashvili has since May 2015 been governor of the Ukrainian region of Odessa and is now a Ukrainian citizen.
17. On the radical police reforms see Devlin (2010); Light (2014) – while a comprehensive analysis of almost all aspects of anti-corruption reform through 2011 can be found in World Bank (2012). For discourse analyses of Georgian anti-corruption see Di Puppo (2010, 2014).
18. It could be countered that Singapore, which the *Democracy Index* also rated until 2013 as a hybrid system, has maintained low levels of corruption for a sustained period, thus challenging our argument. However, Singapore might be the exception that proves the rule. It is also a very affluent society, and there is a strong correlation between affluence and corruption levels (i.e. wealthier societies are generally perceived to have lower levels of corruption). Moreover, Singapore just managed to slip into the 'flawed democracy' category in the 2014 *Democracy Index*.
19. For the record, Georgia formally began to move closer to the EU in 2006. In 2011, President Saakashvili announced that he would like to see his

country join the EU, but no time frame was given. Although Georgia has yet to make a formal application to join the EU, the two sides deepened their relationship with the adoption in 2014 of an Association Agreement.

Bibliography

Anderson, J., & Gray, C. (2006). *Anticorruption in transition 3: who is succeeding… and why?* Washington, DC: World Bank.

BBC. (2008, July 23). EU suspends funding for Bulgaria. *BBC News*. http://news.bbc.co.uk/2/hi/europe/7520736.stm. Retrieved 28 November 2015.

Cheresheva, M. (2016, January 27). EU seeks results from Bulgaria on corruption. *Balkan insight*. http://www.balkaninsight.com/en/article/european-commission-urges-bulgaria-to-speed-up-the-fight-against-corruption-01-27-2016. Retrieved 25 March 2016.

Chiriac, M. (2015, October 7). Romania withdraws bid to join Schengen area. *Balkan insight*. http://www.balkaninsight.com/en/article/romania-bulgaria-face-new-delay-on-joining-schengen-space-10-06-2015. Retrieved 30 November 2015.

Deutsche Welle (2008, July 18). Scathing EU report exposes Bulgaria's high-level corruption. *Deutsche Welle*. http://www.dw.com/en/scathing-eu-report-exposes-bulgarias-high-level-corruption/a-3493169. Retrieved 27 November 2015.

Devlin, M. (2010). Seizing the reform movement: rebuilding Georgia's police, 2004–2006. *Innovations for successful societies*. Princeton NJ: Princeton University. http://successfulsocieties.princeton.edu/publications/seizing-reform-moment-rebuilding-georgias-police-2004-2006. Retrieved 25 August 2013.

Di Puppo, L. (2010). Anti-corruption interventions in Georgia. *Global Crime, 11*, 220–236.

Di Puppo, L. (2014). The construction of success in anti-corruption activity in Georgia. *East European Politics, 30*, 105–122.

Dimitrova, A., & Buzogány, A. (2014). Post-accession policy-making in Bulgaria and Romania: can non-state actors use EU rules to promote better governance? *Journal of Common Market Studies, 52*, 139–156.

Donchev, D., & Ujhelyi, G. (2014). What do corruption indices measure? *Economics and Politics, 26*, 309–331.

EBRD and World Bank. (2010a). *BEEPS at-a-glance 2008 – Bulgaria*. Washington, DC: World Bank.

EBRD and World Bank. (2010b). *BEEPS at-a-glance 2008 – Georgia*. Washington, DC: World Bank.

EBRD and World Bank. (2010c). *BEEPS at-a-glance 2008 – Romania*. Washington, DC: World Bank.

EBRD and World Bank. (2010d). *BEEPS at-a-glance 2008 – Russia*. Washington, DC: World Bank.
EBRD and World Bank. (2013). *BEEPS at-a-glance 2011 – Russia*. Washington, DC: World Bank.
EIU. (2007). *The world in 2007*. London: Economist Intelligence Unit.
EIU. (2009). *Democracy index 2008*. London: Economist Intelligence Unit.
EIU. (2010). *Democracy index 2010: democracy in retreat*. London: Economist Intelligence Unit.
EIU. (2013). *Democracy index 2012: democracy at a standstill*. London: Economist Intelligence Unit.
EIU. (2015). *Democracy index 2014: democracy and its discontents*. London: Economist Intelligence Unit.
European Commission. (1997a). Commission opinion on Bulgaria's application for membership of the European Union. *Bulletin of the European Union*, Supplement 13/97.
European Commission. (1997b). Commission opinion on Romania's application for membership of the European Union. *Bulletin of the European Union*, Supplement 8/97.
European Commission. (2008a, July 23). More efforts needed by Bulgaria and Romania to tackle judicial reform and corruption. http://europa.eu/rapid/press-release_IP-08-1195_en.htm?locale=en. Retrieved 2 December 2015.
European Commission. (2008b, July 23). *Report from the European commission to the European parliament and the council: On the management of EU-funds in Bulgaria*. Brussels: Commission of the European Communities.
European Commission. (2015a, January 28). *Report from the commission to the European parliament and the council: on progress in Bulgaria under the co-operation and verification mechanism*, SWD (2015) 9 final. Brussels: European Commission.
European Commission. (2015b, January 28). *Report from the commission to the European parliament and the council: On progress in Romania under the co-operation and verification mechanism*, SWD (2015) 8 final. Brussels: European Commission.
European Commission. (2016a, January 27). *Report from the commission to the European parliament and the council: on progress in Bulgaria under the co-operation and verification mechanism*, SWD (16) final. Brussels: European Commission.
European Commission. (2016b, January 27). *Report from the commission to the European parliament and the council: on progress in Romania under the co-operation and verification mechanism*, SWD (16) final. Brussels: European Commission.
European Commission. (2016c, January 27). Press release: commission reports on progress in Romania under the co-operation and verification

mechanism. http://europa.eu/rapid/press-release_IP-16-152_en.htm. Retrieved 25 March 2016.

Frankfurter Allgemeine. (2008, July, 24). EU subsidies are frequently misused [Subventionen der EU werden häufig missbraucht]. *Frankfurter Allgemeine FAZ.Net*. http://www.faz.net/s/Rub99C3EECA60D84C08AD6B3E60C4EA807F/Doc~EC7FCC987DB924065A113ABA03461B829~ATpl~Ecommon~Scontent.html. Retrieved 4 July 2009.

Freeman, C. (2008, November 15). Inside Europe's corruption capital: how Bulgaria's crime mafia plunders EU grant money. *Daily Telegraph*.

Fries, S., Lysenko, T., Polanec, S. (2003). The 2002 business environment and enterprise performance survey: results from a survey of 6,100 firms. *European Bank for Reconstruction and Development Working Paper*, No. 84.

Gabanyi, A. (2004). The new business elite: from *Nomenklatura* to oligarchy. In: H. Carey (Ed.), *Romania since 1989: politics, economics, and society* (pp. 353–372). Lanham, MD: Lexington.

Gateva, E. (2013). Post-accession conditionality – translating benchmarks into political pressure? *East European Politics, 29*, 420–442.

Gateva, E. (2015). *European Union enlargement conditionality*. Basingstoke: Palgrave Macmillan.

Gotev, G. (2015, October 19). EU in danger unless Bulgaria joins Schengen, says Sofia. *EurAktiv.com*. http://www.euractiv.com/sections/justice-home-affairs/eu-danger-unless-bulgaria-joins-schengen-says-sofia-318610. Retrieved 30 November 2015.

Gray, C., Hellman, J., Ryterman, R. (2004). *Anticorruption in transition 2: corruption in enterprise-state interactions in Europe and Central Asia 1999–2002*. Washington, DC: World Bank.

Holmes, L. (2006). *Rotten states: corruption, post-communism and neoliberalism*. Durham, NC: Duke University Press.

Holmes, L. (2010). International anti-corruption regimes and corruption levels in European and Eurasian post-communist states. In: S. Wolf & D. Schmidt-Pfister (Eds.), *International anti-corruption regimes in Europe* (pp. 25–45). Baden-Baden: Nomos.

Holmes, L. (2012). Corruption in post-Soviet Russia. *Global Change, Peace and Security, 24*, 235–250.

Holmes, L. (2015). *Corruption: a very short introduction*. Oxford: Oxford University Press.

Hope, K., & Troev, T. (2008, November 26). Bulgaria loses €520m EU funds. *Financial Times*.

Innes, A. (2014). The political economy of state capture in Central Europe. *Journal of Common Market Studies, 52*, 88–104.

Ivanov, K. (2010). The 2007 accession of Bulgaria and Romania: Ritual and Reality. *Global Crime, 11*, 210–219.

Johnston, M. (2014). *Corruption, contention and reform: the power of deep democratization*. Cambridge: Cambridge University Press.
Karosanidze, T. (2007). *National anti-corruption strategy and action plan: elaboration and implementation*. Bergen: U4 Anti-Corruption Resource Centre.
Kaufmann, D., Kraay, A., Zoido-Lobatón, P. (1999a). Aggregating governance indicators. *Policy Research Working Paper No.2195*. Washington, DC: World Bank.
Kaufmann, D., Kraay, A., Zoido-Lobatón, P. (1999b). Governance matters. *Policy Research Working Paper No.2196*. Washington, DC: World Bank.
Kim, L. (2010, August 13). Putin's biggest failure is fight against corruption, poll shows. *Bloomberg Business*. http://www.bloomberg.com/news/articles/2010-08-12/putin-s-biggest-failure-is-fight-against-russian-corruption-poll-shows. Retrieved 23 November 2015.
Knack, S., & Kisunko, G. (2011). *Trends in corruption and regulatory burden in Eastern Europe and Central Asia*. Washington, DC: International Bank for Reconstruction and Development/World Bank.
Levada-Tsentr. (2015, September 10). Perceptions of Vladimir Putin's performance [Vospriyatie deyatel'nosti Vladimira Putina']. *Press-Vypuski*. http://www.levada.ru/2015/09/10/vospriyatie-deyatelnosti-vladimira-putina/. Retrieved 23 November 2015.
Light, M. (2014). Police reforms in the Republic of Georgia: the convergence of domestic and foreign policy in an anti-corruption drive. *Policing and Society, 24*, 318–345.
Lijphart, A. (1971). Comparative politics and the comparative method. *American Political Science Review, 65*, 682–693.
Martini, M. (2014). *State capture: an overview*. Berlin: Transparency International.
Medvedev, D. (2008, February 16). Dmitrii Medvedev nazval chetyre prioriteta blizhaishego chetyrekhletiya: instituty, infrastruktura, innovatsii, investitsii. *Rossiiskaya Gazeta*. https://rg.ru/2008/02/16/medvedev-forum.html. Retrived 31 December 2011.
Medvedev, D. (2011). Message of the President to the Federal Assembly [Poslanie Prezidenta Federal'nomu Sobraniyu]. http://kremlin.ru/news/14088. Retrieved 31 December 2011.
Mishler, W., & Rose, R. (2008). Seeing is not always believing: measuring corruption perceptions and experiences. Paper prepared for the elections, public opinion and parties 2008 annual conference. University of Manchester, 12–14 September.
Mungiu-Pippidi, A. (2007). EU accession is no 'end of history'. *Journal of Democracy, 18*(4), 8–16.
Noutcheva, G., & Bechev, D. (2008). The successful laggards: Bulgaria and Romania's accession to the EU. *East European Politics and Societies, 22*, 114–144.
Novinite (2016, March 23). Romania, Bulgaria, Croatia 'most corrupt EU countries'. *Novinite*. http://www.novinite.com/articles/173680/Romania%2C+Bulgaria%2C+Croatia+%27Most+Corrupt+EU+Countries%27. Retrieved 25 March 2016.

Pradhan, S., et al. (2000). *Anticorruption in transition: a contribution to the policy debate*. Washington, DC: World Bank.

Pridham, G. (2007). The effects of the European Union's democratic conditionality: the case of Romania during accession. *Journal of Communist Studies and Transition Politics, 23*, 233–258.

Putin, V. (2008, February 14). Transcript of annual big press conference. http://www.kremlin.ru/eng/speeches/2008/02/14/1011_type82915_160266.shtml. Retrieved 19 February 2008.

Putin, V. (2015, December 3). Message of the President to the Federal Assembly [Poslanie Prezidenta Federal'nomy Sobraniyu]. http://kremlin.ru/events/president/news/50864. Retrieved 4 December 2015.

Quah, J. (2015). The critical importance of political will in combating corruption in Asian countries. *Public Administration and Policy, 18*(2), 12–23.

RAND Corporation. (2016, March 22). The cost of corruption in Europe – up to €990 billion (£781.64 billion) lost annually. *RAND Corporation*. http://www.rand.org/news/press/2016/03/22.html. Retrieved 25 March 2016.

Rettman, A. (2015, January 28). EU raises alarm on Bulgaria corruption. *EU Observer*. https://euobserver.com/justice/127402. Retrieved 4 December 2015.

Rose, R., & Mishler, W. (2010). Experience versus perception of corruption: Russia as a test case. *Global Crime, 11*, 145–163.

RT (2008, March 24). Corruption's been Putin's biggest failure: opinion poll. *RT*. https://www.rt.com/news/corruptions-been-putins-biggest-failure-opinion-poll/. Retrieved 23 November 2015.

Schiltz, C. (2013, July 26). Europe capitulates to the corruption in Bulgaria [Europa kapituliert vor der Korruption in Bulgarien]. *Die Welt*. http://www.welt.de/politik/ausland/article118431279/Europa-kapituliert-vor-der-Korruption-in-Bulgarien.html. Retrieved 26 November 2015.

Schwab, K. (Ed.) (2009). *The global competitiveness report 2009–2010*. Geneva: World Economic Forum.

Schwab, K. (Ed.) (2011). *The global competitiveness report 2011–2012*. Geneva: World Economic Forum.

Schwab, K. (Ed.) (2014). *The global competitiveness report 2014–2015*. Geneva: World Economic Forum.

Schwab, K. (Ed.) (2015). *The global competitiveness report 2015–2016*. Geneva: World Economic Forum.

Schwab, K., & Porter, M. (Eds.) (2006). *The global competitiveness report 2006–2007*. Geneva: World Economic Forum.

Schwab, K., & Porter, M. (Eds.) (2008). *The global competitiveness report 2008–2009*. Geneva: World Economic Forum.

Spiegel Online. (2008, November 25). Corruption: The European Commission cancels millions in aid to Bulgaria [Korruption: EU-Kommission streicht Bulgarien Hilfen in Millionenhöhe]. *Spiegel*. http://www.spiegel.de/politik/

ausland/korruption-eu-kommission-streicht-bulgarien-hilfen-in-millionen hoehe-a-592707.html#. Retrieved 2 December 2015.
Transparency International. (2015). *Corruption perceptions index 2015: full source description*. Berlin: Transparency International.
Treisman, D. (2007). What have we learned about the causes of corruption from ten years of cross-national empirical research? *Annual Review of Political Science, 10*, 211–244.
Vachudova, M., & Spendzharova, A. (2012). The EU's cooperation and verification mechanism: fighting corruption in Bulgaria and Romania after EU accession. *European Policy Analysis*, Issue #1 2012.
Watt, N. (2006, September 26). Romania and Bulgaria to join EU. *Guardian*.
World Bank. (2012). *Fighting corruption in public services: chronicling Georgia's reforms*. Washington, DC: International Bank for Reconstruction and Development/World Bank.
World Bank and International Finance Corporation. (2012). *Russian federation: country profile 2012*. Washington, DC: The International Bank for Reconstruction and Development, 2011 – updated November 2012.
World Bank and International Finance Corporation. (2013). *Georgia: country profile 2013*. Washington, DC: The International Bank for Reconstruction and Development, 2011 – updated December 2013.
World Bank and International Finance Corporation. (2014a). *Bulgaria: country profile 2013*. Washington, DC: The International Bank for Reconstruction and Development, 2011 – updated April 2014.
World Bank and International Finance Corporation. (2014b). *Romania: country profile 2013*. Washington, DC: The International Bank for Reconstruction and Development, 2011 – updated December 2014.
Zhelev, V. (2015, September 8). Bulgaria fails to adopt key anti-corruption law. *EU Observer*. https://euobserver.com/beyond-brussels/130202. Retrieved 23 November 2015.
Zhelev, V., & Bird, M. (2015, September 11). Bulgaria, Romania tie migrant quotas to Schengen. *EU Observer*. https://euobserver.com/beyond-brussels/130202. Retrieved 23 November 2015.

Leslie Holmes is a Professor Emeritus of Political Science at the University of Melbourne, and a Recurrent Visiting Professor at the Centre for Social Studies (IFiS PAN) in Warsaw, the University of Bologna, and the People's University in Beijing. He has authored 9 books, and his work has been published in 15 languages.

PART II

Central and Eastern Europe

Chapter 5: The V4 Countries and the EU: A Comparative Perspective

Vladimir Baláž, Katarina Karasová and Allan M. Williams

Introduction

The chapter examines both the similarities and the differences in the trajectories of the four V4 (The Visegrád Four) countries. The similarities reflect the enduring influence of structural factors and shared external institutional factors (notably European Union (EU) membership, and the *acquis communautaire* of more than 250,000 pages, Åslund 2013, p. 11) but this is not a simple story of path dependency and lock-in (see Martin and Sunley 2006 for a theoretical overview). Instead, institutions were able to drive new and, to some extent, different pathways, and there are important national differences in say inward investment, migration or engagement with the knowledge economy, which indicate the importance of agency. Transformation theory provides a relatively flexible theoretical framework (Breisinger et al. 2009), which can account for both path dependency and how institutions drive new pathways. Essentially this visualises there being a series of interlocking and repetitive *s*-curves of growth, but also the possibility of break

V. Baláž (✉)
The Institute for Forecasting of the Slovak Academy of Sciences, 81364 Bratislava, Slovakia
e-mail: vbalaz@yahoo.com

Fish, Gill, Petrovic (eds.), *A Quarter Century of Post-Communism Assessed*, DOI 10.1007/978-3-319-43437-7_6

points where change is driven both by external shocks and by institutional changes from within (Martin 2010). The external shocks are manifest in the V4 countries, but there are also institutional changes, as in national economic strategies, and the policies which accompany these. Additionally, this chapter provides a broadly based analysis of the economic journey of the V4 countries, and compares their economic trajectories with those of the three southern European states which became EU members some two decades earlier. Building on the authors' earlier review of the 1990s (Williams et al. 1998), this chapter focuses more on the post-2000 period, when there were illuminating shifts in the experiences of the southern and V4 countries.

Over just 15 years, the central eastern European V4 countries (Czech Republic, Hungary, Poland and Slovakia) transitioned from state socialism to membership of the EU, via a set of often brutal market reforms that were initiated by external shock. They had low growth rates in the final decade of state socialism and the shares of gross fixed capital formation (GFCF) in gross domestic product (GDP) decreased significantly in Slovakia, Poland and Hungary in the late 1980s (Table 5.1).

In contrast, the new southern members of the EU – Portugal and Spain in particular – benefited from inflows of FDI, and growth in GFCF and exports in the same period (Table 5.1, Fig. 5.1). After 1989, there were initially precipitous declines in the V4 economies, with cumulative decreases of 20–25% in their GDPs in 1990–1993 related to the sharp shock introduction of market reforms, the disintegration of traditional CMEA markets and difficulties in reorientating exports to EU15[1] markets, and changes in the product structure of exports.

The economic growth was driven by the EU15-centered exports, strong increases in GFCF, foreign direct investment (FDI), and potential of the market economy in the early 1990s. There was also accelerating inward investment in anticipation of EU accession. Slovakia initially lagged behind, but the end of the Mečiar government in 1998, followed by institutional reforms (economic and political), led to Slovakia joining the accession negotiations, and to major FDI inflows in 2000–2002. Such was the pace of economic change and external reorientation in the V4 group that accession to the EU in 2004 appeared to represent a political formalisation of a process of economic integration that was already largely completed in terms of trade, FDI and migration flows. The transition was even more impressive when these trajectories were compared to those of the southern European

Table 5.1 Economic development in the V4 countries and southern EU members in 1980–2014

	CZ	*HU*	*PL*	*SK*	*EL*	*ES*	*PT*	*V4 avg*	*South avg*
Period	*Average annual growth in GDP (%)*								
1980–1989	1.4	1.5	1.4	1.7	0.8	2.8	3.4	1.5	2.3
1990–2004	1.2	1.2	2.5	1.7	2.9	3.0	2.4	1.7	2.8
2005–2013	2.1	0.9	3.9	3.9	−1.9	0.7	−0.3	2.7	−0.5
	Gross fixed capital formation as % of GDP								
1980–1989	25.5	24.0	20.9	29.4	25.8	22.4	28.1	25.0	25.4
1990–2004	29.3	23.0	19.4	30.3	23.3	24.4	25.2	25.5	24.3
2005–2013	27.2	21.8	20.3	23.8	18.1	24.7	19.6	23.3	20.8
	Average annual growth in total factor productivity (%)								
1980–1989	X	x	x	X	−0.9	1.3	1.6	X	0.7
1990–2004[a]	1.4	1.8	3.1	2.0	1.3	0.2	0.8	2.1	0.8
2005–2013	0.7	−0.2	0.9	2.2	−1.4	0.1	0.1	0.9	−0.4

Notes: [a]1995–2004 for the CZ, HU, SK and PL. Simple averages for the V4 and Southern EU Members.

Source: Eurostat (2015f): ***National accounts***; World Bank (2015): ***World Development Database***. National statistical offices of the V4 countries; Sixta et al. (2013) for the Czech and Slovak Republics in 1980–1990; European Commission, Economic and Financial Affairs (2015): *AMECO* ***database***.

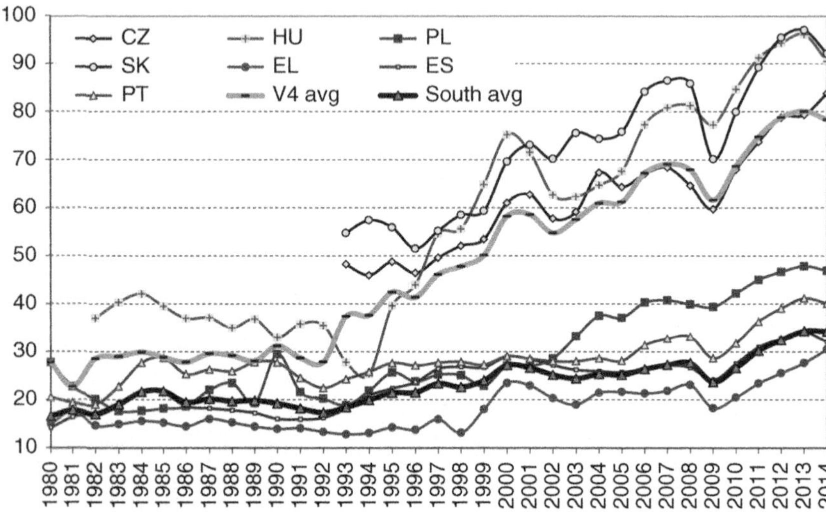

Fig. 5.1 Exports of goods and services in the V4 countries and southern EU member Countries, as % GDP. *Source*: UNCTAD (2015b): *Goods and services (BPM5): Trade openness indicators, annual, 1980–2014, International Trade in Goods and Services, online database*

member states. Although the journey was largely shared, it was also uneven with, for example, Slovakia lagging behind initially, the Czech Republic forging ahead in terms of GDP per capita, Hungary being quicker to open its doors to FDI, and Poland's trajectory being influenced by its earlier partial economic reforms in the 1980s.

By the mid-2000s, there was relatively strong and sometimes spectacular, FDI- and export-led economic growth in the V4 economies. Subsequently, the economic downturn following the 2008 financial crisis exposed the darker economic side of transition and integration in the form of increased vulnerability to external shocks, and a potentially precarious position in the international division of labour. But there were persistent variations in their trajectories, reflecting structural and institutional differences: domestic consumption was a far more important factor of growth in Poland which meant that it was less affected by the 2009 economic recession than the Czech and Slovak Republics and Hungary. Economic growth rebounded in 2010 in all V4 countries, albeit at considerably lower rates than before the crisis, but markedly more strongly than in the southern member states, which experienced deep recessions in the following years.

Having briefly outlined the economic trajectories of the V4 countries, the remainder of the chapter focuses in more detail on foreign trade, FDI, research and development (R&D), and labour migration. The chapter is essentially empirical in content, although framed by an understanding of transformation theory which emphasises the persistence of growth curves in conjunction with the possibility for break points.

Foreign Trade

Under state socialism trade resembled a hub-and-spokes model of bilateral trade between the Soviet Union and the individual eastern bloc countries, with relatively weak trade ties amongst the latter (Dangerfield 1995). After 1989, trade with the Soviet Union collapsed, while trade reorientation to Western Europe was framed by the 1991–1992 Europe Agreements which mapped out a 10-year transition to free trade. Despite the asymmetrical nature of the agreements, which many commentators consider favoured the interests of the EU states (Gowan 1995), there was rapid territorial reorientation of foreign trade in goods after 1989. Whereas the EU15 markets accounted for 32.1% of Polish, 27.1% of Hungarian and 18.5% of Czechoslovak exports in 1989 (United Nations 1995), by 1995 these shares surpassed 60% in Hungary and the Czech Republic and 70% in Poland (Fig. 5.2). The share of direct exports from Slovakia to the EU15 (37.4%) in 1995 were far lower (UNCTAD 2015b), reflecting the importance of direct exports to the Czech Republic, although their ultimate destination was often the EU. By 2004, all the V4 countries exported 60–75% of their goods to the EU15 countries and over 80% to the EU28. The EU members remained the key export markets for the V4 countries also in late 2000s and early 2010s, although multinational branch plants and offices were developing new export markets, especially in Russia and China.

This reorientation occurred against the background of truly spectacular growth in foreign trade after 1989. The shares of exports/imports of goods and services in GDP roughly doubled in 1993–2014 in all the V4 countries (Fig. 5.1). In contrast, the national shares of world exports/imports declined in the GDPs of Portugal and Greece, while stagnating in Spain, in the same period. The most important increases in foreign trade happened in early 1990s, which are related to (i) the EU association

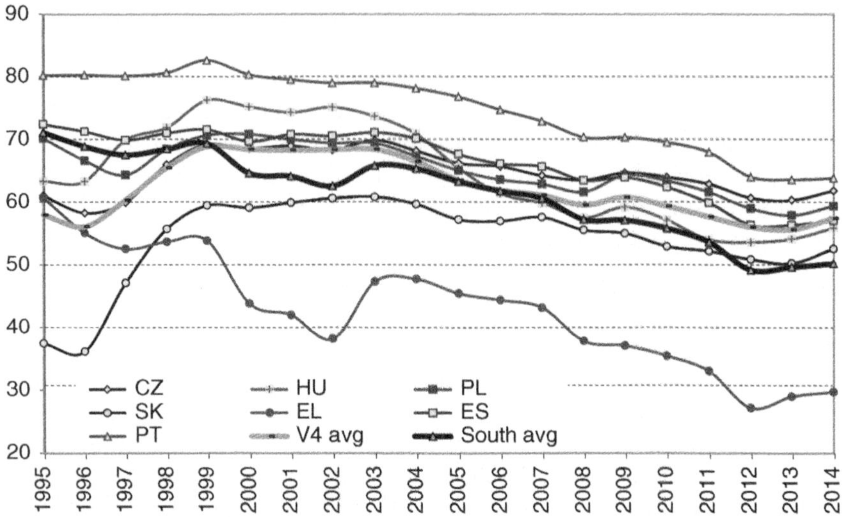

Fig. 5.2 The share of the EU15 in exports of goods and services from the V4 countries and southern EU Member Countries, in %. *Source*: UNCTAD (2015b): *International Trade in Goods and Service in 1995–2014, online database*

agreements in the 1990s, and (ii) the introduction of macroeconomic and structural reforms. This was followed by further increases in export intensity, which are related to (iii) the arrival of multinational companies (MNCs) in the 2000s, and (iv) economic boom in 2001–2007. Within this overall picture, however, we can also see the importance of different national strategies. In 2014, Slovakia and Hungary had the highest degree of openness in foreign trade, equivalent to almost 100% of their GDPs, followed by the Czech Republic (78%), and Poland (48%). These differences only partly reflect country size (trade is usually a smaller share of GDP in larger economies), because Slovakia and Hungary, for example, were more open than the very small Baltic economies. They received more FDI and were more strongly integrated in global value chains. Significant increases in total exports reflected cross-border movements of parts and components (especially in the car industry and consumer electronics) in the V4 countries, and the creation of generally attractive conditions for inward investment in Hungary and Slovakia, in particular. The trade transformation was very much the outcome of the conjunction of external shocks after 1989 and 2008 with institutional changes.

The influx of FDI and the substantial presence of the MNCs influenced the export structures of the V4 countries. Because of their position in the global division of labour, the share of high-tech exports in total exports was low – 21.0% in the Czech Republic, 19.1% in Hungary, 9.7% in Slovakia, and 9.4% in Poland by 2014 – but it was even lower (2.0–6.6%) in the three southern European economies.

Main Trade Partners and Product Groups

Intra-EU trade generated some 79% of total exports of goods in the Czech and Slovak Republics and Hungary, and 72% in Poland, in 2014. The geographical patterns of trade were considerably different to those of the southern EU Members. Spain and Greece, for example, exported only about one half of their goods to the EU.

Germany has been by far the largest partner in intra-EU trade since the early 1990s, and it has also been the largest investor in the V4 economies: these features are interrelated. Germany's FDI helped establish strong export-oriented automotive, electrical engineering and machinery industries in the V4. German- and French-owned subsidiaries of the MNCs ranked amongst the most important importers and exporters of intermediate goods, and final products to/from the V4 countries. In addition, some cross-border trade exchanges reflect continuities from pre-1989 trade patterns. The Czech Republic, for example, remained Slovakia's second most important partner until the mid-2010s.

The concept of comparative advantages provide insights into trade composition. This implies that marginal factor productivities are significantly higher in the exporting than the non-exporting sectors; small open economies should specialise in limited portfolios of exported goods; and foreign investors should prefer export-oriented sectors with above-average marginal factors productivities. These principles seem to apply to the V4 countries. The most important merchandise exports of the V4 countries were concentrated in a relatively limited number of product groups (cars and car parts, consumer electronics and products of electrical engineering), which corresponded with the industries receiving the highest volumes of FDI. The V4 group's competitive advantage in EU export markets is indicated by the Balassa index of revealed comparative advantage (RCA)[2] which, for example, indicates that consumer electronics and electrical engineering accounted for disproportionally high shares of V4 countries exports in the 1990s, 2000s and 2010s.

Cars and car parts, consumer electronics, products of electrical engineering, and basic metals and metal products ranked amongst the most import exports of the Czech and Slovak Republics, and Hungary by 2014. Poland had a similar product structure, but also had strong furniture and shipping exports. Moreover, the concentration index[3] (the degree to which exports and imports are focused in a few products) points to a very high increase in the concentration of exports in a small number of export items for Slovakia, and high increases for the Czech Republic and Hungary in 1995–2013. These small and open economies tended to overspecialise in a relatively small number of export items. Slovakia in particular became extremely dependent on exports of cars and consumer electronics. The concentration indices stagnated in Poland and decreased in Portugal and Spain in the same period. The changes in the concentration indices related to rapid and deep integration of the V4 countries into global value chains. The strategy of export concentration had its own risk, and the overspecialised V4 economies (SK, HU and CZ) experienced deeper slowdown in economic growth after 2008 than Poland, which had more diversified exports (Gurgul and Lach 2013).

Trade in Value Added: Domestic and Foreign Value-Added in Total Exports

Improving productivity and remaining competitive in a world dominated by global value chains requires efficient imports of goods as well as services. Several factors determine the share of domestic value in gross exports. First, large countries, such as the USA and Japan, have greater scope to source inputs from domestic providers and tend to import about one fifth of total production, compared to typically 50–60% in small and medium-sized countries. Second, exports of complex goods (cars and consumer electronics) are usually more demanding on foreign intermediate inputs than exports of simple goods (food products and raw materials) and/or services. Third, countries with extensive and well-embedded value chains tend to have higher shares of domestic content in total exports.

The total value added embodied in exports is broken down to the total domestic versus the foreign value-added contents of exports (see Table 5.2). Slovakia (46.8%), the Czech Republic (45.3%) and Hungary (48.7%), had higher share of foreign content in their total gross exports than Poland

Table 5.2 Domestic and foreign industry value added: share in gross exports in 2011 (%)

	Total industry		*C29: machinery*		*C30: computer, electronics*		*C31: electrical machinery*		*C34: motor vehicles*	
	DVA	*FVA*	*DVA*	*FVA*	*DVA*	*FVA*	*DVA*	*FVA*	*DVA*	*FVA*
Czech Rep.	54.7	45.3	53.6	46.5	32.9	67.1	47.1	52.9	46.4	53.6
Hungary	51.3	48.7	53.8	46.2	25.9	74.1	38.3	61.7	38.6	61.4
Poland	67.6	32.4	63.1	36.9	46.3	53.7	58.0	42.0	50.7	49.3
Slovakia	53.2	46.8	54.2	45.8	39.1	60.9	52.2	47.8	39.2	60.8
V4 average	56.7	43.3	56.2	43.9	36.1	64.0	48.9	51.1	43.7	56.3
Greece	75.1	25.0	76.7	23.3	81.8	18.2	71.2	28.8	76.9	23.2
Spain	73.1	26.9	72.6	27.4	70.9	29.1	64.1	35.9	53.9	46.1
Portugal	67.2	32.8	62.8	37.2	47.6	52.5	50.9	49.1	41.7	58.3
South average	71.8	28.2	70.7	29.3	66.8	33.3	62.1	37.9	57.5	42.5

Notes: DVA = share of domestic value added in the total exports; FVA = share of foreign value added in the total exports. Simple averages for the V4 and southern EU members.

Source: OECD (2015): *Trade in Value Added (TIVA)*.

(32.4%), due to the three factors indicated above. High shares of foreign content in their total gross exports were clearly visible in key exporting industries—computer and electronics, electrical machinery and motor vehicles. The shares of domestic and foreign content in total gross exports indicate that the V4 countries were considerably more integrated into global value chains than the southern EU members (Table 5.2). Moreover, their integration deepened over time. Foreign content, for example, accounted for only 31.9% of the total gross exports in Slovakia, 30.5% in the Czech Republic, 30.1% in Hungary, compared to 16.1% in Poland in 1995 (source: OECD 2015, database on the Trade in Value Added). Inclusion in global value chains enabled fast growth in the exports and GDPs of the V4 economies. It is, of course, much easier to participate in incumbent global value chain than to build new ones but this does not automatically support development of domestic innovations and institutions (Éltető 2014, p. 53). Key industries were linked to the global value chains as suppliers and assemblers of the final products in the V4 countries.

The integration of the V4 countries into global value chains boosted the exports of goods much more than services. While the absolute volume of service exports grew, the relative shares of services in total exports decreased significantly in all V4 countries (1990–2014). This was the opposite of the general EU trends. The concentration on exports of goods is a potential weakness of the V4 economies in contrast to advanced EU and OECD economies which focus more on high value added services. International transport, travel and tourism were the most important items in the service trade of the V4 members rather than knowledge-intensive business services. This reflects the underdevelopment of the knowledge economy sectors of the V4 countries in the mid-2010s.

In the short term, the integration of the V4 countries into the EU boosted their economic growth via the low costs of production inputs and the influx of FDI. However, their integration into global value chains also means that, in the long term, the competitiveness of the V4 countries will depend on the continuing competitiveness of European exporters in the global economy. This will differ between the smaller and more open economies, and Poland. The high degree of openness of small and open economies may have reduced their exposure to domestic shocks (Iossifov 2014) while Poland, on the other hand, remains more exposed to shifts in domestic demand.

Foreign Direct Investment

Changes in foreign trade patterns were inextricably linked to new patterns of foreign investment. FDI was a key element of the neoliberal model of transition. It played an important role in privatisation, deregulation and liberalisation, and was considered essential for ensuring competition in national markets, as well as the transfer of technology, knowledge and capital at a time when national financial markets were weak and deformed (Sheehy 1994). The assumed benefits of FDI did not automatically follow the big bang economic reforms and the Europe Agreements. The V4 countries had to compete for the EU's financial and knowledge resources with incumbent EU members (Spain, Portugal and Greece, in particular), and other Central Eastern European countries such as Slovenia, Romania, Bulgaria and the Baltic countries. However, they had several key advantages. First, they had *favourable geographical locations*, and either bordered or were close to Germany and France, two major EU economies. Portugal, Greece, Romania and/or Baltic countries had more peripheral locations. Strategic locations between Western and Eastern Europe, and geographical proximity to the EU and Russian markets, were valuable assets for their export-oriented industries. Geographical location was particularly important in determining FDI inflows in all the transition economies in Central Eastern Europe (Estrin and Uvalic 2014).

Second, they had favourable *labour costs and educational strengths*. Average nominal gross earnings were 4–5 times lower in the V4 countries than in Spain or Greece in the mid-1990s. The gap somewhat narrowed in the mid-2010s, but gross wages are still 2–3 times lower in the V4 countries than in Spain or Greece (Eurostat 2015a, Average annual gross earnings by economic activity). Educational attainment was also higher in the V4 countries than in the southern EU Members. The southern EU Members, for example, had slightly higher population shares with graduate qualifications, but also much higher shares with less than primary and/or lower secondary education in 2004 (Table 5.3). This reflected the existence of relatively well-developed systems of secondary education and vocational training in the V4 countries. This strong technically oriented secondary education was attractive to foreign investors in manufacturing, the automotive industry in particular. In contrast, the southern EU Members had high rates of early school leavers and lacked secondary school graduates in science and engineering in the mid-2010s.

Table 5.3 Population by educational attainment level, sex and age (%) for the age group 24–35, in 2004 and 2014

	CZ	*HU*	*PL*	*SK*	*EL*	*ES*	*PT*	*V4 avg*	*South avg*
Period	*Less than primary, primary and lower secondary education (ISCED 0 and 2)*								
2004	6.4	16.5	8.5	6.5	23.9	37.4	60.2	9.5	40.5
2014	5.4	13.0	5.8	7.4	17.7	34.4	35.3	7.9	29.1
	Upper secondary and post-secondary non-tertiary education (ISCED 3 and 4)								
2004	80.9	65.0	69.0	79.1	51.3	23.4	21.5	73.5	32.1
2014	64.7	54.9	51.6	62.8	41.6	24.1	33.2	58.5	33.0
	Tertiary education (ISCED 5 and 8)								
2004	12.8	18.6	22.6	14.4	24.8	39.8	18.3	17.1	27.6
2014	29.9	32.1	42.6	29.8	38.7	41.5	31.4	33.6	37.2

Source: Eurostat (2015g): *Population by educational attainment level, sex and age (%25)*; Simple averages for the V4 and southern EU members.

Third, *they had stable macroeconomic environments, and had experienced large-scale privatisations and rapid development of domestic financial markets.* The 'shock therapy' reforms included policies aimed *inter alia* at price deregulation, and liberalisation of trade and capital flows. The liberalisation policies generated high increases in consumer prices but secured relatively stable price environment in the latter phases of the economic transition. Capital asset pricing models recognise two major determinants of the FDI inflows to emerging market economies, internal and external. The former refers to (country specific) 'pull factors', including economic, social and political developments: these can be further subdivided (Lensink and White 1998) into economic performance factors, such as GDP growth, inflation rates, trade and budget balances, saving rates, wage levels, and creditworthiness factors such as the debt to exports and GDP ratios, or international currency reserves to GDP. The latter refer to external (country non-specific) 'push' factors such as developments in international markets, and can be expressed in terms of differences between rates of return on alternative investment on international markets and those in the host country.

A comparative analysis of the V4 countries and newly industrialised Asian economies found GDP per capita, inflation and the ratio of M2 to GDP were the most significant determinants of FDI inflows in the 1990s (Williams and Baláž 2001). This broadly accords with Lensink and White's (1998) findings that FDI tends to be directed to economies with relatively high development levels and relatively developed financial systems (indicated by ratios of broad money to GDP). FDI investors had longer term targets and were less influenced by fluctuations in interest rates and trade balances than speculative investors. Countries like Hungary, which privatised its financial sector early in the transition, enjoyed the advantage of a more sophisticated financial environment in the latter transition stages.

Fourth, there were well-established domestic industrial traditions in the V4 countries, which had strong manufacturing industries under state socialism. The former Czechoslovakia, for example, produced its own car brands (Skoda personal cars and Tatra trucks). Hungary exported Ikarus buses, and Poland produced Fiat cars under licence. The branches of MNCs mostly continued and extended manufacturing industries rather than building these from scratch in the V4 economies.

The average annual net FDI inflows generated 14.2% of the GFCF in the Czech Republic, 23.6% in Hungary, 15.0% in Poland, and 21.3% in Slovakia in 1993–2014. The high proportions in Hungary and Slovakia reflected particularly FDI-friendly national policies at different periods. These shares were substantially higher than those for the EU28 (11.6%), or for, say, India (4.4%), China (8.7%) or Latin America (13.9%). The contribution of FDI to the V4 economies, however, was higher than indicated by the shares of FDI in the GFCF. Financial and capital transfers were accompanied by knowledge transfers in terms of technologies and managerial practices.

The FDI inflows into the V4 economies were uneven, but they were generally positively related to their integration into the EU economy. The annual amounts of FDI reflected the privatisation and sales of domestic enterprises to foreign investors in the early 1990s, greenfield investments in new markets in the late 1990s and early 2000s, and different phases of V4 integration to EU structures (association agreements in 1991–1993 versus accession agreements in 2004). They were also related to business cycles, notably the 2001–2007 boom versus 2008–2009 boom. The first peak was in 1993–1995 while the second in 1998–2002 was related to the expected EU accession of the V4 region. FDI inflows peaked in 2007, when there were not only significantly lower inflows, but also substantial outflows of FDI from the V4 countries. During an economic crisis, 'increased integration may result in more highly correlated business cycles because of common demand shocks or intra-industry trade' (Frankel and Rose 1998). This accords with the notion of break points in transformation theory that are related to external shocks.

The EU15 economies were major investors in the V4 countries and were more severely affected during the economic recession than the USA and/or China. FDI flows from the EU15 to the V4 countries decreased more than the flows from the USA to Latin America and/or flows from China to developing Asia and Africa (UNCTAD 2015a). FDI inflows from the EU15 to the V4 economies resurged after 2010, albeit at a lower level than in 2004–2007. In the intervening period, the economies in Central Eastern Europe (CEE) had become less attractive than the Balkan economies.

Despite the relative slow down, the V4 economies had built substantial stocks of FDI by 2014. This accounted for 54.9% of GDP in the Czech Republic, 41.5% in Hungary, 36.6% in Poland and 55.0% in Slovakia. These were substantially higher than the proportions in the southern EU members in the same year: Greece –0.9%, Spain 4.0% and Portugal 23.9%. FDI in the V4 countries has usually been labour intensive and this provided a competitive advantage both for investors (MNCs) and the recipient countries. The V4 lost relative little foreign capital during the 2008+ economic crisis. European carmakers, for example, used lower cost V4 labour to cut production costs in the period of economic turmoil.

The success of industry-centred FDI in small and open economies (such as the Czech and Slovak Republics and Hungary) is understandable when these economies are well-integrated in global production chains. The Czech Republic and Slovakia had far stronger manufacturing sectors and received more FDI per capita than Hungary and Poland (Table 5.4). However, the low costs of production and proximity to EU markets constituted major competitive advantages for the V4 countries on international markets throughout the 1990s–2010s. The MNCs used the V4 countries as production bases for EU-oriented exports. Foreign capital targeted capital and labour-intensive and export-oriented, sectors such as the automotive and chemical industries. Foreign ownership was also significant in the financial and information and communication technologies (ICT) sectors. In contrast, there was relatively less FDI in those sectors serving domestic markets, such as food processing and transport. The FDI influx was reflected in changes in the ownership structure of the national economies. Eurostat data show that foreign controlled enterprises generated far higher proportions of total value added in the V4 (35.1–51.9%) than in Spain (18.7%) and Portugal (19.7%).

Table 5.4 Average annual net FDI flows in the V4 countries and southern EU members in 1993–2013

	CZ	*HU*	*PL*	*SK*	*EL*	*ES*	*PT*	*V4 avg*	*South avg*
Period	*Average annual net FDI, €m*								
1993–2004	3289	2176	6843	1251	502	-5741	-303	3390	-1847
2005–2013	4048	1718	7323	1814	-97	-13,772	2108	3726	-3920
	Average annual net FDI, € per capita								
1993–2004	322	215	179	233	46	-135	-29	237	-39
2005–2013	390	171	192	337	-9	-302	200	273	-37

Source: Eurostat (2015b): Balance of Payment Statistics; Eurostat (2015c): Financial account – Direct investment; and authors' own computations. Simple averages for the V4 and Southern EU Members.

Most literature on FDI and economic growth identifies a causal relationship between the influx of foreign capital, and increases in exports and in GDP (for example, Makki and Agapi 2004; Alfaro et al. 2004). There is similar evidence for Central and Eastern Europe in the 1990s and 2000s. Kutan and Vukšić (2007) found that FDI contributed to higher exports by increasing supply capacity in the new EU member countries in 1996–2004. In a different study, Śmiech and Zysk (2014) found that the FDI strongly influenced Polish, Slovak and Czech exports and imports in 2001–2011.

FDI boosted the competitiveness of the V4 countries via growth in the stocks of fixed capital, and diffusion of knowledge and advanced technologies. The latter correlated with significant growth in total factor productivity (TFP). According to the EC's Annual Macroeconomic Database (European Commission, Economic and Financial Affairs 2015, AMECO database), the V4 countries enjoyed significant growth in TFP in 1995–2014, increasing annually by 1.1% in the Czech Republic, 0.8% in Hungary, 2.0% in Poland and 2.1% in Slovakia. This was much higher than in Greece (0.4%), Spain (0.1%), Portugal (0.3%) and the EU15 (0.4%) in the same period (Table 5.1). High growth rates in TFP in the V4 countries reflected several factors: low TFP levels in the early 1990s; technology transfers via foreign trade; substantial stocks of human capital; diffusion of knowledge and technology via FDI; and national R&D and innovation efforts. However, the latter were severely affected by the economic and social transition in the early 1990s and contributed less than FDI to national competitiveness.

FDI in the V4 countries also helped to improve the competitiveness of the MNCs. The shares of the automotive industries in total manufacturing employment were significantly lower than the corresponding shares of these industries in gross value added in all the V4 countries (Túry 2014, p. 91). The German and French automotive companies exploited low production costs in the Czech and Slovak Republics and Hungary and reinvested their earnings in the V4 countries. This was different to Spain, where Volkswagen (SEAT) planned to relocate its activities to Slovakia in 2002 leading to a bitter dispute between the Spanish and Slovak governments, and the Spanish government threatening to veto Slovakia's accession to the EU (Medve-Bálint 2014, p. 44).

The contribution of FDI to economic development was not always positive. The V4 countries also received substantial speculative investment in real estate. This was particularly pronounced in Hungary where a market bubble was fuelled by Hungarians taking out mortgages in euros and Swiss francs, leading to up to 40% of mortgages being denominated in foreign exchange in 2006 (Égert and Mihaljek 2007). The collapse of the Hungarian forint exchange rate impacted heavily on mortgage payments. The consumption booms and housing bubbles in the V4 countries, however, were smaller than those in the Baltic countries, Romania and Bulgaria (Bogumil 2014). And, as noted earlier, the openness of the three smaller V4 economies came at the price of considerable vulnerability to external shocks (Smith and Swain 2010).

Research and Development

Labour costs in the V4 countries have risen during the last two decades and have converged on EU15 levels. High labour cost countries can only compete in the increasingly globalised economy if they are specialised in industries that require high knowledge content, high qualification levels and expertise in the labour force. Investments in the knowledge economy increased in the V4 countries, but were far from matching those in the EU15 countries. This is critical because, in the long term, economic growth is primarily defined by technological progress and the accumulation of human capital, which determines the way and the speed at which technological progress penetrates the economy. The three most important issues are the availability of research funding and supply of highly skilled researchers; the creation of a functional national system of innovation; and high shares of innovative enterprises. The V4 countries have struggled with all three elements. R&D was weak under state socialism, due to the preponderance of basic versus applied research (Zon 1996). R&D continued to be relatively weak after 1989, and a Commission of the European Communities report (1995) attributed this to several factors: sharp reductions in public expenditure generally, including R&D; brain drain of highly skilled researchers; short termism in the private domestic sector, exacerbated by the struggle for survival following the sharp shock economic reforms; and the reliance of MNCs on external R&D.

Following EU accession, the V4 countries experienced four major trends. First, there has been an overall increase in gross expenditure on R&D (GERD) in both the EU and the V4 group, including the period of economic turmoil. Some governments have supported business expenditure on R&D (BERD) with tax breaks and grants. The V4 countries had higher growth in GERD compared to the EU28 average, while this stagnated in Greece, Portugal and Spain in the same period. The GERD levels in the V4 countries, however, increased from relatively low levels. The Czech Republic had the most impressive growth in GERD amongst the V4 group, while Slovakia resembled Malta, Cyprus, Romania and Greece in having low growth in GERD.

Second, business expenditure on R&D (BERD) also grew both in the EU28 and V4 in 2008–2013. The Czech Republic and Hungary, in particular, reported high growth in BERD, with the branches of MNCs and domestic firms having broadly similar importance in this. In Poland and Slovakia, expenditure by domestic companies contributed more than MNC expenditure to BERD. The southern EU members, on the other hand, had relatively low inward flows of foreign finance in the business sector.

Third, public expenditure on R&D (government + higher education institutions) decreased in 2008–2013 in the EU28. There were significant cuts in R&D in Spain and Italy in particular, associated with significant reductions in public spending. Public expenditure on R&D has stagnated in Hungary, Poland and Slovakia since 2009, and Slovakia ranked bottom amongst the EU28. The Czech Republic, on the other hand, had the fastest growth of public expenditure on R&D in the EU28 in 2009–2013. Public expenditure on R&D was also affected by cuts in government budgets in Spain, Portugal and Greece.

Fourth, the importance of external international sources of funding for R&D has increased in the V4 countries in the last 10 years. Foreign resources (foreign firms and international organisations) generated about

20% of total GERD in the V4 countries. The Czech Republic in particular had strong growth in such sources, of which two thirds was from the European Commission and one third from foreign companies. The European Commission provided for over 60% of foreign funding in Poland and Slovakia, but also in Greece, Portugal and Spain in early 2010s. The Hungary was rather exceptional, as two thirds of its foreign funding was provided by foreign enterprises in the same period.

Structural Challenges and Integration to the EU's Knowledge Markets

The European Commission's (2015b) annual country reports on research and innovation (R&I) identified a number of persistent challenges for the V4 countries. There is weak national funding and underdeveloped public–private collaboration, as well as the low embeddedness of MNCs in the national economy, and low co-operation between MNCs and national universities and research centres. This is compounded by underdeveloped and/or unstable systems of R&I governance. Other weaknesses include low levels of innovativeness amongst domestic small and medium-sized companies (SMEs), lack of a clear thematic focus in publicly funded research, and hesitant integration of national R&I systems into the European Research Area – for example, low participation in the framework programmes, and in European joint technology initiatives and partnerships.

Some of these structural challenges stem from the history of economic development in the 1990s and early 2000s. The MNCs entered the V4 markets principally because of the low effective costs of production inputs, labour costs in particular. They have tended to retain their research activities and other knowledge-intensive services in their headquarters. Eurostat data on sources of GERD finance do indicate a gradual shift towards more sophisticated activities in the V4 countries, in the Czech Republic and Hungary in particular. However, both the MNCs and domestic enterprises had to cope with a weak supply of high-quality research resources in the V4 countries. Business-oriented research largely disappeared during the turbulent 1990s. Universities and government research facilities tried to insulate themselves from market forces and refocused their attention on basic research and mass education. Research excellence was limited.

There were mixed trends in the internationalisation of R&D in the V4 countries. The Czech Republic and Hungary achieved average success rates in FP7 research projects in 2007–2014, but Poland and Slovakia had quite low success rates. All the V4 countries accounted for below-average patenting activity rates and high-quality scientific publications in the mid-2010s (Table 5.5). Researchers from the CEE countries were also more likely to publish in their national languages and received relatively less citations per paper than authors from the EU15. This may reflect 'poorer knowledge of publication standards and publication strategies as well as inadequate levels of proficiency in English, but also perhaps poorer standards of research resulting, inter alia, from weaker international collaboration' in the CEE countries (Płoszaj and Olechnicka 2015, p. 18).

Table 5.5 Selected indicators of the V4 and southern EU member countries in research and innovation

	*Year**	*GERD, % GDP*	*BERD, % GDP*	*Top publications*	*Patents*	*KIBS exports*	*Innovative SMEs*
CZ	2005	1.17	0.73	4.9	0.72	31.6	35.5
	2014	1.91	1.03	5.6	0.79	35.2	30.9
HU	2005	0.93	0.41	4.8	1.38	21.0	17.6
	2014	1.41	0.98	5.3	1.49	28.8	12.8
PL	2005	0.57	0.18	3.5	0.28	22.6	22.2
	2014	0.87	0.38	3.8	0.42	33.6	13.1
SK	2005	0.49	0.25	2.4	0.54	15.5	19.3
	2014	0.83	0.38	4.2	0.50	31.3	17.7
ES	2005	1.10	x	9.2	1.30	24.0	32.1
	2014	1.24	0.66	10.4	1.57	30.0	18.4
PT	2005	0.76	0.30	9.0	0.26	22.8	38.6
	2014	1.36	0.65	9.9	0.67	35.5	38.3
EL	2005	0.58	x	8.9	0.28	x	34.5
	2014	0.80	0.50	9.2	0.35	53.9	29.6
V4 avg	2005	0.79	0.39	3.9	0.73	22.7	23.7
	2014	1.26	0.69	4.7	0.80	32.2	18.6
South avg	2005	0.81	x	9.0	0.61	x	35.1
	2014	1.13	0.60	9.8	0.86	39.8	28.8
EU28	2014*	2.01	1.29	11.0	3.38	49.5	30.6

Notes: * = or the latest available year. GERD = gross expenditure on research and development; BERD = business expenditure on research and development; top publications = scientific publications within the 10% most cited scientific publications worldwide as percent of total scientific publications of the country; KIBS exports = knowledge-intensive services exports as percent of total service exports; patents = PCT patent applications per billion GDP in current PPS (EUR); innovative SMEs introducing product or process innovations as percent of SMEs. Simple averages for the V4 and southern EU members.

Sources: European Commission (2014): Research and Innovation performance in the EU in 2014; European Commission (2015a): Innovation Union Scoreboard 2015.

Amongst the CEE countries the Czech Republic and Hungary had the best publication results.

Some of the long-term structural challenges to national R&I systems were similar in the V4 and southern Members of the EU. The country reports on the Spanish, Portuguese and Greek national R&I systems, for example, refer to 'fragile and unstable systems of the R&I governance'; 'low business demand and private investment in R&I', and 'low innovativeness by the domestic SMEs' (European Commission 2014).

The V4 countries have tried to overcome these weaknesses with support from the European Commission. A significant part of the structural fund resources, for example, was channelled to national R&I systems in the V4 countries. Their weak national R&I systems, however, had limited absorption capacity. In order to improve spending rates, some national governments allocated most structural funds for research-to-research infrastructure projects. Investments in research infrastructures, however, were not matched by national investments in human resources, or by necessary reforms of national R&I governance. Low levels of research excellence, and poor interconnections between the industry and academia sectors, were evident in the below-EU average values of indicators for commercial and non-commercial research outputs (Table 5.5).

Labour Migration

International labour migration was very limited under state socialism, but thereafter increased significantly. Initially, access to international labour markets was constrained, and there was considerable seasonal working and irregular employment, but there was also significant brain drain, contributing to reduced TFP (Baláž et al. 2004). However, returned migration also ensured that there were some benefits for the V4 countries in the form of knowledge transfers. These were particularly important in the early transition period, when there was a major technology gap between the V4 countries and the EU.

Accession to the EU in May 2004 was a turning point in the migration flows from the V4 countries. Ireland, Sweden and the UK opened their labour markets immediately after EU eastern enlargement in 2004. The UK and Ireland quickly proved to be popular destinations, and the numbers of V4 nationals in the EU15 doubled in 2004–2007. Some EU15 countries negotiated gradual adaptation of their labour markets: Greece, Spain, Italy, Portugal and Finland opened in 2006, Luxembourg in 2007,

France in 2008, and Belgium and Denmark in 2009 but none were prime destinations for the V4 nationals. Finally, Germany and Austria enabled free access to their labour markets for the EU8 nationals in 2011, and their high wages, low unemployment rates and geographical proximity resulted in an increase of 340,000 V4 nationals working in Austria and Germany in 2011–2013.

Poland generated the highest numbers of émigrés in the EU (1.92 m), followed by Hungary (0.30 m), Slovakia and the Czech Republic (0.17 m each) in 2013. Poland, Slovakia, and Hungary, however, had the highest relative intensities of emigration (5.1%, 3.1% and 3.0% of population, respectively) in the same year. Relative emigration from the Czech Republic was significantly lower (1.6%), due in part to its lower unemployment rates and higher wages 1997–2013. Slovakia and Poland, on the other hand, had the lowest wages and the highest unemployment rates in the same period, and had the highest increases in the numbers of émigrés in 1997–2013. Holland et al. (2011, p. 14) assume that 'approximately 75% of the increase can be attributed to the enlargement itself, while the remaining 25% is 'likely to have occurred even in the absence of enlargement'. The 2008 economic crisis somewhat reduced the influx of V4 nationals to the EU15 countries, but the numbers of migrants increased again in 2011.

Migrants from the V4 countries concentrated in a relatively few EU15 destinations. The top six destinations (Germany, Ireland, Italy, Austria, Spain and UK) accounted for over 82% of the total Czech, Slovak, Hungarian and Polish nationals in 1997–2004 and 2005–2013 (Table 5.6). Germany and the UK were by far the most important destinations, accounting for some 55–65% of V4 nationals in these periods.

The concentration was conditional upon wage and employment disparities, language and geographical proximity, and the evolution of labour market policies in the host countries. Jobs and educational opportunities were major motives for the intra-European migration of V4 nationals, and also the relative generosity of the welfare system (Kahanec 2012). Language proximity was of particular importance for the migration of Slovaks to the Czech Republic. The migration to Germany and Austria was informed by geographical proximity and wage differentials. Wage differentials, flexible labour markets and low unemployment rates were important for the migration of V4 nationals to the UK and Ireland. The UK and Ireland also attracted migrants wishing to learn English and/or purse tertiary education.

Table 5.6 Stock of foreign nationals in selected EU countries (period averages)

	Czech Republic		*Hungary*		*Poland*		*Slovakia*	
Period	*97-04*	*05-13*	*97-04*	*05-13*	*97-04*	*05-13*	*97-04*	*05-13*
Germany	25,293	36,686	53,247	74,899	300,873	432,845	15,124	28,081
Ireland	1080	12,450	590	6077	2091	111,814	4292	10,761
Italy	3498	5646	3514	6390	32,508	93,565	2481	7632
Austria	6771	9146	14,009	26,254	22,997	38,882	9208	19,665
Spain	2140	8202	1250	7652	17,722	75,087	1404	7330
UK	12,193	25,850	6355	29,240	33,600	485,778	5250	46,588
EU15 total	56,271	110,797	89,638	173,400	494,846	1,444,151	44,118	134,258
EU28 total	63,214	121,608	92,523	181,121	520,469	1,474,292	98,151	214,420

Sources: Eurostat (2015d): International Migration; Eurostat (2015e): Labour Force Survey; Holland et al. (2011); authors' own computations.

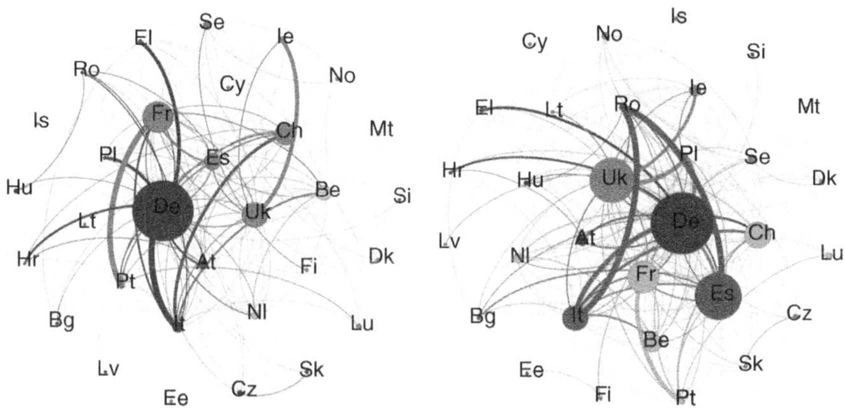

Fig. 5.3 Outflows over 4000 nationals from each country in 1997–2004 (left) and 2005–2013 (right). Country size reflects stocks of the foreign born population from the top partner countries. *Sources*: Eurostat (2015d): *International Migration* and authors' own computations

The network diagrams summarise major intra-European migration movements in 1997–2004 and 2005–2013 (stocks of 4000+ émigrés, Fig. 5.3). The size of the country is proportional to the total stocks of foreign nationals, while each line reflects the magnitude of the connection between the two countries of particular importance is that although the population of the V4 countries was some 6% lower than combined population of Spain, Portugal and Greece. The V4 countries had higher number of émigrés (2.8 million compared to 1.66 million) in 2013. The network diagrams indicate that the major labour migration flows from southern Europe to Western Europe in the 1980s were superseded by flows from the V4 countries in 2000s and later by flows from Bulgaria and Romania by the early 2010s.

The V4 countries had an educated labour force so that deskilling levels were relatively low for the V4 nationals working in the EU15 countries by the end of the 2000s. Holland et al. (2011), for example, found that elementary or basic occupations were only taken by 30% of Poles, 23% of Slovaks, 19% of Hungarians, and 15% of Czechs working in the EU15 in 2010. Most V4 nationals worked in the middle-skilled occupations, such as clerks, service workers and shop and market sales workers, skilled agricultural and fishery workers, craft and related trades workers and plant and machine operators and assemblers. High-skill jobs were taken by about 38% of Czechs, 34% of Hungarians, 30% of Slovaks and 16% of Poles which, together with high numbers of the V4 tertiary students in the EU15 countries (65.7 thousands in 2012), indicate significant brain drain.

Conclusions

The V4 countries experienced a rapid transition from state-controlled to modern market economies. The fast pace of economic reforms in the 1990s, which were partly externally induced through the various agreements with the EU, and partly due to institutional reforms, enabled deep structural changes, such as the introduction of market mechanisms, price deregulation and liberalisation of trade and capital flows. The structural changes facilitated factor movements (capital, investment and knowledge) which contributed to rapid integration of the V4 countries into the EU. In terms of transformation theory, thereafter development did resemble a series of recurrent growth curves, but external shocks (EU accession, the 2009 crisis) and international institutional changes (such as Slovakia's 1998 change of government, or Hungary's creation of a dependence on foreign loans in the housing market) were important turning points.

While changing flows of production factors were the economic trademarks of the post-1989 period, particular factors had distinctive mobility features. Reorientation and integration of the foreign trade was remarkably rapid in the early 1990s, and was complemented by strong influxes of FDI in 1995–2008, conditional on macroeconomic stabilisation, and the prospects of EU eastern enlargement. Most of incumbent EU member countries did not immediately open their labour markets to Central Eastern Europe, but all were obliged to do so by the early 2000s. Knowledge is the most mobile production factor, and driver of productivity, but their integration to the European Research Area was relatively slow. National systems of R&D accounted for the considerable inertia and low speed of transformation in the V4 countries.

The integration of the V4 countries is generally considered a success story in the history of the EU. The comparisons with Greece, Spain and Portugal demonstrate that the V4 countries started their convergence with the incumbent EU members from considerably lower levels of GDP per capita, but achieved higher growth rates. This reflects differences in their starting points, the nature of the external shocks faced, and institutional changes. The future growth of the V4 countries, however, faces risks, some of which are similar to those currently faced by the southern member countries.

First, is likely to pose a major challenge for their future development. They have the highest rates of population ageing in the EU (European Commission 2015b), as well as high rates of emigration by young people, and – until very recently – low levels of immigration. Second, demographic trends indicate that labour productivity growth, in general, and TFP (especially technology), in particular, should be a major source of economic growth in the V4 countries in the coming decades. Since the 1990s, labour productivity growth has benefited from diffusion of technology and organisational innovations by the MNCs. However, this source of growth may diminish as the MNCs relocate some of their production to even lower cost countries. This problem is exacerbated, because the V4 countries have been unable to build strong national innovation systems to support labour productivity growth from domestic resources, yet this is essential for the long-term economic growth, sustainable public finances, and for providing public social services for ageing populations.

Third, the period of the 1990s–2010s was typified by capital-intensive growth and technology transfers assisted by FDI in the V4 countries. They benefited from having an educated but affordable labour force until the mid-2010s. Rising labour costs, however, represent a likely future challenge, especially given the slow transition to knowledge-intensive growth. In this respect, the experience of Portugal may be salutary. Portugal was a favoured FDI destination in the 1980s and 1990s but, having failed to transit to knowledge intensive growth, rising labour costs made Portugal less attractive in the last decade. The V4 countries will have to concentrate more resources in high-tech industries, including making more efficient use of EU structural funds, if they are to make the transition to high value added production. Specifically, they will need to focus more on 'soft' infrastructure projects, such as supporting start-ups, life-long learning and on-the-job training. With wage levels rising, the V4 may also be better able to facilitate the return of their émigrés. There is a considerable potential for turning brain drain to brain gain.

Fourth, overspecialisation is another problem for some V4 countries. Slovakia, for example, hosted four major car-markers and became the largest per capita car producer in the world in 2015. High specialisation in a few export products was also typical for the Czech Republic. While small open economies need to pursue their comparative advantage and specialise, overspecialisation can be problematic in economic downturns, such as that in 2009, or when a few major foreign investors relocate their investments.

Fifth, the V4 countries also are overspecialised in terms of their markets, with the EU taking the vast majority of their exports. Initially, the choice of exchange rate regime was critical for mitigating the impacts of foreign trade on macroeconomic stability. The Czech Republic, Hungary and Poland opted for an external anchor of the fixed exchange rate regime in early 1990s (Szijártó 2014), while Slovakia introduced a mixed exchange rate regime—the crawling peg. However, most CEE countries found the fixed exchange rate regimes were unsustainable during the 1998 crisis, and transited to a managed float or free-float regime. Subsequently, in what became an important turning point in the economic transition, Slovakia adopted the euro, while the three other V4 countries became less enthusiastic about the Eurozone after the outbreak of the 2008 financial crisis. Empirical evidence from the Eurozone indicates the positive effect of common currencies on the intensity of bilateral international trade (Rose and Stanley 2005; Baldwin 2006). The reduction of foreign exchange rate fluctuations and of transaction costs are particularly important for a small country trading intensively with a big Eurozone member. Germany alone accounted for about one third in all V4 countries. Indeed, some studies (Cieślik et al. 2014) found evidence that Eurozone membership was positively related to the probability of exporting.

Finally, institution building is far from complete in the V4 countries. By the mid-2010s, the V4 countries had relatively low rankings in the world leagues tables of the quality of public institutions. The World Bank's Doing Business index and/or World Economic Forum data sets, for example, point to high levels of corruption, significant administrative burdens for businesses, inefficient and corrupt judicial systems, and high shares of the informal sector in the total economy. As these institutions continue to be reshaped in the coming years, transformation theory reminds us that they will constitute important internal sources of turning points in the experiences of the four countries.

Notes

1. EU-15 denotes the fifteen EU Member States that joined the Union before the eastern enlargement in 2004.
2. The Balassa index of revealed comparative advantage (RCA), or normalised market share is defined as (x_{ij}/x_{aj}) / (X_i/X_a) = where x_{ij} is exports of

product *j* from country *i*; x_{aj} is exports of product *j* from the reference area (EU27); X_i is total exports of country *i*; and X_a is total exports from the reference area (EU27). Index RCA higher than 1 indicates a comparative advantage and specialisation of a country in exports of particular good or service. All V4 countries accounted for the Balassa index values higher than 1 in exports of cars and parts, and consumer electronics in mid-2010s.

3. The Herfindahl–Hirschmann index (HHI_j) is a measure of the degree of market concentration. It has been normalised to obtain values ranging from 0 to 1 (maximum concentration), according to the following formula: $HHIj = \Sigma\ (x_{ij}\ /\ i_j)^2$; where x_{ij} = value of export for country *j* and product *i*. An index value that is close to 1 indicates a very concentrated market. On the contrary, values closer to 0, would demonstrate a homogeneous market between the exporters or importers. Source: UNCTAD (2015b).

Bibliography

Alfaro, L., Chanda, A., Kalemli-Ozcan, S., Sayek, S. (2004). FDI and economic growth: the role of local financial markets. *Journal of International Economics, 64*(1), 89–112.

Åslund, A. (2013). *How capitalism was built. The transformation of Central and Eastern Europe, Russia, the Caucasus, and the Central Asia.* Cambridge: Cambridge University Press.

Baláž, V., Williams, A. M., Kollár, D. (2004). Temporary versus permanent youth brain drain: economic implications. *International Migration, 42*(4), 3–34.

Baldwin R. E. (2006). *The euro's trade effect.* Working Paper No. 594. Frankfurt: European Central Bank.

Bogumil, P. (2014). Composition of capital inflows to Central and Eastern Europe (CEE) – is Poland different? *ECFIN Country Focus, 11*(8), 1–9.

Breisinger, C., Diao, X., Thurlow, J. (2009). Modeling growth options and structural change to reach middle income country status: The case of Ghana. *Economic Modelling, 26*(2009), 514–525.

Cieślik, A., Michałek, J., Michałek, A. (2014). Does the common currency increase exports? Evidence from firm-level data. *International Journal of Management and Economics, 4*, 8–22.

Commission of the European Communities. (1995). *Eastern and Central Europe 2000+.* Final Report. Studies 2. Brussels: European Community.

Dangerfield, M. V. (1995). The economic opening of Central and Eastern Europe: continuity and change in foreign economic relations. *Journal of European Integration, 19*(1), 5–42.

Égert, B., & Mihaljek, D. (2007). *Determinants of house prices in Central and Eastern Europe*, BIS Working Paper No. 286, Basel: Bank for International Settlements.

Éltető, A. (Ed.) (2014). Foreign trade trends in the EU10 countries. In *Mind the gap, integration experiences of the ten Central and Eastern European countries* (pp. 41–60). Budapest: Centre for Economic and Regional Studies of the Hungarian Academy of Sciences Institute of World Economics.

Estrin, S., & Uvalic, M. (2014). FDI into transition economies. Are the Balkans different? *Economics of Transition, 22*(2), 281–312.

European Commission. (2014). *Research and innovation performance in the EU in 2014. Innovation Union progress at country level.* European Commission, Directorate-General for Research and Innovation.

European Commission. (2015a). *Innovation Union scoreboard 2015.* Internal Market, Industry, Entrepreneurship and SMEs.

European Commission. (2015b). *The 2015 ageing report, economic and budgetary projections for the 28 EU Member states (2013–2060).* European Economy 3/2015.

European Commission, Economic and Financial Affairs. (2015). *AMECO database* [online database]. http://ec.europa.eu/economy_finance/ameco/user/serie/SelectSerie.cfm. Accessed September 2016.

Eurostat, the Statistical Office of the European Union. (2015a). *Average annual gross earnings by economic activity* [online database]. http://ec.europa.eu/eurostat/web/labour-market/earnings/database. Accessed September 2016.

Eurostat, the Statistical Office of the European Union. (2015b). *Balance of payment statistics* [online database]. http://ec.europa.eu/eurostat/web/balance-of-payments/data/database. Accessed September 2016.

Eurostat, the Statistical Office of the European Union. (2015c). *Financial account – direct investment* [online database]. http://ec.europa.eu/eurostat/web/balance-of-payments/data/database. Accessed September 2016.

Eurostat, the Statistical Office of the European Union. (2015d). *International migration* [online database]. http://ec.europa.eu/eurostat/web/population-demography-migration-projections/population-data/database. Accessed September 2016.

Eurostat, the Statistical Office of the European Union. (2015e). *Labour force survey* [online database]. http://ec.europa.eu/eurostat/web/lfs/data/database. Accessed September 2016.

Eurostat, the Statistical Office of the European Union. (2015f). *National accounts* [online database]. http://ec.europa.eu/eurostat/web/national-accounts/data/database. Accessed September 2016.

Eurostat, the Statistical Office of the European Union. (2015 g). *Population by educational attainment level* [online database]. http://ec.europa.eu/eurostat/web/population-demography-migration-projections/population-data/database. Accessed September 2016.

Frankel, J., & Rose, A. (1998). The endogeneity of the optimum currency area criteria. *Economic Journal, 108*(441), 1009–1025.

Gowan, P. (1995). Neo-liberal theory and practice for Eastern Europe. *New Left Review, 213*, 3–60.

Gurgul, H., & Lach, Ł. (2013). Export diversification and economic growth in transition: lessons from the 2008 financial crisis in CEE. *Quantitative Methods in Economics, 14*(1), 137–149.

Holland, D., Fic, T., Rincon-Aznar, A., Stokes, L., Paluchowski, P. (2011). *Labour mobility within the EU – the impact of enlargement and the functioning of the transitional arrangements.* United Kingdom: National Institute of Economic and Social Research.

Iossifov, P. (2014). *Cross-border production chains and business cycle co-movement between Central and Eastern European countries and euro area member states.* Working Paper No. 1628. Frankfurt: European Central Bank.

Kahanec, M. (2012). *Labor mobility in an enlarged European Union.* Discussion Paper No. 6485. Bonn: Institute for the Study of Labor (IZA).

Kutan, A., & Vukšić, G. (2007). Foreign direct investment and export performance: empirical evidence. *Comparative Economic Studies, 49* (3), 430–445.

Lensink, R., & White, R. (1998). Does the revival of international private capital flows mean the end of aid? An analysis of developing countries access to private capital. *World Development, 26*(7), 1201–1219.

Makki, S. S., & Agapi, S. (2004). Impact of foreign direct investment and trade on economic growth: evidence from developing countries. *American Journal of Agricultural Economics, 86*(3), 795–801.

Martin, R. (2010). Roepke lecture in economic geography-rethinking regional path dependence: beyond lock-in to evolution. *Economic Geography, 85*(1), 1–27.

Martin, R. L., & Sunley, P. J. (2006). Path dependence and regional economic evolution. *Journal of Economic Geography, 6*, 395–438.

Medve-Bálint, G. (2014). The role of the EU in shaping FDI flows to East Central Europe. *Journal of Common Market Studies, 52*(1), 35–51.

OECD, the Organisation for Economic Co-operation and Development. (2015). *Trade in Value Added (TIVA)* [online database]. http://stats.oecd.org/BrandedView.aspx?oecd_bv_id=tiva-data-en%26doi=data-00648-en. Accessed September 2016.

Płoszaj, A., & Olechnicka, A. (2015). *Running faster or measuring better? How is the R&D sector in Central and Eastern Europe catching up with Western Europe?* Working Paper No. 3.06. Growth–innovation – competitiveness: fostering cohesion in Central and Eastern Europe (GRINCOH). Warsaw: Centre for European Regional and Local Studies (EUROREG), University of Warsaw.

Rose, A. K., & Stanley, T. D. (2005). A meta-analysis of the effect of common currencies on international trade. *Journal of Economic Surveys, 19* (3), 347–365.

Sheehy, J. (1994). Foreign direct investment in the CEECs. In: *European economy the economic interpenetration between the European Union and Eastern Europe* (vol. 6, pp. 129–148). European Commission.

Sixta, J., Vltavská, K., Fischer, J. (2013). The development of gross domestic product in the Czech Republic and Slovakia between 1970 and 1989. *Ekonomický časopis, 61*(6), 549–562.

Śmiech, S., & Zysk, W. (2014). The influence of foreign direct investment on foreign trade in the Visegrád countries from 2001 to 2011. *Entrepreneurial Business and Economics Review, 2*(3), 7–18.

Smith, A., & Swain, A. (2010). The global economic crisis, Eastern Europe and the Former Soviet Union: models of development and the contradictions of internationalization. *Eurasian Geography and Economics, 51*(1), 1–34.

Szijártó, N. (2014). Monetary and financial integration in EU10 countries. In: A. Éltető (Ed.), *Mind the gap, integration experiences of the ten Central and Eastern European countries* (pp. 83–105). Budapest: Centre for Economic and Regional Studies of the Hungarian Academy of Sciences Institute of World Economics.

Túry, G. (2014). Automotive industry in the EU10 economies: Developments in the past decade. In A. Éltető (Ed.), *Mind the gap, integration experiences of the ten Central and Eastern European countries* (pp. 41–60). Budapest: Centre for Economic and Regional Studies of the Hungarian Academy of Sciences Institute of World Economics.

United Nations. (1995). Geographical structure of east European trade. *Economic Bulletin for Europe, 47*(5), 109–123.

UNCTAD, United Nations Conference on Trade and Development. (2015a). *World investment report 2015: annex tables* [online database]. http://unctad.org/en/Pages/DIAE/World%20Investment%20Report/Annex-Tables.aspx. Accessed September 2016.

UNCTAD, United Nations Conference on Trade and Development. (2015b). *International trade in goods and services* [online database]. http://unctadstat.unctad.org/wds/ReportFolders/reportFolders.aspx?IF_ActivePath=P,15912. Accessed September 2016.

Williams, A. M., Baláž, V., Zajac, S. (1998). The EU and Central Europe: the reinternationalisation of economic relationships. *Tijdschrift voor Economische en Sociale Geografie, 89*(2), 131–149.

Williams, A. M., & Baláž, V. (2001). Capital mobility in transition countries of Central Europe: macroeconomic performance factors and structural policies. *Ekonomický časopis, 49*(2), 242–271.

World Bank. (2015). *World development indicators* [online database]. http://databank.worldbank.org/data/reports.aspx?source=world-development-indicators. Accessed September 2016.

Zon, H. van (1996). *The future of industry in Central and Eastern Europe.* Aldershot: Averbury Press.

Vladimír Baláž is Research Professor at the Institute for Forecasting of the Slovak Academy of Sciences and a member of the Learned Society of the Slovak Academy of Sciences. The Institute acts both as a research body and government think-thank for design of economic and social policies. Vladimír has three major areas of research interest (1) Innovation and R&D policies, (2) Migration and Regional Development, and (3) Behavioural Economics and Finance.

Katarína Karasová studied quantitative economics with the University of Economics in Bratislava. She currently is a young researcher at the Institute for Forecasting of the Slovak Academy of Sciences. Katarína's research interests include (1) Migration in Europe; (2) Active labour market policies, and (3) Quantitative methods in socio-economic research.

Allan M. Williams is Professor of Tourism and Mobility Studies at the University of Surrey, UK, His research focuses on the relationships between mobility and economic development in Europe. He is the author of 26 books including, most recently, *Migration Risk and Uncertainty* (with Vlado Balaz, Routledge, 2015). He was a founding editor of the journal *European Urban and Regional Studies* (Sage, 1994-) and a fellow of the UK Academy of Social Science.

Chapter 6: Constitutional Identity? The Hungarian Model of Illiberal Democracy

András L. Pap

By connecting to ongoing scholarly discussions on conceptualizing "illiberal democracy" and analyzing the phenomenon of anti-democratic backlash in post-2010 Hungary, this chapter seeks to provide a description and an analysis of the "Hungarian model of illiberal democracy." Throughout this text, "illiberal" is understood as a privative prefix, referring to a constitutional and political condition that creates a unique middle ground between a constitutional democracy and an autocracy. It is argued that the "Hungarian illiberal democracy" is neither a construct of constitutional philosophy, nor a principle for constitutional design, nor is it characteristically illiberal within the interpretative framework of political theory. Rather, it is a tool to channel, define, and dominate general political discourse and to provide a discursive framework for political identification and ideologically biased, yet divergent and ad hoc legislation. It is argued that "illiberalism" is actually a form of constitutional identity, the discursive framework of this new political community that

A.L. Pap (✉)
Department for the Study of Constitutionalism and the Rule of Law, Hungarian Academy of Sciences Centre for Social Sciences at the Institute for Legal Studies, Budapest, Hungary

Slovak Academy of Sciences Institute for Sociology, Bratislava, Slovakia
e-mail: pap.andras.laszlo@tk.mta.hu

Fish, Gill, Petrovic (eds.), *A Quarter Century of Post-Communism Assessed*, DOI 10.1007/978-3-319-43437-7_7

the Orbán-regime claims to have established. The morphosis of this Hungarian model for illiberal democracy manifests itself normatively through value preferences expressed in the new constitution, as well as in a quasi-normative political declaration that serves as a manifesto for the new political community it envisages.

Terminology and Conceptualization

In his seminal essay in which he argues that liberalism, either as a conception of political liberty or as a doctrine about economic policy, does not necessarily coincide with democracy, Fareed Zakaria (1997) defines "liberal democracy" as a political system marked not only by free and fair elections, but also by rule of law, separation of powers, and the protections of basic liberties of speech, assembly, religion, and property. Scholarly discussion on definitions has burgeoned in the past years. As Rupnik and Zielonka (2013) and Collier and Levitsky (1997) argue, authors often qualify the term "democracy" by adding adjectives such as liberal (or illiberal), deliberative, representative, participatory, delegative, façade, direct (or indirect), electoral, hybrid, Western, Islamic, managed (Anderson 2007), etc. Others refer to electoral or competitive autocracies (Shevtsova 2000; Levitsky and Way 2010). Following Mill (1993) and Huntington (1991) in their recent analysis, which serves as a starting point for this assessment, Csillag and Szelényi (2015) define liberalism and democracy as two distinct dimensions of good governance, identifying "liberalism" with separation of powers and the security of private property rights, and "democracy" as majoritarian rule. They do not explicitly define illiberal democracy, but describe the features of the "emergent illiberal post-communist systems" in political terms, and claim that as long as democratic institutions operate and leaders are elected to office, the ruling elites of these "illiberal democracies need a legitimating ideology which can appeal to a broader electorate." In their genealogy of what they call "post-communist managed illiberal democracy," where property relations shift from private property and market capitalism to neo-patrimonial and eventually neo-prebendal property relations, they argue that the core distinguishing feature is this ideology, which they call post-communist traditionalist or neoconservative (pp. 21–22).

To avoid further entanglement in a conceptual and terminological labyrinth, throughout this text "illiberal" should be understood as a privative prefix, referring to a constitutional and political condition that creates a unique middle ground between a constitutional democracy and an autocracy. This reading is not unique in the literature. Csillag and Szelényi claim that the road from democracy to autocracy is paved with the "stones" of illiberalism, and while "illiberalism does not necessarily eliminate democracy, it creates conditions (given the weakness of Constitutional Courts and the legislative branch) for particularly powerful political leaders to flirt with abandoning democratic procedures if they may sense their electoral support eroded and they may not win the next elections" (p. 27). Bozóki (2011) argues that the "system of national cooperation," introduced by Prime Minister Viktor Orbán, which I will analyze in detail later in this chapter in order to make the claim that it is one of the manifestations of the "Hungarian illiberal democracy," has emerged as an alternative to liberal democracy (p. 650). In developing this interpretation, it will be argued that illiberalism in Hungary is a form of constitutional identity, a political discourse that creates the rhetorical and political framework for the newly constructed political community.

Illiberal Developments, Anti-Democratic Backlash

In his earlier writings (Pap 2014, 2015c), this author has demonstrated how the new constitution, titled the Fundamental Law of Hungary (passed in April 2011), has, along with adjacent legislation, set forth several normatively formulated value preferences that can be defined as illiberal in the sense that they either suggest the denial or at least the disregard of individual autonomy and liberty or project a paternalistic conception of society. It has been argued at length that the constitution is not based on individual autonomy or individual liberty, and that the idea of a person is unequivocally and openly based on a paternalistic conception of society and particular values. The new constitution's indications of personhood and of the ideal typical, thus preferred members of the political community were formed to reflect an image of ethnically Hungarian individuals who belong to the middle class, who are employed and active in the labor market, are practicing Christians, or at least belong to a denomination that is recognized by the state, are married heterosexuals living with their spouses, and who are sexually monogamous and naturally fertile. At most, the recognition of individual dignity is conditional on belonging to a community based on the features described earlier, while the dignity of communities – including that of the ethnic majority community – is protected (in ways unknown in liberal democracies) by civil and criminal law, and even against various minorities (be it ethnic, ideological or lifestyle minorities) if need be.

Analysts (Blokker 2013; Tóth 2012; Chronowski 2012; Majtényi 2012), domestic and international human rights monitors, democracy-watchdogs, and other stakeholder organizations have widely documented the FIDESZ-government's process of restructuring the constitutional landscape in Hungary. Based on the so-called Tavares-report prepared by the European Parliament in 2013, which pointed to a clear weakening of the systems of checks and balances required by the rule of law and the democratic principle of the separation of powers, several shortcomings can be identified. The new constitution was adopted on the basis of a bill submitted from an only 35 daylong debate and exclusively by the votes of members of the governing coalition. The Budget Council, a non-parliamentary body with limited democratic legitimacy, has been granted the power to veto the adoption of the state budget, which allows for the president to dissolve the parliament. The new constitution identifies 26 subject matters that need to have cardinal laws, which require a two-thirds majority. Many of these issues, such as specific aspects of family law and the tax and pension systems, habitually fall under the ordinary decision-making powers of a legislature. In the 18 months following the adoption of the new constitution, parliament enacted 49 cardinal laws without adequate consultation with opposition parties and civil society. A 2012 Act on the National Assembly vested the speaker of the Parliament with extensive discretionary powers to limit MPs' free expression, including severe fines applied even for displaying the EU-flag. Severe measures to weaken the competences of the Constitutional Court (a highly esteemed powerful guardian of the post-transition constitutionalism) have been introduced, such as the elimination of *actio popularis* procedures for *ex post* review, powers to review all budget-related legislation, and a repealing all of Court decisions made before 1 January 2012 (when the new Constitution entered into force) so that precedents of the Court are not allowed to be invoked in new cases based on the new Constitution. Additionally, the number of justices has been raised from 11 to 15, and the requirement to try to reach a consensus within parliament regarding their election was eliminated. By now, most of the judges are government loyalists, several having been appointed directly from their positions as members of parliament. In an attempt to weaken the independence of the judiciary, the 6-year-long mandate of the former president of the Supreme Court was prematurely ended after 2 years and the mandatory retirement age for judges was reduced from 70 to 62 years of age, a move that practically removed all of the courts' presidents.

A new, powerful administrative organ for the judiciary titled the National Judicial Office was created with powers to transfer cases from one court to another. The body is presided by the wife of one of the constitution's drafters – who is also a Fidesz member of the European Parliament and a longtime friend of the Prime Minister. A new Act on Churches was passed, making recognition conditional on the prior approval by a two-thirds majority in parliament. Subsequently, 300 registered churches lost their legal status. A restrictive media law was passed, creating a new Media and Telecommunication Authority with overbroad regulatory and sanctioning powers and enabling political influence on public service media. Electoral reforms introduced a remarkable form of gerrymandering that disproportionately favor the governing parties, and the government took political control over the Election Commission.

Most legislation was introduced to parliament as individual members' bills. These introductions avoided any detailed debate, consultation, impact assessment, and traditional venues for negotiation with the civil sector. Laws have often been amended substantially after the parliamentary debate through the use of a special measure aimed at eliminating technical and incoherent provisions. And several pieces of legislation were specifically tailored to accommodate particular acts of favoritism, such as lowering age requirements for ambassadors to enable the appointment of a government loyalist, or changing incompatibility regulations to enable former military service members to run for elected office. Nominally independent institutions have been staffed by government loyalists elected by a two-thirds majority. In many cases, these positions involve 9-year terms with options for tenure and automatically prolonged mandates if successors are not elected. According to Freedom House (2015), by 2014 all major independent institutions were headed by partisan or personal loyalists. A single Office of the Commissioner for Fundamental Rights was created that replaced four formerly independent ombuds institutions. The portfolio of the former Ombudsperson for Data Protection and Freedom of Information was transformed into a quasi-governmental office. Universities were brought under governmental control (Bugarič 2014), and the previously ideologically neutral local government schools were taken over by churches in high numbers, with many settlements only offering faith-based schools. Homelessness and extreme poverty were criminalized. Government rhetoric became hostile toward non-governmental organizations and targeted tax raids have been staged (Amnesty International 2016). The Fundamental Law also sets out that the right to freedom of speech may not be exercised with the aim of violating the dignity of the Hungarian nation or of any national, ethnic, racial, or religious community. Civic and criminal sanctions may ensue speech that is offending, shocking, or disturbing to others, especially to public officials or public figures (Amnesty International 2016). In 2013, the Law on Freedom of Information was amended to allow restricting full access to data concerning governmental institutions.

The right to property has also suffered serious setbacks due to private pension funds being terminated in 2010, and almost all assets (worth 10 billion EUR) were transferred to the state-run pension system. Also, a special 98% tax on certain revenues was introduced retroactively as of 1 January 2010, thus creating a tax obligation for the period preceding the law's promulgation, which also was in breach of the ban on retroactive legislation.[1] Reforms have been extremely swift: in its first 20 months in office, the government pushed through 365 laws, including 12 amendments to the old constitution that together changed more than 50 individual constitutional provisions (Halmai and Scheppele 2012, p. 7). The Fundamental Law, entering into force on 1 January 2012, has already been amended 5 times in 3 years, changing one-fourth of its text (Helsinki Committee 2014).

Illiberalism and the Emergence of a New Political Community: The National System of Cooperation

Unsurprisingly, no normative legal document, formal political manifesto or official government communication ever provided a coherent description of the nature, design, or constitutional philosophy of the Hungarian illiberal democracy model. It is therefore the task and challenge of academic analyses to decipher its normative and analytic content. Thus, this chapter sets forth a thought experiment to fill these gaps and provide a conceptual framework for the Hungarian illiberal democracy. A widely cited and debated speech by the new regime's founding farther, Prime Minister Viktor Orbán, delivered at the Summer Open University of Bálványos in July 2014, will serve as a starting point for this endeavor. Here Orbán identified his regime as illiberal in the following manner:

> ... while breaking with the dogmas and ideologies that have been adopted by the West and keeping ourselves independent from them, we are trying to find the form of community organisation, the new Hungarian state, which is capable of making our community competitive in the great global race for decades to come.... a democracy does not necessarily have to be liberal. Just because a state is not liberal, it can still be a democracy.... until now we have known three forms of state organisation: the nation state, the liberal state and the welfare state. And the question is, what's next? The Hungarian answer to this question is that the era of the work-based state is approaching. We want to organise a work-based society that, undertakes the odium of stating that it is not liberal in character.... we must break with liberal principles and methods of social organisation, and in general with the liberal understanding of society.... ... and forge a new method of Hungarian state organisation..., following (in the sense of bypassing..., ALP) the liberal state and the era of liberal democracy... are attempting to construct Hungarian state life around this idea, that (liberalism) should not be the principle on which society is built.... the Hungarian nation is not simply a group of individuals but a community that must be organised, reinforced and in fact constructed. And... the new state that we are constructing in Hungary is an illiberal state, a non-liberal state.... we want to organise our national state to replace the liberal state, construct a new state built on illiberal and national foundations within the European Union.... the Government has come to a decision according to which within this new state concept, this illiberal state concept, the reorganisation of the Hungarian state is underway, in contrast to the liberal state organisation logic of the previous twenty years.

It has been argued above that the new constitution, the Fundamental Law sets forth several value preferences, but it does not actually take up the task of declaring a new political community. But Orbán claims no less than having created such a political community. This is reflected for example in his change of the official name of the state from "Magyar Köztársaság" to "Magyarország." The former, commonly referred to in English as the "Republic of Hungary," in Hungarian was actually "Hungarian," a grammatical syntax with the noun "republic" ("repiblic") specified with the adjective "Hungarian" ("magyar"). Magyarország, ("Magyarstan") means "Hungarian Country," grammatically a morpheme, a complex word derived by the agglutination of the words "Hungarian" ("magyar" – can be either a noun or an adjective) and "Country" ("ország") (Takács 2015).

The new political community is declared in a formally nonbinding, unique pre-constitutional document, Political Declaration 1 of 2010 (16 June) of the Hungarian Parliament on national cooperation. This document foresees and legitimizes a total break with the preexisting political community and declares the emergence of a new political community, the named National System of Cooperation (NSC), which originates retroactively from a "voting booth revolution," a term used by Orbán to describe the election that created the parliamentary supermajority of the governing coalition (FIDESZ and the Hungarian Christian Democratic Party, the two parties that ran jointly).[2] The political credo of the new regime and the new political community reads as follows:

> At the end of the first decade of the 21st century, after forty-six years of occupation and dictatorship and two turbulent decades of transition Hungary has regained the right and ability of self-determination … In the spring of 2010 the Hungarian nation once again summoned its vitality and brought about another revolution in the voting booths. … The National Assembly declares that a new social contract was laid down in the April general elections through which the Hungarians decided to create a new system: the National Cooperation System. … We, members of the National Assembly declare that we shall elevate the new political and economic system emerging on the basis of the popular democratic will … that connect the members of our diverse Hungarian society. Work, home, family, health and order – these will be the pillars of our common future …. The National Cooperation System is … an opportunity for, as well as a requirement of, everybody who lives, works or has an undertaking in Hungary. We firmly believe that we will be able to change Hungary's future through the solidarity represented by the National Cooperation System and build a strong and successful country. This solidarity that releases tremendous energies and gives great hope to every Hungarian … and … after decades gives a chance to the Hungarians to fulfil their own goals at last.[3]

Arguably, Hungarian illiberal democracy manifests itself in the NSC—a vaguely defined, yet even normatively presented political construct in which majority rule may operate unbounded by the rule of law, separation of powers, and other constraints of liberal democracies. The NSC, which was never actually defined or explained in a normative document or even a political manifesto, is arguably both the conceptualization and a metaphor of the political community. And although it is not a formalized set of political institutions, it is the conceptualization of the illiberal democratic decision-making process, which makes traditional constitutionalism obsolete.

Illiberal Democracy as Constitutional Identity

It is beyond the scope of this chapter to discuss anti-democratic political and legal developments in more detail than the previous subchapter. Suffice it to conclude that most of the criticism pertained not so much to restrictions on individual freedoms and liberties, but rather to the systematic weakening of institutional rule of law guarantees advanced by the meta-institutional practice of cementing government loyalists in most independent constitutional offices. However, as far as strictly normative, grand scale institutional engineering goes, there is no official, authentic (constitutionally declared), sui generis Hungarian illiberal design at play here. In fact, the Orbán regime's constitutional framework does not go directly against the principles of liberal democracies. This constitutional order is built up from elements that are mostly not in clear breach of international human rights standards, nor are individual elements unprecedented in well-functioning constitutional democracies. However, the grand picture emerging from the sum of these individual pieces of the mosaic is one of a constitutional design in which institutional checks and balances are dismantled, the protection of human rights is severely weakened, and political freedom is curtailed (Scheppele 2013).

Also, although the populist rhetoric (of the NSC) aims at targeting and attracting both moderate and far-right voters, the NSC is not inherently and intrinsically racist, misogynist, anti-Semitic, or homophobic. It does, however, neglect and deny the discursive recognition, questions the importance, relevance, and legitimacy of liberal values and fails to adopt an individual freedom and human rights oriented approach that would, for example endorse Roma inclusion, feminism and multiculturalism, post-nationalism, individualism, or a particular vision of modernism – ideals and commitments Hungarian liberal public intellectuals would advocate.[4] In other words, the discourse is not inherently anti-liberal, only a-liberal.

Again, let us torn to the seminal Orbán-speech cited above:

> the Hungarian nation is not simply a group of individuals but a community that must be organised, reinforced and in fact constructed. And... the new state that we are constructing in Hungary is an illiberal state, a non-liberal state. It does not reject the fundamental principles of liberalism such as freedom, and I could list a few more, but it does not make this ideology the central element of state organisation, but instead includes a different, special, national approach.

As Orbán pointed out in his above cited 2014 Bálványos-speech regarding illiberalism and the NSC, "This cannot be entered into law, we are talking about an intellectual starting point now." Thus, it is argued in this chapter that illiberalism in Hungary goes beyond political and legal action. It is a form of ideology and a discursive construct. Even though "unorthodox" legal and political institutions are instrumental for the establishment, solidification and cementing of the Orbán-regime, they are only byproducts. The real product is the (conceptual framework of the) newly established political community. Illiberal democracy and the NSC serve as tools for constitutional identity and an ideological framework for institutionalizing the well-documented process of anti-democratic backlash in Hungary.

This chapter argues that it would be a mistake to identify the Hungarian illiberal democracy model with these constitutional and legal developments. Instead, an alternative, non-institution focused analysis is offered. "Hungarian illiberal democracy" is neither a construct of constitutional philosophy nor is it a principle for constitutional design. It cannot be properly described by the evisceration of classic democratic institutions, and it is also not characteristically illiberal within the interpretative framework of political theory. It would equally not qualify as a *sui generis* un-republican (Niederberger and Schink 2013; Pettit 2013), un-participatory (Garcia 2015), un-agonistic (Wenman 2013), or un-deliberative model (Mansbridge and Parkinson 2012). Despite the political mantra used by Orbán's party of the legitimating force of a parliamentary supermajority being based on a single event of popular vote, the Hungarian model of illiberal democracy cannot be equated with the unfettered freedom of a parliamentary majority to do as it pleases. Rather, it is a tool to channel, define and dominate general political discourse and to provide a discursive framework for political identification and ideologically biased yet divergent and *ad hoc* legislation.

This chapter argues that "illiberal democracy" and "illiberalism" in Hungary are actually forms of constitutional identity guiding the discursive framework of this new political community. Illiberalism is thus the culmination of government discourse along with the discursive framework of the new political community, which in turn reframes politics in terms of nationhood. It is the form and means to construe and express the new and novel (constitutional) identity, which emphasizes cultural particularism and values such as fidelity, faith, and charity as opposed to universal values of equality, human rights, and social inclusion. This creates official historical narratives, but disregards individual autonomy and projects a paternalistic conception of society in which value preferences are not centered around liberty and autonomy. Orbán's illiberal democracy instrumentalizes a special form of nationalism that is built on the uniqueness of the Hungarian "people," where illiberalism is a form of ethno symbolism.[5] Here, the myth of election of the new political community via the NSC is constituted through independence from modernist universalist values, which only brought failure and frustration. This framework for constitutional identity politics centers around the rejection of the liberal political ideology that places individual freedom front and center.

As shown, the morphosis of this Hungarian model for illiberal democracy manifests itself normatively through value preferences expressed in the new constitution, the Fundamental Law, as well as in a quasi-normative political declaration that serves as a manifesto for not only Orbán's new political regime, but also the new political community he and his regime envisages. It is important to highlight that, contrary to what it claims to be, the NSC is not an actual institutionalized modus operandi for the Hungarian illiberal democracy, nor is it a form of political institutional design. It is rather the manifesto of illiberal democracy: the political and quasi-normative declaration of the Orbán-regime's discursive framework.

In sum, the quintessential feature of the Hungarian illiberal democracy is that it is the discursive framework through which the Orbán-government constructed a new national and constitutional identity. It is a form of a constitutional commoditization aimed at selling a political regime, where a significant emphasis is put on authenticity and difference. Thus, illiberalism is not so much a constitutional term describing and legitimizing an overall backlash in democratic control mechanisms and the protection of human rights as it is a discursive framework constructed to describe and mark[6] the new imagined community of the NSC-Hungarian nation and to narrate its shared common belonging.[7] To paraphrase Thierry Balzacq's securitization theory, one may argue that the Hungarian illiberalization process is a perlocutionary constitutional speech act,[8] in which the consequential effects or sequels are aimed to evoke the feelings, beliefs, thought, or actions of the target audience.[9] "Illiberalism" is a mobilizing tactic utilized to question the validity and sustainability of post the WWII (liberal) consensus on human rights centered political language, disenchantment, certain sacred democratic institutions, and neoliberal policies. The term (which is not a coherent concept) can be operationalized by neoconservative movements as an anti-modernist and fundamentalist[10] answer to the neoliberal consensus, similarly, for example, to the ways in which "(anti) gender ideology" is used. As Kováts et al. argue, "gender" has been identified as the common ground, a label amidst diverse political cultures, different party structures and a variety of mobilizing tactics, compressing different fears and values and used against diverse causes (Kováts and Põim 2015; Kováts et al. 2015). Orbán's illiberalism is also very similar to how Hobsbawm (1992) sees nationalism in the twenty-first century – as a substitute, a placebo for disorientation, and a surrogate for integration in a disintegrating society; when society fails, the nation appears as an ultimate guarantee (and in post-communist societies, also as a device to distinguish between the innocent and the guilty). In the Hungarian case, the strategy worked. As Pető and Vasali (2014) point out, the government successfully built a state-funded (pseudo) NGO sector and this, alongside racist and nationalist movements (Feischmidt and Hervik 2015; Wodak et al. 2013; Vidra and Fox 2014), convincingly offered anti-modernism (Kovács et al. 2011), and anti-cosmopolitanism/Europeanism (Melegh 2006) as a viable alternative to neo-liberal democracy and the market economy (Pető and Vasali 2014).

Causes and Explanations

Having provided a possible exegesis of the theoretical construction of the Hungarian model of illiberal democracy, one cannot escape the question: how has one of the leading post-communist democracies transformed into a semi-consolidated Frankenstate? Some of the most appealing explanations will be discussed in the following part of the chapter. In order to understand the evolution and success of Orbán's constitutional capture, two features of post-transition Hungarian political life [will be particularly] highlighted: the domination of political parties in public affairs, and the prevalence of Orbán's long held political strategy to demonize and delegitimize political opponents an polarize politics to its extremes.

Values and Political Culture

Value surveys portray Hungarians as passive, uninterested in politics, isolated, and distrustful, with an especially low trust in democracy, market economy, and transparent, merit-based structures. In 2012, only 40% of Hungarian youth (mostly college and university students) accepted democracy as a legitimate system of government, and roughly one third did not see a difference between dictatorship and democracy (Szabó 2013). According to another survey, only about 20% of respondents were interested in politics (Szabó 2013, p. 22). While in 1991 74% of Hungarians approved of the change from a one-party system to a multiparty system, by 2009 only 56% favored the change, and 77% were dissatisfied with the way democracy was working in Hungary, which was the highest percentage of dissatisfied respondents in the region. While 89% held that politicians have benefited a great deal from the changes since 1989, only 17% believed ordinary people have done so. Seventy-six percent said that corrupt political leaders are a very big problem (Wike 2010). Only 38% believed that voting is a mechanism for affecting politics, and 91% thought the country is on the wrong track (Pew Global 2009).

Hungary is a closed society that is frustrated with the European Union and the development of capitalism, but that also has a high tolerance for corruption and an attraction to charismatic leaders. Regarding values, Hungary is in the vicinity of Orthodox cultures and far from its neighboring countries with similar level of economic development; Hungary is closer to Bulgaria and Moldova than to Slovenia (Keller 2010; Szabó 2013, p. 10; Wike 2010). In a comparative analysis, Hungary was found to be the very last of all European countries, including the former socialist states, in its levels of trust in institutions. Hungarians were found to have especially low levels of trust toward politicians, bankers, and journalists (Hungarian Spectrum 2009). Hungarians also live in social isolation: 81% reported difficulty in finding friends, and according to 85%, relationships often become increasingly unstable. Fifty-eight per cent found little interest in politics, and 41% reported no interest in solving social problems (Til 2015, p. 371).

It is apparent then that the NSC resonates with the expectations of a disillusioned, frustrated, inward-looking, closed Hungarian society that has lost its comparative advantage enjoyed during the time of relative freedom and economic prosperity created by the "Goulash communism" of the pre-transition 1980s. The term "Goulash communism" evokes images of a community-style dish cooked in the open air to symbolize a communist regime with a relatively pleasant overall atmosphere. This term characterizes the mixing of certain elements of the free market with a planned economy that allowed Hungary to have had slightly higher living standards than its Iron Curtain neighbors (Wike 2009) and to be among the rare countries in the Eastern block that did not have a shortage of food (Wike 2010). Paradoxically, Hungarian society retains a sense of superiority, especially toward its neighbors with a significant ethnic Hungarian diaspora traditionally looked down upon by the dominant "Magyars." Still, Hungarians have severely lacked feelings of success in the two decades since the political transition.

It also needs to be added that the conservative political ideology still centers around 1920, when in the post-WWI treaty Hungary lost two-thirds of its territory and the corresponding population. Ever since, the aspiration to reunite the old glory and territorial integrity, or at least a responsibility for ethnic kins in the neighboring countries has been a cornerstone of conservative domestic politics, and after the political transition in 1989, a constitutional responsibility and a foreign policy priority as well. The 1920 Treaty of Trianon also serves a symbol of Hungary's and Hungarians' victimization and mistreatment by the international community. The narratives of victimhood allow for the culture of frustration and refusing responsibility for one's own fate and allowing others to be blamed for failures and the lack of success.

Another important feature of Hungarian political culture is what András Bozóki (2015) describes as "partocracy," or a case in which political parties assume civic duties and dominate public life. Such practices may be for example establishing public benefit foundations, professional groups, club-like community forums called "civic circles" (polgári kör), delegating curators to committees, employing their own journalists and political and market analysts, and self-administering most of the media outlets and think tanks. Similarly to other post-communist states, Hungarian civil society is usually characterized as weak and resource dependent. Additionally, the number of non-government organizations controlled by the government, but being masqueraded as independent NGOs is remarkable (Kövér 2015a). According to Jarábik (2015), although loyalty to political sides and parties is not a Hungarian specialty, nowhere else was the emerging civil society and the media captured by the political parties to such a degree as in Hungary.

Orbán and His Strategy: The Rhetoric and Politics of the "Dark Side"

A contradictory feature of Hungarian politics lies in the fact that despite a significant proportion of the population being in a state of political apathy and disinterest in public affairs, society is nonetheless highly politicized. Polarizing strategies aimed at demonizing and delegitimizing political opponents, initiated and utilized mostly by the right and foremost by Orbán and his party, have set the tone in political debates for over a decade. As Krasztev (2015) shows, private political preferences were transformed to identity issues, widely represented by a variety of commonly displayed symbols of self-definition against those with different political views. As a consequence, families, friendly circles and communities at work were split because of this sophisticated power trick (see also Rupnik 2012).

Thus, a defining feature of the NSC is, as political analyst and former FIDESZ MP Péter Tölgyessy argues, not to form and change society and culture (as Adenauer or Thatcher did), but rather to preserve the dark side of Hungarians' values and orientation such as populism and pessimism, and to blame conspiracy theories and hostile foreign interests for all of the nation's problems. (Lambert 2015; Jarábik 2015, p. 319). Hegedűs (2014) demonstrates the irreconcilable polarization of Hungarian political life and culture through the example of Orbán's strategy for maintaining influence after losing the 2002 election. After this loss, Orbán initiated a political discourse centered on the phrase "the nation cannot be in opposition," and in doing so he relativized the outcome of the democratic elections. His expropriation of the phenomenon of the "nation" established a political environment that excluded any further compromise or cooperation with the governing socialists and liberals, even in important strategic issues. This contributed to the development of Orbán's personal and political charisma but it also created a political cold war, and after 2008 a permanent crisis of governance (p. 4). According to Rupnik (2012), Orbán actively deepened political and cultural divides and transformed transitology to traumatology by not only breaking with the communist past, but also reconnecting with pre-communism by reopening old divides between "urbanists and populists." He positions Western liberal democracy as counter to the rural lifestyle, which he poses as the source of true national values and authentic democracy.

The Rhetoric of Finishing the Political Transition Suspended in 1990

Although it was never part of the 2010 electoral campaign, the cornerstone of the rhetoric of the NSC is that the new constitution finally finishes the political transition and completes the de-communization process that was suspended in 1990 (Sarlo and Otarashvili 2013). In Jenne and Mudde's (2012) words, Fidesz have argued that their proposed transformations represent the realization of the promises of 1989, which went unfulfilled by the communists and dissidents who signed the pacted transitions (p. 8).

Hungary certainly followed a unique path in post-communist transitions: unlike in other states, the first wave of democratization of the "pacted" or "post-sovereign" constitution making, the adoption of an interim constitution, which was designed as the first of a two-step process, was never followed by the adoption of a final constitution sometime after the first democratic elections (Halmai 2013, p. 75). The constitution, to be replaced by the 2011 Fundamental Law, consisted of a vast amendment (involving over 100 provisions) of the communist constitution, originally adopted in 1949 and passed by the communist legislature in 1989 following peaceful negotiations between the representatives of the authoritarian regime and their democratic opposition, in particular by its umbrella organization, the Opposition Round Table (pp. 69–70). The amendment, alongside a correction passed instantly by the first democratically elected parliament in 1990, promulgated on the 33rd anniversary of the 1956 revolution and just 2 weeks before the fall of the Berlin Wall, practically created a new constitution with essentially only one provision remaining from the original Stalinist document: the provision that declared Budapest as the state capitol. The old–new document met most of the criteria liberal constitutional democracies require: a representative government, a parliamentary system, an elaborate system of checks and balances, an independent judiciary, ombuds institutions to guard fundamental rights, and probably the world's most powerful Constitutional Court (Kovács and Tóth 2011, p. 184).

Thus, the unique feature of the Hungarian velvet revolution lies in the fact that the amended constitution was suitable for liberal democracy and a capitalist market academy and that there was no political and legal-technical (or constitutional) pressure to write a new constitution, and the constitutional moment passed. As János Kis (2011) points out, however, this symbolic defect had a price to pay. He claims that the very weakness of the substantially workable constitution lies in the fact that while it was democratic in nature, the 1989 amendment lacked democratic confirmation, and the unfulfilled (and substantially moot) reference in the preamble of the 1989 amendment that stated that a new constitution will be adopted after the first free elections created the impression that the new Hungarian post-communist society is still unfit for constituting a political community (p. 8). The old–new constitution, thus, could not serve as the symbolic glue for the Hungarian Republic, and subsequently, it was too weak to withstand the shocks of the political transition: the shocks of the dark-side of fundamental rights (i.e. hate speech, due process provided for even the guilty, and claims by minority communities – such as the LGBTQ community for example, which is seen as controversial by the conservative majority); shocks brought by the market economy; the shock of weak institutions, which were unable to sustain corruption; and the shock of globalization. The constitution could not stop the erosion of social solidarity, could not build trust in the political class, was incapable of combating skepticism toward market economy and democracy, could not sustain antiestablishment sentiments, and most of all, though being built to foster a constitutional partnership, could not withstand a polarizing and obstructive powerful political party. In sum, the constitution became an easy target and a useful scapegoat (p. 13).

It is noteworthy that despite the fact that Orbán's party played a crucial role in the 1989 negotiations, his rhetoric played on the lack of constitutional-making mandate of the Roundtable talks in 2010. At the end of the day, instead of completing its mission, he created a construct that builds on its negation.

The Rhetoric of Stability and Governance by the People Instead of Debates
As Csillag and Szelényi argue, "liberalism" for Orbán means the excessive emphasis of individual interest over "national" interest (p. 23). In one of his most widely cited speeches, Orbán envisions that in the next 15–20 years Hungary should be dominated by a single, massive right-wing political party that would rule the whole political field without "unnecessary" debates (Rácz 2015). Bánkuti et al. (2012, p. 145) quotes Orbán in 2009, even before the victorious elections visioning a

> ... real chance that politics in Hungary will no longer be tied by a dualist power space ... Instead, a large governing party will emerge in the center of the political stage (that) will be able to formulate national policy, not through constant debates but through a natural representation of interests.

As Lambert (2015) argues, this also relies on the assumption that the rule of law state built in 1989 never belonged to the people. It was an elite project, manifested in the activism of the Constitutional Court, which brought only legalism instead of justice, wealth and prosperity for former communist elites, and the ordinary people were left behind and unattended. Halmai points out that his rhetoric also reinforces that there was no real transition in 1989–1990, only the communist nomenclature converting its lost political power to an economic one, which Orbán exemplified by claiming that the last two Socialist prime ministers in office before his takeover in 2010 both became rich after the transition through the privatization process (p. 72).

Furthermore, Hegedűs (2014, p. 8) cites Orbán's infamous speech stating that

> The political and intellectual program of 1848 proclaimed: we will not be a colony! The program and the desire of Hungarians in 2012 is: we will not be a colony! Hungary could not have stood against the pressure and dictats from abroad in the winter of 2011–2012 if it were not for those hundreds of thousands of people who stood up to show everyone that Hungarians will not live as foreigners dictate, will not give up their independence or their freedom, therefore they will not give up their constitution either, which they finally managed to draft after twenty years. Thank you all!

A Little Help from the Constitutional Structure...

As mentioned above, the institutional structure set forth by the 1989 constitution envisioned a constitutional partnership, relying on a broad consensus that could not withhold the political cold war FIDESZ instrumentalized (Kis 2012 p. 19). The founding fathers (who, in fact, were mostly male) institutionalized the qualified two-third majority consensus for a wide variety of issues, and this has enabled the opposition to obstruct structural reforms for decades. Following the German chancellor-type model, the Prime Minister, on the other hand, could have only been removed by constructive vote of non-confidence, which in turn created a strong government with a limited responsibility to the strong opposition. This in practice meant that no incumbent government was ever removed. As Bozóki argues, the illusion of stability brought a plethora of informal practices as a modus operandi: tax evasion and party finance stalling democratic institution-building (p. 5).

It is not as much a cause as it is an illuminating signifier how deeply post-transition Hungarian politics have failed to fulfill the goals of constitutional partnership. Hungary has maintained a political culture that continues to lack commitment to substantive gender equality. Before the 1990s the ratio of female parliamentarians was at about 30%; after the transition, it has yet to exceeded 10% (Kövér 2015b, p. 114). In 2007 only 18% of mayors were women: this number being the lowest among Budapest districts, with most elected in the strategically least important settlements – poorly founded small, disadvantaged villages – where there is no money, only lots of work.[11]

Economic Hardship

According to a 2009 poll, a half a year before the "voting booth revolution," 72% of Hungarians actually felt to be worse off economically than under communism. Ninety-four per cent described the country's economy as bad, and 42% disapproved of the move from a state-controlled economy to a market economy (Pew Global 2009; Wike 2010), even though in 1991, 80% answered just the opposite to the same question (Wike 2010). Not only have Hungarians felt as though they have been the losers in the political transition to free market democracy, but also, as Hegedűs points out, though Hungary carried out widely recognized economic reforms during the late state socialist era and was the first post-socialist state to pave the way for liberal economic reforms in East Central Europe during the 1990s, in the 2000s its competitiveness continuously decreased. The country's external debts and economic imbalances soared during the first decade of the new millennium (Hegedűs 2014, p. 3; Eurostat 2016; Knoema 2016). In 2010, Hungary's GDP was further from Austria's (the former sibling-state apropos the Austro-Hungarian Monarchy, dismantled in the post-WWI treaties) than it was in 1990 (Lambert 2015, p. 9). Since 2002, government gross debt as percentage of GDP has grown by approximately 3% annually, from a level of 55.9% in 2002 to 58.6% in 2003, and 82.2% in 2010 (Hegedűs 2014, pp. 4–5; World Bank 2016). In the years 2002–2008, the budget deficit varied between –5% and –9% annually and all initiatives to create structural reforms and restore the balance of public spending remained unsuccessful. This was partly due to the then-opposition FIDESZ torpedoing education and healthcare reforms with a "social referendum" in 2009, which pressed the government to suspend the system of individual financial contributions to healthcare and higher education. Thus, by the time when the economic crisis hit, Hungary was greatly in debt both in the public and private sectors, and was without feasible crisis management strategies (Hegedűs 2014, pp. 4–5). Additionally, the lack of appropriate structural reforms led Hungary to lose its earlier competitive advantages over other post-socialist states in the region (p. 6). Being in public and private debt, as well as a structural economic and competitiveness crisis, Hungary was hit hard by the global economic crisis and was endangered both by the collapse of the national currency the forint (HUF), and in 2009 by state insolvency (World Bank Group 2016; INSOL). Before Orbán's takeover, his predecessors focused mainly on spending cuts and the securing of the IMF-EU-IBRD loan package amounting to approximately 20 billion euros for 2008 (International Monetary Fund 2008).

Shift and Legacy: Concluding Remarks

To sum up, this chapter made the following arguments: (i) the Orbán-government's self-proclaimed revolutionary regime claims to have reconstituted and re-conceptualized the relationship between the state and its citizens, both in institutional and normative terms. For example, the Republic of Hungary was renamed Hungary. (ii) The new regime in several fields of life made a significant departure from constitutional standards generally held in liberal democracies. However, neither its creators argued convincingly, nor could an academic analysis support the claim that this would indeed constitute a new, coherent, sui generis illiberal democracy model from the constitutional legal or the political theoretical point of view. (iii) This self-identified illiberal regime, however, sets forth a political discourse and a discursive framework that also materializes in the form of legal, constitutional documents, which reject ideological and policy commitments toward human rights and a liberal concept on personhood.

Notes

1. It needs to be noted that due to criticism by international organizations such as the EU, the Council of Europe, or judicial organs, like the European Court of Human Rights (ECHR) or the European Court of Justice, some of these legislation has been amended. For example in April 2014, the European Court of Justice ruled that the abrupt termination of the data protection commissioner's term in 2011 infringed on the authority's independence, and that the church law violated the European Convention of Human Rights. The ECHR also declared that the early removal of the former Supreme Court president in 2012 violated his rights, and also condemned Hungary for violating the freedom of expression because opposition party MP's were sanctioned. Likewise, the 98 % retroactive tax was found to be contrary to the Convention.
2. Retroactivity refers to the fact that the idea of creating a new political community (or even the adoption of a new constitution) was not part of the political campaign in the elections, and, needless to say, the principles of this new regimes were not up to political deliberation either.
3. The Declaration, adopted shortly after the new government took office, was ordered to be displayed in all government facilities in Hungary. The president, the speaker of the parliament, the presidents of the Constitutional Court and the Supreme Court, the Central Bank, mayors, the ombudspersons, chief prosecutors and judges were requested in the form of a Government Resolution to follow suit. Most state institutions, such as hospitals or universities, also complied.

4. This is not to argue that liberalism is necessarily multicultural, or that any form of collectivistic constitutionalism would be inherently liberal, only that these would be the most characteristic and typical commitments by Hungarian liberal public intellectuals (who, in the absence of a visible liberal party, can be identified as relevant "liberal" voices.)
5. According to the concept of ethno-symbolism, nations are based on ethnic groups, where cultural cohesion is built on myths and symbols. Anthony D. Smith (1996, 1999, 2009) explains how myths are highly significant factors in nation building. Also consider John Armstrong (1982) arguing that "A most significant effect of the myth recital is to arouse an intense awareness among the group members of their 'common fate' " (p. 9).
6. For the concept, see Comaroff and Comaroff (2009).
7. For scholarly assessments on the role of discursive action in the process of identity formation see Fox and Miller-Idriss (2008) and Wodak (2009).
8. For the original theory, see Austin (1962).
9. Balzacq (2010) argues that three different aspects should be considered when analyzing perlocutionary speech acts: (i) the centrality of the audience; (ii) the co-dependency of agency and context; (iii) the dispositive and structuring force of practices.
10. For more on this see Vidra et al. (2012).
11. According to the 2014 World economic forum Global Gender Gap Report Hungary is placed 128 out of 143 in the field of political empowerment, with a 93rd overall gender-gap rank.

Bibliography

Amnesty International. (2016). Annual report: Hungary 2015–2016. https://www.amnesty.org/en/countries/europe-and-central-asia/hungary/report-hungary/. Accessed June 2016.

Anderson, P. (2007). Russia's managed democracy. *London Review of Books, 29*(2), 2–12.

Armstrong, J. (1982). *Nations before nationalism.* Chapel Hill: University of North Carolina Press.

Austin, J. L. (1962). *How to do things with words.* Oxford: Clarendon Press.

Balzacq, T. (2010). *Securitization theory: how security problems emerge and dissolve.* Milton Park, Abingdon: Routledge.

Bánkuti, M., Halmai, G., Scheppele, K. L. (2012). Hungary's illiberal turn: disabling the constitution. In: A. T. Gábor (Ed.), *Constitution for a disunited nation on Hungary's 2011 fundamental law.* Budapest: CEU Press.

Blokker, P. (2013). *New democracies in crisis? A comparative constitutional study of the Czech Republic, Hungary, Poland, Romania and Slovakia.* London and New York: Routledge.

Bozóki, A. (2011). Occupy the state: The Orbán regime in Hungary. *Journal of Contemporary Central and Eastern Europe, 19*(3), 649–663.

Bozóki, A (2015). Broken democracy, predatory state, and nationalist populism. In: P. Krasztev & J. V. Til (Eds.), *The Hungarian patient. Social opposition to an illiberal democracy*. Budapest: Central European University Press.

Bugarič, B. (2014). Protecting democracy and the rule of law in the European Union: The Hungarian challenge, LSE "Europe in question". *LEQS Discussion Paper Series*, No. 79, 1–44.

Chronowski, N. (2012). The new Hungarian fundamental law in the light of the European Union's normative values. *Revue Est Europa, 1*(2), 111–142.

Collier, D., & Levitsky, S. (1997). Democracy with adjectives: conceptual innovation in comparative research. *World Politics, 49*(3), 430–451.

Comaroff, J. L., & Comaroff, J. (2009). *Ethnicity, Inc.* Chicago: University of Chicago Press.

Csillag, T., & Szelényi, I. (2015). Drifting from liberal democracy: Traditionalist/neoconservative ideology of managed illiberal democratic capitalism in post-communist Europe, intersections. *East European Journal of Society and Politics, 1*(1), 18–48.

Eurostat. (2016). Real GDP growth rate – Volume. http://ec.europa.eu/eurostat/web/products-datasets/-/tec00115. Accessed June 2016.

Feischmidt, M., & Hervik, P. (2015). Mainstreaming the extreme: intersecting challenges from the far right in Europe, intersections. *East European Journal of Society and Politics, 1*(1), 3–15.

Fox, J. E., & Miller-Idriss, C. (2008) Everyday nationhood. *Ethnicities, 8*(4), 536–563.

Freedom House. (2015). Hungary: nations in transit. https://freedomhouse.org/report/nations-transit/2015/hungary. Accessed 1 June 2016.

Garcia, L. B. (2015). *Participatory democracy and civil society in the EU. Agenda-setting and institutionalisation*. Basingstoke: Palgrave.

Halmai, G. (2013). The rise and fall of Hungarian Constitutionalism. In: S. Benhabib, D. Cameron, A. Dolidze, G. Halmai, G. Hellmann, K. Pishchikova, R. Youngs (Eds.), *The democratic disconnect citizenship and accountability in the transatlantic community* (pp. 67–77). Washington, DC: Transatlantic Academy.

Halmai, G., & Scheppele, K. L. (Eds.) (2012) *Opinion on Hungary's new constitutional order: Amicus brief for the Venice commission on the transitional provisions of the fundamental law and the Key Cardinal Laws*. Princeton: Princeton University.

Hegedűs, D. (2014). From front-runner's "Euphoria" to Backmarker's "pragmatic adhocism"? Hungary's ten years within the European Union in a Visegrad comparison. *DGAPanalyse (7)*. https://dgap.org/en/article/getFullPDF/25438. Accessed 1 June 2016.

Helsinki Committee. (2014). Disrespect for European values in Hungary 2010–2014. http://helsinki.hu/wp-content/uploads/Disrespect_for_values-Nov2014.pdf. Accessed June 2016.

Hobsbawm, E. J. (1992). *Nations and nationalism since 1789: programme, myth, reality*. Cambridge: Cambridge University Press.

Hungarian Spectrum. (2009). Value structure of Hungarian society, 2009. http://hungarianspectrum.org/2009/10/13/value-structure-of-hungarian-society-2009/. Accessed June 2016.

Huntington, S. (1991) *The third wave: democratization in the late twentieth century*. Norman, Oklahoma: University of Oklahoma Press.

International Monetary Fund. (2008, October 28). IMF, EU, and World Bank line up $25 billion for Hungary. IMF Survey Online. http://www.imf.org/external/pubs/ft/survey/so/2008/car102808b.htm. Accessed June 2016.

Jarábik, B. (2015). From Belarus to Hungary: lessons from a traditionalist revolution. In: P. Krasztev & J. V. Til (Eds.), *The Hungarian patient. Social opposition to an illiberal democracy* (pp. 319–324). Budapest: Central European University Press.

Jenne, E. K., & Mudde, C. (2012). Can outsiders help? *Journal of Democracy, 23*(3), 147–155.

Keller, T. (2010). Hungary on the world values map. *Review of Sociology, 20*(1), 27–51.

Kis, J. (2012). Introduction: from the 1989 constitution to the 2011 fundamental law. In: A. T. Gábor (Ed.), *Constitution for a disunited nation on Hungary's 2011 fundamental law*. Budapest: CEU Press.

Knoema. (2016). World Data Atlas: Hungary – Gross Domestic Product. http://knoema.com/atlas/Hungary/GDP. Accessed June 2016.

Kováts, E., & Põim, M. (2015). Gender as symbolic glue: the position and role of conservative and far right parties anti-gender mobilizations in Europe. Foundation for European Progressive Studies and the Friedrich-Ebert-Stiftung.

Kováts, E., Põim, M., Tánczos, J. (2015). Beyond gender? Anti-gender mobilization and the lessons for progressives. FEPS-FES Policy Brief.

Kovács, A., Horváth, A., Vidra, Z. (2011). The Ferry-Country between East and West: debates on modernity and Europe in Hungary. In: A. Ichijo (Ed.), *Europe, nations and modernity* (pp. 158–182). Basingstoke: Palgrave Macmillan.

Kovács, K., & Tóth, G.A. (2011). Hungary's constitutional transformation. *European Constitutional Law Review, 7*(2), 183–203.

Kövér, A. (2015a). Captured by state and church: civil society in democratic Hungary populism. In: P. Krasztev & J. V. Til (Eds.), *The Hungarian patient. Social opposition to an illiberal democracy* (pp. 81–90). Budapest: Central European University Press.

Kövér, A. (2015b). Timike and the Sweetie Pies: fragmented discourses about women in Hungarian public life. In: P. Krasztev & J. V. Til (Eds.), *The Hungarian patient. Social opposition to an illiberal democracy*. Budapest: Central European University Press.

Krasztev, P. (2015). Social responses to the "hybridization" of the political system: the case of Hungary. In: P. Krasztev & J. V. Til (Eds.), *The Hungarian patient. Social opposition to an illiberal democracy*. Budapest: Central European University Press.

Lambert, G. (2015). Azután egyszer csak beütött a mennyko – interjú Tölgyessy Péterrel [And then all Hell Broke loose: An interview with Péter Tölgyessy]. Figyelo Online. http://m.figyelo.hu/cikkek/427802-azutan-egyszer-csak-beutott-a-mennyko—interju-tolgyessy-peterrel. Accessed 1 June 2015.

Levitsky, S., & Way, L. A. (2010). *Competitive authoritarianism: hybrid regimes after the cold war*. Cambridge: Cambridge University Press.

Majtényi, B. (2012). Legislative stupidities in the New Hungarian Constitution. *Peace Human Rights, 1*(9), 105–110.

Mansbridge, J. J., & Parkinson, J. (Eds.). (2012). *Deliberative systems*. Cambridge: Cambridge University Press.

Melegh, A. (2006). *On the East/West slope: globalization, nationalism, racism and discourses on Eastern Europe*. New York: Central European University Press.

Mill, J. S. (Ed.) (1993 [1859]). On liberty. In *Utilitarianism, liberty, and representative government* (pp. 69–185). London: Everyman's Library.

Niederberger, A., & and Schink, P. (2013). *Republican democracy liberty, law and politics*. Edinburgh: Edinburgh University Press.

Pap, A. L. (2014). Személyiségkép és alkotmányos identitás a Nemzeti Együttműködés Rendszerében (I. rész), [Personhood and constitutional identity under the new constitution]. *Közjogi Szemle 2014(4)*, 1–11.

Pap, A. L. (2015a) Who are "we, the people"? Biases and preferences in the Hungarian fundamental law. In: Z. Fejes, F. Mandák, Z. Szente (Eds.), *Challenges and pitfalls in the recent Hungarian constitutional development – discussing the new fundamental law of Hungary* (pp. 53–75). Paris: L'Harmattan.

Pap, A. L. (2015b). Személyiségkép és alkotmányos identitás a Nemzeti Együttműködés Rendszerében [Personhood and constitutional identity under the new constitution] Part II., *Közjogi Szemle, 2015*(1), 1–11.

Pap, A. L. (2015c). Személyiségkép és alkotmányos identitás a Nemzeti Együttműködés Rendszerében (Personhood and constitutional identity under the new constitution) Part III., *Közjogi Szemle* (*1*).

Pető, A., & Vasali, Z. (2014, January 20). The "laboratory" called Hungary: a challenge for understanding protest movements. *OpenDemocracy*. https://www.opendemocracy.net/can-europe-make-it/andrea-pet%C5%91-zolt%C3%A1n-vasali/%E2%80%98laboratory%E2%80%99-called-hungary-challenge-for-understanding. Accessed June 2016.

Pettit, P. (2013). *On the people's terms: a republican theory and model of democracy*. Cambridge: Cambridge University Press.

Pew Global. (2009, November). End of communism cheered but now with more reservations. http://www.pewglobal.org/2009/11/02/end-of-communism-cheered-but-now-with-more-reservations/. Accessed June 2016.

Rácz, A. (2015). Multi-vectorialism failing? The Russia-policy of the Orbán-government. *Russkii Vopros (1)*. http://www.russkiivopros.com/?pag=one&id=619&kat=7&csl=69. Accessed June 2016.

Rupnik, J. (2012). How things went wrong. *Journal of Democracy, 23*(3), 132–137.

Rupnik, J., & Zielonka, J. (2013) Introduction: the state of democracy 20 years on: domestic and external factors. *East European Politics and Societies, 27*(1), 3–25.

Sarlo, A. W., & Otarashvili, M. (2013, July). Can the EU rescue democracy in Hungary? *Foreign Policy Research Institute*. https://www.files.ethz.ch/isn/167427/Wiktorek_Otarashvili_-_EU_and_Democracy_in_Hungary.pdf. Accessed June 2016.

Scheppele, K. L. (2013). The rule of law and the Frankenstate: why governance checklists do not work. *Governance, 26*(4), 559–562.

Scheppele, K. L. (2014, May 6). Hungary and the end of politics. *The Nation*. https://www.thenation.com/article/hungary-and-end-politics/. Accessed June 2016.

Shevtsova, L. F. (2000) Can electoral autocracy survive? *Journal of Democracy, 11*(3), 36–38.

Smith, A. D. (1996). Culture, community and territory: the politics of ethnicity and nationalism. *International Affairs, 74*(3), 451–452.

Smith, A. D. (1999). Ethnic election and national destiny: some religious origins of nationalist ideals. *Nations and Nationalism, 5*(3), 331–355.

Smith, A. D. (2009). *Ethno-symbolism and nationalism. A cultural approach*. New York and London: Routledge.

Szabó, A. (Ed.) (2013). Political orientations, values and activities of Hungarian University and College Students. In *Active Youth in Hungary Research Group*. Prague: Heinrich-Böll-Stiftung.

Takács, P. (2015). *A rózsa neve: Magyar Köztársaság – Az államok nevéről és a magyar állam átnevezéséről (The name of the rose: Hungarian republic: on the names of states and the renaming of the Hungarian state)*. Budapest: Gondolat.

Tavares Report. (2013, June 25). Report A7-0229/2013 on the situation of fundamental rights: standards and practices in Hungary (pursuant to the European Parliament resolution of 16 February 2012). Report prepared by the European Parliament. (2012/2130(INI)).

Til, J. V. (2015). Democratic resurgence in Hungary: challenges to oppositional movement (an open-ended conclusion). In: P. Krasztev & J. V. Til (Eds.), *The Hungarian patient. Social opposition to an illiberal democracy*. Budapest: Central European University Press.

Tóth, G. A. (2012). *Constitution for a disunited nation: on Hungary's 2011 fundamental law* (pp. 1–21). Budapest: Central European University Press.

Vidra, Z., & Fox, J. (2014). Mainstreaming of racist anti-Roma discourses in the media in Hungary. *Journal of Immigrant and Refugee Studies, 12*(4), 437–455.

Vidra, Z., Horváth, A., Fox, J. (2012). Tolerance and cultural diversity discourses in Hungary. In: R. Zapata-Barrero & A. Triandafyllidou (Eds.), *Addressing tolerance and diversity discourse in Europe comparative overview of 16 European countries* (pp. 317–43). Barcelona: Barcelona Centre for International Affairs.

Wenman, M. (2013). *Agonistic democracy, constituent power in the era of globalisation.* Cambridge: Cambridge University Press.

Wike, R. (2010, April 7). Hungary dissatisfied with democracy, but not its ideals. *Pew Global Attitudes Project.* http://www.pewglobal.org/2010/04/07/hungary-dissatisfied-with-democracy-but-not-its-ideals/. Accessed 1 June 2016.

Wodak, R. (2009). *The discursive construction of national identity.* Edinburgh: Edinburgh University Press.

Wodak, R., Khosravinik, M., & Mral, B. (2013) *Rightwing populism in Europe: politics and discourse.* London: Bloomsbury Academic.

World Bank. (2016). Data: Hungary. http://data.worldbank.org/country/hungary. Accessed June 2016.

World Bank Group. (2016). Resolving insolvency in Hungary. http://www.doingbusiness.org/data/exploreeconomies/hungary/resolving-insolvency/. Accessed June 2016.

World Economic Forum. (2014). Insight report: the global gender gap report 2014. http://www3.weforum.org/docs/GGGR14/GGGR_CompleteReport_2014.pdf. Accessed June 2016.

Zakaria, F. (1997, November–December). The rise of illiberal democracy. *Foreign Affairs, 76*(6), 22–43.

András L. Pap is Research Chair and Head of Department for the Study of Constitutionalism and the Rule of Law at the Hungarian Academy of Sciences Centre for Social Sciences Institute for Legal Studies, and a SASRO-Marie Skłodowska-Curie Fellow at the Institute of Sociology of the Slovak Academy of Sciences in Bratislava. He is also Professor of Law at the Law Enforcement Faculty of the National University of Public Service and a Recurrent Visiting (Adjunct) Professor at the Nationalism Studies Program at Central European University in Budapest, Hungary. He has published 6 books, 6 textbooks and over 200 articles on constitutional law, human rights, minority rights and law enforcement issues.

Chapter 7: Establishing the Rule of Law in Kosovo and Bosnia and Herzegovina: The Contribution of the EU Civilian Missions

Efstathios T. Fakiolas and Nikolaos Tzifakis

Introduction

Peace seems to have taken roots in the Western Balkans. The European Union (EU) has spearheaded to stabilize the region through humanitarian and post-conflict assistance instruments, the most effective and enticing of which remains the award of integration. The EU still feels confident that it is the soft "power of attraction" of the membership perspective that primarily induces the region's leadership to accept the adaptation costs of hard reforms and resolve outstanding disputes (Petrovic 2013; Fakiolas and Tzifakis 2008). But stability overall is far from complete, especially in Kosovo and Bosnia and Herzegovina (BiH), in which security challenges persist. Scarcely surprising, in the former the EU keeps deployed a Common Security and Defence Policy

E.T. Fakiolas (✉)
Department of Political Science and International Relations,
University of the Peloponnese, Corinth, Greece
e-mail: fakiolas@uop.gr

Fish, Gill, Petrovic (eds.), *A Quarter Century of Post-Communism Assessed*, DOI 10.1007/978-3-319-43437-7_8

(CSDP) civilian mission, the European Union Rule of Law mission (EULEX); while in the latter a respective mission, the European Union Police Mission (EUPM), closed down in 2012.

In this context, the chapter examines the efforts of EULEX and EUPM to push through state-building transition and democratization by restructuring and upholding constituents of the rule of law sector. By focusing on the scope of mandate, the resources reserved for the task, and the results achieved, it pursues to map out successes and deficiencies. The main finding of this track record investigation is that the more focused and specific the activities taken up by EULEX and EUPM have been on the ground, the more efficient and rewarding their contribution has been to advancing the rule of law and public order in Kosovo and BiH, respectively. Equally important, the two missions have proved able to smoothly work to the benefit of their operational objectives whenever they have both stayed tuned with local interests and streamlined their practices with other EU policies active in the area.

But before we proceed with the two case studies, two preliminary remarks are appropriate. First, the EU appears to understand the rule of law both as a condition and a principle in which ruling institutions and authority, individuals, state and society, public and private entities are all bound and accountable to law; which in turn is consistent with human rights and is enforced and adjudicated in the name of citizens. From this angle, the rule of law is taken to pertain to an "overarching concept" for CSDP civilian missions deployed in crisis and conflict-ridden situations to strengthen weak or failed authorities through monitoring, mentoring, and advising (MMA) operations or executive engagement functions in state building and ruling. The central objective is to develop a strong and effective judiciary, reinforce public order, and fight the organized crime and corruption (European Commission 2015a, pp. 12, 16, 18; Winkelhofer 2015, pp. 118–119; Opitz 2014, pp. 151–153). Second, the selection of the two CSDP civilian missions is not accidental. It concerns the two Balkan post-conflict countries in which the EU has devoted all these years more energy and resources than anywhere else. EUPM, on the one hand, marks the first and longest running EU civilian operation. As Javier Solana (2013, p. 3) put it, it is the EU's first example of "learning by doing," in that it "became the template for other missions." And EULEX, on the other, represents the EU's largest ever deployed civilian mission.

EULEX in Kosovo

Mandate

On 4 February 2008, the EU decided the deployment of EULEX in Kosovo to assist in developing independent multiethnic justice, police and customs institutions. EULEX was called to MMA Kosovo's institutions "on all areas related to the wider rule of law" (Council of the European Union 2008, p. 93). It was tasked with contributing to the maintenance of the rule of law, public order, and security while ensuring that all activities of Kosovo's institutions remain free from political interference and in line with international standards concerning gender equality and human rights (Council of the European Union 2008, p. 93). EULEX was also expected to support the fight against organized crime, corruption, and interethnic and other serious crimes. Interestingly, most EULEX tasks were preceded by the verb "ensure," a word choice indicating that the mission was held directly responsible for making progress in reforms. Indeed, EULEX was vested with "certain executive responsibilities" to carry out its own operations where these seemed necessary, as well as the authority to annul or reverse operational decisions of the Kosovo institutions (Council of the European Union 2008, p. 93). Therefore, it received extensive powers and a quite ambitious mandate to improve the rule of law and restore police, judicial, and customs institutions in Kosovo.

The mandate of EULEX was not so straightforward. The mission's deployment evolved into a daunting task in itself, despite the fact that an almost 3-year-long preparation phase preceded the adoption of the relevant Joint Action. EU leaders seemed to presume that the Ahtisaari plan previewing Kosovo's "supervised independence" would be accepted by all parties, and has been preparing EULEX to assist the institution building of the rule of law sector until the end of international supervision (Papadimitriou and Petrov 2012, p. 756). Nevertheless, the deadlock in the Kosovo "final status" talks changed the context of the mission's deployment. Russia was opposed to the Ahtisaari plan and claimed that the United Nations Security Council (UNSC) Resolution 1244 (that had placed Kosovo under UN administration in 1999) was still in force. Similarly, Russia also disapproved the replacement of the UN Mission in Kosovo (UNMIK) by EULEX owing to the fact that the latter was designated to contribute to Kosovo's supervised independence.

At the EU level, the failure of the status talks divided the member-states over the question of Kosovo's independence. While 22 EU members supported the recognition of Kosovo's statehood and the implementation of the Ahtisaari plan, five EU countries (i.e., Cyprus, Greece, Romania, Slovakia, and Spain) kept reservations and abided by UNSC Resolution 1244 (Tzifakis 2013, pp. 45–46; Petrovic 2013, pp. 154–155). At the same time, the Kosovars and Serbs maintained their irreconcilable perspectives on the region's status and nurtured different expectations from EULEX's work.

EULEX, eventually, deployed in December 2008 and reached full operational capacity on 6 April 2009. Not only did it take an entire year for EULEX to assume its duties, it was also plagued by internal contradictions and tensions. In particular, the Russian opposition was circumvented by the UN Secretary General, Ban Ki-moon, who proposed making EULEX a constituent part of UNMIK (United Nations Security Council 2008, p. 5). As a result, EULEX has been set to operate within the "status-neutral" framework of UN policies in observance of UNSC Resolution 1244. This was indeed a convenient solution for EU members too, that did not wish to openly clash over the question of Kosovo's statehood. The problem, however, is that although EULEX was designated as a "status neutral" mission, its job description has required of it to strengthen emblematic institutions of independent statehood. Its operations have been rightly depicted as "squaring the circle" (Richter 2009, p. 34). The mission has responded to the challenge by downplaying the rule of law as a manifestation of sovereignty and, instead, emphasizing the services it provided to people. In particular, it proclaimed that it intended to work on the field to improve the standards and the routine performance of police and justice institutions rather than adopt a "top-down" approach to those institutions' restructuring (Richter 2009, p. 34). In this regard, it has tried to portray itself as a technical, apolitical mission. Yet, its work has increasingly implied decisions that presupposed a clear position on Kosovo's status (e.g., the selection of body of law to be applied in justice). EULEX, indeed, proceeded very slowly and cautiously with the implementation of its program, prompting some analysts to qualify its work as an EU "face-saving exercise," or a "continuation of UNMIK policy" (Gregor Mayer, quoted in Džihić and Kramer 2009, p. 20; Richter 2009, p. 18). Furthermore, it adopted a defensive posture and dedicated much energy and work to render its policies compliant (at least at a discursive level) with the contradictory expectations of different domestic and international stakeholders. For instance, while EULEX remarked to the Kosovo Albanians that it advanced local ownership of rule of law institutions, it emphasized in its communications with the Kosovo Serbs that it worked to improve law and order for everyone living in the multiethnic society of Kosovo (Musliu and Geci 2014, pp. 72–75).

Although the EU renewed three times EULEX's mandate during the researched period (in 2010, 2012, and 2014), it has refrained from revising the mission's tasks (Council of the European Union 2010, p. 14, 2012, p. 46, 2014a, p. 42). The EU has, apparently, avoided running the risk of upsetting the delicate balance among recognizers and nonrecognizers of Kosovo independence that permitted the mission's deployment. However, in practice, much innovative thinking has been employed to adjust EULEX's operations to changing conditions on the ground, especially following the end of Kosovo's supervised independence in September 2012. For instance, in 2014, the EU diminished the scope of the jurisdiction and competences of EULEX judges and prosecutors (with respect to the exercise of executive functions on new cases) in order to secure the approval of Kosovo institutions to the extension of the mission's deployment until June 2016. These changes were, nevertheless, written down merely in a national law adopted by the Kosovo Parliament (Assembly of the Republic of Kosovo 2014a). Whereas the Kosovo authorities claimed that the renewal of EULEX mandate in 2014 resulted from an international agreement with the EU (Assembly of the Republic of Kosovo 2014b), the latter cautiously confined itself to just an exchange of letters between Atifete Jahjaga, Kosovo's President and Catherine Ashton, EU High Representative for Foreign Affairs and Security Policy (see Annex I in Assembly of the Republic of Kosovo 2014b).

Resources

The capabilities that the EU and its members dispose in a CSDP mission can be indicative of the extent of their commitment to improve conditions on the ground. This is especially true when a great discrepancy exists between pledges of resources at the time of a mission's launch and actual allocations at the operational phase.

To begin with economic resources, EULEX has received all these years more than €890 million from the EU budget (Council of the European Union 2014a, p. 43, 2014b, p. 52, 2015, p. 21). Its annual budget from

June 2015 to 2016 was set to €77 million (Council of the European Union 2015, p. 21). To this amount should also be added the payments made by the contributing EU members for the salaries of their seconded staff. This is a substantial expense, whose exact size is not known to the EU itself. Overall, EULEX has been the most expensive EU civilian mission so far, and this fact could be taken to constitute a proof of the Union's commitment to the improve rule of law in Kosovo.

With respect to its personnel, EULEX has brought together police officers, judges, prosecutors, and custom officers from EU and non-EU countries and Kosovo itself. Its staff was originally planned to consist of around 3200 people (1950 internationals and 1250 locals). However, it has never reached to its full strength. According to the European Court of Auditors (2012, p. 37), in the years 2010–2011 EULEX operated at approximately 75% of its authorized strength. In the justice sector, for instance, where there was a great need of assistance and a backlog of more than 210,000 cases, the secondments were short of the authorized strength by 40% (KIPRED 2013, p. 12). EU members have seconded fewer staff than what they had pledged, with their pledges being already fewer than what the EU had initially authorized. Although some progress has been made on that count and despite the fact that the EU pragmatically decided in 2012 to downsize the mission by 25% to 2250 people, David Lidington, UK Minister for Europe, disclosed in 2013 before the European Union Sub-Committee of the House of Lords, that "there are frankly still too many unoccupied positions" (House of Lords 2013, p. 11).

Another constraint in EULEX human resources is the high turnover of its international staff. Most secondments have been for a year. This timeframe is insufficient for officers to get acquainted with the Kosovo field of operations and contribute to the management of complicated issues such as the investigation of cases of organized crime and corruption (KIPRED 2013, p. 13). The occurrence on many occasions of delays in finding people to replace outgoing staff members has implied that posts have frequently remained vacant for some time and, when these posts were filled, incoming staff members did not receive their dossiers directly from their predecessors (Jacqué 2015, p. 18). The EULEX's high turnover of personnel has also undermined the transfer of expertise to local authorities and, by extension, the efficient implementation of the mission's overall MMA work (European Court of Auditors 2012, p. 38). More worryingly, the quality of human resources seconded in Kosovo has been rather poor.

EU members have usually paid little attention to properly screening candidates for the mission's positions and have not provided them with sufficient training (European Court of Auditors 2012, pp. 38–39; Jacqué 2015, p. 17). They have also offered little incentives to their qualified people to apply and, thus, their seconded staff has featured many trainees and young professionals who lacked the necessary experience and knowledge to MMA the local officers, let alone to investigate complex cases of serious crimes or award justice (KIPRED 2013, p. 13; Jacqué 2015, p. 18). Not accidentally, 11 contributing EU countries were alleged to have dispatched unqualified staff to work with the mission (European Court of Auditors 2012, p. 38). On the whole, the mission's deficiency in sufficient and adequately qualified staff has compromised its effort to improve rule of law in Kosovo.

Last, but not least, the mission has not managed to foster among its members a "sense of belonging" with many of its staff members operating along national contingents, or even worse, individually. In the words, of Jean-Paul Jacqué (2015, p. 19), the expert who was appointed by Brussels to evaluate the mission's mandate implementation, "it appears that there is no real team of prosecutors, or prosecution service (what the French would call a 'parquet'), but merely a collection of individuals." Having briefly analyzed the mission's mandate and resources, the next section assesses its track record.

Results

EULEX has tangibly assisted to the strengthening of Kosovo's rule of law sector institutional capacity. With the guidance of the EU mission, the Kosovo authorities have adopted more than 110 laws, administrative instructions, and regulations (EULEX 2015, p. 2). The Kosovo Police has been reorganized and its patrol management and crime persecution capabilities have been enhanced (EULEX 2011, pp. 9, 18–19; Joint Rule of Law Coordination Board 2013, p. 7, 2014, p. 8). The Kosovo Police has also achieved "ethnic balance" in its human resources with 16.10 % of posts being filled by people coming from nonmajority communities (Joint Rule of Law Coordination Board 2015, p. 11). Moreover, it has taken over, along with other relevant Kosovo institutions, the management and control of the borders with Albania, Montenegro and the Former Yugoslav Republic of Macedonia and it has carried out joint border patrols with the police authorities of these countries (European Commission 2015b, p. 57).

The Kosovo Customs has been restructured and it has adopted a new system for the recruitment, appraisal, and career progression of its officers (Joint Rule of Law Coordination Board 2015, p. 14). In addition, it has adopted a Customs Code in accordance with European standards (EULEX 2011, pp. 52–54). The Kosovo rule of law institutions have also introduced integrated management practices in the country's borders and, thus, the Kosovo Customs Office has been collecting more than 70% of the country's revenues (Joint Rule of Law Coordination Board 2015, p. 14).

In the justice sector, EULEX has assisted the Kosovo institutions to adopt several much needed pieces of legislation, such as the Law on Courts, the Law on the Kosovo Judicial Council, the Law on the State Prosecutor, and the Law on the Kosovo Prosecutorial Council (Joint Rule of Law Coordination Board 2015, p. 22). The Kosovo judges and prosecutors have been scrutinized, rated, and reappointed while 60% of related posts were filled by new applicants (EULEX 2011, pp. 33–34). The security of the Kosovo Correctional Service facilities has been upgraded, and its staff has been trained on best practices (EULEX 2011, pp. 47–48). Furthermore, the Kosovo Correction Service has adopted new rules aiming at the diminution of nepotism and contraband in its facilities (Joint Rule of Law Coordination Board 2015, p. 19). EULEX has also extensively exercised its executive powers and has contributed to the adjudication of 42,000 conflict-related property cases in the Kosovo Property Claims Commission (KPCC); several hundreds of appeals (to KPCC decisions) in the Appeals Panel of the Supreme Court for Kosovo Property Agency; and more than 10,000 cases in the Special Chamber of the Supreme Court of Kosovo (Joint Rule of Law Coordination Board 2015, p. 26; EULEX 2015, p. 1). More importantly, EULEX prosecutors have also handled hundreds of cases of serious crimes and EULEX judges have in a few cases reached verdicts against high-profile officials such as politicians, judges, and prosecutors (EULEX 2015, p. 1).

However, on a more negative note, the Kosovo rule of law institutions have not developed the capabilities to address on their own complex issues such as outbreaks of serious disorder and investigations of serious crimes (Rozée 2015, p. 108; Jacqué 2015, p. 22). As the European Commission (2015b, pp. 15, 18) diplomatically put it, the Kosovo institutions are "at an early stage of preparations" in the struggle against corruption and organized crime. Having said that it is not implied that Kosovo has not taken any institutional steps in the right direction (Weber and West 2014, p. 17). Rather that instruments have not been exploited and policies have not been genuinely executed. For instance, although the Kosovo Police has signed an agreement on the electronic exchange of information with the Financial Intelligence Unit (FIU) of the Ministry of Economics, cooperation between the FIU, the police, and prosecution has been insufficient (Joint Rule of Law Coordination Board 2014, p. 12; European Commission 2015b, p. 58). Likewise, notwithstanding that the country's rule of law institutions have jointly established a National Coordinator on Economic Crime, they have failed to act upon the latter's recommendations (Joint Rule of Law Coordination Board 2015, p. 25). For instance, the Kosovo authorities have not yet adopted an "anti-Mafia law" that would enable the confiscation of illegally acquired property pending trial (Gazetta Express 2015). In a similar manner, cooperation among the Police Inspectorate and prosecution has been poor. The two institutions have not harmonized their data systems and they have not elaborated their action plans sufficiently enough to determine common objectives (Joint Rule of Law Coordination Board 2015, p. 13). What is more, the police has been accusing the Prosecutor's Office of adopting an noncooperative position when it comes to the investigation of serious crimes such as corruption (Avdiu and Perteshi 2015, p. 12). As a result, in cases of organized crime and corruption (especially when high-profile officials are involved), very few investigations have been launched; convictions have been rarely decided; and confiscations of assets have been almost never executed (European Commission 2015b, pp. 15–18, 58–60; Joint Rule of Law Coordination Board 2015, pp. 13, 24).

The deficiency of the country's rule of law institutions in the field of serious crime (i.e., war crimes, organized crime, and corruption) is mainly owed to the lack of political will of the country's authorities. The latter have understaffed rule of law institutions, leaving unfilled key posts for those institutions' operation (Weber and West 2014, p. 17). In addition, the Kosovo authorities have not consistently implemented necessary reforms and have even facilitated the prevalence of impunity. To illustrate, the Kosovo government used the opportunity in mid-2013 of the adoption of EU-suggested amnesty law for crimes of Serbs in North Kosovo (a necessary step for the integration of North Kosovo in the country) in order to give amnesty for several types of crimes committed throughout the entire territory of Kosovo. In this way, several members of the ruling party who were under investigation were cleared of charges (Weber 2015, p. 6). In addition, the Kosovo Police has remained at all times under the control of the political party in power (Weber 2015, p. 17). Similarly, concerns have been raised about the judiciary's impartiality; its vulnerability to threats, intimidation, and political interference; its weak management of cases and data; and the transparency of allocation of cases to judges and prosecutors (European Commission 2015b, pp. 12–16; European Court of Auditors 2012, p. 22). The overall backlog of unresolved cases has been growing from 218,000 at the end of 2012 to 400,000 in July 2015 (European Commission 2013b, p. 11, 2015b, p. 35). What is more, the actual law implementation has been problematic as most court rulings were hardly enforced (European Court of Auditors 2012, p. 22).

To be sure, EULEX too, bears some responsibility for the policy failure in the fight against serious crime. In terms of exercising their executive powers, EULEX prosecutors and judges have been recurrently accused of handling serious cases with incompetence and for having avoided for some time lodging investigations or prosecutions against high-profile officials (Capussela 2011). The most emblematic case of EULEX negligence has been the mismanagement of a corruption allegation inside the mission's ranks. While Maria Bamieh, an EULEX prosecutor, gave evidence to her superiors in June 2012 concerning a bribery case involving EULEX officials, the mission's leadership did not take seriously her allegations and delayed for a year to launch an internal investigation. As a result, when Bamieh was suspended from the mission in 2014, she went public and asserted that she had been punished for her revelations (Jacqué 2015). Notwithstanding that the EU has initiated criminal and administrative proceedings to investigate these allegations, the mission's credibility has been seriously impaired.

More worryingly, following the EU–Kosovo deal of April 2014 concerning the revision of the mission's mandate, EULEX prosecutors and judges have been stripped of the authority of taking on new cases. Considering the weakness of the country's rule of law institutions, an EULEX officer argued with disappointment: "no high-profile persons will ever be prosecuted again. [...] All the senior guys can now feel safe" (quoted in Weber 2015, p. 8). Indeed, to demonstrate that the EU itself has not vested with trust the country's rule of law institutions, suffice it to mention the European stance concerning the investigation of the crimes conducted during the Kosovo war. Notwithstanding that the Kosovo Police Witness Protection Directorate has been declared operational (Joint Rule of Law Coordination Board 2015, p. 17), the EU has insisted on the establishment of a Specialist Chambers and a Specialist Prosecution's Office for the war crimes that would operate outside the territory of Kosovo (i.e., in Hague) and would be solely staffed with international staff.

The limited progress in the struggle against serious crime has additionally highlighted some of the failures of EULEX to transfer adequate expertise to the local institutions. To illustrate, an EULEX action on "intelligence-led policing" had limited impact owing to the fact that the EU mission had not earlier secured that a sufficient number of Kosovo officers would participate (Weber and West 2014, p. 17). More importantly, the lack of results in the efforts of EULEX to raise the capacities of the Kosovo rule of law institutions has manifested the limited reach of the mission's MMA activities. Deprived of any instruments of conditionality, EULEX MMA activities have inevitably depended on the willingness of the Kosovo political authorities to improve rule of law in their country (Radin 2014, p. 188). However, as earlier explained, the Kosovo authorities have been reluctant to combat serious crime, apparently, owing to the fact that, according to various reports, many leading figures in the country have been themselves involved in organized crime groups (see inter alia Sudetic 2015; McAllester 2011; Marty 2010, p. 14).

Another area where EULEX-inspired rule of law reforms have had limited impact is in North Kosovo, where Serbs have opposed any attempt to shore up Kosovo's institutions, maintaining their own parallel rule of law structures. The Kosovo Police has been operational in the region, but it has not secured the trust of the local population, even though most of its officers were Serbs (International Crisis Group 2011, p. 16). In the justice sector, Kosovo judges and prosecutors have not been allowed to work in North Kosovo; and thereby, they have been replaced by EULEX judges who, however, have pragmatically focused on criminal cases, neglecting civil suits. Lastly, EULEX and Kosovo Customs could monitor the traffic, but not collect duties in the two checkpoints in North Kosovo.

In this context, it has been the EU-facilitated dialogue between Belgrade and Pristina (having as milestone the "Brussels agreement" of April 2013) that has provided the ground for some timid progress toward the establishment of Kosovo rule of law institutions in the region. In particular, EULEX has provided technical support for the integration until mid-2015 of 288 police officers, 105 civil protection officers, and 26 customs officers of Serb ethnicity into the corresponding rule of law structures of Kosovo (Joint Rule of Law Coordination Board 2014, p. 23, 2015, pp. 15, 29; European Commission 2015b, p. 29). Moreover, with the assistance of EULEX, the Kosovo Police has established in North Kosovo a Quick Response Team, a Crowd and Riot Control unit, and a special multiethnic unit for the protection of religious and cultural heritage sites (EULEX 2015, pp. 1–2; Joint Rule of Law Coordination Board 2015, pp. 14, 29). EULEX has also assisted the Kosovo Customs to introduce full controls and collect levies in the northern borders with Serbia and it has facilitated the implementation of the freedom of movement agreement between Kosovo and Serbia (EULEX 2015, p. 2; Joint Rule of Law Coordination Board 2014, p. 27, 2015, p. 29). Finally, in the justice sector, the Kosovo institutions have integrated 65 Kosovo Serb judges and prosecutors (International Commission of Jurists 2016, p. 12).

Nevertheless, the Kosovo Serbs have not abolished their parallel structures and crucial aspects of the operation in North Kosovo of the country's rule of law institutions have not been ironed out (Schwartz 2016; International Commission of Jurists 2016, pp. 19–22). In addition, fear and insecurity among people living on both sides of the divide has not diminished (ECMI Kosovo 2015, p. 2). More worryingly, the dysfunction (not to say absence) of rule of law institutions in North Kosovo has all these years contributed to the emergence of an environment of general impunity and lawlessness, with serious crime taking gigantic proportions much alike in the rest of Kosovo (Prelec and Rashiti 2015, p. 6). Therefore, even though the improvement of interethnic relations in Kosovo is beyond EULEX's mandate, we can safely conclude that the mission's work has had limited results in the country. Having analyzed the track record of EULEX in Kosovo, the next section turns to EUPM and its work for the improvement of rule of law in BiH.

EUPM in BiH

Mandate

Upon a formal request by the authorities of BiH, the EU launched EUPM on 1 January 2003 and, after four renewals of mandate, drew it to a close on 30 June 2012. EUPM replaced the UN-mandated International Police

Task Force (IPTF) which, having stepped in BiH, in late December 1995, did its share on the ground in securing post-conflict stability, law enforcement, and compliance with the Dayton Peace accords (Aitchison 2007, pp. 328, 331–334).

EUPM was initially intended to operate until the end of 2005. Starting out from premise that "the future of BiH lying in integration into the European structures," it was assigned to address "the whole range of Rule of Law aspects, including institution building programs and police activities," with a view to contributing "to the overall peace implementation [...] as well as to the achievement of the EU's overall policy in the region" (Council of the European Union 2002a, p. 16). This mandate was rather general than precise and focused. The EUPM strategic goals were set to provide high-quality advisory and inspection services; assist local police authorities to revamp institutional structures and streamline operational processes; and "monitor the exercise of appropriate political control over the police" (Council of the European Union 2002b, p. 5). EUPM was essentially directed to strengthen professionalism, efficiency, and accountability of the BiH police, and make the local authorities able to uphold the rule of law, fight corruption and organized crime, and safeguard public order (Council of the European Union 2002b, p. 5). In truth, EUPM aimed to help stabilizing BiH by supervising the reform of a critical constituent of its rule of law sector that is, policing arrangements.

In addition to its wide scope of mandate, however, the problem was that EUPM was not entrusted with "executive powers" or the authority to deploy "an armed component" (Council of the European Union 2002b, p. 5). The practice, as aptly pointed out, resulted in a considerable "confusion regarding what was supposed to be the role of EUPM on the ground and an outstanding tendency to conceive police operations in an executive way" (Juncos 2007, p. 53). This was exacerbated by the "diversity of the legal and operational traditions and structures governing policing within the EU," which posed serious hurdles in the efforts of EUPM to standardize law enforcement process and institutionalize common policing practices and norms (Flessenkemper 2013a, p. 28). What is more, in December 2004 the start of EUFOR *Althea*, the EU's military mission in BiH, complicated the division of tasks; as, on the one hand, EUPM had no right to push through compliance measures and, on the other, EUFOR *Althea* was also commanded to counter illegal and criminal activities. This led to a perplexing duplication of roles with regard to the political oversight of the fight against organized crime, which affected negatively the coordination of the civilian and military actions at the operational level (Kirchner 2013, p. 41; Dari et al. 2012, p. 36, 48; Gross 2012, p. 3; Juncos 2007, pp. 58–59).

In 2005, EUPM's presence in BiH was extended up to the end of 2007 "in full complementarity with other components of the EU's engagement" in the country (Council of the European Union 2005a, p. 9, 2005b, pp. 55, 58). This time the mandate, while standing firm on its wide scope, was better framed. One critical aspect was that it was upgraded to the effect that the EU credited EUPM with a "unified chain of command as a crisis management operation"; thereby giving the power to the mission to "take the lead" in concerting the policing and law-enforcement actions of EU bodies against organized crime (Council of the European Union 2005b, pp. 56–57). The result was that though still lacking executive competencies, EUPM was wholly empowered to authorize EUFOR *Althea* to go to the assistance of BiH agencies (Ioannides 2013, p. 58). The other crucial aspect was that EUPM was specifically refocused on, first, setting up a professional police service in which all three ethnic communities would be represented; and, second, supporting local authorities in organized crime investigations (Council of the European Union 2005b, pp. 55–56).

In 2007, the mandate of EUPM was once again renewed until end-December 2009. In the context of the same wide scope and strategic goals as in the two previous mandates, EUPM was additionally tasked with helping the BiH agencies run more efficiently their criminal justice system and improve their police prosecution capabilities (Council of the European Union 2007, pp. 40–41, 44). Afterward, in 2009, the mission's engagement in the country was agreed to continue for an additional 2-year period. Yet, holding firm to the same tasks as previously and, in particular, to police reform and police accountability enhancement, the fourth mandate was slightly modified to center its attention more closely on assisting the "BiH relevant law enforcement agencies in the fight against organized crime and corruption" (Council of the European Union 2009, pp. 22, 25). Following a positive assessment review of its work, in late 2011 the EU decided to direct for fifth time EUPM to get through a 6-month phase of exit and wrap-up the mission in mid-2012 (European Union External Action 2012, p. 2).

In principle, encapsulating a widely held view, the command of EUPM was to conduct MMA activities (Kammel 2015, 107; Garcia-Perez and Glume, 2015, pp. 162–163). The lexicon of the EUPM mandates persistently exemplified a broad policy perspective. In terms of textual discourse,

EUPM was directed to carry out "crisis management" operations within a "broader rule of law approach" (Council of the European Union 2002b, p. 2, 2005b, pp. 55, 57, 2007, pp. 40, 42, 2009, pp. 22, 24). But in practice, during its lifespan, EUPM appeared to have gradually adapted its ways of acting from generally helping reform the policing constituent of the rule of law sector to specifically helping re-establish police institutions, develop managerial capacities, and fight organized crime and corruption. That EUPM's mandate was extended four consecutive times might be taken as a measure of success in one respect; in that, however fragile, the progress was each time achieved toward police reform needed to further consolidate and carry on. Indeed, the more the enhancement of the policing capacity in BiH appeared to take shape and substance, the more the mission demonstrated that it had been able to accomplish the task; and, therefore, the more it was assigned to keep contributing to building local capabilities to improve police provision and tackle serious crime.

Resources

As EUPM was the first ever EU cross-border civilian operation, its preparation took almost a year. In this time span, a planning team was deployed for 8 months on the spot to concert the transfer of the command from IPTF and prepare the ground for the inception of the mission (Matthiessen 2013, pp. 16–17). After EUPM was deployed, it was sustained by sufficient financing. Over the entire period of its operation, the mission's budget was set to amount to €110 million. To this sum allocated by the EU budget should be added the funds that were provided by the contributing countries to bear all seconded personnel-related costs (Flessenkemper and Helly 2013, p. 81). On the whole, EUPM evolved into an "adequately financed" operation (Flessenkemper 2013b, p. 65).

However, EUPM met serious human resources constraints. To begin with, the planning team – consisting of 17 police officers, six civilian experts, and five local people – lacked qualified and experienced people in finance and procurement management and capacity building with good knowledge of the local situation (Council of the European Union 2003, pp. 9–10). During the first stages of deployment in the field, EUPM was fortunate enough to recruit seconded personnel who had served in the IPTF and had acquired much-needed skills and experience (Flessenkemper 2013b, p. 59; Juncos 2007, pp. 52–53). By then, the mission had staff strength in between 750 and 900 people of whom less than two-thirds were police officers seconded by the contributing states (Flessenkemper and Helly 2013, p. 82; European Union External Action 2012, p. 2). Over the years, all in all, EUPM employed a workforce of some 2300 persons of whom 1786 were police officers, 154 were civilians with diverse educational background and expertise, and 487 local practitioners (EU Press Release 2012, p. 2).

Paradoxically, the quality of the EUPM personnel started deteriorating once mission mandate became more specific, coincided as it was with its transformation from a "traditional police peacekeeping operation" to a "rule of law mission" (Flessenkemper 2013a, pp. 30–31, 2013b, pp. 59–60). After the mission modified its focus on law enforcement and criminal justice system restructuring, several rule of law professionals were hired (Dari et al. 2012, p. 36). But as competent and experienced experts were required to provide consultancy in areas related to the investigation of organized crime and corruption and the operation of penitentiary institutions, recruitment procedures became more demanding. This development inevitably complicated force generation, which was further affected negatively by the practice of contributing states to reserve skillful senior functionaries for their home services. This also gave birth to a phased shortage of qualified specialists (Flessenkemper 2013b, pp. 60–61, 64–65; Dari et al. 2012, p. 36; Juncos 2007, pp. 55–56, 72). It is no coincidence that during the mid and last stages of deployment, EUPM was staffed with seconded and contracted advisors whose number ranged between 430 and 75 (Flessenkemper and Helly 2013, p. 82; European Union External Action 2012, p. 2).

From this angle, that the majority of EUPM personnel were seconded by the contributing states was a constraining fact in point. One important dimension is that recruiting and deploying experts from the government sector of various countries is a complex challenge hardly easy to get through (Antolovic-Tovornik 2015, pp. 241–242; Rehrl 2014, p. 71). Not rarely did strained relations occur between the EUPM qualified staff members because of the fact that they had similar job skills and experience but differing national origin and ensuing policing standards, norms, and rules of engagement. Another key dimension is that it is the EU's greatest countries, which are most likely to determine, in accordance with their national interests and "on a case by case basis," whether the EU can initiate a CSDP mission and if they can commit skillful personnel to it (Asseburg and Kempin 2011, p. 182; Malešič 2011, pp. 169–171). Yet, another critical dimension was that EUPM had been provided with insufficient human resources to fight organized crime until the third renewal of its mandate because EU member states believed that this "hands-off approach" was the most effective way to force the BiH authorities to become more responsible and build local ownership competencies (Tolksdorf 2014, pp. 61–62).

In principle, the operational capabilities reserved for a CSDP civilian mission should be matched to the mandate it is ordered to pursue. In practice, EUPM, on the one hand, was supplied with adequate financing facilities to support the restructuring of the BiH police institutions. Personnel capabilities, on the other, have been quite limited; in the sense that little emphasis was placed on employing civilian specialists with knowledge and experience in building local capacities, leveraging the fight against organized crime, and managing politics at all levels of mission engagement. Like in other CSDP civilian missions, the EUPM international officers were probably appropriate for police activities, but they lacked the political awareness and flexibility to advise and instruct government bodies at all levels (central state, entity, local) to reconstruct obsolete policing arrangements and establish the rule of law. This explains in part why, in general, the EU has started placing much emphasis on the recruitment and training of the CSDP's civilian staff throughout the phase of planning (Antolovic-Tovornik 2015, pp. 242–243); and, in particular, the EUPM efforts to deal with organized forms of criminal activities met fierce resistance among the BiH policy-makers and functionaries, especially at the entity and local levels, who extensively used the police to their partial benefit as an institutional instrument for political manipulation, economic appropriation, and even ethnic cleansing during the civil war (Berenskoetter 2008, pp. 186–194). Scarcely surprising, for instance, in 2010 only two of 215 charges of money laundering were not ultimately filed by the relevant police offices (Berenschot 2013, p. 49).

To come full circle, the strengthening of BiH police and its functioning performance were closely interrelated to the specific capabilities committed by EUPM. What is more, the latter's resources were provided in the name of a police operation that gradually evolved into a rule of law mission. But the decisive aspect that should not be overlooked is that EUPM's rule of law experts had no executive mandate and, thereby, had no explicit jurisdiction over the BiH authorities. This meant that EUPM was not vested with the power to ensure law enforcement, let alone mobilize its assigned capabilities on its own for the consolidation of the rule of law.

Results

It was not before, as already discussed, EUPM's mandate was renewed for first time, and it was entrusted, in addition to assisting local authorities in reforming police services, with the power to coordinate initiatives of all EU agencies engaged in BiH against organized crime and corruption that results started looking promising and encouraging. Indeed, as the mission's efforts to synchronize activities intensified in parallel to recurring extensions of its enhanced presence in the country, so the situation on the ground showed increasing signs of improvement, and so EUPM proved all the more capable of taking on tasks.

EUPM, for instance, made good progress in strengthening the capacities of relevant BiH authorities to harmonize regulations of organization and functioning between police services at the state and local levels, pass legislation relating to recruitment, career advancement and disciplinary issues, and inspect and enforce their implementation even though this compliance was dependent on whether it encroached on political interference and local interests (Fréjabue 2013, pp. 39–41). Also, EUPM delivered some satisfactory results in reinforcing police accountability, training senior officers, and establishing or rebuilding domestic security- and border-related institutions at the state level, among others the Ministry of Security, the State Investigation and Protection Agency (SIPA), and the State Border Service (SBS) (Tolksdorf 2014, pp. 64–66; Moore 2014, pp. 288–290; Juncos 2007, pp. 62–63). But despite the steps forward, today the BiH police bodies are reported to be transparent and carrying out their work well and independently, mostly unless public figures in the high echelons of the country's political, economic, and social life are implicated in cases of organized crime and corruption (Kovačević and Visca 2015).

In addition, EUPM was instrumental in underpinning attempts at harmonizing BiH's policing mentalities, procedures, management, and practices with best European standards and norms (Merlingen 2009, pp. 162, 169). Indeed, local police agencies were aided to streamline administrative processes, improve coordination and chain of command, and enhance operational efficiency. But while the institution building of police services appeared to have largely been successful at the entity and local levels, the restructuring and centralization of police institutions at the central state level failed to secure substantial advances. BiH's police system remained fragmented, with weak central state-level bodies and structures that were unable to combat organized crime, deal with corruption, and uphold the rule of law (Tolksdorf 2014, pp. 65–68; Flessenkemper 2013a, pp. 30–33; Fréjabue 2013, p. 42; Kirchner 2013, p. 45; Gross 2012, p. 3). This could be argued to result in part from the fact that the EUPM staff avoided both getting engaged with local stakeholders and facilitating local and junior police officers to take ownership not only of the reform design and implementation efforts but also of a variety of inspection and enforcement activities (Moore 2014, pp. 296–300). However, to be fair, the failure of the centralization of police institutions (a reform that was fervently advanced by Paddy Ashdown, the UN High Representative in BiH although it, admittedly, lay beyond the limits of the *acquis communautaire*) should not be attributed to EUPM predominantly (Tzifakis 2012, p. 137). Rather, it should be related to its politicization as a symbol of external "authoritative state-building" within the framework of a policy that has firmly placed the protection of each ethnic community's rights and interests ahead of governance efficiency (Hayden 2005, pp. 253–254; Knaus and Cox 2005, pp. 48–49).

Not accidentally, EUPM ended its operations shortly after it faced the denial of the BiH authorities at the entity level to adopt a law that would eliminate political interference in police work (Bassuener and Weber 2013, p. 4). This development, nonetheless, by no means cancels out the fact that EUPM made headway in transferring legal consultancy, technological knowledge, and capacity-building experience which enabled state functionaries and local-level police forces to lay the foundations for rule of law structures (Penksa 2013, pp. 69–71; Bećirević and Ćehajić 2013, p. 49). After all, EUPM played its part in enabling the BiH leadership to complete the Stabilization and Association Agreement in early 2008, even though the latter eventually entered into force in June 2015. In addition, at the time that EUPM was closed down, such constituent parts of the rule of law sector as the judicial system and the fight against organized crime and corruption had been "at an early stage" of reform having achieved limited progress. And three years later, they are reported to have reached "some level of preparation" (European Commission 2013a, pp. 12–15, 2014, pp. 12–16, 2015a, pp. 12–20).

Streamlining commands in BiH's police services, as well as enhancing their professionalism, transparency, and accountability, is still reported to be a key policy issue that needs further, urgent reform (Marijan and Guzina 2014, pp. 2–3, 8). Yet, the transformation of the police and criminal justice system was an enormous challenge that lied outside the mandate and competence of EUPM (Penksa 2013, p. 70; Kirchner 2013, p. 45). This required a more comprehensive action on the part of the EU who did not realize that resetting up the police in an ethnically split society was a highly sensitive and complex issue (Gross 2012, p. 3). Likewise, the fight against organized crime and corruption was such a great problem that exceeded EUPM's "problem-solving capacity" (Merlingen 2009, p. 162).

If anything, as mentioned before, EUPM was a police mission assigned to MMA. It was directed to assist and support, not to act and run law-enforcement operations on its own. It was not executively mandated to restructure BiH's police system and root out criminal and corruptive networks. Neither was it authorized, nor provided the expertise, to take the lead in enlisting the support of the BiH elites and people to the cause. The gist of the matter is that this was undeniably beyond its mission horizons, whether it was the crux of the problem or not. Still, one cannot ignore the fact that EUPM was not depicted by its creators, and contributing states as an operation aimed at taking full ownership of state building and ruling in BiH. In this respect, taking the slow pace of reforms as a measure of lack of progress toward mandate implementation would do little justice to a thorough assessment of the mission's contribution. Despite deficiencies and shortfalls, EUPM did its share in improving policing services and the rule of law in BiH.

In *Lieu* of Conclusions

This chapter examined the effort of the EU to improve the rule of law in Kosovo and BiH through the deployment of CSDP civilian missions. The presentation in parallel of the features and the work of EUPM and EULEX allows us to reach some comparative conclusions.

With respect to their mandate, both missions were directed to MMA the corresponding local authorities in order to improve the professionalism and efficiency of those countries' rule of law institutions. The latter were expected to become emancipated from political interference and grow capabilities to preserve public order and fight organized crime and corruption in their respective countries. Nevertheless, beyond sharing a very general set of common objectives, those missions' mandates featured important differences as well. In particular, unlike EULEX, EUPM was initially designated to narrowly focus on reforming the police rather than all rule of law institutions in BiH. Still, contrary to EULEX (whose very deployment was controversial), the mandate of EUPM has been subsequently adjusted to changing conditions on the ground and, thus, the CSDP mission in BiH has over time assumed tasks that were not related to policing such as assisting the reform of the criminal justice system. Another important difference is that, in sharp contrast to EUPM, EULEX has been also vested with certain executive powers to initiate, where necessary, action on its own. Specifically, EULEX police has intervened to restore order and make arrests; EULEX prosecutors have conducted hundreds of crime investigations; EULEX judges have adjudicated thousands of cases in court; and EULEX custom officers have collected duties on the borders with Serbia.

In terms of material resources, both CSDP missions have benefited from generous and adequate financing as well as the supply of all necessary equipment and logistical support to carry out their work. However, the personnel of both missions has been deficient in experienced and highly qualified experts who could mentor the local authorities on institutional reforms aiming at the increase of operational capacity and efficiency. As earlier illustrated, whereas EULEX never reached full strength with a large number of vacancies being disproportionally evident in the justice sector, the transition of EUPM from a predominantly police to a fully fledged rule of law mission was not followed by a substantial increase in the number of its civilian officers. Moreover, both missions have at times suffered from a lack of coherence with different national contingents and individual officers applying dissimilar norms and practices in their work. But in terms of overall resources, EUPM appeared to have been much smaller and less ambitious. A striking measure of this difference, as already demonstrated, is the fact that EUPM's allocated budget and active staff accounted for about one-ninth and one-third of EULEX's so far, respectively.

The track record of EUPM and EULEX has also featured similar accomplishments and failures. In principle, both missions have successfully transferred much-needed expertise and technical assistance to local authorities in BiH and Kosovo to strengthen the rule of law. In particular, the police forces in both countries have adopted new administrative and operational procedures, methods of work, and best practices in line with European standards. Indeed, both polices have become more efficient in the management of routine day-to-day operations (e.g., petty crimes and instances of small-scale disorder). Moreover, the CSDP missions have assisted local authorities in BiH and Kosovo to establish new rule of law institutions (e.g., for the fight against serious crime and the management of borders) and draft essential pieces of legislation.

Nevertheless, on a more negative note, the ability of the Bosnian and Kosovar institutions to deal with serious crimes has not been substantially improved. As it was elaborated, in both countries, newly established and reformed rule of law institutions have not efficiently coordinated their work. In addition, adopted laws have not been consistently implemented. To illustrate, while both countries reformed their recruitment and career advancement procedures, they have not ceased following nontransparent promotion procedures in disregard of the newly established professional and education criteria (Avdiu and Perteshi 2015, p. 15; Kovačević and Visca 2015, p. 13). In addition, the political authorities in both countries have not been eager to take the necessary steps to fight organized crime and corruption. Likewise, the progress for the adoption of reforms that touched upon issues of ethnic discord in these two countries such as the police restructuring in BiH and the institution building in North Kosovo has been very poor. Indeed, what these failures demonstrate is that the success of MMA activities depends heavily on the consent of the local authorities to EU-prescribed reforms. And, whereas both CSDP missions have been bestowed with international legitimacy, they have neglected to build their downward legitimacy in BiH and Kosovo, in the sense of seeking for the consent and/or support of local stakeholders to their policies (Yabanci 2016, p. 350). In this context, if the local authorities have not been willing to change their countries, EUPM and EULEX could do little more than expected that the EU would mount external pressure on the former through the coordination of its instruments and the introduction of policies of conditionality. Therefore, the EU civilian missions neither can be held responsible for the interest of local leaderships in meddling in the operation of rule of law institutions. Nor can the CSDP missions be criticized for the lack of commitment of the local authorities to the fight against serious crime. And, certainly, it has been beyond the scope of those missions' mandate to resolve the ethnic disputes that have impeded the centralization of BiH police structures and the establishment of rule of law institutions in North Kosovo.

To conclude, all other things being equal, the more the work of the two missions has been technical and did not impinge upon the interests of local authorities, the greater have been the chances that it would be successful. Alternatively, the greater the coordination of EU means and instruments in these two countries (e.g.. the linkage of the EU-facilitated

Belgrade–Pristina dialogue with the policy of enlargement and the work of EULEX), the larger have been the possibilities that CSDP objectives would be advanced on the ground.

Acknowledgments The authors would like to acknowledge that research for this chapter was conducted with the support of a grant (Pelopas) provided by the Research Committee of the University of the Peloponnese. The authors would also like to thank the book editors for their comments and suggestions.

Bibliography

Aitchison, A. (2007). Police reform in Bosnia and Herzegovina: state, democracy and international assistance. *Policing and Society, 17*(4), 321–343.

Antolovic-Tovornik, N. (2015). Civilian capability development. In: J. Rehrl & G. Glume (Eds.), *Handbook on CSDP missions and operations. The Common Security and Defence Policy of the European Union.* (pp. 241–243). Vienna: Directorate for Security Policy of the Federal Ministry of Defence and Sports of the Republic of Austria.

Asseburg, M., & Kempin, R. (2011). ESDP in practice: crisis management without strategic planning. *Journal of International Peacekeeping, 15*(1–2), 178–199.

Assembly of the Republic of Kosovo. (2014a, April 23). *On amending and supplementing the laws related to the mandate of the European Union rule of law mission in the Republic of Kosovo.* Law No. 04/L-273.

Assembly of the Republic of Kosovo. (2014b, April 23). *On ratification of the international agreement between the Republic of Kosovo and the European Union on the European Union Rule of law mission in Kosovo.* Law No. 04/L-274.

Avdiu, P., & Perteshi, S. (2015). *Assessment of police integrity in Kosovo.* Belgrade and Pristina: Belgrade Centre for Security Policy & Kosovar Centre for Security Studies.

Bassuener, K., & Weber, B. (2013). *House of cards: the EU's "reinforced presence" in Bosnia and Herzegovina. Proposal for a new policy approach* (DPC Policy Paper). Sarajevo & Berlin: Democratization Policy Council.

Bećirević, E., & Ćehajić, M. (2013). Politics, policing and security sector reform in post-war Bosnia and Herzegovina. In: T. Flessenkemper & D. Helly (Eds.), *Ten years after: lessons from the EUPM in Bosnia and Herzegovina 2002–2012* (Joint Report, pp. 43–50). Paris: European Union Institute for Security Studies.

Berenschot. (2013, February). *Thematic evaluation of rule of law, judicial reform and fight against corruption and organised crime in the Western Balkans-Lot 3,* Final Main Report, Service Contract Ref. No 2010/256638.

Berenskoetter, F. (2008). Under construction: ESDP and the "fight against organized crime". *Journal of Intervention and Statebuilding, 2*(2), 175–200.

Capussela, A. (2011, April, 9). Eulex in Kosovo: a shining symbol of incompetence. *The Guardian*. http://www.guardian.co.uk/commentisfree/2011/apr/09/eulex-kosovo-eu-mission. Accessed 20 November 2015.

Council of the European Union. (2002a, February 18–19). *Council general affairs (2409th meeting, 18/19 February 2002)*.C/02/30, 6247/02 (Presse 30). Brussels.

Council of the European Union. (2002b, March 13). *Council joint action 2002/210/CFSP (11 March 2002)*, Official Journal of the European Communities, L 70/1.

Council of the European Union. (2003, July 14). *Lessons from the planning of the EU police mission in Bosnia and Herzegovina (EUPM), Autumn 2001–December 2002*.11206/03 LIMITE CIVCOM 94 PESC 412 COSDP 408 RELEX 275 JAI 206 PROCIV 84 EUPM 3. Brussels.

Council of the European Union. (2005a, July 18). *Council general affairs (2674th meeting, 18 July 2005)*.C/05/177, 10813/05 (Presse 177). Brussels.

Council of the European Union. (2005b, November 25). *Council joint action 2005/824/CFSP (24 November 2005)*. Official Journal of the European Union, L 307/55.

Council of the European Union (2007, November 21) *Council joint action 2007/749/CFSP (19 November 2007)*. Official Journal of the European Union, L 303/40.

Council of the European Union. (2008, February 16). *Council joint action 2008/124/CFSP of 4 February 2008 on the European Union rule of law mission in Kosovo, EULEX Kosovo*. Official Journal of the European Union EN, L42.

Council of the European Union (2009, December 9) *Council decision 2009/906/CFSP (8 December 2009)*. Official Journal of the European Union, L 322/22.

Council of the European Union. (2010, June 11). *Council decision 2010/322/CFSP of 8 June 2010 amending and extending joint action 2008/124/CFSP on the European Union rule of law mission in Kosovo, EULEX Kosovo*. Official Journal of the European Union EN, L145.

Council of the European Union. (2012, June 6). *Council decision 2012/291/CFSP of 5 June 2012 amending and extending joint action 2008/124/CFSP on the European Union rule of law mission in Kosovo, EULEX Kosovo*. Official Journal of the European Union EN, L146.

Council of the European Union. (2014a, June 13). *Council decision 2014/349/CFSP of 12 June 2014 amending joint action 2008/124/CFSP on the European Union rule of law mission in Kosovo, EULEX Kosovo*. Official Journal of the European Union EN, L174.

Council of the European Union. (2014b, September 30). *Council decision 2014/685/CFSP of 29 September 2014 amending joint action 2008/124/CFSP on the*

European Union rule of law mission in Kosovo, EULEX Kosovo. Official Journal of the European Union EN, L284.

Council of the European Union. (2015, June 12). *Council decision (CFSP) 2015/901 of 11 June 2015 amending joint action 2008/124/CFSP on the European Union rule of law mission in Kosovo (EULEX Kosovo)*. Official Journal of the European Union EN, L147.

Dari, E., Price, M., Van Der Wal, J., Gottwald, M., Koenig, N. (2012, April). *CSDP missions and operations: lessons learned processes* (Policy Department, PE457.062). Brussels: Directorate-General for External Policies of the Union.

Džihić, V., & Kramer, H. (2009). *Kosovo after independence: is the EU's EULEX mission delivering on its promises?* Berlin: Friedrich-Ebert-Stiftung, International Policy Analysis.

ECMI Kosovo. (2015, April 21). *Incidents and tensions in Mitrovica: The need for unbiased reporting and the strengthening of the rule of law*. Pristina: European Centre for Minority Issues Kosovo, Information Bulletin.

EU Press Release. (2012, June 30). EU completes its police mission in Bosnia and Herzegovina. Brussels: EN, Press. http://www.consilium.europa.eu/uedocs/cms_data/docs/pressdata/EN/foraff/131440.pdf. Accessed 20 August 2013.

EULEX. (2011). EULEX programme report 2011: bolstering the rule of law in Kosovo. A stock take. http://www.eulex-kosovo.eu/docs/tracking/EULEX%20ProgrammeReport%202011.pdf. Accessed 8 July 2012.

EULEX. (2015). Implementation of rule of law. http://www.eulex-kosovo.eu/eul/repository/docs/missionaccomplishments_2.pdf. Accessed 13 December 2015.

European Commission. (2013a, October 16). *Bosnia and Herzegovina 2013 progress report*. SWD(2013) 415 Final. Brussels.

European Commission. (2013b, October 16). *Kosovo 2013 progress report*. SWD (2013) 416 Final. Brussels.

European Commission. (2014, October 8). *Bosnia and Herzegovina 2014 progress report*. SWD(2014) 305 Final. Brussels.

European Commission. (2015a, November 10). *Bosnia and Herzegovina 2015 report*. SWD(2015) 214 Final. Brussels.

European Commission. (2015b, November 10). *Kosovo 2015 report*. SWD(2015) 215 final, Brussels.

European Court of Auditors. (2012, October 16). *European Union assistance to Kosovo related to the rule of law*. Special Report No 18/2012.

European Union External Action. (2012, June). *Common security and defence policy. European Union police mission in Bosnia and Herzegovina* (Press). http://consilium.europa.eu/uedocs/cms_data/docs/missionPress/files/EUPM%20fact sheet%20EN%20latest%20FINAL.pdf. Accessed 20 August 2013.

Fakiolas, E., & Tzifakis, N. (2008). Transformation or accession? Reflecting on the EU's strategy towards the Western Balkans. *European Foreign Affairs Review, 13*(3), 377–398.

Flessenkemper, T. (2013a). Support to the fight against organised crime and corruption: between standards, structural reform and pragmatism. In: T. Flessenkemper & D. Helly (Eds.), *Ten years after: lessons from the EUPM in Bosnia and Herzegovina 2002–2012* (Joint Report, pp. 27–33). Paris: European Union Institute for Security Studies.

Flessenkemper, T. (2013b). Lessons from staffing and equipping EUPM. Learning by doing? In: T. Flessenkemper & D. Helly (Eds.), *Ten years after: lessons from the EUPM in Bosnia and Herzegovina 2002–2012* (Joint Report, pp. 58–65). Paris: European Union Institute for Security Studies.

Flessenkemper, T., & Helly, D. (Eds.) (2013). *Ten years after: lessons from the EUPM in Bosnia and Herzegovina 2002–2012* (Joint Report). Paris: European Union Institute for Security Studies.

Fréjabue, E. (2013). Lessons from EUPM: a legal approach. In: T. Flessenkemper & D. Helly (Eds.), *Ten years after: lessons from the EUPM in Bosnia and Herzegovina 2002–2012* (Joint Report, pp. 34–43). Paris: European Union Institute for Security Studies.

Garcia-Perez, M., & Glume, G. (2015). Scope of missions and operations. Civilian CSDP missions. In: J. Rehrl & G. Glume (Eds.), *Handbook on CSDP missions and operations. The common security and defence policy of the European Union* (pp. 162–168). Vienna: Directorate for Security Policy of the Federal Ministry of Defence and Sports of the Republic of Austria.

Gazetta Express. (2015, November 4). O'Connell: The corrupted are going unpunished. *Gazetta Express.* http://www.gazetaexpress.com/en/news/oconnell-the-corrupted-are-going-unpunished-142224/. Accessed 25 February 2016.

Gross, E. (2012). *The end of the EU police mission in Bosnia and Herzegovina: what lessons for the common security and defence policy?* (EPC Policy Brief, 13 June), Brussels: European Policy Centre.

Hayden, R. M. (2005). "Democracy" without a Demos? The Bosnian constitutional experiment and the international construction of nonfunctioning states. *East European Politics and Societies, 19*(2), 567–594.

House of Lords. (2013, April 25). *Unrevised transcript of evidence taken before the select committee on the European Union Sub-Committee C (external affairs) inquiry on EULEX KOSOVO.* Evidence Session 2.

International Commission of Jurists. (2016, February 24). *Uncharted transition: the "integration" of the justice system in Kosovo – a briefing paper.* Geneva. http://icj.wpengine.netdna-cdn.com/wp-content/uploads/2016/02/Kosovo-Integration-of-the-justice-system-Publications-2016-ENG.pdf. Accessed 19 March 2016.

International Crisis Group. (2011, March 14). *North Kosovo: dual sovereignty in practice*. Europe Report 211.

Ioannides, I. (2013). EU peace support operations in the Western Balkans since 2003. In: E. Prifti (Ed.), *The European future of the Western Balkans. Thessaloniki@10 (2003–2013)*. (pp. 55–62). Paris: European Union Institute for Security Studies.

Jacqué, J. P. (2015, March 31). *Review of the EULEX Kosovo mission's implementation of the mandate with a particular focus on the handling of the recent allegations*. Report to the attention of High Representative/Vice President of the European Commission, Ms Federica Mogherini.

Joint Rule of Law Coordination Board. (2013, September). *Compact progress report*.

Joint Rule of Law Coordination Board. (2014, June). *Compact progress report*.

Joint Rule of Law Coordination Board. (2015, September). *Compact progress report: assessing progress between July 2014–July 2015*.

Juncos, E. A. (2007). Police mission in Bosnia and Herzegovina. In: M. Emerson & E. Gross (Eds.), *Evaluating the EU's crisis missions in the Balkans* (pp. 46–80). Brussels: Centre for European Policy Studies.

Kammel, A. (2015). From EUPM Bosnia to EUMAM RCA. Snapshot of ongoing and past CSDP missions and operations. In: J. Rehrl & G. Glume (Eds.), *Handbook on CSDP missions and operations. The common security and defence policy of the European Union*. (pp. 106–111). Vienna: Directorate for Security Policy of the Federal Ministry of Defence and Sports of the Republic of Austria.

KIPRED. (2013, January). *A comprehensive analysis of EULEX: what next?* Policy Paper 1/13.

Kirchner, E. (2013). Common security and defence Policy peace operations in the Western Balkans: impact and lessons learned. *European Security, 22*(1), 36–54.

Knaus, G., & Cox, M. (2005). The "Helsinki Moment" in Southeastern Europe. *Journal of Democracy, 16*(1), 39–53.

Kovačević, A., & Visca, H. (2015). *Assessment of police integrity in Bosnia and Herzegovina*. Belgrade & Sarajevo: Belgrade Centre for Security Policy & Centre for Security Studies.

Malešič, M. (2011). Civilian crisis management in the EU-structural and functional aspects. *Journal of International Peacekeeping, 15*(1–2), 152–177.

Marijan, B., & Guzina, D. (2014, June). The politics of the "unfinished business': Bosnian police reform (Cigi Policy Brief, 42). https://www.cigionline.org/sites/default/files/cigi_pb_42.pdf. Accessed 18 November 2015.

Marty, D. (2010, December 12). *Inhuman treatment of people and illicit trafficking in human organs in Kosovo*. Strasbourg: Council of Europe,

Parliamentary Assembly, Committee on Legal Affairs and Human Rights, AS/Jur (2010)46.

Matthiessen, M. (2013). The institutional genesis of the EUPM. In: T. Flessenkemper & D. Helly (Eds.), *Ten years after: lessons from the EUPM in Bosnia and Herzegovina 2002–2012* (Joint Report, pp. 13–19). Paris: European Union Institute for Security Studies.

McAllester, M. (2011, March 27). Kosovo's Mafia: how the US and allies ignore allegations of organized crime at the highest levels of a new democracy. *Global Post*. http://www.globalpost.com/dispatch/news/regions/europe/110321/kosovo-hashim-thaci-organized-crime. Accessed 8 March 2016.

Merlingen, M. (2009). EUPM (Bosnia and Herzegovina). In: G. Grevi, D. Helly, D. Keohane (Eds.), *European security and defence policy: the first ten years (1999–2009)* (pp. 161–171). Paris: The European Union Institute for Security Studies.

Moore, A. (2014). CSDP police missions: comparing bottom-up and top-down approaches. *European Foreign Affairs Review, 19*(2), 283–306.

Musliu, V., & Geci, S. (2014). Deconstructing and defining EULEX. *Central European Journal of International & Security Studies, 8*(1), 66–80.

Opitz, A. (2014). Rule of law. In: J. Rehrl (Ed.), *Handbook for decision makers. The common security and defence policy of the European Union* (pp. 151–153). Vienna: Directorate for Security Policy of the Federal Ministry of Defence and Sports of the Republic of Austria.

Papadimitriou, P., & Petrov, P. (2012). Whose rule, whose law? Contested statehood, external leverage and the European Union's rule of law mission in Kosovo. *Journal of Common Market Studies, 50*(5), 746–763.

Penksa, S.-E. (2013). Measuring impact: specific achievements and outcomes. In: T. Flessenkemper & D. Helly (Eds.), *Ten years after: lessons from the EUPM in Bosnia and Herzegovina 2002–2012* (Joint Report, pp. 66–72). Paris: European Union Institute for Security Studies.

Petrovic, M. (2013). *The democratic transition of post-communist Europe. In the shadow of communist differences and uneven Europeanisation*. Basingstoke, Hampshire: Palgrave Macmillan.

Prelec, M., & Rashiti, N. (2015, March 19). *Serb integration in Kosovo: after the Brussels agreement*. Balkans Policy Research Group.

Radin, A. (2014). Analysis of current events: "towards the rule of law in Kosovo: EULEX should go". *Nationalities Papers, 42*(2), 181–194.

Rehrl, J. (2014). Training and recruitment. In: J. Rehrl (Ed.), *Handbook for decision makers. The common security and defence policy of the European Union* (p. 71). Vienna: Directorate for Security Policy of the Federal Ministry of Defence and Sports of the Republic of Austria.

Richter, S. (2009, December). Promoting rule of law without state-building: can EULEX square the circle in Kosovo? In: M. Asseburg & R. Kempin, (Eds.),

The EU as a strategic actor in the realm of security and defense? A systematic assessment of ESDP missions and operations (pp. 30–45). Berlin: Stiftung Wissenschaft und Politik, Research Paper 14.

Rozée, S. (2015). Order-maintenance in Kosovo: the EU as an increasingly comprehensive police actor? *European Foreign Affairs Review, 20*(1), 97–114.

Schwartz, S. (2016, March 7). Brussels sparks political showdown in Kosovo. *The Weekly Standard.* http://www.weeklystandard.com/brussels-sparks-political-showdown-in-kosovo/article/2001446. Accessed 17 March 2016.

Solana, J. (2013). The closure of EUPM: back to the future. In: T. Flessenkemper & D. Helly (Eds.), *Ten years after: lessons from the EUPM in Bosnia and Herzegovina 2002–2012* (Joint Report, pp. 3–5). Paris: European Union Institute for Security Studies.

Sudetic, C. (2015, July 21). The bullies who run Kosovo. *Politico.* http://www.politico.eu/article/kosovo-hashim-thaci-un-special-court-tribunal-organ-trafficking-kla-serbia-milosevic-serbia-ramush/. Accessed 18 August 2015.

Tolksdorf, D. (2014). Incoherent peacebuilding: the European Union's support for the police sector in Bosnia and Herzegovina, 2002–8. *International Peacekeeping, 21*(1), 56–73.

Tzifakis, N. (2012). Bosnia's slow Europeanisation. *Perspectives on European Politics and Society, 13*(2), 131–148.

Tzifakis, N. (2013). The European Union in Kosovo reflecting on the credibility and efficiency deficit. *Problems of Post-Communism, 60*(1), 43–54.

United Nations Security Council. (2008, June 12). *Report of the secretary-general on the United Nations interim administration mission in Kosovo.* S/2008/354.

Weber, B. (2015, November). *Progress undone? Trading democracy for solving the status dispute in Kosovo.* Berlin: Democratization Policy Council, DPC Policy Paper.

Weber, B., & West, L. (2014, April). *EULEX – Towards an integrated exit strategy: strengthening the rule of law through EU-integration.* Pristina and Berlin: Group for Legal and Political Studies (GLPS) and Democratization Policy Council (DPC), Policy Report 05/14.

Winkelhofer, R. (2015). Human rights and rule of law. In: J. Rehrl & G. Glume (Eds.), *Handbook on CSDP missions and operations. The common security and defence policy of the European Union* (pp. 116–119). Vienna: Directorate for Security Policy of the Federal Ministry of Defence and Sports of the Republic of Austria.

Yabanci, B. (2016). The (Il)legitimacy of EU state building: local support and contention in Kosovo. *Southeast European and Black Sea Studies, 16*(3), 345–373.

Efstathios T. Fakiolas (PhD, Department of War Studies, King's College London) is Assistant Professor in the Department of Political Science and International Relations at the University of the Peloponnese. Prior to joining the academia, he had been working for 12 years in units of strategic planning and analysis in the Greek banking sector.

Nikolaos Tzifakis is Assistant Professor at the Department of Political Science and International Relations of the University of the Peloponnese. His research interests are in IR theory, EU external policies and Balkan politics. His recent publications include articles in *Cambridge Review of International Affairs*, *Global Society* and *Problems of Post-Communism.*

Chapter 8: Old Paradigms of Ethnicity and Post-Soviet Transition in the Baltic States

Šarunas Liekis

In contrast to the majority of the post-Soviet states, which have over the years sunk into (mainly consolidated) authoritarian regimes, the Baltic countries of Estonia, Latvia and Lithuania are nowadays considered consolidated democracies by many experts and specialized organizations (such as Freedom House or the Global Ranking Association). They have also been members of the European Union (EU) since 2004. To achieve this, the Baltic countries had to undergo both de-Sovietization and Europeanization together with the painful process of political and economic transition from totalitarian societies and centrally planned economies to democracies and modern market economies. Although the process of post-communist political and economic transformation only had a limited impact on minority policies and interethnic relations in the three Baltic countries, these have been the focus of constant criticism coming from the (less democratized) Russian Federation; they have also received considerable international attention on these matters.

Š. Liekis (✉)
Political Science and Diplomacy Faculty, Vytautas Magnus University, Kaunas, Lithuania
e-mail: s.liekis@vdu.lt

Fish, Gill, Petrovic (eds.), *A Quarter Century of Post-Communism Assessed*, DOI 10.1007/978-3-319-43437-7_9

Historically, the fate of the three Baltic countries substantially diverged from the thirteenth century onwards. At that time, only the Lithuanian tribes managed to consolidate their resources and establish their own feudal state. A very different fate befell their northern Latvian and Estonian neighbours, who fell prey to their militarily and technologically advanced neighbours from Scandinavia and the German fiefdoms. The predecessors of the modern nations of Estonia and Latvia were not part of the German ruling class, and most of the ancestors of present-day Lithuanians were not part of the Polish–Lithuanian Commonwealth's (1569–1795) own nobility. On the other hand, the elites of the former Polish–Lithuanian Commonwealth and the German-speaking Livonian elites had nothing in common either. The distance between them was comparable to the distance existing between Russians and French elites in the eighteenth century (Liekis et al. 2008, 2009; Berenis 2008, p. 67; Potašenko 2009, pp. 275–299).

The Livonian Confederation, which included most of the territories that make up present-day Latvia and Estonia, was established in 1435, but it ceased to exist by the end of the sixteenth century. Its northern parts were ceded to Sweden and formed into the Duchy of Estonia, while its southern territories became part of the Grand Duchy of Lithuania – and thus eventually of the Polish–Lithuanian Commonwealth. The Russians took control of all of former Livonia and partitioned the Polish–Lithuanian Commonwealth in the historic partnership with the Habsburg Empire and Prussia of 1795, later marginalizing and pushing Sweden into neutrality. The incorporation of former Livonia into the Russian Empire and the ethnically Lithuanian part of the Grand Duchy of Lithuania did not create a common identity between the peoples and its elites (Kasekamp 2010, pp. 1–251).

Modern Estonian, Latvian and Lithuanian nationhood, which is based on linguistic nationalism, correlates with each state's peasant origins and the eventual emancipation of this estate. Surfacing in the mid-nineteenth century, the new ethno-nationalist ideologies had pro-Russian as well as anti-Western tendencies and overtones from the very beginning. There were many similarities between the Estonian and Latvian ethno-nationalist movements, both of which contained a strong pro-Russian stance. Estonian and Latvian nationhood developed exclusively on the basis of social identity and opposed the dominant culture of the German elites. A kind of Russophilia looked to the Russian authorities and officialdom, yearning to finally be relieved of the oppression and exploitation of the German nobility. The leaders of the Latvian national awakening, Kritjanis Valdemars and Krišjanis Barons, and the first overtly nationalistic Latvian newspaper *Peterburgas Avizes* (the Saint Petersburg Newspaper), which began publication in 1862, openly expressed pro-Russian sentiments. In the case of the Estonians, the same sentiments were expressed by Johan Koler and Carl Robert Jakobson, the editor of *Sakala* from 1878. Anti-serfdom sentiments were strongly mixed with anti-German sentiments, based on the self-government traditions of the land-owning estates and German Baltic regionalism (Švabe 1991, p. 1; Pivoras 2000, p. 152; Kasekamp 2010, pp. 76–83).

The situation in Lithuania was substantially different. Although the population spoke different languages and there was an enormous social distance between the estates, the descendants of the Grand Duchy of Lithuania behaved as one whole and there was no difference in geopolitical orientation between the nobility and the peasants. Later, Lithuanian nationalism, based on its peasant identity, developed in the second part of the nineteenth century. The 1897 Russian census in the territory of present-day Lithuania revealed that 59.5 % of inhabitants ethnically identified themselves as Lithuanian (Eberhardt 1997, p. 56).[1]

By the end of the nineteenth century, the Estonian, Latvian and Lithuanian ethno-nationalist movements paradoxically featured an overall geopolitical and civilizational orientation towards Russia. In opposition, the traditional elites identified themselves to a greater degree with the new Polish or German nations (Laurinavičius et al. 2005, p. 88).

The Lithuanian nationalist movement before the First World War did not avoid geopolitical gravitation towards Russia at the expense of its split with the Polish nationalist movement over social and linguistic issues. All three Baltic peoples finally became engulfed in confrontation with the people and cultures that had lived among them for centuries. The genesis of both the nationalist and socialist ideologies in the Baltics had demonstrated substantial dependency on Russia and witnessed a major role for it, while at the same time these movements were striving for emancipation from the German subculture (for Estonians and Latvians) and the Polish one (for Lithuanians, Laurinavičius et al. 2005, pp. 89–90). The Lithuanian ethnic revival accentuated the political nation at its initial stage, while their northern neighbours placed more focus on the change of social status of ethnic Latvians and Estonians. The first spokespersons of the Lithuanian national movement in the nineteenth century, Simonas Daukantas and Motiejus Valančius, foresaw that the Lithuanian nation and people were not different in terms of estate or social standing, as long as they upheld political values and maintained loyalty to the ethnic values of language and culture (Merkys 2006, pp. 35–40). However, the conservatism of the ruling elites, alienation and positivist tendencies in social surveys led very soon to ethnic categorization, which was reflected in statistics concerning social status. The ethnicities defined by the first census gatherers in the first part of the nineteenth century were usually ethno-social communities. Thus, social researchers and pollsters simply imposed their definitions.

The Baltic States in their present form became a reality after the major powers of Germany and Russia and the Western maritime powers (the United Kingdom, France and the United States) clashed in the region during the First World War. The consolidation of the Baltic ethnicities continued during the interwar years. All the elements of an ethnic confrontation with the minority ethnic groups living among the general population still prevailed. The confrontational nature of the interethnic relationship, combined with the rise of authoritarian regimes in these countries – Lithuania became authoritarian in 1926, and Latvia and Estonia did so in 1934 – did not encourage civic integration or the consolidation of political nations in the Baltic States. However, the negative implications of authoritarian rule were offset somewhat by non-violent forms of oppression, with there being a very small number of deaths among political opponents. For example, some authors have counted 13 attempts to overthrow Antanas Smetona's (1874–1944) regime from the onset of the authoritarian regime in 1926 until the end of 1938. Despite this, a total of only 209 persons were tried, and 11 were executed by firing squad during the period of his dictatorship on politically related charges (Liekis 2010, p. 33).

Obviously – sociologically, culturally and even as civilizations – all three countries have many similarities. The interwar development helped to consolidate nationhood, although all three resorted to dictatorships when faced with civilizational and cultural challenges, which prevented civic consolidation and merely strengthened ethnic divisions, especially in Latvia and Lithuania. After the Soviet occupation in 1940, contrary to expectations, the Baltic countries and their elites internalized their Western civilizationalism. It was subordinated to the Soviet identity and geopolitically tuned against the Western powers.

Regaining independence in 1990 and 1991, the Baltic States, despite being integrated into NATO and the EU, continued to be volatile, relatively small and young states possessing a comparatively low degree of power; they were committed to their role of acting as a geopolitical barrier between the West and East as well as a connecting region for integrating both parts of the continent. However, this is just a superficial assessment. If thoroughly applied, a comparative historical analysis should demonstrate more differences than similarities.

The ethnic minority issue became instrumental in maintaining and assuring independence. The Baltic States were not bound by any substantial international agreement at the initial stage of their fight to become a part of the international community. However, these countries joined international organizations and their impact has been felt to varying degrees. Their ethnic makeup did not turn out to be an asset of diversity but rather a heavy liability, a sign of potential trouble in the future and a weakness at the time of the restitution of their independence.

Another significant aspect which is important for issues related to the Baltic States is the fate of democracy in heterogeneous societies. Ethnic differences in themselves do not diminish self-identification with a political community. Any democratic state may flourish with a very heterogeneous body of citizens. The work of scholars may encourage ethnicity to become the most important means of self-identification. Therefore, one type of ethnicity may be promoted and strengthened by state authorities in long-term policies, while another is seen as destined for eradication (Moreno Morales 2008, pp. 55–84).

The situation in the Baltic States after regaining independence in 1991 is a good example of this kind of self-strengthening identity scheme, which may be activated and made more visible in public discourse in opinion polls or population censuses. For instance, it is apparent that surveys hardly ask respondents to show whether one identifies with "Lithuania", "Estonia" or "Latvia" in a political sense. Hence, there is no possibility of straying beyond the traditional ethnic makeup of the country. One must be an ethnic Estonian, Latvian or Lithuanian in order to identify with the political project of Estonia, Latvia or Lithuania. For others (e.g. an ethnic Pole, Russian or Finn), there is no ideology of self-identification, only a "loyalty" to one's country of citizenship. Multilayered identities, often centred around political identity, are as a rule excluded from data collection surveys in the Baltics. There is no universally valid remedy for multi-ethnic states for avoiding ethnic conflicts.

In times of transition, we are usually concerned with the relationship between ethnicity and a situation possibly becoming prone to conflict. There is a range of factors which influence ethnic conflicts, and we cannot predict when and under what circumstances ethnic conflicts emerge. The only productive strategy is to pursue policies which aim to help prevent ethnic conflicts. The policies of conflict avoidance have made the greatest impact on ethnic animosities and conflicts in the Baltic States, resting on the success of their post-communist transition.

Estonia and Latvia

Identities as well as social reality are constructed using a discursive structure in which cultural memories and history are essential elements. Therefore, it cannot be dismissed as a matter of secondary importance, even if it disregards economic interests or status in international relations. At the same time, even if this aspect is often missing in the larger picture, we should not overemphasize or simplify the importance of socio-economic factors (Ehin and Berg 2009, p. 9).

How are ethnic identities related to radical transformations in the post-Soviet period? Traditionally, transformations in transition have described change in predominantly material terms. For example, political attitudes, social attitudes and perceptions were of secondary importance in these first analyses (Knudsen 1996, p. 186). The transformations radically changed the status of those countries that went from being an integral part of the Soviet Union to independent nation states. As a result, the economic (monetary and fiscal) model of the country changed. The political model's development was altered fundamentally as well. However, it should not be understood that with transformation there is also the birth of values, convictions, opinions or norms never seen before. As extensive research in Lithuania has demonstrated, transformation usually takes place by reshuffling the hierarchy, and in the strength and importance of values. We should not exclude the idea that this usually includes the formation of new institutions (Šaulauskas 2000, p. 17).

There are four types of orientation: a focus on restitution, imitation, continuation and innovation. These became the basis for ideological polarization under post-communist conditions in all three Baltic States. The ideological tensions in the initial stage after regaining independence could be described as a fundamental tension between the restitution mode of transition, represented mainly by the Conservative and Christian Democratic political parties (copying the institutions, values and norms of the interwar republics), and those which were continuity oriented (represented by the former communist groups which enforced the Soviet forms and norms of existence). The later period was marked with a greater impact from political forces (liberals, centre movements and social democrats) clearly following innovative trends (Šaulauskas 2000, p. 27). In other words, the changes in the countries that followed the same patterns as in the years before the loss of independence have been defined as restitution. On the other hand, imitation took place when part of the social reality and norms became things which had never existed before in the country and which might have been copied from elsewhere. The first stage of initial revolutionary change, abundant with restitution, imitation and continuation, changed into evolutionary continuation, imitation and innovation (Šaulauskas 2000, p. 29).

This pattern was followed in all the Baltic countries after 1990, when the new governments had to cope with the de facto postcolonial situation, and during the few decades of annexed existence that had altered the social and ethnic composition of each country's respective population. Their ethnic and social structure had changed enormously as a result of the Soviet occupation. Questioning the legality of these changes became fundamental to relations between the Baltic States and the Russian Federation. Table 8.1 illustrates population changes in the Baltic countries during the years of Soviet rule.

Table 8.1 Ethnic composition of the Baltic States (in thousands)

a) Latvia *Nationality*	*1959*	*1989*	*Difference*
Latvians	1,297.9	1,387.8	+89.9
Russians	556.5	905.5	**+349.0**
Belarusians	61.6	119.7	+58.1
Ukrainians	29.4	92.1	+62.7
Others	148.1	161.5	+13.4
Total	2,093.5	2,666.6	+573.1

Over a period of 30 years, the number of Russian-speaking immigrants increased in Latvia to 41.9 % of the total population.

b) Estonia *Nationality*	*1959*	*1989*	*Difference*
Estonians	892.7	963.3	+70.6
Russians	240.2	474.8	**+234.6**
Ukrainians	15.8	48.2	+32.4
Belarusians	10.9	27.7	+16.8
Others	37.2	51.7	+14.5
Total	1,196.8	1,565.7	+368.9

In 1989, Russians made up 30.3 % of the total population, and with the remainder of the Russian speakers they represented almost half the country's population.

c) Lithuania Nationality	*1959*	*1989*	*Difference*
Lithuanians	2,150.8	2,924.3	+773.5
Russians	231.0	344.5	+113.5
Poles	230.0	258.0	+28.0
Belarusians	30.3	63.2	+32.9
Others	69.3	84.8	+15.5
Total	2,711.4	3,674.8	+963.4

Lithuania was not affected by the general trends experienced in Latvia and Estonia. Its own population growth was characteristic of that seen in pre-urban societies.
Source: Gosudarstviennyj Komitet SSSR po Statistikie (1991); Centralnoje Statisticheskoje Upravlenie (1963); Ligenzowska and Piecuch (2015, pp. 169–171).

The change in the ethnic makeup of the population has been perceived as a political and social problem in Estonia and Latvia. At the same time, ingrained social practices reproduce intersubjective meanings that constitute the meanings of interethnic relations, and reproduce the past patterns of international relations and the rationale for ethnically based interstate relations (Muižnieks 2011, p. 1). This is exacerbated by the continuing memory of political and social conflicts fought in the Baltic–Soviet area (perceived by the Balts as "Russian") from the beginning of Baltic independence in the 1990s and even earlier. However, after the withdrawal of troops of the former Soviet Union, Latvia and Estonia could not refuse international involvement in their minority problems. Ethnic minority issues became related and hostage to Latvia's and Estonia's relations with the Russian Federation. The Soviets had their hands free when it came to ethnically related issues internationally, as these were beyond the reach of the international community and were only very vaguely and indirectly mentioned within the Soviet international commitments. Contemporary, Russian policies and institutions have also managed to stay immune, to a larger extent, to the critiques of international organizations and foreign governments (Pohl 2014; Hoynck 2011, p. 11). This in itself creates a lack of balance in Baltic–Russian relations and gives the Russian side a strategic initiative in bringing forward cases against the Baltic governments. The continued stationing of Russian troops in the Baltic States from 1991 to 1994 left an impact on the ethnic minorities in Estonia and Latvia. The Russian Federation tried to link withdrawal of their troops with guarantees to the Russian-speaking populations (CSCE 1994).

The Russian Federation has raised the question of the status of human rights in Estonia and Latvia in the United Nations (UN) several times.

The first representative offices of the United Nations Development Program (UNDP) were opened in the Baltic States in 1992. The Baltic States delivered their first reports on the status of human rights to the UN Human Rights Committee in 1993–1996 and received positive acceptance. The Organization of Security and Cooperation in Europe (OSCE) Office for Democratic Institutions and Human Rights (ODIHR) and the Council of Europe have also provided assistance to the Baltic countries. Overall, all international organizations conveyed a positive view of the situation in the Baltic States.

The military withdrawal from Latvia in 1994 did not change the tense security agenda and awareness of the Russian Federation's connection to ethnic minority-related problems. Baltic–Russian ethnic minority issues were gradually heating up. Before the final worsening of relations, in the hope of countering the Baltic States' attempts to join NATO, the Russian Federation proposed security guarantees and the Regional Stability Pact in 1997. However, the Latvian government, as did Estonia and Lithuania, rejected the Russians' advances. Soon after, the Baltic governments signed A Charter of Partnership among the United States of America and the Republic of Estonia, Republic of Latvia and Republic of Lithuania on 16 January 1998. Already in the years of 1997–1998, under the right-wing Prime Minister Guntars Krasts, the government resisted pressure from the EU and the OSCE to liberalize its minority policy and the citizenship law in particular. The arguments of the Russian Federation claimed "discrimination against Russian speakers" and lamented the "revival of fascism". Russia's criticism of Latvia's treatment of ethnic minorities has been a steady feature, as has the constant effort to link the situation with other issues. However, Russian efforts were insufficiently substantiated and did not receive greater support in Europe or elsewhere. The signing and ratification of the Framework Convention of the Council of Europe by Estonia (ratified on 6 January 1998), Lithuania (ratified on 23 March 2000) and Latvia (ratified on 6 June 2005) channelled debates on ethnic minorities towards a pan-European and international framework. In conjunction with other convention bodies and non-convention organizations like the European Commission against Racism and Intolerance (ECRI), these efforts pushed bilateral relations with the Russian Federation into the background.

Though other pragmatic, economic and security issues have arisen between the Russian Federation and the Baltic States, the focus remained on both sides with the implicit issues related to ethnic identity and disagreements over the past events. History issues (or more precisely, cultural memory) are important for ethnic identity formation and very much define the nature and patterns of international relations. The cultural memory issues constantly raised by the Russian Federation and its proxies (e.g. Belarus) systematically manufactured an enemy image of the Baltic countries. The most pronounced negative portrayal concerned the treatment of Russian speakers in Latvia and Estonia, the approach to the history of the Soviet Union, and accession to NATO. According to Nils Muižnieks, the situation of Russians and Russian speakers in Latvia is a theme that cuts across all other themes, and features in virtually every other issue (Muižnieks 2008, p. 161). According to Dmitri Trenin and Bobo Lo, the Russian establishment treats Baltic ethnic policies as a pressure point for the EU as well as an issue on which the Russian elite can easily agree (Trenin and Lo 2005, p. 16). The enemy image of the Baltics was a good fit in terms of the Russian Federation's general anti-Western sentiment widely promulgated for internal consumption and internationally. The Baltic countries accession to NATO in 2004 became a matter of concern to Russia and helped blur anti-Western rhetoric with anti-Baltic stereotypes and sentiments. While Russia does portray the Baltic countries as weak, unable to afford NATO and meet the standards of a democratic regime, it does nonetheless see NATO as a threat.

Russian core policy documents linking bilateral relations with the Baltic States do in fact directly or indirectly confirm these observations. The Russian National Security Strategy to 2020 claims: the Russian Federation is willing to interact with Latvia, Lithuania and Estonia in the spirit of good-neighbourliness and on the basis of reciprocal consideration of interests. Of fundamental importance for Russia are the matters relating to the rights of the Russian-language population in accordance with the principles and norms of European and international law. The importance of history is also mentioned in the National Security Strategy, where it is said "Negative influences on the state of national security in the cultural sphere are intensified by attempts to revive perspectives on Russia's history, its role and place in world history" (Ministry of Foreign Affairs of the Russian Federation 2000, 2009). Similar claims, for example, that the Estonian government's decision on Russian-language schooling runs counter to recommendations by international human rights institutions on guaranteeing national minorities the right to preserve and develop their language are promulgated not only in the statements of the Ministry of Foreign Affairs (MFA) of the

Russian Federation, but also in the extensive new media coverage of the situation of Russian speakers in the Baltics.

It is no surprise that the societal attitudes towards perceptions of threats and geopolitical orientations of society diverge among ethnically Latvian or Estonian and non-Estonian or non-Latvian populations. However, the strongest ethnolinguistic divide is on the stance towards Russia. Recent surveys demonstrate that while close to 90 % of Russian speakers have positive views of Russia; the figure for ethnic Latvians is less than 50 %. Russian soft power is greater for Russian speakers who have ethnic, linguistic and historical links to Russia and consume Russian media products (Muižnieks 2011, p. 66). On this occasion, it should be noted that in line with the conclusions of sociologist Aivars Tabuns, we should underline that: “the bottom line is that there are substantial differences between the political identities of the various ethnic groups” (Tabuns 2010) in Latvia. The same applies in Estonia to a lesser degree as well.

Overall, ethnic tensions eased with the departure of the former Soviet military personnel. Many ethnic and social tensions also eased with emigration from the Baltic States, especially after joining the EU in 2004 when not only minorities but also large parts of the main groups left, especially from Latvia and Lithuania. The total population in the Baltic States decreased from 7.9 million in 1990 to just over 7 million in 2007, or by 11 %. The share of the minority population which formed 33 % of the total population in the Baltics in 1989 decreased further by the year 2000 and has continued to do so since (Central Statistics Bureau of the Republic of Latvia 2003).

The transition in both Estonia and Latvia has been dominated by ethnic issues. Very differently from the Lithuanian case where all inhabitants have been given Lithuanian citizenship, the inhabitants of Estonia and Latvia who moved there during the Soviet period were excluded from automatically receiving citizenship rights. They were not allowed to vote in post-independence parliamentary elections. The dividing and formal issue was the question of naturalization. However, naturalization issues also reflected different visions of statehood and debates on the nature of society and its relationship with “the other”. As it happened, the “others” clearly identified with the Russian-speaking community in Estonia and Latvia. Naturalization was only in part related to ethnicity issues that dominated with the changing ethnic structure and analysis of the formation of different social segments within ethnic groups. It has a dimension of social space rather than an issue of quantitative proportions between ethnic groups. Therefore, the stance of the majority of the population, as well as of state institutions, becomes very important. The variety of ethnic backgrounds in schools supports the imperative to separate the language of instruction from the assumption that a certain school belongs to a particular ethnic community merely based on which language is used in the classroom. Preferential treatment of certain population groups, and the ethnicity of the Latvians, Estonians and Lithuanians the state claimed to represent has been deeply ingrained in institutional thinking for nearly two decades since the restoration of independence. Only recently, for example, the Latvian Ministry of Foreign Affairs has started to pursue the principle of open Latvian-ness; the term diaspora includes all Latvian nationals, both citizens and non-citizens, and the descendants of émigrés until the third generation, regardless of ethnicity or native language (Krapane 2016, p. 108). Similar changes started to occur in the rest of the Baltic countries, taking multiculturalism as a European value at the political establishment level. One of the main incentives for taking a new direction in the Baltics was the resurgence of Russian revisionism that had ideological connotations. Ideological confrontation with the Russian Federation, and the Russian authorities support for exclusiveness, isolationism and ethnic nationalism in East Central Europe has strengthened attacks on European values and multiculturalism.

The present-day policy practitioners image of ethnic transformations in the Baltics is reflected in the Polity IV Country Report series (Center for Systemic Peace 2010b). The report claims that in Estonia there is serious disenfranchisement of Russian, Ukrainian and Belarusian residents. In 1991, the Estonian parliament passed a restrictive citizenship law which, in effect, granted citizenship only to those people who were citizens of the interwar republic and their descendants (approximately 60 % of the population). By the end of the decade, less than 1 million residents (out of 1.3 million) were citizens, resulting in the political disenfranchisement of almost one-third of the population. The report also provided statistics. More than 25 % of Estonia's people are ethnically Russian and speak Russian. As of 2006, 35 % of Russian speakers hold Estonian citizenship, 30 % hold Russian citizenship and 35 % are "undefined". Residents without citizenship may not vote in elections for either national or EU parliaments but are eligible to vote in local elections. Given these electoral requirements, in 2007, 16.3 % of the total population was disenfranchised in national and EU elections. This disenfranchisement, along with allegations of persistent job, salary and housing discrimination, continued to fuel ethnic Russian resentment in Estonia. Since then, despite substantial changes in the legislation and introduction of better suited practices of integration, according to an Amnesty 2015 report, approximately 6.8 % of Estonia's population are still not citizens of the country (Tambur 2015).

As in the Estonian case, Polity IV claims that an obstacle to fully competitive elections in Latvia is the remaining persistence of discriminatory practices against Russian residents of this former Soviet republic. New legislation passed in 2006 specifies that candidates for citizenship who fail a Latvian language test three times would be denied legal national citizenship status. People without citizenship are neither entitled to vote, nor to obtain an EU passport. Government data from 2007 indicates that 56.5 % of the 650,000 ethnic Russians living in Latvia now have Latvian citizenship (Center for Systemic Peace 2010a). Over 18 % of the population of Latvia continues to be non-citizens. Despite this ethnic cleavage, since Latvia joined the EU and NATO in 2004, concern over the threat posed by Russian-speaking residents has begun to wane. The population overall started to benefit from EU and NATO membership, which also had a profound impact on how threats were perceived.

The report claims that Latvia is undergoing a relatively peaceful transition to institutionalized competitive participation. The tension between Latvians and ethnic Russians, while less severe than in the early years of independence, continues to be a source of political division. Since regaining its independence in the early 1990s, language and citizenship laws tailored to preserve the disappearing Latvian national identity have been the cornerstone of post-Soviet Latvian politics. The report claims that Latvian citizenship and language laws are in accordance with the European Union's standards. Nonetheless, many Russian speakers continue to claim that they face significant political discrimination (Center for Systemic Peace 2010a).

Difficulties in acquiring citizenship made some of the Russian-speaking aliens take up Russian citizenship. Sustainable development in all the Baltic countries has made it a much more predictable option for its inhabitants than the Russian Federation. The number of "non-citizens" in both Latvia and Estonia has dropped sharply over the past two decades (from 715,000 in 1991 to 290,000 in 2011 in Latvia, and from 340,000 in 1991 to 94,000 in 2011 in Estonia) (Kramer 2012, p. 3). However, at present the requirements to acquire citizenship are not extraordinarily tough in the European context. According to the citizenship act, non-citizens have to reside in the country for 8 years and demonstrate knowledge of the language (Estonian Parliament 1995).

The changes took place because of EU integration and the human rights monitoring mechanisms in place, and were also due to direct pressure from international organizations and governments. The 1997–1998 crisis in Latvia, which endangered its accession to the EU, revealed that the country was in danger of becoming a "binational society". Extensive research revealed significant differences between the attitudes and values of Latvians and national minorities, and citizens and non-citizens. As a consequence, the National Programme for the Integration of Society was established (Rozenvalds 2010, p. 52). A few years later, the Social Integration Policy Guidelines 2008–2018 were prepared by the Latvian Integration Secretariat. This new document stressed the importance of a democratic, inclusive civil society in social integration processes, as well as multiculturalism. Despite positive developments, it remains to be seen if the policy guidelines will remain the basis for harmonizing interethnic relations and further sustainable development in society (Rozenvalds 2010, p. 59). However, in the final analysis, the need for democratic legitimization with adequate communication helped to change the scope of the problem in practical terms, and received the support of nearly 80 % of the population in Latvia, increasing pressure concerning integration in both countries (Tabuns 2010, p. 257). According to the data, in August 1989 less than 10 % of the Russian-speaking population supported the independence of Estonia; by March 1991 this had grown to 30 % of ethnic Estonians and 38 % of the Russian-speaking population living there. The results of research conducted by Vihalemm and Lauristin demonstrate that within less than a year the share of supporters of Estonian independence increased from 30 to 72 %, that is, almost 2.5 times (Simonyan 2013, p. 170). Research from Latvia indicates that the voter participation differences between ethnic Latvians and non-Latvians are negligible. When it comes to other forms of political participation, the differences are much more obvious. Ethnic Latvians have been more hesitant to sign petitions, demand the dismissal of the government or participate in consultative bodies or civil society organizations (Kehris Brandis 2010, pp. 115–118).

Unnoticed Transformation of Lithuania

Lithuania has no mention of ethnicity-related issues at all in the Polity IV country reports. No wonder that in 2004, Eleonora Mitrofanova, the First Deputy Minister of Foreign Affairs, noticed:

> The situation of the Russian-speaking populations in the three Baltic States differs. Lithuania, as you know, in 1991 automatically granted citizenship to

> all its permanent residents; it has signed and ratified the Council of Europe's Framework Convention for the Protection of National Minorities, and consistently relies on its provisions in its legislation and nationalities policy. The example of Lithuania once more confirms the correctness of our thesis of the unacceptability of references to historical circumstances for justifying discrimination against large groups of non-titular population, as is the case in Latvia and Estonia (Ministry of Foreign Affairs of the Russian Federation 2004).

Lithuania was a showcase of a civilized and Russian-approved solution to the minority issue introduced on their soil by the Soviet occupation of the Baltic States from 1940 to 1991. As we have discussed, there are many differences between the Lithuanian case on the one hand, and the Estonian and Latvian cases on the other. This attitude has been deeply ingrained in popular and scholarly publications. However, nobody has pointed out or noticed that these policies underwent substantial changes and became similar in terms of content to the situation in the rest of the Baltic nations. As in the Estonian and Latvian cases, the immediate post-Soviet Lithuanian concept of the "other" was equally about breaking down the traditionally existing linguistic-cultural and confessional pluralism. The history of the Grand Duchy of Lithuania, especially its parts inhabited by people speaking Lithuanian dialects, was very different from the ideological vision of contemporary nationalism that saw ethnolinguistic borders overlapping with political borders. The aim of the Lithuanian national movement founded at the end of the nineteenth century was to establish a national state where people speaking Lithuanian would become the majority and be supported, promoted and protected from "others" by the future state. The vision was idealistic but detached from reality, with the hope of turning it into political practice in the future. This was not an easy dream to realize.

During the years of the interwar Lithuanian Republic (1918–1940), there was a conviction that ethnolinguistic minorities would object to the establishment of a Lithuanian state for Lithuanian speakers. Mistrust and suspicion towards ethnolinguistic minorities was often combined with a paternalistic attitude towards them and became one of the main obsessions of the Lithuanian state's administration. The state tried all kinds of measures to ensure loyalty which all served specific purposes, for example, subsidies for minority organizations, direct administrative and police control, censorship and a policy of assimilation.

The Soviet transformations from 1940 onwards did not change identity policies much in Lithuania. They promoted and enforced the lay-folk forms of identity and the myth of linguistic exclusiveness. Moreover, they further elaborated on the themes of Lithuanian identity, going beyond the Christian and European traditions, which were always under pressure from Christendom. The Lithuanians as the last pagans resisting Europeans in the times of the Crusaders and the negative social and historical stereotypes against Poland were beloved topics of Soviet Lithuanian officialdom. Lithuania under the Soviets was a small micro-cosmos of the Soviet Union. It was a ground of competition for the cultures of the Lithuanian and Russian peoples, which competed for attraction among the other minority pupils.

On the other hand, it was almost impossible for a pluralist identity to find its place in the sun. All the inhabitants of Lithuania were framed into one or another kind of identity. The only alternative to the traditional ethnicity was the Soviet type of socio-economic identity, which denied the importance of local language, culture and ethnicity. The Russian culture was often identified with this kind of "homo sovieticus", because this ambiguity was the safest strategy in the world of essentialist Soviet policies, which defined ethnicity as monistic and inherited. In practice, it meant the objectivization of ethnicity, very often mutually denying identity, a ban on professions, and discrimination not only of minorities but of the majorities as well (Kobeckaitė 1989). Only with the collapse of the Soviet Union and the restoration of Lithuanian independence did multiculturalism and universalism start to receive wider acknowledgement.

However, the pedigree of statehood in Lithuanian ethno-nationalism made Westernization and gravitation into a postmodern type of political nationhood difficult during the post-communist transition. The regaining of statehood in 1990 was closely related to the *Sąjūdis* movement, based on restitution of the pre-war statehood and ethno-nationalism. Naturally, ethnic minorities became a focus of attention immediately because of historical, political, legal and psychological reasons stemming from a paternalistic Lithuanian attitude deeply ingrained in the cultural memory. On the other hand, minority organizations (which suddenly found themselves as Georgians, Russians, Poles, etc.) tried to find a consensus with representatives and organizations of the ethnic majority in Lithuania and to understand its relationship with the future sovereignty of Lithuania (Kobeckaitė 1989).

Articulation of ethnic interests and self-organization took place in parallel with the process of legalizing the presence of minorities in the political framework of the country. It took some effort on the part of the new authorities in the Lithuanian Republic in 1990–1993 to resist the temptation of establishing national autonomy for minorities. This turn of events would have meant turning Lithuania into a partner of the corporate minorities, as in the initial years of the interwar independence (Laurinavičius and Sirutavičius 2008, p. 128; Liekis 2003). Despite the failure of ethnic minority federalization, the minorities had to be integrated through the preservation of ethnic and organizational–institutional separateness. This kind of integration, preserving separate ethnic institutions, appeared first in the *Sąjūdis* Popular Front and later in the new Lithuanian state structure.[2] An association uniting all ethnic organizations had been established already in 1988. It became the only association which aimed to re-establish the traditional culture and appreciate the ethnic identities of their members. The decree by the Supreme Soviet of the Lithuanian Soviet Socialist Republic over Temporary Order for Registration of Citizen Voluntary Organizations issued on 17 February 1989, helped to promote self-expression and development of civil society and a larger number of organizations.

However, all of the official rhetoric of the time was full of anthropomorphisms when discussing nation, national identity and ethnicity. The Lithuanian nation (ethnicity), as it was understood in pre-independent Lithuania, became a substitute for the non-existing independent statehood and the hegemonic figure in the country. At the same time, very rarely did anybody remember the role of state institutions or even the sociological makeup of society. A radical step in the opposite direction was the Law on Citizenship of 23 November 1989, which entitled all inhabitants of Lithuania to citizenship and equal rights. The first Minorities Law of Lithuania was passed on 23–24 November 1989. The discussions that hindered rapid acceptance of the law were about the willingness of the local Polish politicians to have national territorial autonomy, and the debates about the necessity to offer university education in minority languages. On 18 November 1988, the Supreme Soviet of the Lithuanian Soviet Socialist Republic introduced an article proclaiming the Lithuanian language as the state language, with an option to use minority languages in the territories of their compact inhabitance.

According to Vladas Sirutavičius (2008), one of the researchers of the period, Lithuanian ethnic minorities representatives met the law with hesitation. For example, the Polish minority representatives were not concerned that Lithuanian was proclaimed the state language, but that regulations on using the Polish language in the eastern part of the country where there was a high percentage of a Polish speaking population were introduced. The first contacts between Lithuanian politicians and representatives of the Polish Union of Lithuania took place on 30 June 1989. These were discussions which at the initial stage did not contribute much to mutual understanding. Nevertheless, it did point to a very different understanding of the nature of the new state. On what basis did it plan to regain independence? For Lithuanian politicians, it sounded natural that the new state would be ethno-national, a state for Lithuanians, but not that ethno-nationalism would constitute a political principle of the democratic state. In other words, only Lithuanian ethno-nationals could restore Lithuanian independence and the core of the new Lithuanian nation would be made up of ethnic Lithuanians. In a sense, ethnic Lithuanians became the new owners and subjects of the new state and they had to establish their relationship with their ethnic minorities.

Integration of the multicultural ethnic heritage became conceptually problematic. The problem of how ethnically diverse cultures should become part of Lithuania's culture was an underlying current during the whole period. Plus, there were serious tensions between two contradictory principles: giving priority to an ethnic group, or being democratic towards the entire majority and minorities in all aspects of politics. Despite the difficulties in being convinced about the democratic intentions of Lithuanians, Polish politicians finally found themselves in a position that was not so different to all the other minorities. The attempts to acquire special status for the Polish minority did not succeed. In the later years after regaining independence, politicians were also selective in promoting a certain ethnic identity. This was very much reminiscent of the interwar and Soviet Lithuanian-type of Lithuanian ethnic identity, based on folk culture and lacking the continuity of the historical dimension entrenched in the culture of the elites in the Polish–Lithuanian Commonwealth. Naturally, attempts to promote identity based on narratives of exclusivity should be defined as counterproductive.

Integration is not a separate method to deal with ethnic relations, but rather the state of affairs between different ethnic groups. Acculturation is more appropriate in describing the ethnic policies which result in integration. Because integration and acculturation are intermediate stages before assimilation, in real terms both might be interpreted as an attempt to introduce assimilationist policies. The policies of the Lithuanian state can be described through government programmes. The first elements for the implementation of ethnic policies were introduced in the programme of the III Lithuanian Government (13 January 1991–21 July 1992). It has a chapter about migration policies by establishing an institution which was to take care of migration processes. Apart from the focus on regulating the flow of people leaving the country, for the first time the historical-cultural tradition and a willingness to act in the former historical boundaries of Lithuania was mentioned. There was a plan to implement a programme for fostering the culture of Lithuania Minor. There were also intentions for another programme for fostering the culture of south-eastern Lithuania, which had to be based on the continuity of the traditions of the Grand Duchy of Lithuania as a polycultural state.

However, in the final analysis, during this period observers witnessed active cultivation and fetishization of ethnic identity. Moreover, the state's attention to ethnicity issues was also related to helping compatriots in learning the Lithuanian language and, generally, culture was seen as the sphere which might help build historical continuity. Prioritizing Lithuanian language and support for its study abroad automatically meant prioritization and exclusive support for only one of Lithuania's ethnic cultures.

The first attempt in 2003 to produce a draft ethnic policy of the Lithuanian Republic, based on positive interculturalism, drew criticism from traditionally oriented opponents. They were against multi-ethnicity in the country. According to them, minorities had at best to be ascribed the status of a traditionally understood national minority in return for having limited civic participation, which implied marginality in society. The drafters of the concept well understood that uneven and ethnically charged policies did not have the potential to level different interpretations of history, values and points of view between the ethnic majority and minorities in the state. Moreover, the previous policies of ethnicization did not strengthen a sense of belonging to the Lithuanian state, and might have been interpreted as hindering the formation of social contacts and dialogue (Potašenko 2009, pp. 280–283).

These tendencies prioritizing Lithuanian ethnic nationalism continued unabated until November 2006, when the Lithuanian Constitutional Court issued a decree confirming the Concept of the Lithuanian Civic

Nation. The decision forced change in as many as 23 articles of the Law on Citizenship of 2002 (Constitutional Court of the Republic of Lithuania 2006). The decision turned against ethno-nationalist nationalism. Later, attempts in the political domain to undermine the decision of the Constitutional Court through legislation and everyday public practices did not make an impact on the legal interpretation. A different turn of events continued in the public policy formation process. Any attempts to construct positive multiculturalism or interculturalism drew criticism from the followers of an ethno-nationalist interpretation of Lithuanian identity.

Many observers might be able to claim that "categorical nationalism" united everyone, and that rejection of the Soviet system, which was heavily identified with Russification, prevailed (Venclova 1994, p. 17). Actually, the factor of perceiving the Soviet order as threatening Lithuanian identity was of crucial importance for the national movement in capitalizing on the advantages offered by Gorbachev's Perestroika. However, let us keep in mind the patterns and circumstances of change where there was not a single ethnic conflict and only an instrumental, festive and short-lived anti-Russian argument in place. According to Šaulauskas, it well suited the eclectic nature of the development.

Thus, the reality was more complex. The elites understood that civic (political) nationalism is more favourable to multiculturalism and recognition of societal diversity. However, the tensions still existing in the political field and ideological manifestations between two visions – the ethno-nationalist and civic nationalism – contribute to political mobilization of ethnic minorities, their radicalism and social distance.

Neither of these visions are effective in light of the inconsistency facing the political mobilization of minorities. All this is even more exaggerated with the absence of modern consultative politics at the governmental level. However, the tendencies at least from 2003 were very visible in the legal field and were fruitful in the formation of the political nation.

Lithuania moved much further away in changes with civic self-identification, catching up with the population's predominantly ethnic world view. Research by Nadezhda Lebedeva from 1996 revealed that already a few years after regaining independence in 1991, identifying oneself as a citizen of one's respective country was the most frequent among Lithuanians (23.5 %) and significantly less so among Estonians. A certain parity between two types of self-identification (ethnic and civic) is noticeable only between Lithuanians. Among the Estonians, ethnic identity clearly dominates, followed by civic and European options (Lebedeva

2004, p. 52). The lesser emphasis on ethnicity in Lithuania in terms of self-identification is matched by the close social distance to Russians (Lebedeva 2004, p. 62). Genealogical heritage manipulation and balancing economic and political interests are seen as the most successful prescriptions that governments can apply under certain circumstances (Statkus 2003, p. 278). The Lithuanian government employed these policies to a certain degree, in respect to its Polish minority.

Among other things, this tendency to identify with civic nationalism contributed enormously to Polish–Lithuanian rapprochement and political partnership until 2008. Lithuanian ethno-nationalist identity has been constructed on selective negation of its intimate relationship and its roots in the Polish–Lithuanian Commonwealth, and to a certain degree in the Polish language (Mačiulis 2005).

Ever since the 1990s, the Polish minority has been viewed horizontally as constituting a challenge to Lithuanian statehood and as an offspring of the former Polish cultural dominance in the Lithuanian territories. The shift in Lithuanian policies in 2000 was a good example of how ethnic politics in the country could help to encourage international cooperation and closer collaboration. The new Polish–Lithuanian narrative of closeness helped to legitimize the policy of Polish–Lithuanian cooperation. Also, the identity narrative helped mobilize the political public. Moreover, it helped to build and maintain alliances, encouraged (re)constructing identity claims in international relations and encouraged formation, projection and reception of a Lithuanian strategic and civilizational narrative for foreign policy purposes.

The surveys demonstrated that 24 % of Lithuanians felt a relationship of identity with Poles, while around 20–30 % of Lithuanian Poles did not mind being called Lithuanians. The Lithuanian and Polish identities, as in premodern times though having a different content, at times supplement one another (Leončikas 2007, p. 89). The politicization of minority issues became possible after a worsening of Polish–Lithuanian relations in 2008, following the election victory of the Civil Platform in Poland and the Conservative Party in Lithuania. Many issues of real and of secondary importance and sometimes of symbolic value (e.g. the writing of Polish names in the original language, with Polish diacritical letters) started to be exaggerated and politicized on both sides in the period 2008–2016. The Lithuanian Conservative Party, joining with the Lithuanian Nationalist Party that represented the ethno-nationalist worldview, also exaggerated in a bad sense the Lithuanian stance towards the

Polish–Lithuanian rapprochement. The victory of the social democrats in the 2013 elections in Lithuania did not change bilateral relations much from the perspective of minority politics. It might have indicated also the failure of deeper integration, limiting its success only to legal phraseology. Especially, since scholars from the Lithuanian Social Research Institute have noticed the negative trend of Lithuanian Russians sliding into the social exclusion zone. Russians demonstrated that they felt more discriminated against than others, and were mostly negative in self-evaluation of their social status and opportunities for social mobility, which was a substantial change from the pro-integrationist attitude of Russians in the 1990s (Leončikas 2007, p. 128). This might have certain correlations with the feelings and segregationist strategies of the Polish ethnic political elites in Lithuania from 2008, which also saw electoral cooperation with Russian ethnic political movements in Lithuania in the national and municipal elections in 2013.

An ethnicity-centred analysis and geopolitical narrative of a civilizational stand against Russia with increasing consolidation, linguistic assimilation and an amalgamation of ethnic markers is not the only topic of interest to researchers. Other areas of interest include social divisions and the formation of the "winning" and the "losing" sectors of society with, for example, modernists opposing traditionalists, liberals opposing nationalists and pro-Europeans opposing Eurosceptics. (Švarplys 2013, p. 278).

The power balance with the neighbours and their influence on their co-ethnics in Lithuania seemed to have greater influence on the actions of the state than other considerations. The vertical relationship with the Russian ethnic minority based on cultural memory constructs underwent changes with Vladimir Putin's rise to power in 1999, when Lithuania's perception of Russia changed enormously, especially after the annexation of Crimea from Ukraine in 2014. The vague identification of local Russians with present-day Russia started to be seen as being related to the agenda of the Russian Federation.

Within the framework of the worsening international situation, with the Russian Federation playing an increasingly more assertive role since 2014, the present-day situation in Lithuania is almost playing into the hands of Russian propaganda and its strategic anti-European narrative to the same extent. The Russian Federation's propaganda war has been based on the premise that the policies of the Baltic States and East Central European countries seek to subvert the status of Russian speakers in the post-Soviet area. Recent Russian propaganda efforts resorted to instigating the separatism of Russians and Poles using social media. Thus, such an instigation of separatism in the Baltic States has to be placed in the context of the entire post-Soviet space.

Conclusions

As suggested above, since the collapse of the Soviet Union in 1990–1992, several developments in the Baltics have taken place. The first was the resurgence of old essentialist concepts of ethnicity in the Baltic countries and changes in ethnic relations. Ethnic policies were manifested in several forms – at the symbolic level, in politics, in stereotypes and in the increased activities of ethnic groups during the initial stage of articulation of ethnic "interests" by radical nationalist organizations. Conflict prevention and stability formed the backbone of policies in the Baltic States, effectively diverting attention away from integration policies.

Since the Baltic States accession to the EU and NATO and even earlier, Russia exerted considerable effort to discredit the policies of the Baltic States internationally and at home. Interethnic relations are also affected by the international situation – this was clearly evident immediately after independence and in further development dynamics after accession to the EU, when rates of naturalization increased in Estonia and Latvia.

The historical record demonstrates that the interplay of the international situation with ethnic policies must be supplemented by a nuanced understanding of the historical and cultural context in each of the countries. The histories of these countries, combined with contemporary mistrust of ethnic minorities and the inability to engage in sustained dialogue do make a difference. Minority policies in the Baltic States were a compromise formed largely as the result of international pressure and home-grown tendencies. The Lithuanian example demonstrates that less intense demands from the international community and less direct pressure from Russia did not ultimately create a favourable climate for the integration of minorities into this small country.

Although the Baltic countries started off in the 1990s with different policies towards ethnic minorities, having the Russian "factor" as the locus of their fears and policies during the 25 years of independence brought them closer. The policies enacted abandoned extremes and pursued the common denominator of ensuring the legal equality of minority rights in Estonia, Latvia and Lithuania.

Notes

1. In 1897 in the territory of the present-day Lithuania, 58.3 % of people spoke different Lithuanian dialects, 13.3 % were Yiddish speakers, 10.3 % were Polish speakers, the other 14.6 % spoke other Slavic languages. Very differently from the opinion of the contemporary Lithuanian population, among Polish speakers, peasants constituted 40.9 % of this ethnic group, the gentry 30.2 % and city dwellers 26.4 % (Aleksandravičius and Kulakauskas 1996, pp. 232–233).
2. People of different ethnic backgrounds started cooperating in the name of Lithuanian statehood from various organizations: Tatjana Michniova, Natalija Kasatkina, Medardas Čobutas, Česlovas Okinčicas, Eusėjus Jacovskis, Halina Kobeckaitė and others.

Bibliography

Aleksandravičius, E., & Kulakauskas, A. (1996). *Carų valdžioje –XIX amžiaus Lietuvoje* (p. 359). Vilnius: Baltos lankos.

Berenis, V. (2008). LDK istorinis paveldas ir nacionalinio tapatumo problema. In: A. Andrijauskas & V. Rubavičius (Eds.), *Nacionalinio tapatumo tęstinumas ir savikūra eurointegracijos sąlygomis* (pp. 60–75). Vilnius: Kronta.

Center for Systemic Peace. (2010a). Latvia. http://www.systemicpeace.org/polity/Latvia2010.pdf. Accessed 25 December 2015.

Center for Systemic Peace. (2010b). Estonia. http://www.systemicpeace.org/polity/Estonia2010.pdf. Accessed 25 December 2015.

Centralnoje Statisticheskoje Upravlenie. (1963). *Itogi vsesojuznoj perepisi nasielienija 1959 g.* Moskva.

Central Statistics Bureau of the Republic of Latvia. (2003). http://www.csb.gov.lv/en. Accessed 25 December 2015.

Coakley, J. (2009). Comparing ethnic conflicts: common patterns, shared challenges. *Nationalism and Ethnic Politics, 15*(3/4), 261–271.

Constitutional Court of the Republic of Lithuania. (2006). Lietuvos Respublikos Konstitucinio Teismo nutarimas Dėl teisės aktų, reguliuojančių Lietuvos Respublikos pilietybės santykius, nuostatų atitikties Lietuvos Respublikos Konstitucijai, 2006 m. lapkričio 13 d., Byla Nr. 45/03-36/04.

CSCE. (1994). CSCE mission to Latvia, activity report, No. 9 (1994, October 3), pp. 1–4 and No. 10 (1994, October 27), pp. 1–7.

Eberhardt, P. (1997). *Przemiany narodowosciowe na Litwie* (p. 307). Warsaw: Przegląd Wschodni.

Ehin, P., & Berg, E. (2009). Incompatible identities? Baltic–Russian relations and the EU as an arena for identity conflict. In E. Berg & P. Ehin (Eds.), *Identity and foreign policy Baltic-Russian relations and European integration*. Surrey: Ashgate.

Estonian Parliament. (1995). Citizenship act passed 19 January 1995. http://legaltext.ee/text/en/x40001K6.htm. Accessed 2 January 2016.

Gosudarstviennyj Komitet SSSR po Statistikie (1991). *Nacjonalyj sostav nasielienija SSSR. Po danym vsesojuznoj perepisi nasielienija 1989 g.* Moskva.

Hoynck, W. (2011). Elements for success of the OSCE Mission in Latvia. unpublished presentation made at the conference "OSCE and Latvia: past, present and future". In N. Muižnieks (Ed.), *Latvian–Russian relations: Dynamics since Latvia's accession to the EU and NATO.* Riga: University of Latvia Press (Riga, Latvia on 20 March 2002).

Kasekamp, A. (2010). *A history of the Baltic States.* Houndmills: Palgrave Macmillan.

Kehris Brandis, I. (2010). Citizenship, participation and representation. In: N. Muižnieks (Ed.), *How integrated is Latvian society? An audit of achievements, failures and challenges* (pp. 93–123). Riga: University of Latvia Press.

Knudsen, K. (1996). Lithuania in a period of transition. Forkskningsstiftelsenfafo, Fafo Report.

Kobeckaitė, H. (1989, December 9). Chairman of the minorities committee at the LSSR Ministers Council speech at the 11th Lithuanian Supreme Council session, Galvė.

Kramer, M. (2012). *The Baltic countries after two decades of independence. Achievements, setbacks, internal challenges.* PONARS Eurasia Policy Memo No. 200, pp. 1–88.

Krapane, A. (2016). Latvia's cooperation with diaspora in 2015. In: A. Sprūds & I. Bruģe (Eds.), *Latvian foreign and security policy yearbook 2016.* Riga: Latvian Institute of International Affairs.

Kuklys, M., & Carstocea, R. (2015). *Instigations of separatism in the Baltic states.* Flensburg: ECMI, ISSUE BRIEF No. 35.

Laponce, J. (2008). Research on ethnies and nations: comparing is the way, but comparing what? *Nationalism and Ethnic Politics, 14*(2), 223–238.

Laurinavičius, Č., Motieka, E., Statkus N. (2005). *Baltijos valstybių geopolitikos bruožai XX amžius* (p. LII). Vilnius: Lietuvos istorijos instituto leidykla.

Laurinavičius, Č., & Sirutavičius, V. (2008). Sąjūdis: Nuo „Persitvarkymo" iki Kovo 11-osios. In *Lietuvos istorija* (Vol. XII, Part I). Vilnius: Lietuvos istorijos instituto leidykla.

Lebedeva, N. (2004). *Inter-ethnic relations and the acculturation of the non-titular population in Estonia and Lithuania: a socio-psychological perspective in ethnicity studies* (T. Leončikas ed.). Kaunas: Vytautas Magnus University.

Leončikas, T. (2007). Asimiliacija šiuolaikinėje Lietuvos visuomenėje: švietimo sektoriaus pasirinkimas. Etniškumo studijos, 1, Vilnius: Socialinių tyrimų institutas/Eugrimas.

Ligenzowska, J., & Piecuch, J (2015). National minorities' integration in the Baltic States. *Studia Ekonomiczne. Zeszyty Naukowe*, Uniwersytetu Ekonomicznego w Katowicach, No. 228, pp. 167–175.

Liekis, Š. (2003). *A state within a state? Jewish Autonomy in Lithuania 1918–1925.* Vilnius: Versus Aureus.

Liekis, Š. (2010). *1939: the year that changed everything in Lithuania's history.* Amsterdam and New York: Rodopi.

Liekis, Š., Bumblauskas, A., Potašenko, G. (2008). *Lietuvos Didžiosios Kunigaikštijos tradicija ir paveldo "dalybos".* Vilnius: Vilniaus Universiteto Leidykla.

Liekis, Š., Bumblauskas, A., Potašenko, G. (2009). *Naujasis Vilniaus perskaitymas: didieji Lietuvos istoriniai pasakojimai ir daugiakultūrinis miesto paveldas.* Collection of articles. Vilnius: Vilniaus Universiteto Leidykla.

Mačiulis, D. (2005). *Valstybės Kultūros Politika Lietuvoje 1927–1940 metais* (p. LII). Vilnius: Lietuvos Istorijos Institutas.

Merkys, V. (2006). *Tautiniai Santykiai Vilniaus Vyskupijoje 1798–1918 m.* Vilnius: Versus Aureus.

Ministry of Foreign Affairs of the Russian Federation. (2000). Concept de la Securite Nationale de la Federation de Russie. http://www.mid.ru/fr/web/guest/foreign_policy/official_documents/-/asset_publisher/CptICkB6BZ29/content/id/589768/pop_up?_101_INSTANCE_CptICkB6BZ29_viewMode=print&_101_INSTANCE_CptICkB6BZ29_qrIndex=0. Accessed 06 January 2016.

Ministry of Foreign Affairs of the Russian Federation. (2004). http://www.mid.ru/en/web/guest/activity/compatriots/min/-/asset_publisher/evi8j0czyac3/content/id/4913866. Accessed 28 December 2015.

Ministry of Foreign Affairs of the Russian Federation. (2009). Стратегия национальной безопасности Российской Федерации до 2020 года. http://www.mid.ru/ru/foreign_policy/official_documents/-/asset_publisher/CptICkB6BZ29/content/id/294430. Accessed 26 December 2016.

Moreno Morales, D. E. (2008). National political community and ethnicity: evidence from two Latin American countries. *Nationalism and Ethnic Politics, 14*(1), 55–84.

Muižnieks, N. (Ed.) (2008). *Manufacturing enemy images? Russian media portrayal of Latvia.* Riga: University of Latvia Press.

Muižnieks, N. (2011). *Latvian–Russian relations: dynamics since Latvia's accession to the EU and NATO.* Riga: University of Latvia Press.

Norkus, Z. (2014). *Du Nepriklausomybės dešimtmečiai.* Vilnius: Aukso žuvys.

Pivoras, S. (2000). *Lietuvių ir latvių pilietinės savimonės raida.* Kaunas: Vytauto Didžiojo Universiteto Leidykla.

Pohl, O. J. (2014). Colonialism in one country: the deported peoples in the USSR as an example of internal colonialism. *Journal of Race, Ethnicity, and Religion, 5*, 1–27.
Potašenko, G. (2009). Istorijos kultūra šiuolaikinėje Lietuvoje: daugiakultūriškumo samprata visuomenėje ir Lietuvos Didžiosios Kunigaikštijos tyrimuose. *Lietuvos Didžiosios Kunigaikštijos tradicija ir tautiniai naratyvai. V* (pp. 275–301). Vilnius: Vilniaus universiteto leidykla.
Rozenvalds, J. (2010). The Soviet heritage and integration policy development since the restoration of independence. In: N. Muižnieks (Ed.), *How integrated is Latvian society? An audit of achievements, failures and challenges* (pp. 33–61). Riga: University of Latvia Press.
Šaulauskas, M. P. (2000). Socialinė kaita: metodologija ir bendrosios tendencijos. In: A. Dobryninas, V. Gaidys, B. Gruževskis, A. Poviliūnas, V. Skapcevičius, M. P. Šaulauskas, & S. Žukas (Eds.), *Socialiniai pokyčiai:Lietuva 1990–1998* (Collective Monograph). Vilnius: Garnelis.
Simonyan, R. (2013). The history of the formation of the Russian diaspora in the Baltic states. *Filosofija. Sociologija, 24*(4), 161–170.
Statkus, N. (2003). *Etniškumas ir Nacionalizmas.* Vilnius: Vilniaus Universitetas.
Švabe, A. (1991). *Latvijas vesture 1800–1914.* Sej.1 Riga. Avots.
Švarplys, A. (2013). Who is telling it to whom? Economical, political, and cultural conditions for national narrative in after-post-communist Lithuania. In: E. Aleksandravičius (Ed.), *Darbai ir Dienos* (vol. 60), pp. 265–279.
Tabuns, A. (2010). Identity, ethnic relations, language and culture. In N. Muižnieks (Ed.), *How integrated is Latvian society? An audit of achievements, failures and challenges* (pp. 253–279). Riga: University of Latvia Press.
Tambur, S. (2015, February 26). Estonian public broadcasting. Media release. http://news.err.ee/v/news/politics/society/48f806ac-8d6f-4375-9eee-2ab66da19ef4/91000-stateless-people-have-limited-political-rights-in-esto nia-amnesty-2015-report-says. Accessed 8 April 2016.
Trenin, D., & Lo, B. (2005). *The landscape of Russian foreign policy decision-making.* Washington, DC: Carnegie Endowment for International Peace.
Uhlin, A. (2011). Civil society and problems of democratization in post-communist states in democracy in Lithuania. Civil spirit versus totalitarianism at the defining moments of the twentieth century. In: M. Jurkutė & N. Šepetys (Eds.), *Naujasis Židinys – Aidai* (pp. 233–249). Vilnius: Naujasis Židinys-Aidai.
Venclova, T. (1994). *Penktieji Laisvės Metai.* Vilnius: Metmenys.

Šarunas Liekis is Dean and Professor at the School of Political Science and Diplomacy at Vytautas Magnus University and a member of the Board of the Lithuanian Human Rights Monitoring Institute. He has published 6 authored or co-authored books and over 50 journal articles and book chapters. His most recent book is *Jews in the Former Grand Duchy of Lithuania since 1772* (with Polonsky, 2013).

PART III

Ukraine, Russia and Kazakhstan

Chapter 9: Ukraine's Democratisation Path Post-Orange Revolution: Examining the Internal and External Impediments to Successful Democratic Reform in Ukraine

Nicholas Ross Smith

Introduction

The chapter assesses Ukraine's attempted democratisation since its Orange Revolution which occurred at the end of 2004. The Orange Revolution raised high hopes for a positive upsurge in Ukraine's post-Soviet democratisation efforts, a transition which had previously stagnated and faltered. However, a decade after the Orange Revolution, Ukraine has made little progress with regard to democratisation. Invoking a liberal definition of democracy,[1] it is argued that while Ukraine has had largely free and fair elections since the Orange Revolution, it has fallen well short of democratic standards in other, more substantive 'liberal' areas of democracy such as civil society, independent media, rule of law and state-level corruption. Thus,

N.R. Smith (✉)
National Centre for Research on Europe, University of Canterbury,
Christchurch, New Zealand
e-mail: nrsmith@outlook.co.nz

Fish, Gill, Petrovic (eds.), *A Quarter Century of Post-Communism Assessed*, DOI 10.1007/978-3-319-43437-7_10

despite numerous statements and pledges by high-ranking officials to undertake greater democratisation, Ukraine has continued to stagnate as a kind of illiberal (or managed) democracy.

This chapter is demarcated into three main sections. The first section examines Ukraine's history with democratisation from independence until present day. It is argued that while the 2004 Orange Revolution produced hope for a positive democratic turn in Ukraine, it became clear by 2010 that no significant democratic gains were made, and eventually regression occurred under the rule of Viktor Yanukovych thereafter. The second section asks the question 'Why has Ukraine failed to democratise' and identifies two key impediments. Internally, it is argued that the role of elites – specifically in this case, the oligarchisation of power – has been detrimental to Ukraine's democratisation efforts. Externally, it is argued that Ukraine's geopolitical positioning in Eastern Europe is a bulwark to the potential external diffusion of democracy. The last section builds on the first two and discusses what the democratic prospects of Ukraine are moving forward. It is argued that the oligarchisation of power is an internal impediment which shows no signs of changing in the near future. However, if the European Union (EU) could improve its external democracy promotion, it might conceivably incentivise elites into making democratic concessions. Ultimately, given the EU's flaws as an agent of democratisation and Russia's strong strategic anti-democratic interests in Ukraine, Ukraine's continued democratic underachievement seems set to remain in the foreseeable future.

Ukraine's History with Democratisation

When Ukraine gained independence from the crumbling Soviet Union in 1991, there was cautious optimism – both in Ukraine and in the West – that a fully liberal democracy could eventually emerge in lieu of the totalitarian system which preceded it (Karatnycky 1992; Zlenko 1992). Leonid Kravchuk (1991), the first ever elected president of Ukraine, stated in his inauguration speech on 1 December 1991:

> I would like to congratulate all of you on the greatest event in the history of our people – the birth of New Ukraine which has been created by the will of her people, pursuing the highest standards of democracy.

Conversely, leaders from the West, arguably enchanted by the perceived ideological victory of Western values over Soviet ones with the end of the Cold War, expressed their own desire for a democratic Ukraine as part of a wider post-Soviet wave of democratisation. George H. Bush (1991), in a speech which was later dubbed a 'chicken Kiev' by detractors because of its cautious treatment of Ukrainian statehood, emphasised that the United States would 'support those who want to build democracy…and by democracy we mean a system of government in which people may vie openly for the hearts and yes, the votes of the public'.

However, severely hampered by pressing issues surrounding Ukraine's flimsy sovereignty coupled with the stark realities of undertaking simultaneous social, economic and political transitions, Ukraine's 'democratic dream' failed to materialise in its first decade of independence (Dobriansky 1994; Karatnycky 1995; Kubiček 1994; Kuzio 1994). Consequently, in the absence of a functioning democratic system, Ukraine was rendered a kind of illiberal democracy; a system that was neither purely democratic nor purely authoritarian (Beichelt 2004).[2] Thus, Ukraine's only real democratic gain in the first dozen years of independence was the establishment of relatively free and fair elections (Carothers 2002; Rose 2001). This was exemplified by the electoral defeat of Ukraine's first president, Kravchuk, in the 1994 presidential election, the first post-Soviet leader to be defeated at the ballot box (Kuzio 1996). However, in the more substantive areas of democracy – namely, a vibrant civil society, protection of civil liberties and low levels of corruption – Ukraine made meagre advancement, thus, remaining something of an illiberal entity (Kubiček 2001).

It was not until the events of the Orange Revolution in late 2004, early 2005, that enthusiasm as to the democratic prospects of Ukraine returned to the fore. In a nutshell, the Orange Revolution came about after allegations of electoral violations against Viktor Yanukovych in the 2004 presidential election, who was running as the chosen successor of the incumbent Leonid Kuchma, which resulted in mass protests in Kiev (Karatnycky 2005). The protests lasted more than 2 months, eventually leading to a rerun of the election which ended with opposition candidate Viktor Yushchenko winning. The Orange Revolution, as part of the broader Colour Revolutions wave of the early 2000s, was expected by many to be the watershed moment that catapulted Ukraine towards a liberal democracy (Åslund 2009a; Christensen et al. 2005; McFaul 2007).

Like other countries that experienced Colour Revolutions – arguably the same can be said for the countries affected by the Arab Spring too – the Orange Revolution demonstrated genuine popular demand for more democratisation in Ukraine (Hale 2013). However, despite rhetoric from Yushchenko and other key Orange revolutionaries (e.g. Yulia

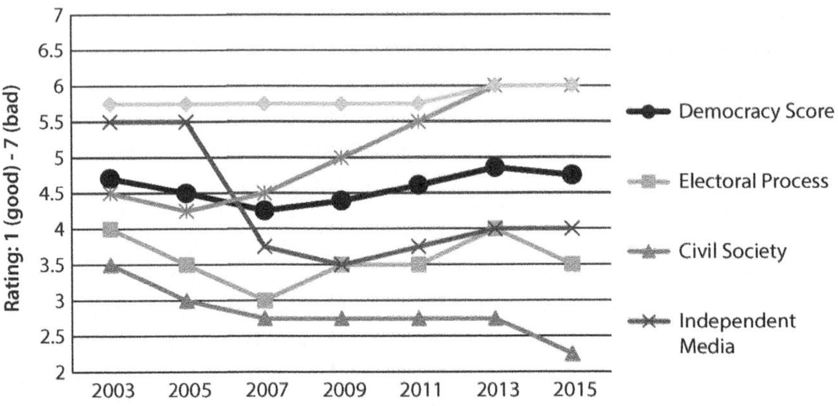

Fig. 9.1 Ukraine's nations in transit ratings 2003–2015

Tymoshenko), by the end of their tenure in power in 2010, no substantial democratic gains had been achieved (Haran 2011). Indeed, two of the major democratic ratings indexes – Freedom House's Nations in Transit ratings (Fig. 9.1) and Bertelsmann Stiftung's Transformation Index ratings (Fig. 9.2) – chart, after an initial positive spike in the aftermath of the Orange Revolution, a gradual waning of Ukraine's democratic rating over the past decade (Freedom House n.d.; Bertelsmann Stiftung n.d.).

Concerning the formal aspects of democracy – namely elections, rule of law and separation of powers – Ukraine arguably regressed in the 5 years of Orange rule. Despite some initial attempts to reform in all three areas, from 2007 onwards, Ukraine experienced notable failures. Certainly, the two parliamentary elections (2006 and 2007) and one presidential election (2010) that occurred in this period were considered free and fair by the major election observation monitors: the Organization for Security and Co-operation in Europe (OSCE), Council of Europe (CoE) and the EU (Katchanovski 2008; Casier 2011). However, regarding rule of law and separation of powers, the Orange revolutionaries' tabled constitutional and judicial reforms were delayed, altered and eventually ineffectively implemented (Kubiček 2009).

In the more substantive (or informal) areas of democracy – especially civil society, civil liberties and corruption – the Orange Revolution resulted in few advances. As promoting substantive democracy is arguably harder and requires a long-term focus, it would be unrealistic to expect significant improvement in Ukraine in such a short period of time (Casier 2011).

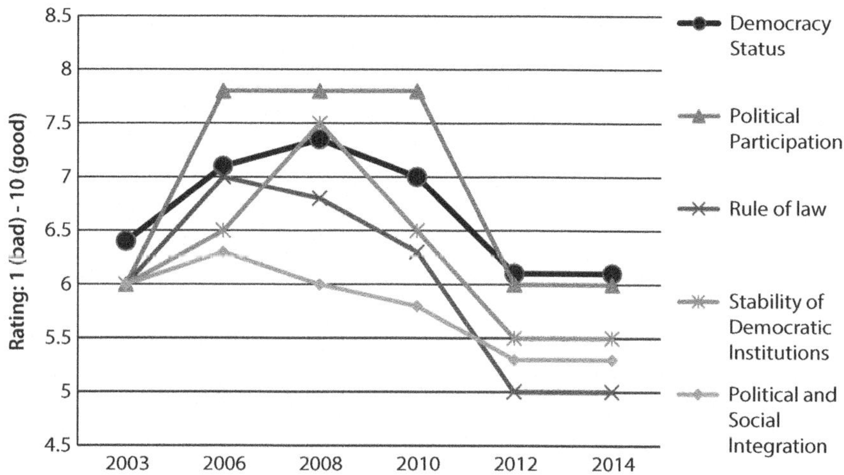

Fig. 9.2 Ukraine's Transformation Index ratings 2003–2014

Consequently, although the functioning of civil society and the protection of civil liberties remained adequate in Ukraine during the Orange regime's tenure, neither showed signs of marked improvement (Kuzio 2010). Regarding corruption, reduction of which was one of the key promises of the Orange Revolution, the high levels of corruption failed to be properly addressed and remained a key hurdle to Ukraine's democratisation prospects (Kubiček 2009).

Indeed, the democratisation goals of the Orange Revolution were partly undermined by the global financial crisis which placed extraordinary pressure on Ukraine; Ukraine's economy contracted by 15% in 2009 (Åslund 2009b; Kubiček 2009). However, the internal power struggles between Yushchenko and Tymoschenko were arguably more damaging to Ukraine's democratisation (Flikke 2008). In the aftermath of the defeat of the Orange revolutionaries in the 2010 presidential election at the hands of Yanukovych, Ukraine's democracy moved from stagnation to regression.

By the time of Yanukovych's flight from power in early 2014, Ukraine had backslid democratically across the board to pre-Orange Revolution levels (Kudelia 2014; Motyl 2013). Yanukovych's reign as president was particularly blighted by two key democratic failings: the rise of selective justice (i.e. inadequate rule of law) and the problematic 2012 parliamentary elections. Cases of selective justice became more noticeable (even egregious) under Yanukovych as he sought to marginalise political competitors. The imprisonment of Tymoshenko and her ally Yuri Lutsenko, among roughly 15 individuals from the opposition targeted by Yanukovych, on corruption charges in 2011 were the most blatant (Burlyuk 2015). This demonstrated a clear regression of the rule of law in Ukraine under Yanukovych (Kudelia 2014). Regarding the electoral process, the 2012 parliamentary elections represented a noticeable step backwards from the preceding three elections. Prior to the elections a mixed voting system was implemented, a system previously used pre-Orange Revolution, which was, according to critics, designed to give Yanukovych's Party of the Regions a parliamentary majority (Kovalov 2014). Additionally, the post-election setting was rife with issues ranging from accusations of electoral violations in Kiev to the decision to require repeat elections in five constituencies.

With the flight of Yanukovych and the subsequent election of Petro Poroshenko as President in 2014 (during the first few months of the Ukraine crisis), Ukraine has once again started a new phase of attempting to democratise under a different leader (Gershman 2015; Snyder 2015). Despite strong rhetorical commitments to democratisation, Poroshenko is significantly hamstrung by the ongoing Ukraine crisis which has resulted in the annexation of Crimea by Russia and civil war in the Donbass region not to mentioned producing significant economic, political, diplomatic and social strife (Wilson 2015). Additionally, as this chapter will argue deep-seated impediments, both internal and external, to Ukraine's democratic prospects remain even greater challenges to overcome. Consequently, Ukraine's prospects for achieving its democratic dream are perhaps at its lowest point in its history with few people, internally or externally, confident about its democratic trajectory.

Why Has Ukraine Failed to Democratise?

The democratisation literature remains highly contested as to why some states successfully democratise and why others do not. Traditional democratisation theories have tended to look at the internal conditions as to whether a state democratises or not, with a particular focus on the prerequisites required in implementing democracy, the role of elites in choosing democratisation (or not) and the constraints of internal power structures (Potter 1997). However, since Huntington's (1991) 'waves of democratisation' argument in the early 1990s, the body of literature has added an external focus to the traditional internal focus as to why states democratise. Thus, this body of literature broadly argues that external (and international) factors play a prominent role in democratisation as transitions are not random occurrences but are linked to the external environment (Gleditsch and Ward 2006).

This chapter holds that understanding both internal and external factors is important when examining why a state, such as Ukraine, has failed to democratise. Although a number of variables deserve examination in the context of Ukraine, one key internal and one key external variable will be examined in this chapter. The chosen key internal variable is the unwillingness of the Ukrainian political elite to embrace substantial democratisation. Elites, it is argued, are a crucially important variable for the undertaking of democratisation, particularly in the post-Soviet context of Ukraine where the 'oligarchisation of power' has occurred. Thus, it is argued that it has not been in the interests of Ukraine's 'oligarchic class' to undertake deep democratic reform to date. The chosen key external variable is Ukraine's geopolitical position in Eastern Europe wedged between two powers with competing regime preferences for it, the EU and Russia. On the one hand, the EU attempts to promote democracy in Ukraine through its Eastern Partnership initiative. However, on the other hand, Russia has a countervailing regime promotion strategy in Ukraine, a kind of autocracy promotion. Consequently, Ukraine's precarious geopolitical position creates an external impediment to the diffusion of democracy from the West.

Internal Impediment: The Oligarchization of Power in Ukraine

In truth, Ukraine has numerous domestic obstacles to achieving a functioning liberal democracy. Ukraine's economy, which was significantly hit during the 2008 global financial crisis, has more recently taken a further turn for the worse with the ongoing Ukraine crisis and destruction of the Donbass region, its industrial heartland (Wilson 2015). Thus, not only is Ukraine's economic outlook dire (a 12% drop is forecast for 2015), inequality is also on the rise (inflation is expected to hit 23.6% in 2016), both of which do not bode well for democratisation prospects (RT 2015). Additionally, although Ukraine's civil society is rated as having decent functionality (see Figs. 9.1 and 9.2), it clearly has a lacking substantive critical mass needed for organic democratisation to develop (Kuzio 2010).

Unsurprisingly, after numerous failed democratic movements, political apathy amongst average Ukrainians is growing and few seem genuinely convinced of an achievable democratic future for Ukraine (Yanevskyy 2015). However, while the aforementioned issues are problematic and certainly need addressing, if successful democratisation is to be achieved the biggest internal hurdle is undoubtedly rectifying the role of elites in Ukrainian politics.

Elites, as a variable for understanding democratisation, were a key component of the transitional theory of democratisation first introduced by Rustow (1970) in the 1970s and later added to by O'Donnell and Schmitter (1986), and Higley and Burton (1989) in the 1980s. The main argument of this school of thought was that democracy comes about through elite-managed transitions, generally occurring in stages and ending in a 'habituation stage' where democracy is consciously adoption (Potter 1997). As Grugel and Bishop (2002, p. 56) note, for transitologists, democracy is not 'a question of waiting for economic conditions to mature or the political struggles unleashed by economic change to be one', but rather democracy is the outcome of intentional actions pursued by elites. While the step-by-step transition argument holds little weight in more recent scholarship (Carothers 2002; Lynch and Crawford 2011) the importance of elites as to whether concrete democratisation occurs or not is undeniable (Hale 2005; Tolstrup 2012).

In the context of the transitions that have occurred in the independent states that emerged from the Soviet Union's collapse, all of which have ostensibly attempted some level of democratisation, the role of elites has been important as to whether democracy has occurred or not. Although, popular mobilisations demanding democracy, like what occurred at the fall of the Soviet Union or more recently in the Colour Revolutions, have often grabbed the headlines. Hale (2005, p. 161) argues that in the majority of post-Soviet states, 'political contestation is at root an elite affair where powerful groups compete to manipulate mass opinion through biased media and machine politics'. Thus, it is elites which represent the crucial variable when assessing the democratisation prospects of post-Soviet countries, such as Ukraine, which have entrenched illiberal (what Hale calls, patronal) regimes (Hale 2005).

The influence of elites on Ukraine's politics and governance in its two and a half decades of independence has been significant. Initially, in the early years of independence under Kravchuk, the Ukrainian political elite was made up mostly of former high-ranking figures from the Communist apparatus (Puglisi 2003). However, due to wide-ranging economic reforms, especially privatisation, implemented when Kuchma came to power in 1994, a new breed of elite emerged in Ukraine: oligarchs. The term oligarch, in this context, refers to business magnates who acquired huge amounts of wealth, often through criminal connections or activities, during the privatisation process. Along with the acquisition of immense wealth naturally came significant political influence and power, making the management of the oligarchs a key priority of the president (Kuzio 2007).

The literature on whether the emergence of powerful oligarchs is good or bad for democracy is contested, with examples of emerging groups of oligarchs' unwittingly aiding liberalisation in Japan and Malaysia (Puglisi 2003). In the Ukrainian context, however, the rise of oligarchs, occurring at time when economic and political transitions were failing, has been a largely negative development for democracy (Burlyuk 2015; Kuzio 2007). Beyond the obvious problems with triggering rising corruption (Transparency International documented worsening perceptions of corruption in Ukraine between 1996 and 2004), Kubiček (2009, p. 620) argues that the rise of oligarchs undermined the potentially positive impact of trade unions which could have reverted the 'overcentralisation of authority and lack of checks on both political and economic power'. Furthermore, this negative impact was exacerbated with the emergence politically of key oligarchs in Kuchma's second term in 1999 which went hand-in-hand with the democratic backsliding that eventually reached a crescendo with the electoral violations preceding the Orange Revolution (Kuzio 2007).

Unsurprisingly, one of the key pledges of the Orange Revolution was to address the high levels of corruption (read: oligarchs) in Ukraine's politics in order to foster greater democratisation. Yushchenko (2005), in his inauguration speech, stated that:

> We will eliminate corruption and bring economy out of shadow. Taxes will be reduced but everybody will pay them. Business to be separated from power. Only those people who declared their incomes will assume state offices.

However, instead of addressing the problem of oligarchs and corruption, the Orange Revolution led, ironically, to what Hovshovsurka (2006) termed the 'oligarchisation of power' in Ukraine. Importantly, because a number of key Orange revolutionaries were themselves, for all intents and purposes, oligarchs (or linked to oligarchic factions) – most notably Yulia Tymoshenko and Petro Poroshenko – the Orange Revolution actually represented the further encroachment of oligarchs into politics (Kuzio 2007). Furthermore, soon after the 2005 'Orange divorce' between Yushchenko and Tymoshenko and abetted by Tymoshenko's agenda-driven corruption crusade against perceived oligarchic rivals, Ukraine became a political battleground between different oligarchic factions vying for power (Kubiček 2009).

The end of Orange rule at the hands of Yanukovych in the 2010 presidential election had very little effect on the role of oligarchs in Ukrainian politics. Yanukovych himself was an oligarch of sorts, albeit a relative newcomer to his wealth and was, more importantly, heavily backed by a group of oligarchs from the Donbass region of Ukraine, most notably billionaires Rinat Akhmetov and Dmitry Firtash (Kudelia 2014). Contrary to the Orange revolutionaries, Yanukovych did not make bold democratic reform aims for his presidency, rather promising, first and foremost, stability after 5 years of chaotic Orange rule (Motyl 2013). Indeed, rhetorical commitments to fighting corruption and pursuing democratic reforms followed, but this was little more than placation of the EU's prescribed democratic reform demands for Ukraine (Smith 2014).

Unlike long periods of Kuchma's presidency, or Vladimir Putin's rule in Russia, it became apparent near the end of Yanukovych's reign that the oligarchisation of power has reached a point where the power of the President was impotent in the face of oligarchic interests. Although Yanukovych spent much of his reign attempting to acquire enough financial and political capital in order to insulate himself from the power of his Donbass backers, when Ukraine became unstable at the end of 2013, Yanukovych's grip on power proved to be weak (Kudelia 2014). Notwithstanding mounting popular pressure on his position as president orchestrated by the Euromaidan movement, it was the removal of support from key oligarchs, especially Akhmetov and Firtash, which led to Yanukovych fleeing in late February 2014 (Neef 2014).

Despite the flight of Yanukovych and the election of a new president, Petro Poroshenko, in 2014 who openly stated his desire for Ukraine to pursue a European pathway, signing an economic and political deal with the EU which requires concrete democratisation, few are optimistic as to Ukraine's immediate democratic prospects. Not only is Poroshenko an oligarch – a billionaire chocolate magnate – but also his rule to date has been blighted by the same problems that have affected Ukrainian politics since the emergence of oligarchs in the late 1990s, namely allegations of infighting, corruption and nepotism (Pond 2015). Indeed, the momentum generated by the Euromaidan movement seems to have been co-opted by Poroshenko and his oligarchic supporters as zero of the key grassroots figures in that movement were represented in the positions of real power in the new regime (Andreyev and Wilson 2014). Thus, despite promises to de-oligarchise Ukrainian politics, Poroshenko's first year in power illustrates that history is once again repeating itself in Ukraine (Kononczuk 2015).

Ultimately, as Hale (2005) observed during the Orange Revolution, the current political system in Ukraine, which has not been significantly altered in design by the ongoing Ukraine crisis to date, means that rather than moving towards democracy or autocracy, power will merely perpetually vacillate between competing elite groups, creating cycles of 'regime behaviour'. Thus, breaking this embedded system which serves oligarchic interests appears to be the key challenge impeding Ukraine's prospects for achieving greater democratisation from within, because without significant alteration, not matter what happens economically or in other areas of democratisation (i.e. civil society growth, elections, rule of law), a liberal democracy is largely impossible.

External Impediment: The Competing Regime Promotion Strategies of the EU and Russia in Ukraine

The external dimension of Ukraine's democratisation challenges has received a significant amount of attention over the past decade, particularly as the EU has actively sought to promote democracy in Ukraine in the last decade (Solonenko 2009; Gawrich et al. 2010; Casier 2011). Additionally, with the increased interference of the Kremlin in Ukrainian politics, starting in the wake of the Orange Revolution and reaching a crescendo with the Ukraine crisis, Russia's role as a kind of autocracy promoter (or at the very least, a bulwark against democratisation) in Ukraine (and its broader 'near abroad') has become a more recent focus of literature (Ambrosio 2010; Bader et al. 2010; Melnykovska et al. 2012). Certainly, the external impediments to democracy are not as critical as the current internal impediments in Ukraine, particularly the impact of oligarchs, but nevertheless the geopolitical setting Ukraine currently resides in has important implications for its democratisation prospects.

Various external variables have been cited as having the potential to impact the democratisation trajectories of a given state. The diffusion argument, which held that because instances of democratisation tend to occur in temporal and spatial clusters (i.e. waves) states are susceptible to what is occurring in their region, lost much of its appeal after the failures of the Colour Revolutions and Arab Spring waves which did not result in the spread of democracy, although it did, arguably, spread regime change (Beissinger 2009; Hale 2013). While the jury is out as to whether democracy via diffusion occurs, the role of external democracy promoters is something that has been more concretely evaluated in the past two decades (Tolstrup 2012). Certainly, it is unsurprising that large international powers, whether on an international or regional level, have specific regime preferences for strategically important smaller states and often undertake actions to promote one specific regime-type over another (Smith 2015).

In the post-Cold War setting, regime promotion has predominately been undertaken under the guise of international democracy promotion led by Western powers such as the United States and the EU. However, more recently, it has been asserted, particularly in the foreign policies of Russia and China, that autocracies have also started promoting their own regime type (Bader et al. 2010; Melnykovska et al. 2012). Crudely, both democracy and autocracy promotion strategies attempt to, in part, induce their preferred regime by using the mechanism of conditionality; appealing directly to strategic calculations of political elites in a target state (Tolstrup 2012). Indeed, much of the EU's apparent success in facilitating democratic transitions in 10 post-Communist countries in Central Eastern Europe (CEE) and the Baltics through its enlargement process which began in the 1990s was due to the offer a 'golden carrot' of membership in the EU which made the benefits of undertaking the prescribed democratic reforms outweigh the costs (Schimmelfennig and Sedelmeier 2004).

In the context of Ukraine, it was not until the events of the Orange Revolution that it became an explicit target state for both democratic and autocratic promotion from outsiders. Certainly, prior to the Orange Revolution, democracy promotion (and perhaps autocracy promotion) by external actors did occur in Ukraine, but this was mainly a softer form of promotion, undertaken by state agencies (e.g. USAID) in conjunction with local NGOs, that appealed not to the strategic calculations of elites but to their 'logic of appropriateness' through socialising them with Western democratic norms. Consequently, the impact of the various external democracy promotion strategies on Ukraine's democratisation was relatively minor in the first dozen years of its independence.

Preceding the Orange Revolution, Europe's geopolitical setting changed significantly in 2004 with the enlargement of the EU eastwards which coincided with a re-assertiveness of Russia in its near abroad, generating a corridor of states between the two; a shared neighbourhood of Belarus, Moldova and Ukraine (Averre 2009). Subsequently, when the Orange Revolution materialised in late 2004 in this newly emerged geopolitical setting of Eastern Europe, both the EU and Russia had interests in the regime outcome in Ukraine. The EU played an important role (in conjunction with the United States) in securing a rerun of the election while proactively funding pro-Yushchenko NGOs in order to support the Orange revolutionaries secure power (Wilson 2006; Youngs 2009). Conversely, Russia strongly backed Yanukovych as its preferred presidential candidate with Russian Prime Minister Putin calling the Orange Revolution 'unconstitutional' while stating that 'a repeat of the second round would yield nothing' (Schneider 2004).

The Orange Revolution represented something of a watershed moment for regime promotion conflict between external actors in Ukraine. Shortly, after the revolution in 2005, the EU involved Ukraine in its European Neighbourhood Policy (ENP) which aimed at promoting European-style democratisation in Ukraine through offering trade and economic incentives in return for successful reform (Gawrich et al. 2010). As outlined in a jointly agreed action plan, 'further strengthening the stability and effectiveness of institutions guaranteeing democracy and the rule of law' was deemed the top priority of the relationship, with additional mention of electoral performance, judicial performance, freedom of media and the fight against corruption as well (European Commission 2005). However, crucially, instead of offering eventual membership in the Union as an incentive for reform, the EU offered only vague economic and political incentives. Indeed, this was somewhat rectified with the EU's attempted upgrading of the policy through initiating the Eastern Partnership (EaP) in 2009, which sought to offer more concrete incentives for the tabled reform, namely a Deep and Comprehensive Free Trade Agreement (DCFTA), but even so, this still fell significantly short of a 'membership perspective' (European Commission 2009).

Conversely, after Yushchenko's ultimate victory in the rerun of the presidential election, Russia sought to discredit, through utilising 'dezinformatsiya' tactics, and punish, through energy and trade squeezes, the new regime while actively supporting the main opposition parties: the Party of the Regions and the Communist Party (Kuzio 2005). Stent (2008, p. 1101) argued that the Kremlin's post-Orange Revolution policy aimed to 'ensure that Russian youth does not catch the virus that had infected Ukrainian youth'. Later, Russia upped its regime promotion ante through employing its own form of conditionality, offering Ukraine a membership opportunity in its Eurasian Economic Union project, a politically and economically less demanding alternative to the EU's EaP initiative (Dragneva and Wolczuk 2012). Although not officially designed to promote autocracy, Russia's insistence on a loyal Ukrainian regime did have important democratic implications, particularly in relation to lessening the impact of the EU's prescribed reforms. As Ambrosio (2010, p. 376) argues, Russia has endeavoured, particularly in its periphery, to create 'conditions under which democracy promotion is blunted and state sovereignty (understood as the ability of leaders to determine the form of government for their country) is further entrenched'.

The competing regime preferences of the EU and Russia made life incredibly difficult for Ukraine's rulers, particularly given the necessity of Ukraine's long-held multi-vector foreign policy (maintaining strong relations with multiple foreign partners) to its functioning (Gnedina 2015). With regards to democracy, the geopolitical pressures on Ukraine produced an external environment far from conducive to undertaking democratic reform. During the reign of Yushchenko (2005–2010), the EU's ENP policy had little effect, particularly due to its ambiguity and lacking incentives on offer. This was exacerbated by Russia's support for anti-government factions during this reign which worsened the infighting amongst Orange revolutionaries while strengthening opposition figures, eventually aiding, in part, Yanukovych's election victory in 2010.

In Yanukovych's subsequent reign (2010–2014), regime promotion competition between the EU and Russia became more zero-sum and contributed to the onset of the Ukraine crisis (Smith 2015). The EU's EaP process, which was to reach its zenith in late 2013 with Ukraine signing an Association Agreement at the Vilnius Summit, initially seemed to have won out over Russia's competing Eurasian Economic Union offer. However, out of desperation, Russia utilised its trade and energy leverage, along with financial support (a proposed $15 billion loan), to assuage Yanukovych into reneging on the EU deal in favour of an alternative Russian deal (Pridham 2014). The ensuing fallout from this decision eventually led to Yanukovych's flight from power in March 2014 and sparked the deterioration of the Ukraine crisis. Although it is too early to assess the external dimension of the post-Yanukovych setting as it pertains to democratisation (and regime promotion), it appears that Ukraine is destined to become something of a static buffer state between the EU and Russia, and thus, remain an illiberal democracy.

Consequently, in the decade since the Orange Revolution, Ukraine's geopolitical setting, where the EU and Russia openly competed to secure their own regime preferences in Ukraine, significantly pacified any opportunity for external influence on the democratisation process. The EU's democracy promotion policies were hamstrung by its lack of tangible incentives on offer for Ukraine to undertake its prescribed reform, most notably the failure to provide a clear membership perspective. Additionally, Russia's countervailing regime promotion strategies further undermined the EU's democracy promotion and helped entrench illiberal practices in Ukraine's governance. Ultimately, the strategic calculations of key elites in Ukraine continued to deem the costs of undertaking Ukraine's democratic reform targets (as prescribed by the EU) as higher than the benefits, particularly when the added costs of Russia's threats and actions were factored in, leading to only half-hearted attempts at pursuing democratisation during this period.

Rectifying the Internal and External Impediments to Democratic Ukraine: A Plausible Future Pathway?

There has been little evidence in the 25 years of Ukrainian independence to suggest that a fully functioning liberal democracy is within Ukraine's immediate grasp. As illustrated in the first section of this chapter, Ukraine's attempts to democratise have been flawed and ultimately unsuccessful, leaving few optimists amongst commentators or scholars. As examined in greater detail in section two, two ongoing key impediments, one internal and one external, severely undermines Ukraine's ongoing democratisation efforts. Indeed, the oligarchisation of power in Ukraine (the internal impediment) is a far greater hurdle to its democracy prospects than the current geopolitical setting (the external impediment). However, as the internal and external settings are inextricably linked, it is argued that altering the external setting perhaps holds the key to fixing the internal, anti-democratic quagmire in Ukraine.

This chapter made the claim that the elites, acting on a logic of consequences, make rational decisions as to whether undertake democratic reform or not. In the context of Ukraine, this was seen as a major challenge because the oligarchisation of power had brought to the fore of Ukrainian politics a group of elites with strong anti-democratic interests. Thus, as it currently stands, for those in power in Ukraine, as was the case with the previous two regimes, the costs of implementing democratic reform clearly outweigh the benefits. As Schimmelfennig and Sedelmeier (2004) argued, democratic reform represents a tricky matter for ruling elites because strict adherence to undertaking the prescribed reforms essentially requires leaders to reform themselves out of power.

Given the entrenchment of the oligarchs in Ukraine coupled with a lacking substantive critical mass for democracy, expecting rapid democratic change to be propelled solely from within is somewhat naïve. Historically, functioning liberal democracies generally emerge from long-term evolution – that is, the gradual organic growth of democracy (which may be triggered by an initial revolution or shock) – rather than resulting from the instantaneous revolution-style adoption of a democratic system (Garrard 2001; Tilly 2000). Certainly, Ukraine has experienced impressive popular mobilisation in both the Orange Revolution and more recently during the Euromaidan movement which makes the prospect for long-term evolutionary democratisation plausible, as long as rising apathy does not curtail it. However, as the absence of key Euromaidan figures in any prominent positions in the new Poroshenko regime demonstrates, Ukrainian elites do not seem ready to pursue a democratising path driven by the desires of the general population (Kononczuk 2015).

While organic democratisation appears a long way off in Ukraine, it would not be beyond the realms of possibility that positive democratic changes in Ukraine could be fomented through an external democracy promoter, such as the EU, incentivising elites to adopt democratic reforms. Indeed, something of a precedent exists for this, as the EU's democracy promotion in Slovakia illustrates. In the mid-to-late 1990s, Slovakia, under the leadership of Prime Minister Vladimir Mečiar, experienced something of an authoritarian turn. The EU, concerned by this development, made Slovakia's place as an accession candidate conditional on an immediate reversal of Slovakia's authoritarian trends (Schimmelfennig 2005). While this failed to coerce Mečiar, it did succeed in galvanising a pro-EU group of elites, led by Mikuláš Dzurinda, who eventually triumphed over Mečiar and allies in the 1998 elections. Thus, the EU, through dangling the golden carrot of membership in the Union, was able to appeal directly to key elites in Slovakia, and of course, in the other nine post-Communist countries that acceded to the EU in 2004 and 2007, in order to foster the desired democratic reform (Schimmelfennig 2005).

Could conditionality of this nature also work for Ukraine? The EU's poor track record as an agent of democratisation since it stopped offering membership as the main incentive for a target state to undertake tabled reforms, a kind of post-enlargement era, suggests that it can only be effective when membership is offered. The EU's anaemia in facilitating any sort of positive democratic trends in Ukraine through the ENP or EaP policies, both of which explicitly rule out any future Ukrainian membership in the EU, is testament to this. Indeed, when comparing the levels of Ukraine's current economic and political development vis-à-vis the EU's Copenhagen criteria, the benchmarks used by the EU to accept a new member state, Ukraine does appear light years away from being ready to accede into the Union (Petrovic and Smith 2013). However, as can be illustrated in the Western Balkans states, all of which were given formal membership perspectives by the EU, the acknowledgement of a potential membership scenario in the future can be a strong incentive for reform (Gawrich et al. 2010; Petrovic and Smith 2013).

Unsurprisingly, the lack of a clear membership perspective has long blighted the EU's democracy promotion efforts in Ukraine. Indeed, the power of offering a membership perspective was not lost on then Polish Foreign Minister Radek Sikorski (2009), who, in lobbying for a membership perspective to be added to the EaP, argued that 'the alluring prospect of joining the European Union is one of the main sources of EU influence and "soft power"'. Additionally, an interviewed Ukrainian official stated in September 2013 that:

> of course we would like to have a membership perspective in our relations, first of all due to its encouraging effects [but] also membership perspective means that EU will be more engaged on expert, financial and technical levels… so what can be done in 100 years can be done in 10 years.[3]

However, given the EU's refusal to give any sort of membership perspective, partly due to diverging internal interests amongst member states, and only offer an Association Agreement in lieu, Ukraine's reform progress languished noticeably comparatively to the CEE and Baltic countries involved in the enlargement process a decade earlier or the Western Balkan countries given explicit membership assurances in the mid-2000s.

Undoubtedly, offering Ukraine a clear membership perspective would aid the EU's democracy promotion efforts in Ukraine. However, as illustrated by the events of the ongoing Ukraine crisis, Russia's reactions to the perceived encroachments of the EU cannot be underestimated. Therefore, given that Russia views Ukraine as a vital national interest, one which has to be protected at all costs, any greater commitment by the EU will be met with strong reaction by the Kremlin. Additionally, there is a noticeable incoherence in the EU's foreign policy towards both Ukraine and Russia, a product of the conflicting national interests of its member states. Evidence of this emerged in the wake of the Ukraine crisis, where a clear division emerged between member states that wanted to punish Russia for its perceived inflammatory actions – this cohort was led by Poland, Sweden and the Baltics – and a group of member states which all had strong strategic and commercial relations – this cohort included Greece, Cyprus and Hungary, but also, at times, Italy, Germany and France – who favoured a more lenient response (Smith 2016).

Ultimately, a change in the EU's approach to promoting democracy in Ukraine is likely contingent on two key developments, both of which appear less than likely in the current climate: an improvement in its foreign policy coherency while making Ukraine a pivotal strategic interest. Until this happens, Russia seemingly has the upper hand in undermining the EU's democracy promotion efforts in Ukraine because when 'the chips are on the table', as has been evident in the Ukraine crisis to date, Russia is prepared to incur more costs than the EU is in Ukraine. Therefore, while in theory, external democracy promotion by the EU could appeal to Ukrainian elites to undertake lasting democratic reform, in practice it has proven difficult, if not impossible. Consequently, Ukraine's geopolitical positioning will remain a bulwark to external democratic diffusion meaning that any positive democratic gains will have to be driven from within Ukraine, which, given its entrenchment of oligarchs in key political positions, presents itself as a difficult, if not impossible task.

Notes

1. A liberal definition of democracy goes beyond mere elections as a benchmark as it also requires the existence of the rule of law, a free press, basic human rights and active political participation (through a vibrant civil society) on the part of the general population (Dahl 1973; Diamond

1995). Thus, liberal democratic system allows a polity to exert effective control over their elected political leaders (who themselves become the de facto and de jure rulers of the country).

2. Fareed Zakaria (1997, p. 22) first coined the term illiberal democracy after noticing that many putatively functioning democracies were 'routinely ignoring constitutional limits on their power and depriving their citizens of basic rights and freedoms' (see Andras Pap's chapter in this volume for a deeper discussion on illiberal democracy and the emerging Hungarian model of illiberal democracy). Numerous other terms have also been used to describe this kind of failing democratic system: semi-democracy, pseudo-democracy, managed democracy, competitive authoritarianism, hybrid regime and delegative democracy (Diamond 2002).
3. The interview with a Ukrainian Ministry of Foreign Affairs (MFA) official took place in Brussels on 25 September 2013.

Bibliography

Ambrosio, T. (2010). Constructing a framework of authoritarian diffusion: concepts, dynamics, and future research. *International Studies Perspectives, 11* (4), 375–392.

Andreyev, O., & Wilson, A. (2014, April 7). Ukraine's May Presidential election and the politics of East and West. *European Council on Foreign Relations.* http://www.ecfr.eu/article/commentary_ukraines_may_presidential_election_and_the_politics_of_east_a244. Accessed 12 October 2015.

Åslund, A. (2009a). *How Ukraine became a market economy and democracy.* Washington, DC: Peterson Institute.

Åslund, A. (2009b). Ukraine's financial crisis, 2009. *Eurasian Geography and Economics, 50*(4), 371–386.

Averre, D. (2009). Competing rationalities: Russia, the EU and the "shared neighbourhood." *Europe-Asia Studies, 61*(10), 1689–1713.

Bader, J., Grävingholt, J., Kästner, A. (2010). Would autocracies promote autocracy? A political economy perspective on regime-type export in regional neighbourhoods. *Contemporary Politics, 16*(1), 81–100.

Beichelt, T. (2004). Autocracy and democracy in Belarus, Russia and Ukraine. *Democratization, 11*(5), 113–132.

Beissinger, M. R. (2009). An interrelated wave. *Journal of Democracy, 20*(1), 74–77.

Bertelsmann Stiftung. (n.d.). Transformation index. http://www.bti-project.org/index/. Accessed 20 November 2015.

Burlyuk, O. (2015). The introduction and consolidation of the rule of law in Ukraine: domestic hindrances at the level of the demand for law. *Hague Journal on the Rule of Law, 7*(1), 1–25.

Bush, G. H. (1991, August 1). Remarks to the Supreme Soviet of the Republic of the Ukraine. *Speech to the Ukrainian parliament*. http://www.kyivpost.com/opinion/op-ed/george-bush39s-chicken-kyiv-speech-39freedom-is-no-9437.html. Accessed 12 October 2015.

Carothers, T. (2002). The end of the transition paradigm. *Journal of Democracy, 13*(1), 5–21.

Casier, T. (2011). The EU's two-track approach to democracy promotion: the case of Ukraine. *Democratization, 18*(4), 956–977.

Christensen, R. K., Rakhimkulov, E. R., Wise, C. R. (2005). The Ukrainian Orange Revolution brought more than a new president: what kind of democracy will the institutional changes bring? *Communist and Post-Communist Studies, 38*(2), 207–230.

Dahl, R. A. (1973). *Polyarchy: participation and opposition*. New Haven: Yale University Press.

Diamond, L. J. (1995). *Promoting democracy in the 1990s: actors and instruments, issues and imperatives*. New York: Carnegie.

Diamond, L. J. (2002). Thinking about hybrid regimes. *Journal of Democracy, 13*(2), 21–35.

Dobriansky, P. J. (1994). Ukraine: a question of survival. *The National Interest*, 65–72.

Dragneva, R., & Wolczuk, K. (2012). Russia, the Eurasian customs union and the EU: cooperation, stagnation or rivalry? *Chatham House Briefing Paper*.

European Commission. (2005). EU-Ukraine action plan. http://www.enpi-info.eu/library/content/eu-ukraine-action-plan-0. Accessed 15 December 2015.

European Commission. (2009). EU-Ukraine association agenda. http://eeas.europa.eu/ukraine/docs/2010_eu_ukraine_association_agenda_en.pdf. Accessed 15 December 2015.

Flikke, G. (2008). Pacts, parties and elite struggle: Ukraine's troubled post-orange transition. *Europe-Asia Studies, 60*(3), 375–396.

Freedom House. (n.d.). Nations in transit. https://freedomhouse.org/report/nations-transit/nations-transit-2015. Accessed 20 November 2015.

Garrard, J. (2001). *Democratisation in Britain: elites, civil society and reform since 1800*. Basingstoke: Palgrave Macmillan.

Gawrich, A., Melnykovska, I., Schweickert, R. (2010). Neighbourhood Europeanization through ENP: the case of Ukraine. *JCMS: Journal of Common Market Studies, 48*(5), 1209–1235.

Gershman, C. (2015). A fight for democracy. *World Affairs, 177*(6), 47–56.

Gleditsch, K. S., & Ward, M. D. (2006). Diffusion and the international context of democratization. *International Organization, 60*(4), 911–933.

Gnedina, E. (2015). "Multi-vector" foreign policies in Europe: balancing, bandwagoning or bargaining? *Europe-Asia Studies, 67*(7), 1007–1029.

Grugel, J., & Bishop, M. L. (2002). *Democratization: a critical introduction*. New York: Palgrave Macmillan.

Hale, H. E. (2005). Regime cycles: democracy, autocracy, and revolution in post-Soviet Eurasia. *World Politics, 58*(01), 133–165.

Hale, H. E. (2013). Regime change cascades: what we have learned from the 1848 revolutions to the 2011 Arab uprisings. *Annual Review of Political Science, 16*, 331–353.

Haran, O. (2011). From Viktor to Viktor: democracy and authoritarianism in Ukraine. *Demokratizatsiya, 19*(2), 93–110.

Higley, J., & Burton, M. G. (1989). The elite variable in democratic transitions and breakdowns. *American Sociological Review, 54*(1), 17–32.

Hovshovsurka, V. (2006, January 31). How to stop the oligarchization of power? *The Day Weekly Digest*. http://www.day.kiev.ua/en/article/close/how-stop-oligarchization-power. Accessed 12 October 2015.

Huntington, S. P. (1991). *The third wave: Democratization in the late twentieth century* (Vol. 1). Norman: University of Oklahoma press.

Karatnycky, A. (1992). The Ukrainian factor. *Foreign Affairs, 71*(3), 90–107.

Karatnycky, A. (1995). Ukraine at the crossroads. *Journal of Democracy, 6*(1), 117–130.

Karatnycky, A. (2005). Ukraine's Orange Revolution. *Foreign Affairs, 84*(2), 35–52.

Katchanovski, I. (2008). The Orange Evolution? The "Orange Revolution" and political changes in Ukraine. *Post-Soviet Affairs, 24*(4), 351–382.

Kovalov, M. (2014). Electoral manipulations and fraud in parliamentary elections: the case of Ukraine. *East European Politics & Societies, 28* (4), 781–807.

Kononczuk, W. (2015, February 16). Oligarchs after the Maidan: the old system in a "new" Ukraine. *OSW Commentary No. 162*. http://www.osw.waw.pl/en/publikacje/osw-commentary/2015-02-16/oligarchs-after-maidan-old-system-a-new-ukraine. Accessed 12 October 2015.

Kravchuk, L. (1991, December 5). Our goal – a free Ukraine. *The inauguration meeting of the Supreme Council of Ukraine*. http://www.artukraine.com/old/buildukraine/kravchuk.htm. Accessed 20 November 2015.

Kubiček, P. (2001). The limits of electoral democracy in Ukraine. *Democratization, 8*(2), 117–139.

Kubiček, P. (2009). Problems of post-post-communism: Ukraine after the Orange Revolution. *Democratization, 16*(2), 323–343.

Kubiček, P. (1994). Delegative democracy in Russia and Ukraine. *Communist and Post-Communist Studies, 27*(4), 423–441.

Kudelia, S. (2014). The house that Yanukovych built. *Journal of Democracy, 25*(3), 19–34.

Kuzio, T. (1994). The multi-party system in Ukraine on the eve of elections: Identity problems, conflicts and solutions. *Government and Opposition, 29*(1), 109–127.

Kuzio, T. (1996). Kravchuk to Kuchma: the Ukrainian presidential elections of 1994. *Journal of Communist Studies and Transition Politics, 12*(2), 117–144.
Kuzio, T. (2005). Neither east nor west: Ukraine's security policy. *Problems of Post-Communism, 52*(2), 59–68.
Kuzio, T. (2007). Oligarchs, tapes and oranges: "Kuchmagate" to the Orange Revolution. *Journal of Communist Studies and Transition Politics, 23*(1), 30–56.
Kuzio, T. (2010). Nationalism, identity and civil society in Ukraine: understanding the Orange Revolution. *Communist and Post-Communist Studies, 43*(3), 285–296.
Lynch, G., & Crawford, G. (2011). Democratization in Africa 1990–2010: an assessment. *Democratization, 18*(2), 275–310.
McFaul, M. (2007). Ukraine imports democracy: external influences on the Orange Revolution. *International Security, 32*(2), 45–83.
Melnykovska, I., Plamper, H., Schweickert, R. (2012). Do Russia and China promote autocracy in Central Asia? *Asia Europe Journal, 10*(1), 1–15.
Motyl, A. J. (2013). Yanukovych's choice. *Foreign Affairs*, 46–51.
Neef, C. (2014, February 25). Yanukovych's fall: the power of Ukraine's billionaires. *Spiegel Online International*. http://www.spiegel.de/international/europe/how-oligarchs-in-ukraine-prepared-for-the-fall-of-yanukovych-a-955328.html. Accessed 15 December 2015.
O'Donnell, G., & Schmitter, P. C. (1986). *Transitions from authoritarian rule: tentative conclusions about uncertain democracies*. Baltimore: Johns Hopkins University Press.
Petrovic, M., & Smith, N. R. (2013). In Croatia's slipstream or on an alternative road? Assessing the objective case for the remaining Western Balkan states acceding into the EU. *Southeast European and Black Sea Studies, 13*(4), 553–573.
Pond, E. (2015). Will Ukraine snatch defeat from the jaws of victory? *Survival, 57*(6), 59–68.
Potter, D. S. (1997). Explaining democratization. In: D. S. Potter, D. Goldblatt, M. Kiloh, P. Lewis (Eds.), *Democratization* (Vol. 2). Cambridge: Polity.
Pridham, G. (2014). EU/Ukraine relations and the crisis with Russia, 2013–14: a turning point. *International Spectator, 49*(4), 53–61.
Puglisi, R. (2003). The rise of the Ukrainian oligarchs. *Democratization, 10*(3), 99–123.
Rose, R. (2001). A diverging Europe. *Journal of Democracy, 12*(1), 93–106.
RT. (2015, October 5). World Bank sharply downgrades Ukraine's GDP forecast. *RT question more*. https://www.rt.com/business/317664-ukraine-gdp-world-bank/. Accessed 20 November 2015.
Rustow, D. A. (1970). Transitions to democracy: Toward a dynamic model. *Comparative Politics, 2*(3), 337–363.
Schimmelfennig, F. (2005). Strategic calculation and international socialization: membership incentives, party constellations, and sustained compliance in Central and Eastern Europe. *International Organization, 59*, 827–860.

Schimmelfennig, F., & Sedelmeier, U. (2004). Governance by conditionality: EU rule transfer to the candidate countries of Central and Eastern Europe. *Journal of European Public Policy, 11*(4), 661–679.

Schneider, W. (2004). Ukraine's Orange revolution: a victory for Viktor Yushchenko in Ukraine would confirm the West's increasing influence there. *The Atlantic.* http://www.theatlantic.com/magazine/archive/2004/12/ukraines-orange-revolution/305157/. Accessed 15 December 2015.

Sikorski, R. (2009). The EU's "Eastern partnership" with former Soviet states holds the key to relations with Russia. *Europe's World.* http://europesworld.org/2009/06/01/the-eus-eastern-partnership-with-former-soviet-states-holds-the-key-to-relations-with-russia/. Accessed 15 December 2015.

Smith, N. R. (2014). The underpinning realpolitik of the EU's policies towards Ukraine: an analysis of norms and interests in the EU-Ukraine association agreement. *European Foreign Affairs Review, 19*(4), 581–596.

Smith, N. R. (2015). The EU and Russia's conflicting regime preferences in Ukraine: assessing regime promotion strategies in the scope of the Ukraine crisis. *European Security,* 24(4), 525–540.

Smith, N. R. (2016). The EU under a realist scope: Employing a neoclassical realist framework for the analysis of the EU's deep and comprehensive free trade agreement offer to Ukraine. *International Relations, 30*(1), 29–48.

Snyder, T. (2015). Ukraine: the edge of democracy. *The New York Review of Books.* http://www.nybooks.com/daily/2014/05/22/ukraine-edge-democracy/. Accessed 12 October 2015.

Solonenko, I. (2009). External democracy promotion in Ukraine: the role of the European Union. *Democratization, 16*(4), 709–731.

Stent, A. E. (2008). Restoration and revolution in Putin's foreign policy. *Europe-Asia Studies, 60*(6), 1089–1106.

Tilly, C. (2000). Processes and mechanisms of democratization. *Sociological Theory, 18*(1), 1–16. doi:10.1111/0735-2751.00085.

Tolstrup, J. (2012). When can external actors influence democratization? Leverage, linkages, and gatekeeper elites. *Democratization, 20*(4), 716–742.

Wilson, A. (2006). Ukraine's Orange Revolution, NGOs and the role of the West. *Cambridge Review of International Affairs, 19*(1), 21–32.

Wilson, A. (2015, April 27). Ukraine's economic pressures. *European Council on Foreign Relations.* http://www.ecfr.eu/article/commentary_ukraines_economic_pressures3008. Accessed 15 December 2015.

Yanevskyy, O. (2015, October 13). Poll: Ukrainians unhappy about corruption, incomplete reforms. *Voice of America.* http://www.voanews.com/content/poll-ukrainians-unhappy-about-corruption-incompete-reforms/3004595.html. Accessed 15 December 2015.

Youngs, R. (2009). "A door neither closed nor open": EU policy towards Ukraine during and since the Orange Revolution. *International Politics, 46*(4), 358–375.

Yushchenko, V. (2005, January 24). Inaugural address of the President of Ukraine Victor Yushchenko to the Ukrainian people on independence square. http://www.kmu.gov.ua/control/en/publish/article?art_id=11100895. Accessed 20 November 2015.

Zakaria, F. (1997, November–December). The rise of illiberal democracy. *Foreign Affairs, 76* (1997), 22–41.

Zlenko, A. (1992). Independent Ukraine: risk or stability? *The RUSI Journal, 137*(2), 38–42.

Dr Nicholas Ross Smith is a postdoctoral fellow at the University of Canterbury's National Centre for Research on Europe. He is an expert in International Relations and currently has a specific focus on geopolitics in Eastern Europe. Recent journal publications include an examination of the EU's foreign policy towards Ukraine under a realist scope (International Relations) and assessing the competitiveness of the EU and Russia's regime preferences in Ukraine (European Security).

Chapter 10: Post-Communist Russia and the West: From Crisis to Crisis?

James Headley

In 1994, the first major post–Cold War crisis between Russia and the West occurred over the North Atlantic Treaty Organization's (NATO) threat to bomb the Bosnian Serbs. Five years later, a worse crisis erupted over the Kosovo war, culminating in a stand-off between Russian and NATO troops at Pristina airport. In 2003, Russia strongly opposed the US-led invasion of Iraq, and the following year tensions emerged over the disputed election in Ukraine. In 2008, Russia's war against Georgia was strongly condemned in the West. Disagreements have continued over the war in Syria since 2012. And in late 2013 the most severe crisis of all broke out, over Ukraine. In one sense, then, the post–Cold War period can be seen as a succession of crises in Russian–Western relations after the initial "honeymoon period". In each case, there was talk of a new "Cold War" and soul-searching in the West over what approach should be taken towards Russia. However, after each crisis, a rapprochement followed, such that the whole period cannot be considered one of continual antagonism between Russia and the West. Nevertheless, the severity of the Ukrainian crisis suggests a more serious and possibly permanent schism.

This chapter examines the continuities and changes in post-communist Russian foreign policy as reflected in Russia's relations with the West.

J. Headley (✉)
Department of Politics, University of Otago, Dunedin, New Zealand
e-mail: james.headley@otago.ac.nz

Fish, Gill, Petrovic (eds.), *A Quarter Century of Post-Communism Assessed*, DOI 10.1007/978-3-319-43437-7_11

It argues that key features of Russia's foreign policy approach were already in place in the early Yeltsin period: assertion of Russian national interests distinct from those of the West, insistence on Russia's status as a great power, maintenance of Russia's role in international institutions, and resistance to Western unilateralism and hegemony. These features clashed with key developments in Western foreign policy approaches, helping to explain the recurrent crises. Hence, the chapter also argues that there was much continuity from the Yeltsin to the Putin periods, although an economically stronger and politically more stable Russia could back up its assertive rhetoric more effectively after the chaotic first decade of post-communism. However, changing political circumstances in Russia and changing international circumstances explain why the Ukrainian crisis may mark a turning point in Russian–Western relations: a more authoritarian and conservative nationalist Russia aiming to reintegrate areas of the former Soviet space is coming up against a European Union (EU) that is seeking to engage more actively in the "shared neighbourhood", and a United States that regards Russia as a renewed antagonist.

I will look first at the similarities and differences between Russian responses to the Yugoslav conflicts and the war in Syria. I will then consider what this shows us about the main tenets of Russian foreign policy and how they have developed in the intervening years in response to crises and as a result of political change. Then, I will show how these developments have culminated in the serious crisis in Russian–Western relations over Ukraine. I will conclude with some observations on what lessons we might draw from 25 years of post-communist Russian relations with the West.

Cycle of Crises? Bosnia, 1994, to Syria, 2013

On 5 February 1994, a mortar shell was fired into the Markale marketplace in Sarajevo, Bosnia–Herzegovina, killing 68 people and wounding a further 200. Five days later, NATO issued an ultimatum to all forces fighting within 20 km of Sarajevo to hand over their heavy weapons and to refrain from attacks within the area; if they failed to do so within 10 days, heavy weapons of any of the parties found within the exclusion zone, along with their military support facilities, would be subject to NATO air strikes. This led to the first major crisis in Russian–Western relations after the Cold War (Headley 2003). Although Russian policymakers approved of the aims of the declaration, they criticised the threat of force, the fact that it would be carried out by NATO, and the fact that Russia had been sidelined in taking the decision. Instead, the Russian envoy Vitalii Churkin gained the agreement of Slobodan Milošević (President of Serbia) and Radovan Karadžić (leader of the Bosnian Serbs) to withdraw Serb heavy weapons, while 400 Russian peacekeepers were transferred from Croatia to Sarajevo. This defused the crisis without recourse to air strikes. Both NATO and Russia claimed the credit.

Russian policymakers drew lessons from the crisis, which contributed to the consolidation of broader principles in relation to the wars not only in former Yugoslavia but also in Russian foreign policy more generally (Headley 2003). They argued that NATO had no right to threaten force without a United Nations Security Council (UNSC) resolution; that although the language of the ultimatum was neutral, it was clearly aimed against the Bosnian Serbs even though their responsibility for the mortar shell had not been established; that it was the fact that Russia had asked the Serbs to withdraw their heavy weapons, not the threat of force, that had made the difference; and that the crisis showed the importance of Russia to the resolution of such situations. These conclusions displayed key elements of the Russian position on the Yugoslav conflicts which had been established over the preceding year: that there should be a peaceful resolution to the conflicts through negotiations without preconditions; that there should be no threat or use of force by outside powers; that the UNSC should play the lead role in conflict resolution, not NATO; that the conflict in Bosnia was a civil war in which it was "impossible… to determine who is right and who is wrong", in the words of Sergei Lavrov, then Russian ambassador to the UN (Headley 2008, p. 123); that since the conflicts were taking place in a region of Russian interests, but also had implications for European and global security, Russia should be involved as an equal partner in resolving them; that Russian interests might differ from those of Western powers, who were also pursuing their own interests; but that it was important to avoid a great power conflict, including outside powers supporting proxies in the conflict.

On 21 August 2013, a chemical attack in Ghouta, Syria, focused international attention on the Syrian conflict and led to calls in a number of Western states for intervention against the Bashar al-Assad regime. The following month, after a UN investigation confirmed the use of sarin, Russian diplomats played a lead role in brokering a deal by which the Syrian government would destroy its chemical weapons stocks and sign up to the Chemical Weapons Convention. This deal averted intervention by Western powers, although debates in the US Congress and the UK House of Commons showed that there was significant reluctance to get involved, even though the atrocity had crossed President Obama's "red line". Russia's position was that it was essential to verify which side had used chemical weapons before taking any action; that the crisis should only be resolved by peaceful means (that there should be no threat or actual use of force against the regime); that the crisis showed the importance of Russian diplomacy; and that although Russia did not rule out the future use of force if the government side did not comply with the agreement, any such action must be approved by the UNSC (e.g. Russian Ministry of Foreign Affairs [MFA] 2013a).

These responses to the chemical weapons crisis also reflected wider Russian policy towards the Syrian conflict at that time. First, there should be a peaceful resolution to the conflict, and no preconditions to negotiations (such as the immediate resignation of Assad); second outside powers should neither threaten nor use force to bring about a resolution to the conflict; third the war was a civil war with no side in the right or wrong (except the extreme Islamists) – as President Putin (2013) argued in an article in the *New York Times*, "Syria is not witnessing a battle for democracy, but an armed conflict between government and opposition in a multi-religious country"; fourth decisions must involve Russia, through the UNSC or an institution or conference in which Russia was an equal participant; fifth the war was taking place in an area of Russian interests,[1] but it was also of global concern with implications for world order; and finally Russia's interests might diverge from those of Western powers, yet it was important to cooperate in finding a common position and preventing it from becoming a proxy war or even a direct war between outside states.

There are many significant differences between the earlier situation in Bosnia and the current conflict in Syria, and also in Russia's policy towards them. In practice, for example, Russia was less supportive of the Bosnian government and more favourable towards the "rebels" (Serbs) than in Syria because of sympathy for the Serb side, domestic pressure and a tendency to view Bosnia as an artificial construct, although formally Russia continued to support Bosnia's territorial integrity. Russia was also bound by existing UNSC resolutions that it had voted for in its initial post-Soviet "liberal Westernizing" foreign policy phase – sanctions against Serbia, the "safe areas", the no-fly zone and the International Criminal Tribunal for former Yugoslavia. Russia also favoured upholding the arms embargo, whereas in Syria, it was arming the government side.

Nevertheless, the similarity of policies across a 20-year gap is striking, indicating the long-term continuities in Russian foreign policy. A statement by a representative of the Russian Ministry of Foreign Affairs on 30 August 2013 could have been taken from any official statement in relation to the Yugoslav conflicts after 1992:

> Any unilateral forceful action bypassing the UN Security Council, however "restricted" it is, will become a direct violation of international law, will disrupt the prospects of a political and diplomatic resolution of the conflict in Syria, and will lead to a new turn of confrontation and new victims. We cannot allow such [a] development of events. (Russian MFA 2013b)

We can see here the insistence on international law, in terms of due process (through the UNSC) and observation of principles of non-intervention and sovereignty, and on a Russian role in resolution of international crises. What this amounted to in terms of Syria, as with former Yugoslavia previously, was the use of the UNSC to block external intervention in a civil war and to avert any action outside a UNSC framework (Charap 2013; Hahn 2012). It reflected scepticism about the notion of "humanitarian intervention" or a "responsibility to protect", which Russian policymakers saw as a mask for self-interest on the part of Western states.

Russia propounded these principles in other key crises in the intervening period, with policymakers demanding that Russia be involved in their resolution, resisting Western interventionism and standing up for what they perceived to be Russian interests. First, the Russian response to Operation "Deliberate Force", NATO's air campaign against the Bosnian Serb forces in August–September 1995, was a logical extension of its position in relation to the Sarajevo crisis: Russia objected to the use of force by NATO without a clear-cut Security Council resolution (policymakers argued that existing resolutions creating the "safe areas" did not permit such extensive action) (Headley 2008). The same applied when the Kosovo crisis emerged a few years later. Russia objected to NATO threats of force against Serbia, and then its actual use of force from March to June 1999, Operation "Allied Force". In addition, it saw NATO's intervention and the terms of the peace agreement that ended it as paving the way for Western-backed independence for Kosovo, and also a mechanism to bring about "regime change" in Belgrade. Policy thereafter became focused on resisting moves towards Kosovo independence, in line with the principle of territorial integrity as set out in, for example, the Helsinki Final Act, and in line with the rather ambiguous UNSC Resolution 1244 that ended the conflict (Headley 2008).

In each of these cases, a key factor was NATO. It was not just that NATO was pushing Russia aside, but that such actions gave NATO a raison d'ětre in the post–Cold War world. Hence, the issue of NATO action in former Yugoslavia became tied up in the wider question of the role of NATO in post–Cold War Europe and the increasingly divisive question of NATO enlargement (NATO in fact admitted its first former Warsaw Pact members in April 1999, during Operation "Allied Force"). Furthermore, in Kosovo, Russia rejected Western claims that existing resolutions permitted military action, and regarded as spurious the argument that the fact that a draft resolution condemning the bombing was defeated in the UNSC gave it legitimacy. Fundamentally, Russian policymakers believed that Western powers were not respecting international law, were dismissing out of hand objections by other states and were motivated by self-interest rather than humanitarian impulses (Headley 2008).

Similar issues arose with the US-led invasion of Iraq in 2003, with the difference that the West was more divided in this case. Again, Russia objected to intervention in a sovereign state against its government's wishes and without explicit UNSC approval. Russian policymakers did not accept the argument that existing resolutions allowed for such action, and were unconvinced by the claims that Iraq possessed weapons of mass destruction; instead, they attributed the Bush-administration's policy to geopolitical calculations. There were, however, additional features in relation to Iraq that concerned Russia, which I will discuss in more detail below: regime change and the attempted imposition of liberal democracy; and the belief that such action might create a failed state and encourage Islamic fundamentalism.

In each of the previous crises, the downturn in Russia's relations with the West was gradually reversed and a relative rapprochement occurred as each side recognised the importance of maintaining cooperative relations built on mutual interests. The Iraq war, however, added to building resentment among Russian policymakers at the disregard for Russia's objections, and wariness about backing resolutions in the Security Council that might be used as a pretext for intervention, especially as the pattern was later repeated in relation to Libya. Russia abstained on UNSC Resolution 1973 authorising a no-fly zone in Libya in 2012, but subsequently objected to the way in which certain NATO states exceeded the mandate. As Lavrov, now Foreign Minister, put it in response to an interview question of whether Russia had been misled on the resolution:

> We stated clearly that the mandate given by the resolution on which we and the Chinese abstained was grossly violated. The no-fly zone is about not allowing the military aircraft flying, and that's it. And that's it. The coalition was not patrolling the no-fly zone and was not ensuring the no-fly zone. It was taking out targets on the ground, directly participating in the internal conflict. (Glasser 2013)

And in a speech later that year at MGIMO university he reiterated the point:

> In the case of Libya, where, as you know, there was declared a task to establish a no-fly zone and only afterwards the rule of democracy, there took place a simple transformation of this no-fly zone into elementary, cynical occupation of the aviation of NATO member countries involved in the internal conflict that were on the side of the opponents of the regime of Gaddafi. This was evident in the shocking fact that Gaddafi was savagely killed by NATO forces. (Lavrov 2013).

These developments help to explain Russia's subsequent reluctance to allow more extensive international action over Syria, and also contributed to deepening its already entrenched distrust of Western interventionism.

Norms and Interests in Russian Foreign Policy

What can we conclude from this brief survey of international crises involving Russia? I have suggested that we can see a fairly consistent defence of a set of norms of non-intervention, sovereignty and territorial integrity (I will discuss below problems in the Russian position in practice from 2008). These are traditional state-centric norms, reflecting scepticism about ideas of humanitarian intervention, but still couched in principled terms.[2] For example, the 2013 Russian Foreign Policy Concept states (31[b]) under the heading "Rule of Law in International Relations":

> Arbitrary and politically motivated interpretation of fundamental international legal norms and principles such as non-use of force or threat of force, peaceful settlement of international disputes, respect for sovereignty and

> territorial integrity of states, right of peoples to self-determination, in favour of certain countries pose particular danger to international peace, law and order. Likewise, attempts to represent violations of international law as its "creative" application are dangerous. It is unacceptable that military interventions and other forms of interference from without which undermine the foundations of international law based on the principle of sovereign equality of states, be carried out on the pretext of implementing the concept of "responsibility to protect". (Russian MFA 2013c)

Russia claimed not to object in principle to action on the basis of humanitarian concerns, but believed that it should not undermine the general basis of international relations, and also should be decided through due process (the UNSC). For example, in the context of the debate over Syria and the Libya events preceding it, Lavrov answered the question, "do you think there are any situations in which humanitarian intervention is justified?" as follows:

> Well, you know this issue has been discussed a lot, including at the United Nations. It is a generally accepted rule and norm of international law that sovereignty cannot be used as a pretext for gross violations of human rights, ethnic cleansing, genocide, military crimes. And all this has been clearly spelled out in 2005 when the United Nations General Assembly was convened at the summit level and adopted a declaration where this "responsibility to protect" concept was described. That declaration clearly stated, that the priorities given to the efforts of the states themselves who have the obligation – the primary obligation – to protect their population, that the priority must be given to political means. And that only in case when a state exhausts all its possibilities and is not able to protect the population, it is only then that the international community can interfere, but only when the Security Council so decides. So this issue is closed. The rules have been agreed. (Glasser 2013)

In practice, throughout the period, Russia has held the bar very high in terms of what is required for the use of force, even to uphold resolutions it has supported, especially where policymakers believe Russia's interests to be at stake. For example, in early 1994, in his capacity of Deputy Foreign Minister, Lavrov explained to the Duma the Russian position on air strikes in Bosnia: existing resolutions allowed force only in the event of an attack on a convoy delivering humanitarian aid, a violation of the no-fly zone or "direct obstruction of the UN peace-keeping forces in carrying out their mandate" for the maintenance of the "safe areas". And a special procedure was required for force then to be used:

> In all the enumerated decisions the question is only about a threat of the use of force against a violator. Its actual use requires a special additional procedure – consultations between the secretary general and the members of the Security Council. Our position in the course of such consultations, if they begin, will be negative. (Headley 2003, p. 215)

This would seem to indicate a predetermined rejection of the use of air strikes in any circumstances. Similarly, in 2013, Russia opposed the use of force in Syria by outside powers even to enforce the weak UNSC resolutions 2042/3. As suggested above, this was partly the consequence of what had happened in Libya, and also genuine concerns about the security vacuum that might be created if Syrian government forces withdrew (as with Kosovo in 1999).

It is easy to see, however, that Russia had interests in preventing Western action in each of the situations discussed. In former Yugoslavia, Russian policymakers perceived those interests to include restricting NATO's role and, increasingly, to nurture Serbia as a potential ally in the Balkans (there was an increasing trend towards supporting the Serb side which, while not an explicitly pro-Orthodox/Slav policy, did reflect such sympathies among the elite and was a consequence also of domestic pressure). In Iraq, Russia resisted being pushed out of a Middle Eastern country with which it had strong ties, including lucrative contracts for oil extraction. In addition, as I explore below, opposing the idea of "regime change" became paramount under Putin. In the case of Syria, the standard account of Russia's position was that Russia was supporting an authoritarian ally, and protecting arms sales and its naval base at Tartus (its only one in the Mediterranean) (Charap 2013, p. 35). All of this is in line with the dominant realist outlook in Russian foreign policy which stresses the pursuit and defence of Russian interests even when they may conflict with those of the West, and attributes Western foreign policy to a corresponding pursuit of self-interest.

There is clearly tension between the principled rhetoric and the realist outlook on foreign affairs. I cannot explore this contradiction in further detail here, but would suggest, first, that it is not uncommon for self-interest and defence of norms to be intertwined, and in terms of international theory we should not consider them to be in contradiction or mutually exclusive. In the Russian case, policymakers believed that Russia is better off with traditional state-centric principles in international affairs, but also that these principles are best for the world as a whole. Second, the Russian realist-based claim that all states are equally pursuing their self-interest has been a rhetorical strategy that masks the fact that Russia often is making principled arguments (Averre 2009; Casier 2013; DeBardeleben 2012). It seems to have convinced many analysts who take it at face value and contrast it with the West's normative approach. For example, in response to the Wikileaks, Farrell and Finnemore (2013) wrote:

> Indeed, the United States could take a page out of China's and Russia's playbooks: instead of framing their behaviour in terms of the common good, those countries decry anything that they see as infringing on their national sovereignty and assert their prerogative to pursue their interests at will. Washington could do the same, while continuing to punish leakers with harsh prison sentences and threatening countries that might give them refuge.

My analysis challenges the claim that Russia does not frame its behaviour in terms of the common good, but it is an empirical matter whether, in the case of Russia and Western states, such rhetoric merely masks self-interest.

Third, and connected to the previous point, Western refusal to acknowledge Russia as an equal interlocutor in developing international norms and in deciding international policies has fed into Russian resentment and increased assertiveness over the past two decades. Russian policymakers have shown growing frustration over Western claims to a special knowledge of the moral truth based on various forms of exceptionalism. We get a hint of Russian frustration in Lavrov's interview in 2013:

> And speaking of the Syrian situation in general and about the American position and the Russian position, we have been listening for a couple of years during the previous administration of President Obama. We have been hearing appeals to us to change our position. All the time the official representatives of the State Department or the White House will be saying, "We call on Russia and China to change their position", which meant the conviction of Washington that their position was right. (Glasser 2013)

The Russian rejection of US exceptionalism was later well summed up by Putin (2013) in response to President Obama's address to the US nation over Syria:

> I would rather disagree with a case he made on American exceptionalism, stating that the United States' policy is "what makes America different. It's what makes us exceptional". It is extremely dangerous to encourage people to see themselves as exceptional, whatever the motivation. There are big countries and small countries, rich and poor, those with long democratic traditions and those still finding their way to democracy. Their policies differ, too. We are all different, but when we ask for the Lord's blessings, we must not forget that God created us equal.

Russian policymakers, then, have been sceptical about the concept of a "responsibility to protect", but also about the way Western powers assume the sole moral authority to judge its applicability in specific cases. In order to undercut this presumption, Russian policymakers have increasingly accused their Western counterparts of displaying double standards in their policies across a range of areas – for example, in recognition of Kosovo, in upholding minority rights and in supporting authoritarian allies in some countries, but seeking regime change in others (Headley 2015a). For example, Lavrov (2013) complained:

> If we talk about the Middle East and North Africa, there was what we call a "double standard", as well as personal attitude i.e. personal animosity to a single authoritarian leader results in the agreement that he must be toppled by all means, and authoritarian leaders who do not cause such dislike and who are allies of our Western partners and assist them, are not taken into consideration at all.

Finally, my analysis challenges the common tendency among commentators to argue that Russia's assertive approach occurred only under President Putin. For example, many analysts point to Putin's speech at the Munich security conference in 2007 as evidence of a turning point towards an aggressively assertive Russian policy. Yet, the essentials of that speech have formed the basis of foreign policy since around 1993/1994: pursuit of multipolarity, opposition to NATO enlargement, resistance to Western interventionism and the undermining of sovereignty, especially when carried out unilaterally and without regard for the UNSC, and so on. There was little new here that had not been heard in complaints throughout most of the post–Cold War era, and can be seen in successive versions of the Russian Foreign Policy Doctrine, for example. It was merely stated more directly than usual, but Putin (2007) explained why:

> This conference's structure allows me to avoid excessive politeness and the need to speak in roundabout, pleasant but empty diplomatic terms. This conference's format will allow me to say what I really think about international security problems. And if my comments seem unduly polemical, pointed or inexact to our colleagues, then I would ask you not to get angry with me. After all, this is only a conference.

Nevertheless, we cannot ignore the changes that have occurred during Putin's rule, especially as they connect to his domestic consolidation of power; and we also need to explain the dramatic developments in relation to Syria and Ukraine since 2013. I will turn now to a more detailed analysis of the Putin period, before focusing on those recent developments.

The Putin Era

Three key interrelated factors in the Putin era shed light on Russia's increasingly strained relations with the West, each one linking domestic and foreign policy developments: Chechnya, terrorism and Islamic fundamentalism; increased authoritarianism in Russia, legitimised through the notion of "sovereign democracy" and connected to resistance to "regime change"; and emphasis on the former Soviet space with the aim of reintegrating it economically.

Putin rose to power on the back of crushing Chechnya. Although the renewed war resulted in more terrorist atrocities across Russia, the pretext for the invasion in 1999 was the apartment bombings in Moscow and Volgodonsk as well as incursions by Islamic fundamentalists from Chechnya into neighbouring Dagestan. After the interim peace agreement in 1996, Chechnya had been de facto independent, but was ruled by warlords and fundamentalists intent on trying to expand their control. Hence, Putin's rhetoric in the early 2000s linked the threat of separatism, Islamic fundamentalism and terrorism, and he saw these as connected across an "arc of instability" spreading from Afghanistan across the Middle East (and Russia's southern tier) to the Balkans (Headley 2005). He argued that Russia and the West shared a common interest in resisting this threat, and justified military action on this basis. In early September 2001, one of the major international news items was the rising tension between Russia and Georgia as Russian airplanes conducted strikes against Chechen fighters based in the Pankisi Gorge, an area of Georgia neighbouring Chechnya. When the terrorist attacks occurred in the United States on 11 September, Russia offered sympathy and support against a "common enemy", including allowing transit of goods by the US military across Russia to support the war in Afghanistan. The common threat was used as a basis to repair relations severely strained after the Kosovo conflict and NATO enlargement and to divert criticism away from Russia's conduct of its operations in Chechnya (although two years later, Russia, like other states, rejected the claim that Iraq was linked to terrorism, and as we have seen, the Iraq invasion led to a renewed crisis in relations).

Chechnya laid the basis for Putin's rise to power but also contributed to the authoritarian shift in Russian politics (Headley 2005). First, there was the indiscriminate attack on Chechnya with little regard for loss of civilian lives, and the subsequent repression there under President Kadyrov. Second, outspoken critics of the Chechnya campaign, and individuals who have investigated the questionable actions of the Federal Security Service (FSB) in the apartment bombings preceding the second Chechen war have been silenced (Alexander Litvinenko, Anna Politkovskaia). Third, the Chechen war has been used by Putin to consolidate and centralise power (e.g. after the Beslan massacre in 2004, governors of federal entities were appointed rather than elected, and Duma election rules were changed to favour larger parties).

These measures fed into the broader trend towards authoritarianism, which was couched in ideological terms as "sovereign democracy", the assertion of the right of each sovereign state to its own form of democracy against pressure from the West and international organisations in promoting universal human rights and liberal representative democracy (Headley 2015b). As a result, a normative gap arose between Russia and the West, including between Russia and the European Union over the degree to which pan-European norms should be developed to shape the domestic and international behaviour of all European states, over who should develop such norms, and how (Headley 2012a). Increasingly, the Russian authorities clamped down on non-governmental organisations based in Russia that were portrayed as agents of Western states, contributing to the narrowing of civil society. Such organisations were accused of promoting "regime change" in Russia itself, so that the idea of a domestic threat to the Putin regime became tied to Russian foreign policy in resisting "regime change" in the Middle East and particularly in the former Soviet space.

Increasing emphasis on the former Soviet space as the priority area for Russian foreign policy was a feature of the more assertive approach in the 1990s after the initial "liberal Westernizing" phase. Under Putin, it became more than a declaration of intent, as signified by his famous statement in his 2005 address to the Federal Assembly that the "collapse of the Soviet Union was a major geopolitical disaster of the century" (Putin 2005). Putin acknowledged that the former Soviet space remained highly integrated in many ways – movement of people and goods, for example – particularly with the Russian economic boom in the 2000s. But by the early 2010s, Russian policymakers were actively pursuing regionalism (the deliberate policy of developing intra-regional ties) through specific integrationist projects (Putin 2011). This has been accompanied by rhetorical emphasis on the idea of a "civilizational identity", although this is in tension with the simultaneous promotion of specifically Russian language and culture and support for ethnic Russians in the "near abroad" (Headley 2012b, 2015b).

Such developments have contributed to recurrent crises with the West during the Putin era. First, the "Orange Revolution" in Ukraine in 2004 challenged the apparent manipulation of the election there, including direct Russian interference in support of Viktor Yanukovych, while Russia accused Western states of engineering "regime change" and overturning democratic results in order to get pro-Western forces into power. This crisis prefigured the 2013 crisis and prompted similar fears of a new Cold War. Then, in 2008, Russia fought its first war in the post-Cold War era outside the borders of the Russian Federation, against Georgia. Russian actions were clearly intended to protect perceived interests in the former Soviet space: to block the pro-Western Georgian President Saakashvili's attempt to reclaim South Ossetia and Abkhazia and to show the credibility of Russian commitments to breakaway regions (Russia had explicitly stated that Russia would prevent any forceful attempt by Georgia to reclaim them). They were also tied to the wider issue of NATO enlargement, as Ukraine and Georgia were pushing for NATO membership, encouraged by the Bush administration (Mearsheimer 2014).

Although the subsequent report by the Independent International Fact-Finding Mission on the Conflict in Georgia (2009) held Georgia primarily responsible for initiating the conflict,[3] Russia's willingness to use force and apparent incitement of Georgia confirmed for many Western commentators and policymakers that there had been a major shift in Russian policy under Putin and that his Munich rhetoric was now being applied in practice. Furthermore, when Russia recognised the breakaway regions as independent states it seemed to signify a major departure: after all, in rhetoric at least, Russia had previously insisted on the territorial integrity of the former Yugoslav and former Soviet republics. This remained the basis of Russian objections to Kosovo's declaration of independence in February 2008 and its subsequent recognition by most Western states, as well as the legitimation for Russia's own reabsorption of Chechnya into the Russian Federation.

Nevertheless, these developments again need to be understood within the context of longer-term developments in Russian foreign policy. It is true that by recognizing South Ossetia and Abkhazia, Russian policymakers abandoned any real claim to consistency of defence of such principles (though, like Western powers with Kosovo, they portrayed it as a unique case that had no implications for those principles), but they had warned repeatedly that Western recognition of Kosovo against Russia's (and Serbia's) objections would have implications elsewhere (Headley 2012a). They had also warned that they would uphold their role as peacekeeper in "frozen conflicts" in the former Soviet space (although Russian troops have in fact provided support for de facto states since the early 1990s). In addition, Russia had had to accept NATO enlargement as a *fait accompli*, including the accession of the Baltic states, but Russian policymakers have repeatedly warned against any further NATO encroachment into the former Soviet space, viewed as an area of vital and special Russian interests.

The war with Georgia showed that Russia was now prepared and able to back up its rhetoric of standing up for its interests, especially in the former Soviet space. So, although the rhetoric and overall outlook had not changed, Putin was more willing to implement it in practice even if it meant a deterioration of relations with the West. This was partly because, as a result of the economic recovery, Russia was now more capable of doing so and less dependent on economic ties with the West (the reintegration process within the former Soviet space was also designed to reinforce the economic revival and Russia's independence from the West). However, as with previous crises, there was a subsequent attempt to emphasise shared interests with the West and to promote a rapprochement. One move in this direction was the proposal to develop a European Security Treaty that would help resolve the disputes over Kosovo and Georgia (Russian MFA 2009). As with earlier attempts to invigorate the Conference/Organization for Security and Cooperation in Europe (CSCE/OSCE) as the key security institution in Europe, the Russian initiative fell on deaf ears in the West. By now, Russia was seen as acting against European norms rather than as an equal participant in European affairs, and although there was more caution about further NATO enlargement,[4] alternative ways of bringing former Soviet states into the Western fold were now pursued (the Eastern Partnership). Such a rebuttal merely contributed to further Russian resentment and assertiveness.

Hence, the cycle of crisis and rapprochement between Russia and the West seemed to be developing into a spiral of deepening mutual distrust.

Ukraine and Syria, 2013–

The developments outlined above came to a head with the Ukraine crisis. There is no room here to go into detail about internal Ukrainian politics;[5] I will focus instead on how the crisis there turned into a wider clash between Russia and the West, and specifically on the Russia–EU dimension.

For much of the post-Soviet period, Russian policymakers viewed the European Union as the benign West in contrast to the United States and NATO (there are echoes here of Cold War wedge driving). Russia was fairly positive about European Union integration and did not object in principle to EU enlargement, unlike NATO enlargement. Nominally at least, Russian policymakers hoped that EU enlargement would also promote closer ties between Russia and the EU, and insisted that Russia was a European power. As suggested above, there were clashes over norms, however, and specific tensions as a result of EU criticism of Russia's Chechnya campaign, over certain issues related to enlargement (Kaliningrad; the rights of ethnic Russians in the Baltic States), as well as between Russia and individual EU Member States such as the United Kingdom and Poland. These tensions were a prelude to the dramatic clash over Ukraine which resulted from an assertive Russia seeking reintegration in the Soviet space meeting an EU that was emboldened to act in its neighbourhood and regarded Russia as a disruptive influence.

In one respect, the Ukraine crisis was the result of two contradictory integration projects (Headley 2012c, 2013). Although Ukraine was not being offered actual membership of the EU, the Association Agreement (AA) incorporating a Deep and Comprehensive Free Trade Agreement (DCFTA) was designed to extend many features of membership and incorporate Ukraine into the wider EU orbit, tied to conditionality in a way that was familiar from the enlargement process. The AAs grew out of the EU's

Eastern Partnership, developed partly in response to the Georgia crisis. Ukraine was key for Russia, however: Putin believed that Ukrainian membership was vital for the success of reintegration initially as a Customs Union and more ambitiously as a Eurasian Economic Union; Russian oligarchs were intimately involved in Ukraine, and Ukraine was central to Russian energy exports; culturally and historically, eastern Ukraine at least was considered part of a common space with Russia, and ethnic Russians lived there in large numbers; and Sevastopol in the Crimean peninsula, controversially leased from Ukraine, was the home to Russia's Black Sea Fleet.

Both sides made it clear that Ukraine could not be a member of the Customs Union and sign an FTA with the EU. This points to problems with the narrative of EU integration as a peace project, since a deep integration project of this sort creates similar issues to those that emerged with the nation state: breaking up existing common economic and cultural spaces and making borders more significant. Furthermore, the EU's foreign policy was conducted in a way that did not promote peace: it ignored Russian concerns about the agreement, and, convinced of its own inherent goodness and the benefits an FTA would bring to Ukraine, equated a pro-EU orientation with democracy, neglecting legitimate concerns among many Ukrainians about the proposed agreement (these problems with the divisive effect that integration could have, and with EU foreign policy, echoed aspects of the Yugoslav conflict in the early 1990s; Woodward [1995]).

Furthermore, the AA also required Ukraine to align with the EU's Common Foreign and Security Policy, which Russia increasingly perceived as a way to build close ties with NATO and as being antagonistic towards Russia. Combined with US support for the Maidan protestors and its apparent attempt to engineer the removal of President Yanukovych and replace him with Arseniy Yatsenyuk – whose "Open Ukraine" organisation (http://openukraine.org/en/about/partners) was sponsored by, among others, the US State Department, the National Endowment for Democracy, the Polish Embassy, Chatham House and the NATO Information and Documentation Centre in Kiev – such policies led Russian policymakers to perceive events in Ukraine as a Western attempt to push Russia out of an area of vital interests, implemented through the now familiar method of regime change – in this case the removal of a democratically elected president through a popular protest campaign orchestrated in part by anti-Russian Ukrainian nationalists.

Consequently, when Yanukovych fled (apparently against Putin's wishes) and the future orientation of Ukraine became clear, it is perhaps not fully surprising that Putin moved surreptitiously to annex Crimea – an opportunistic move to solve once and for all the Sevastopol issue (Mearsheimer 2014). Once again this was a blatant violation of the norm of territorial integrity that was supposedly still central to Russian foreign policy. Although arguments could be made, as with Kosovo, that Crimea is a special case (it has a majority of Russian speakers, and it was only part of Ukraine due to its arbitrary transfer from Soviet Russia to Soviet Ukraine by Nikita Khrushchev in 1954), Russia had clearly come a long way from its stance of 1991/1992 – that the constituent republics of the Socialist Federative Republic of Yugoslavia and of the Soviet Union were now independent states entitled to their territorial integrity. Subsequently, Moscow played Belgrade to eastern Ukraine's Republika Srpska, again in stark contrast to the Yugoslav wars when Russia had voted for sanctions against Serbia for supporting Serb secessionists in Bosnia – even if, unlike with Crimea, Russia formally claimed not to support independence or accession to the Russian Federation for the self-declared Donetsk and Lugansk "republics", urging instead substantial autonomy within Ukraine.[6]

The Ukraine crisis is the culmination of Russia's more assertive attitude – especially in its "near abroad" – now backed up with a willingness to stand up for its interests even with force, despite the isolation and economic repercussions it entails. At the same time, Russian policymakers still attempt to defend their actions in terms of shared principles, and to accuse the West of abrogating those principles (in manufacturing a coup against an elected leader by those who threatened the rights of the Russian minority) and displaying double standards; and they object to the lack of consultation with Russia or consideration of Russian interests. For example, Putin (2014) told the Duma in December 2014:

> ...in the case of the Ukraine-EU Association Agreement, there was no dialogue at all. We were told that it was none of our business or, to put it simply, we were told where to go. All the arguments that Russia and Ukraine are members of the CIS free-trade zone, that we have deep-rooted cooperation in industry and agriculture, and basically share the same infrastructure – no one wanted to hear these arguments, let alone take them into account.

Similarly, with Syria, Russia refused to back down from its support of Assad and then, later, provided direct military support to his regime. This was a demonstration of the assertiveness and geopolitical thinking (supporting an ally) that has been the mainstay of Russian rhetoric, including in relation to the Middle East where it displays the influence of the former Foreign Minister Evgenii Primakov, a Middle Eastern specialist. Theoretically, it does not signify a reversal of Russia's opposition to Western intervention in 2013 (and subsequently), or its earlier anti-interventionist position, because Russia was invited to join the campaign by what it sees as the legitimate government. However, as in Ukraine, Russia seems prepared to risk a confrontation with the West, this time by openly entering the war, thereby going beyond supporting a proxy, which is a far cry from the caution in Bosnia in the 1990s. This willingness can be explained in part by two developments discussed previously: the vision of Russia as a fighter against Islamic fundamentalism and terrorism, tying the Syrian conflict to Russia's own struggle internally,[7] and the attempt to match great power rhetoric with action, backed by renewed military capability. In this context, the multifaceted intervention in the Syrian war serves as a demonstration of Russia's "return" to military "greatness" (Myers and Schmitt 2015). Yet, it is still justified in terms of existing international principles: support for a legitimate government that Russia portrays as the most effective bulwark against Islamic extremism, offering also the potential for cooperation with the West against Islamic State.

Conclusion

I have argued that the main principles of Russian foreign policy have been fairly consistent since the early 1990s. These principles help to explain the periodic clashes with Western states, particularly over issues or in areas that Russian policymakers perceive to be important to Russian interests. In broader terms, a Russia seeking to re-establish its great power status, which depends particularly on key strategic areas, is coming up against a West that regards Russia as an irritant in its promulgation of norms and approaches to resolving international crises. This is exacerbated by the tendency of Western policymakers to ignore Russian objections to their policies and not to engage seriously with the principles their Russian counterparts espouse. Until recently, crises tended to be followed by rapprochements, but the circumstances of Russian domestic developments, and developments in the former Soviet Union and Middle East involving Western states, have created a more permanent freezing of relations.

How can we interpret post-communist Russian foreign policy and its relations with the West? Firstly, I would argue that it is misleading to frame the tensions in terms of a new "Cold War". Russia is not the Soviet Union, in borders or in politico-economic system, and does not present an alternative system to liberal democratic capitalism. Although Russia wants to be recognised as a great power, it does not have the global pretensions or global capability of its predecessor, nor the ideological drive to compete globally with the United States. The prime area of attention is the "near abroad", the former Soviet space, which is both an area of primary Russian interests and a means for Russia to assert its great power status. The dominant realist thinking in foreign policy sees Russia as a regional hegemon and as a major power because of its dominant sphere.

A second, alternative interpretation is that Russia is a rising power, challenging Western hegemony. The idea of the BRICS suits this interpretation, moving beyond the Cold War paradigm. Russia, along with the other rising powers, is a revisionist power, seeking to challenge the dominant Western-led order. While there is some truth in this account, it is problematic to view such a diverse range of countries as a coherent group, regardless of attempts by policymakers to make it into one. Regarding Russia, although foreign policy over the past 20 years has been geared towards re-establishing Russia's status after the collapse of the Soviet Union and its empire, its former status and its level of development place it in a different position to other members of the group.

We can see then that Russia is a revisionist state in terms of power - it wants to be acknowledged as a great power, to be heard and to be one of the major powers making key decisions in the international arena. But this desire in fact manifests itself as a defence of the existing order of international politics based on the United Nations and especially the Security Council in which, as a permanent veto-wielding member, Russia can be an equal participant with other major powers. Similarly, defence of the idea of non-intervention and sovereignty suits the Putin regime's interests but is also presented as a defence of fundamental principles of the world order under threat from Western interventionism and hegemony in the widest sense. So, Russia is more of a status quo power than a revisionist power regarding the principles of the international order. Nevertheless, when it comes to the immediate neighbourhood, Russian policymakers have increasingly contravened such principles in pursuing specific Russian and regime interests, in line with the realist idea of great power regional hegemony. Such actions only serve to undermine the principled stance promulgated in other contexts.

This makes it harder for Western policymakers as the normative gap between Russia and the West widens. Yet, Russia has become more assertive partly because it has been ignored in the past. Western policymakers have too often disregarded Russian opinions on international matters, and have then been surprised by Russian assertiveness. This is partly a matter of ignorance (House of Lords European Union Committee 2015), but also a habit developed during the Yeltsin period of assuming that Russian objections to Western policy are mere bluster for a domestic audience. Too often, also, Western policymakers are convinced of the rectitude of their own policies and disregard legitimate concerns from Russia. In this regard, Russia is not alone in demanding more equal consideration in international affairs and challenging Western hegemony in the post-Cold War era.

Notes

1. According to Hahn (2012), "being in the immediate neighbourhood", Russia is "caught even more tightly" in the Syrian crisis than the United States.
2. In his detailed analysis of Russian approaches to military intervention, Allison (2013) also argues that Russia has defended a particular set of norms, leading to "normative friction" (p. 208) with the West.
3. The report wrote: "The shelling of Tskhinvali by the Georgian armed forces during the night of 7 to 8 August 2008 marked the beginning of the large-scale armed conflict in Georgia, yet it was only the culminating point of a long period of increasing tensions, provocations and incidents" (p. 11).
4. NATO's invitation to Montenegro in December 2015 to begin accession talks sparked an angry Russian reaction, showing that Russia remains opposed to NATO enlargement even outside the former Soviet Union.
5. For detailed analysis of the Ukrainian crisis from contrasting perspectives, see Sakwa (2015) and Wilson (2014).
6. In practice, Putin's control of events and of the secessionist forces is probably exaggerated in mainstream accounts, as was Milošević's control over Serb nationalists outside Serbia; but as with Milošević, Putin is trapped by his own nationalist rhetoric which is instrumental to his popular support.
7. Although a report by Elena Milashina (2015) in *Novaia gazeta* suggested that the Syrian conflict has also been seen as an opportunity for Russia, with special services helping Islamists from the Russian Caucasus to go to fight in Syria, hoping thereby to remove a domestic threat.

Bibliography

Allison, R. (2013). *Russia, the West, and military intervention*. Oxford: Oxford University Press.

Averre, D. (2009). From Pristina to Tskhinvali: the legacy of operation allied force in Russia's relations with the West. *International Affairs, 85*(3), 575–591.

Casier, T. (2013). The EU-Russia strategic partnership: challenging the normative argument. *Europe-Asia Studies, 65*(7), 1377–1395.

Charap, S. (2013). Russia, Syria and the doctrine of intervention. *Survival 55*(1), 35–41.

DeBardeleben, J. (2012). Applying constructivism to understanding EU-Russian relations. *International Politics, 49*(4), 418–433.

Farrell, H., & Finnemore, M. (2013). The end of hypocrisy: American foreign policy in the age of leaks. *Foreign Affairs, 92*(6), 22–26.

Glasser, S. B. (2013, April 29). "The law of politics" according to Sergei Lavrov: an exclusive interview with Russia's top diplomat. *Foreign Policy Magazine*.

Hahn, G. (2012, February 16). Russia's hard-nosed realism in Syria: the roots and reasoning. *Fair Observer*. http://www.fairobserver.com/region/europe/russias-hard-nosed-realism-syria-roots-and-reasoning/. Accessed 10 December 2015.

Headley, J. (2003). Sarajevo, February 1994: the first Russia-NATO crisis of the post-Cold War era. *Review of International Studies, 29*(2), 209–227.

Headley, J. (2005). War on terror or pretext for power? Putin, Chechnya, and the "terrorist international". *Australasian Journal of Human Security, 1*(2), 13–35.

Headley, J. (2008). *Russia and the Balkans: Foreign policy from Yeltsin to Putin*. London and New York: Hurst and Co.; Columbia University Press.

Headley, J. (2012a). Is Russia out of step with European norms? Assessing Russia's relationship to European identity, values and norms through the issue of self-determination. *Europe-Asia Studies, 64*(3), 427–447.

Headley, J. (2012b). Near abroads and arcs of instability: conceptualising the region in the South Pacific and Eurasia. *Canterbury Law Review, 18*, 15–40.

Headley, J. (2012c). National and transnational challenges in the former Soviet Union and former Yugoslavia. *Global Change, Peace & Security, 24*(2), 251–269.

Headley, J. (2013). A divided democracy/contested kleptocracy between two unions. *Australian and New Zealand Journal of European Studies, 5*(2), 98–101.

Headley, J. (2015a). Challenging the EU's claim to moral authority: Russian talk of "double standards". *Asia Europe Journal, 13*(3), 297–307.

Headley, J. (2015b). Russia's complex engagement with European Union norms: sovereign democracy versus post-Westphalianism? In: A. Björkdahl, N. Chaban, J. Leslie, A. Masselot (Eds.), *Importing EU norms: conceptual framework and empirical findings* (pp. 211–230). New York: Springer.

House of Lords European Union Committee. (2015). *The EU and Russia: before and beyond the crisis in Ukraine*. http://www.publications.parliament.uk/pa/ld201415/ldselect/ldeucom/115/115.pdf. Accessed 6 January 2016.

Independent International Fact-Finding Mission on the Conflict in Georgia. (2009, September). *Report*. http://echr.coe.int/Documents/HUDOC_38263_08_Annexes_ENG.pdf. Accessed 10 December 2015.

Lavrov, S. V. (2013, September 2). Speech by S.V. Lavrov, Russian Federation Ministry of Foreign Affairs, in front of the students and professors of MGIMO (University) MFA of Russia. http://www.rusemb.org.uk/foreignpolicy/1215. Accessed 10 December 2015.

Mearsheimer, J. J. (2014). Why the Ukraine crisis is the West's fault. *Foreign Affairs, 93*, 77–89.

Milashina, E. (2015, July 29). Khalifat? Primarka dlia durakov! *Novaia gazeta*. http://www.novayagazeta.ru/inquests/69364.html. Accessed 7 January 2016.

Myers, S. L., & Schmitt, E. (2015, October 14). Russian military uses Syria as proving ground, and West takes notice. *International New York Times*. Accessed 17 December 2015.

Putin, V. V. (2005, April 25). Annual address to the Federal Assembly of the Russian Federation. http://archive.kremlin.ru/eng/speeches/2005/04/25/2031_type70029type82912_87086.shtml. Accessed 10 December 2015.

Putin, V. V. (2007, February 10). Speech and the following discussion at the Munich Conference on Security Policy. http://en.kremlin.ru/events/president/transcripts/24034. Accessed 10 December 2015.

Putin, V. V. (2011, October 3). A new integration project for Eurasia: the future in the making. *Izvestiia*. English translation at http://www.russianmission.eu/en/news/article-prime-minister-vladimir-putin-new-integration-project-eurasia-future-making-izvestia-3-. Accessed 6 January 2015.

Putin, V. V. (2013, September 11). A plea for caution from Russia. *New York Times*.

Putin, V. V. (2014, December 4). Presidential address to the Federal Assembly. http://en.kremlin.ru/events/president/news/47173. Accessed 6 January 2016.

Russian Ministry of Foreign Affairs. (2009). Draft European Security Treaty. http://en.kremlin.ru/events/president/news/6152. Accessed 6 January 2016.

Russian Ministry of Foreign Affairs. (2013a, September 4). Comment by the Information and Press Department of the Russian Ministry of Foreign Affairs regarding a possible forceful action by the United States against Syria. http://en.mid.ru/en_GB/web/guest/foreign_policy/international_safety/conflicts/-/asset_publisher/xIEMTQ3OvzcA/content/id/98022. Accessed 7 January 2016.

Russian Ministry of Foreign Affairs. (2013b, August 30). Comment by the official representative of the Ministry of Foreign Affairs of Russia Alexander Lukashevich regarding the statements of the United States about the forceful action against Syria. http://en.mid.ru/en_GB/web/guest/posledniye_dobavlnenniye/-/asset_publisher/MCZ7HQuMdqBY/content/id/98312. Accessed 10 December 2016.

Russian Ministry of Foreign Affairs (2013c, February 12). Concept of the Foreign Policy of the Russian Federation. http://archive.mid.ru//brp_4.nsf/0/76389FEC168189ED44257B2E0039B16D. Accessed 10 December 2016.

Sakwa, R. (2015). *Frontline Ukraine: crisis in the borderlands*. London: I.B. Tauris.

Wilson, A. (2014). *Ukraine Crisis: what it means for the West*. New Haven: Yale University Press.

Woodward, S. L. (1995). *Balkan tragedy: chaos and dissolution after the cold war*. Washington, DC: Brookings Institution.

Dr James Headley is a Senior Lecturer in Politics at the University of Otago, New Zealand. He has published academic articles and book chapters on Russia–EU relations, and nationalism in the former Soviet Union and Yugoslavia. He is the author of *Russia and the Balkans: Foreign Policy from Yeltsin to Putin* (Hurst and Co./Columbia University Press, 2008).

Chapter 11: Russia's Security-Related Decision-Making: The Case of Crimea

Stephen Fortescue

There are two big issues in the political science of post-communist transition. First, the relationship between rulers and ruled; second, governance arrangements within the executive. The first could be summed up as "politics," the second as "policy." The first has received the most attention: are regimes democratic, and if not what other feedback and accountability mechanisms exist? The general consensus is that post-Soviet Russia, particularly under Putin, is not democratic, in that – among other shortcomings – it does not have genuine electoral contests that can potentially produce a change in government.

Our concern here is not with "politics," but with "policy." Does the Russian state have the policy-making arrangements to allow it to respond wisely and efficiently to policy challenges? Doubts on that score focus on an overly presidential constitution, and the reliance on personalist, "crony" methods of rule by the overly powerful president (Minchenko 2014; Gaaze 2014). In studies of the policy-making process, the author has devoted considerable attention to the other side of the coin: the split structure that comes from a semi-presidential constitution and the

S. Fortescue (✉)
University of New South Wales and Australian National University,
Canberra, Australia
e-mail: s.fortescue@unsw.edu.au

Fish, Gill, Petrovic (eds.), *A Quarter Century of Post-Communism Assessed*, DOI 10.1007/978-3-319-43437-7_12

highly bureaucratic nature of policy-making (Fortescue, 2010a, 2012). In this view, a large number of individually powerful, specialized agencies participate, utilizing elaborate consultation and sign-off procedures. The result has been slow decision-making in many cases, with "lowest common denominator" policy outcomes, something that has encouraged Putin to turn, somewhat half-heartedly, to more direct personal involvement, the so-called *ruchnoe upravlenie* (hands-on management).

In earlier work, I concentrated on important but not directly security-related issues (Fortescue 2006, 2009, 2010b, 2014, 2015). There was an almost complete absence of security agencies in at least the public record of these policy processes. My concern here, however, is not with the possible presence of security agencies in nonsecurity policy-making. Rather, I look at a security-related policy decision – to annex Crimea – in order to ascertain whether security policy is decided differently from nonsecurity policy, and, if it is, whether the difference explains Russia's rather adventurous foreign policy in recent times.

One expects security-related policy to be treated differently, not least because of the division of state agencies into those with security and nonsecurity responsibilities with the former being directly subordinate to the president. Thus, the semi-presidential issue is relevant in a different way from nonsecurity policy-making. There the question is how the president involves himself in policy areas for which the prime minister-led government is responsible; on security issues, the question is how nonsecurity agencies compete for policy influence against the special presidential status of the security agencies.

The special status of the security agencies is accentuated by the personal status of the so-called siloviki who head those agencies. There are those who explain Russia's foreign policy adventurism in terms of a hyper-version of the crony model of governance, that policy is made in a small circle of Putin's silovik cronies who share with him a highly aggressive view of global order and Russia's place in it (Renz 2012, pp. 214–215). In this chapter, the question posed is: was the Crimean decision a reckless one made by Putin within a small group of ideologically driven cronies operating on the basis of a narrow range of distorted information; or was there a bureaucratic process that ensured that action followed discussion among a range of participants with varying expertises and policy responsibilities and based on all relevant information?[1] The latter does not exclude the possibility of aggressive, securitized policy outcomes, if the bureaucratic agencies engaged in the policy process share a single approach or if the leader is able to impose his/her will regardless of the bureaucratic process. But there is at least a greater opportunity for moderated policy outcomes if policy-making involves a wide range of participants, with procedures which encourage the exchange of opinions, bargaining, and compromise. Two stages of the decision-making process are examined: what I call the "actual" decision, the moment when it was decided to annex Crimea; and any preliminary consideration of options, implications, costs, and benefits.

Crimea: The Timeline

Crimea is a peninsula in the Black Sea which, despite having no land connection to it, was part of the Russian Federation within the Soviet Union until 1954, when Khrushchev notoriously "gave" it to Ukraine (Kramer 2014). When the Soviet Union disintegrated, Crimea remained within the now independent Ukraine, with the naval port of Sevastopol – a special administrative zone leased to Russia.

The status of Crimea occasionally appeared on the fringes of Russian politics over the following years. The long-time mayor of Moscow, Yurii Luzhkov, attracted attention with his calls for its return to Russia (Hill 2001), with similar talk by the likes of nationalist philosopher Aleksandr Dugin who was seen at the time as on the political fringe (Allison 2014, pp. 1270–1271). Zygar' (2016) claims that at the Bucharest NATO summit in April 2008 Putin threatened the seizure of Crimea if Ukraine were to join NATO. While unofficial texts of his address – an official transcript was not released – are not that explicit (Putin 2008), the tone could be taken as threatening and Zygar' could be right that such a scenario became a mantra for Putin and some close colleagues in the following years. But, despite the complexity of Russia's relationship with Ukraine, the status of Crimea was never a matter of official dispute, and even the arrangements for Russia's military presence in Sevastopol, while far from trouble free, were generally kept under control (Allison 2014, p. 1278).

Things changed radically in November 2013, with the Euromaidan response to Ukrainian president Yanukovich's last-minute decision not to sign an association agreement with the European Union (EU). The street protests against the decision triggered a ferocious Russian propaganda campaign, accusing the protestors of being US-inspired fascists, threatening not just a legitimately elected government but also carrying out anti-Russian pogroms in eastern Ukraine and Crimea.

Matters came to a head on 21 February 2014 with the immediate collapse of a peace agreement negotiated by Germany, France, Poland, and Russia (although the Russian representative had refused to sign). The next day Yanukovich fled Kiev. A year later, Putin claimed that it was at the end of a meeting of security advisers through the night of 22–23 February, called ostensibly to discuss how to ensure Yanukovich's safety, that he expressed the need to secure Crimea's accession to Russia (Kondrashov 2015). We will discuss that meeting in more detail later. On 23 February, rallies were held in Crimea calling for unification with Russia. Zygar' (2016) claims that on that day Oleg Belaventsev, a protégé of Minister of Defence Shoigu who became the Kremlin's head of Crimean operations and subsequently Putin's formal representative there, arrived on the peninsula. On 25 February, the pro-Russian Crimean Front demanded a referendum on unification. The following day saw the first open appearance of the "little green men" or "polite people," military personnel without identifying insignia but widely believed to be Russian soldiers.[2]

Early the next morning, 27 February, pro-Russian gunmen, backed by Russian military personnel, seized government buildings, including the parliament. Later that day the parliament – in a meeting to which observers were not admitted – voted to hold a referendum on Crimean self-determination within Ukraine. On 1 March, the new Crimean prime minister Sergei Aksenov asked for assistance from Russia, and Putin formally requested of the upper house of the Russian parliament the power to send troops to Ukraine, as pro-Russian demonstrations erupted throughout east Ukraine.

At a press conference on 4 March, Putin stated that Russia would do nothing to encourage sentiments of self-determination in Crimea, and avoided a question on how Russia would respond to the outcome of the planned referendum (kremlin.ru/events/president/news/20366). Two days later, the Crimean parliament voted to change the wording of the referendum, so that Crimeans would now be asked whether they supported accession to the Russian Federation. The referendum was held on 16 March, and according to official figures 83.1 % of Crimean residents voted, with 96.77 % supporting accession (in Sevastopol 89.5 % turned out, with 95.60 % voting in favor). The next day, the Crimean parliament asked to be admitted to the Russian Federation. Russia's legislature moved efficiently and by 21 March Putin had signed the relevant law.

Crimea: The Motives

What drove the decision to annex Crimea? The sequence of events began with the Euromaidan protest against Yanukovich's decision not to sign the EU association agreement, and for Russia took a serious turn for the worse when Yanukovich's government was replaced by a determinedly pro-Western one. There was a strong desire to prevent Ukraine formally aligning itself with the West, whether the EU or NATO. Ukraine remaining outside Russia's economic integration project, the Eurasian Economic Union, would be a major blow. Another major concern was the status of Sevastopol in a Ukraine governed by pro-Western and indeed radically anti-Russian forces. For a regime determined to raise its geostrategic status globally and particularly in the region, no threat to its military presence in the Black Sea could be countenanced (Allison 2014, pp. 1273–1274).

Putin subsequently claimed that Russia's actions were responses to requests from the residents of Crimea for protection from "specific and tangible threats" (en.kremlin.ru/events/president/news/20796). His vague claims were made in the context of persistent Russian propaganda highlighting the violent repression of Russian speakers on Ukrainian territory, the implication being that such behavior was taking place in Crimea. There is too little evidence of that being so to take this justification seriously (Allison 2014, p. 1296).

Later still Putin justified the annexation in terms of the deep historical importance of Crimea for the Russian people (through the claimed baptism of Vladimir, the founding prince of the Kiev state, on Crimean territory) and the righting of a historical wrong (kremlin.ru/events/president/news/47173). While one might question the veracity of Putin's claims and whether, even if true, they would justify seizing the territory of another state, he nevertheless expressed sentiments widely held within Russia, and it might well be the case that they drove his own personal approach.

Some argue that because of those popular sentiments, Putin was able to use the annexation of Crimea to restore flagging popularity at home. As part of a general campaign to arouse patriotic enthusiasm by "getting

Russia off her knees," the dramatic seizure of "sacred soil" increased his poll ratings (Levinson 2015).

The Actual Decision

Putin has sketchily described the decision-making process on a few occasions, the first during an open-line event on 17 April 2014 (en.kremlin.ru/events/president/news/20796). It was then that he admitted that Russian troops had been present, claiming that their dispatch was decided – without specifying when – because Crimean residents felt "threatened" and "oppressed" and therefore interested in self-determination. This might suggest, the trigger for a Russian decision was the demonstrations calling for unification on 23 February, or more formally the 27 February Crimean parliament vote to conduct a referendum on self-determination or the 1 March request by prime minister Aksenov for Russian assistance.

In a documentary film trailered in March 2015, Putin suggested very different timing (Kondrashov 2014). He related how he had said at the end of an all-night meeting on 22–23 February 2014: "We are forced to begin work to bring Crimea back into Russia."[3] It is not clear from his words that this conclusion was reached following discussion of such a possibility at the meeting. Nevertheless, by this point, before both the demonstrations of the 23rd and the formal requests just mentioned, a decision had been made to annex, even if only in Putin's own mind. He added that actual steps would be taken only when it became clear that the Crimean people supported Russian action. We will return to the expression of the people's will, and whether there was another "actual" decision at that point.

Participants

Putin specifies in the documentary that four people were present when he made the statement. Those involved in the meeting were "the leaders of our special services and the defence ministry." It is not clear whether only the four were present throughout, or whether they were a rump kept behind to hear Putin announce his intentions.

Whatever the nature of their presence, who might the four have been? Zygar' (2016) suggests secretary of the Security Council Patrushev, head of the Federal Security Service (FSB) Bortnikov, head of the Presidential Administration Ivanov, and Minister of Defence Shoigu. They indeed seem the most likely four. The first three have solid backgrounds in the security agencies and personal links with Putin.[4] Neither can be said of Shoigu. With a background in civil engineering and low-level komsomol and party work in the Soviet period, he took over what became the Ministry of Emergency Situations in 1991, until after a brief interlude as governor of the Moscow region he was appointed Minister of Defence in 2012. Despite lacking a classic silovik background and personal ties with Putin, and indeed having the dangerous liabilities of personal popularity and even being described as a possible successor, he appears to enjoy Putin's trust. That, plus the relevance of his formal position, suggests he would have been present.

The Security Council

Putin's statement was made at the end of an informal meeting. Is it possible that his expressed belief in the need to move toward the annexation of Crimea had been or was then subjected to discussion and decision within a formal body? Commentators have pointed out that Russia lacks an equivalent body to the Soviet Union's Politburo, which was universally recognized as the peak decision-making body in all areas of policy-making – security and nonsecurity – for most of the Soviet Union's existence. Others claim that the Security Council is the Russian equivalent of the Politburo (Jones and Brusstar 1993, p. 355; Kryshtanovskaya and White 2003, p. 297; Vendil Pallin 2009, p. 25). Yet others, while not drawing that precise comparison, see the Security Council as filling a decision-making vacuum left by a weak government and the abandonment of Putin's effort to create a "second government" in the Presidential Administration when he returned to the presidency in 2012 (Stanovaia 2016).

The Security Council is like the Politburo in that it exists within a bifurcated executive. Contemporary Russia, like the Soviet Union, has a cabinet chaired by a prime minister. In both cases, the cabinet and prime minister are clearly inferior to the party leadership in the Soviet case and the presidency in the Russian case, with the Security Council firmly subordinated to the president.

In the Soviet case, the inferiority of the state hierarchy left the Politburo as the dominant decision-making body. The situation regarding the Security Council is less straightforward. It has nothing like the ideological authority of the party hierarchy at the peak of which stood the Politburo; indeed it has no equivalent hierarchy. Also it has a specific responsibility only for national security matters. While national security is defined broadly (Polozhenie 2011), nevertheless, the Security Council clearly does not enjoy the undisputed right of the Politburo to discuss everything. Serious policy-making across a wide range of important areas is conducted at cabinet level. How the president participates in that policy-making is institutionally a complex matter, but there is little evidence that the Security Council is involved. Further, while the Central Committee apparatus was clearly subordinate to and served the Politburo, there is no sense that the Russian equivalent, the Presidential Administration, serves and is subordinate to the Security Council.

The Security Council's decisions are given force through decrees, orders (*rasporiazheniia*), and instructions (*porucheniia*) of the president (Polozhenie, Para.15). The president's decree powers are somewhat limited in that they cannot contradict existing legislation, and relatively few policy-related decrees are issued (Fortescue 2012, p. 123). Orders are used for relatively routine administrative matters. Instructions are usually addressed to the government, with implementation being notoriously patchy (Fortescue 2012, pp. 133–134). Although not specifically mentioned in the Security Council Statute, the president has the right to send legislation directly to parliament, and has done so in recent times on some controversial security-related issues. Nevertheless, most presidential governance is carried on through the government and the legislation which it sends to parliament (Shul'man 2015).

While there are good reasons not to see the Security Council as a modern-day Politburo,[5] the annexation of Crimea was a national security matter by any definition, and if any formal institution were involved it was surely the Security Council.

Indeed, in April 2014 Putin claimed that he had obtained the agreement of the Council's members to action in Crimea (en.kremlin.ru/events/president/news/20796). The Council has what are called permanent members and members. We are interested only in the permanent members, since only they attend the regular meetings (*soveshchaniia*) which would have been the forum for any decision-oriented discussion of Crimea. Ordinary members attend only the rarer and showpiece *zasedaniia*. The permanent members are listed in Table 11.1

Membership is dominated as one might expect by siloviki, in many cases with a history of personal and professional links with Putin. As an exception, Medvedev has long links with Putin, but no silovik background. Indeed, he is often seen as possessing a less "securitized"

Table 11.1 Permanent members of the Russian Security Council at the time of the events in Crimea

Name	*Post*
Putin	President, Russian Federation (chair)
Medvedev	Prime Minister, Russian Federation
Bortnikov	Director, Federal Security Service (FSB)
Gryzlov	Chair, Supreme Council, "Edinaia Rossiia"
Ivanov	Head, Presidential Administration
Kolokol'tsev	Minister of Internal Affairs
Lavrov	Minister of Foreign Affairs
Matvienko	Chair, Council of the Federation
Naryshkin	Speaker, State Duma
Nurgaliev	Deputy secretary, Security Council
Patrushev	Secretary, Security Council
Fradkov	Director, Foreign Intelligence Service (SVR)
Shoigu	Minister of Defence

policy approach. There is no other member representing nonsecurity structures. Of the three "parliamentary" members – Matvienko, Gryzlov and Naryshkin – the last two have claims to a silovik/crony background, while Matvienko has often expressed sentiments consistent with such an outlook.[6]

The Security Council is unlikely to cause Putin difficulties when it comes to adventurous decision-making. It also has considerable relevant expertise. Does this suggest that it was used as a collective body in the decision-making around Crimea? The timing of its meetings might provide some clues. Its Statute (Polozhenie, Para. 14) says that "in order to discuss current issues in the provision of national security that require managerial (*upravliaiushchie*) decisions, the chairman of the Security Council holds with the permanent members of the Security Council operational meetings (*operativnye soveshchaniia*) of the Security Council, as a rule weekly."

As events on Kiev's Maidan unfolded in late 2013 the Security Council met for operational meetings on a fortnightly, not weekly, basis until 14 November (19 October, 1 and 14 November). Ukraine was not in the summaries on the presidential website of what was discussed. It then did not meet for nearly a month, holding a meeting on 11 December to consider Putin's state of the union address and another on 27 December to sum up the events of the year. There was then another break of nearly a month, with meetings held on 24 and 31 January. These were the first at which events in Ukraine were said to have been discussed. There was then a fortnight break until 14 February, when the Geneva-2 negotiations on Syria were discussed. A truce had been declared in Kiev the day before, something which, judging by the presidential website summary, was not discussed at the meeting. The next meeting was held on 21 February, the day of dramatic events in Kiev. (The meeting was not described on the Kremlin website as *operativnoe*. The significance of the absence of that word is not clear.) The meeting was reported on the presidential website at 13.30 Moscow time as having taken place and as having discussed Ukraine. The signing of a peace agreement was announced by the official Ukrainian news agency at 16.40 Kiev time, that is, 17.40 Moscow time. Thus, the Security Council meeting took place before any agreement was reached in Kiev, before the Russian representative refused to sign the agreement, and before it became clear that it was not going to hold. Thus, it is possible that the Russian approach to the negotiations in Kiev were discussed, but it is unlikely that there was any decision on the annexation of Crimea, given that it was entirely unclear how events would develop in Kiev. It seems unlikely that the permission sought of Security Council members to move toward the annexation of Crimea that Putin referred to in April 2014 was obtained at this meeting.

The next announced meeting of the permanent members of the Council took place on 25 February. This is the only meeting throughout the period that in terms of timing was out of sequence. It was described as *operativnoe*, and the account on the presidential website said simply that the situation in Ukraine was discussed. Unusually, no list of participants was published, perhaps to hide the absence of Medvedev. He is not sitting in his usual place in the two photographs of the meeting on the presidential website, and his own website lists no official engagements for that day (although one decree is listed as having been signed by him). If Medvedev were absent because he had been excluded (it is possible that he was ill – he had no official engagements the following day as well), that would be very significant. Those visible in the photographs are Patrushev, Lavrov, Bortnikov, Ivanov, Kolokol'tsev, and Matvienko, a list which includes some who are not generally considered as being in the inner core.

It was over the following two days that the "little green men" appeared, public buildings were seized, and the parliament decided to hold a referendum on Crimea's future. It is possible that it was decided at the 25 February meeting that such events should occur.[7] It is also possible that the meeting was called so that members (or those not already in the know) could be informed of the decision announced by Putin at the end of the all-night 22–23 February meeting and the preparations subsequently undertaken. It could have been at this meeting that Putin received the approval from Security Council members that he referred to the following month.

It is also possible that it was decided at this meeting to change the referendum question from self-determination within Ukraine to accession to the Russian Federation, something which the Crimean parliament did on 6 March. This would suggest that the decision arrived at early in the morning of 23 February, to prepare for annexation, was conditional, and that another decision, to take that step rather than settle for some form of Crimean autonomy, came sometime after (Zygar' 2016). If so, and if it were conditional, as claimed by Putin after the event, on secret polling demonstrating support for such a move among the residents of Crimea, it is hard to link it to any publicized meeting of the Security Council, including that on 25 February. There is evidence – to be presented below – that such polling was done in early March. The Council next met on 6 March, the same day but after the Crimean parliament decided to change the referendum wording. We have no clue, from Putin or other sources, when or by whom a second decision might have been made.

The situation in Ukraine was discussed among other things at the next meeting of the Security Council on 13 March. The Crimean referendum and resulting request of the Crimean parliament that the peninsula be accepted into the Russian Federation took place precisely half-way between that meeting and one on 21 March. For some reason that meeting, at which the situation in Ukraine was said to have been discussed in detail, was not described as *operativnoe*. The discussion could only have been of the processes of integration, since the formal annexation itself was now all but complete. The meeting was reported on the presidential website at 12.30, before Putin signed the accession document later that afternoon.

In summary, the rarity of meetings and apparent lack of consideration of Ukrainian affairs at those meeting held from October through to mid-February are striking, at a time when one might have expected issues and options to be discussed in a broad "policy" sense. The body then became more active, and Ukraine was frequently discussed. On occasion the timing was such that a meeting closely preceded significant events, that of 25 February being the most striking example. But more often that was not the case. Lack of strong evidence of the use of the Security Council as a decision-making body suggests that it played no such role.

Rather, the decision was taken by Putin after the gravity of the situation became clear at the meeting of 22–23 February. That was not a meeting of a formally constituted body and indeed involved a very small number of people at its most crucial stage. But it was more than a fire-side chat with some cronies. Those present had responsibility in terms of formal position for the operations that were carried out soon after. By the nature of the Russian system they were also people with close personal connections with Putin. The decision was neither made by a small bunch of dilettantes nor was it made in the broadly representative circumstances that might encourage moderation.

What happened was not unlike controversial security-related decisions in other systems. For example, an early account of the Soviet decision to intervene in Czechoslovakia in August 1968 stressed the bureaucratic nature of the decision-making process, with outcomes decided by the push and pull of powerful agencies and bureaucratic interests within the Politburo (Valenta 1979). Later accounts based on archive evidence suggest a decision made within a narrow circle of key participants (Williams 1996). In the case of the US decision to drop nuclear bombs on Japan, a relatively formal and representative so-called Interim Committee provided recommendations to Truman. But he relied heavily in making his decision, and on his diplomatic use of the bomb, on his long-time mentor, Joseph Byrnes, whom he appointed Secretary of State (with Byrnes in turn relying on a narrow group of key advisors) (Malloy 2008, pp. 9–10, 93, 118).

Information Input

If the actual decision was made within a small group of security-related officials with personal ties to Putin, on the basis of what information obtained from what sources did they make their decision? The types of information plausibly needed to make a decision in the case of Crimea come in four categories. Not all issues noted here will be considered in detail.

1. Operational feasibility: essentially military considerations, including the capacity and willingness of Ukrainian military units to respond aggressively.

2. Reaction of Crimean and Russian populations: would the former support the process on the ground; how would it affect Putin's popularity in the case of the latter?
3. Foreign reactions: how far would the West go in supporting Ukraine militarily, diplomatically, and economically, including through sanctions on Russia? Would Russia have supporters?
4. Economic costs: the general cost of militarization that formed a backdrop to the decision, the costs of sanctions and isolation from the global economy that might ensue, and the costs of integration.

As with the actual decision, two forms of information provision are possible. First, the small group of Putin cronies, who were involved in taking the actual decision and who also headed the major security agencies, relied on their own views of the world plus information received from their own agencies; that is, the information input was narrow. Second, even if the actual decision was taken within a small group, they received information from a broad range of sources that had gone through a process of analysis, debate, and consolidation.

Regarding the second possibility, the most likely institution to have played such a role is the Security Council. Monaghan puts it thus:

> Bringing these representatives [of various security and non-security agencies] together as it does, the Security Council is the central locus for forging consensus and the coordination of strategic planning and expert preparation of the concepts, doctrines, strategies and programmes (Monaghan 2014, pp. 9–10).[8]

Vendil Pallin puts it more conditionally – "certain directorates of the Security Council are probably used for preparing new plans and programme documents simply because it is one of the few coordinating institutions with a sizeable analytical staff" (Vendil Pallin 2009, p. 126). Galeotii rejects such a view, in terms that make clear the implications for our purposes:

> The Security Council is essentially an administrative rather than policy body, agencies brief the president individually, and there is no independent national security advisor to help identify questionable findings. As a result, they [intelligence agencies] may encourage Putin's increasingly assertive and risk-taking policies abroad (Galeotii 2015, p. 10).

Those who see it playing a policy information role point to its apparatus, interdepartmental committees and Scientific Council. At deputy secretary level the apparatus is heavily dominated by people with a background in the intelligence community. Little information is available on the apparatus at department level. Departments identified include Economic Security, Defence Industry and Military-Technical Cooperation, Military Security, the Commonwealth of Independent States (CIS), Information Technology, Analysis and Warning of Terrorist Threats and Conflict Situations, State and Public Security. The Economic Security Department was headed for many years until his retirement in 2015 by Valentin Valiukov. No full biography is available, but he was a graduate of the Moscow Aviation Institute (1974) and took up lecturing at the Moscow State Technical University of Civil Aviation on retirement. His 1994 candidate's dissertation was in economics, on migration processes in the R&D sector. He was closely involved in the Security Council campaign of the mid-2000s to revive minerals exploration through stronger state involvement (info.tatcenter.ru/print/21192). A 2008 publication on inequalities between regional economies was moderately dirigiste in its vague policy recommendations (*Vestnik analitiki*, no. 1, 2008, pp. 154–167). There was nothing to suggest a hard-core silovik from what little we know of him.

The following interdepartmental committees exist (with chairperson in brackets): Economic and Social security (deputy secretary SC), Information Security (deputy secretary SC), Public Security (Minister of Internal Affairs), CIS (deputy secretary SC), Strategic Planning (secretary SC), Ecological Security (member presidium Academy of Sciences), Military Security (no membership, including chair, published). Membership is broad, with a wide range of security and civilian ministries represented, usually at deputy minister level. The Scientific Council has nearly 150 members across a wide range of disciplines, and has reasonably active sections and working groups on a wide range of issues. At least one of them has provided a forum for what could be described as anti-Western economic policies, to be outlined below, at which point some general comment on the possible information input role of the Security Council will be offered.

We now turn to information-input issues across the four categories.

Military-Operational

The smooth success of the seizure and annexation suggests that the action was conceived well in advance. Putin has been adamant that it was not preplanned (en.kremlin.ru/events/president/news/20796), but it is impossible to believe that there had not been at least some scenario planning.[9]

The scenario was well worked out, in terms of the capacity of Russian personnel to operate in Crimea in deniable mode, the presence of local activists who could be controlled and utilized, and the estimation of Ukrainian capacity and willingness to respond. Military reform had long been on Putin's agenda, with conflicts in Chechnya and Georgia ramming home the need for not just a modernized military but one proficient at hybrid war fighting (Ven Bruusgaard 2014, pp. 83–84). There is debate among military specialists as to the relative role of the General Staff, Security Council and Presidential Administration in the determination of military doctrine and tactics (Vendil Pallin 2009, pp. 12–13; Bjelakovic 2008, pp. 537–578). We will not engage in that debate, but will simply conclude that military specialists were sufficiently involved in preparatory planning, even if only of a scenario type, that when the decision to act was made the plan was ready and worked well.

Political

Putin said after the event that the final decision to annex Crimea was taken only after the mood of the people became clear through secret polling, which revealed that 80 % of the residents of Crimea wanted accession to the Russian Federation. He gave no clue as to when the polling might have been done (kremlin.ru/events/president/news/20753). In April 2014, hackers released thousands of e-mails between officials of the Domestic Politics Division of the Presidential Administration, and various PR consultants and *polittekhnologi* (specialists in what in Russian is known as "political technology," the application to the relationship between rulers and ruled of sophisticated methods of propaganda and monitoring) (Surnacheva 2014). They included experienced professionals without clear institutional affiliation, a well-connected Moscow PR agency, and an academic researcher at the Tauride University in Crimea. Polls seemingly carried out in early March and with results similar to those mentioned by Putin were described. It was presumably these results that Putin claimed to rely on.

Sociologists, to say nothing of experts in international law, might question the validity of such polls. But we should not be surprised that they were conducted and their results considered important. This is a regime which is strongly committed to political technology, for which activities it has significant capacity, centered in and contracted out by the Domestic Politics Division of the Presidential Administration. There is no suggestion that the Security Council or any organizations other than those contracted by the Presidential Administration were involved.

Despite the apparently small number of people engaged in the secret polling, they seem to have got it right. Although there is understandable skepticism among many as to the very high levels of support claimed for unification, there was no significant expressed opposition except from the Crimean Tatars.

International Reaction

The Western reaction to the annexation was not aggressive in a military sense and had an element of "what's done is done" about it. Nevertheless, it was reasonably robust and united – in the form of condemnation and sanctions – and arguably more so than Putin expected, particularly when strengthened following events in Donbas. The Chinese and other would-be Russian sympathizers, such as members of the BRICS and the Eurasian Economic Union were cautious if not cool (Sherr 2015, p. 15).

Seemingly, Putin misread the international reaction and Russia is suffering greater economic consequences than he anticipated. Such a misreading of the Western reaction was probably caused by a view of the West that Putin had long propagated, that it is weak politically, economically, and morally (Sherr 2015, p. 13). Added to that, in the period leading up to the events in Crimea there had been a lot of publicity in the Russian press regarding the popularity of Putin among European elites and the general population, while the Sochi Olympics – in progress while events in Crimea were unfolding – were presented as a personal global triumph. If such popularity were believed to exist, a vigorous reaction to Crimean events would have seemed unlikely.

It is not hard to believe that this view is a personal one derived by Putin from his background, and reinforced by meetings with Western leaders and the impression he might have gained from reading press summaries of Western political and economic dysfunction. But might he have been reinforced in his views by the small group of cronies with similar backgrounds who surround him? Certainly the expressed views of most of them are aggressively anti-Western, although perhaps with some leaning toward the threat posed by the West rather than its weakness.

These people have access to Putin on a personal basis, and most of them also head important security bodies which have access to considerable analytical capacities in their own right (Sherr 2015, pp. 12, 18; Dneprov 2015). Stanovaia (2016) suggests that their access to Putin is such that he has less capacity to treat the information they provide on its merits than he might himself believe.

In this area of information input the only agency that might be in a position to temper the views of the siloviki is the Ministry of Foreign Affairs. Minister Lavrov is a member of the Security Council and active in the conduct of Russian foreign policy. The Ministry appears well-placed to have an informed view of foreign capabilities and expectations. However, it is generally not seen as a key player in policy formation. While noting its Moscow-based foreign policy expertise and network of embassies abroad, Vendil Pallin concludes that Lavrov, a career diplomat rather than someone with a silovik background or personal ties to Putin, "probably heads a relatively weak power ministry with little say in policy formulation" (Vendil Pallin 2007, p. 7; Sherr 2015, p. 19).

Economic Implications

The economic implications of the Crimean annexation should be seen within the context of broader debates over the costs of an aggressive and militarized foreign policy. In nonsecurity areas the so-called economic block, in particular the Ministry of Finance, but also the Central Bank and in a more ambiguous way the Ministry of Economic Development, exercises significant bureaucratic control over policy actors that want to spend money. The Ministry of Finance plays the standard fiscal custodian role, protecting tax revenues at all costs and attacking expenditure at every opportunity. Putin often supports the ministry, placing major emphasis on the need to balance the budget. Highly sensitive national security debates are less open to the public, but we have evidence that the Ministry of Finance at least tries to contain military expenditures. Long-time minister Aleksei Kudrin seemingly lost his job over it, and current minister Anton Siluanov occasionally indicates that he is no happier than Kudrin (minfin.ru/ru/press-center/?id_4=33034).

But it is not just Kudrin's fate that suggests that the economic block has limited influence over military expenditures. The Ministry of Finance has some dedicated capacity for the analysis of security-related spending, with a Department of Budgetary Policy in the Area of State Military and Law

Enforcement Services and Military Procurement.[10] But both Monaghan and Cooper point to the lack of institutions and mechanisms for linking socioeconomic and security planning, with Cooper suggesting that the security block has a greater capacity to influence socioeconomic planning than vice versa (Monaghan 2013, p. 1233; Cooper nd, pp. 7–8).

Other than Medvedev as prime minister, the economic block has no permanent membership of the Security Council.[11] There is no reason to believe that senior figures in the economic block do not have direct access to Putin on an individual basis (Gabuev et al. 2013), and Putin could well be willing to hear their views on the economic implications of national security actions. But the fate of Kudrin is enough for them to know that there is a limit to how hard they can push such matters. On top of that, the Security Council has its own claims to economic expertise, briefly outlined above.

At this point we return more specifically to Crimea. Among the most significant consequences of the Crimean annexation were economic sanctions. They appear to have been unexpected, a failure of foreign policy rather than economic analysis.[12] Nevertheless, the response, as ad hoc as it appeared, derived from long-standing economic debates with an ideological dimension. The view that sanctions could be readily made up for by deals with the Chinese or by domestic effort fitted within the heavily pushed "turn to the East" policy and a long-standing debate over industry policy and import substitution. It could be argued, on the basis of slight evidence, that the Security Council apparatus was a supporter of the Chinese option, through its interest in new reserve currencies and BRICS as an anti-Western organization, an issue considered by the economic and social security section of the Council's Scientific Council (Fortescue 2014, pp. 230–231). The pros and cons of a domestically oriented industry policy had been exhaustively debated and generally rejected by policy-makers over many years, with the Security Council through its Interdepartmental Commission on Economic and Social Security being one of the platforms for presentation of the pros (Butrin 2015).

It is likely that to the extent that sanctions were recognized as a possibility in advance of the decision to annex Crimea, the response – the turn to China and import substitution – was attractive to decision-makers keen to justify to themselves an action they wanted to take regardless, despite both elements of the response having always been regarded with scepticism in extensive analysis and debate over many years. Putin was clearly aware of the arguments against the two policy responses; to a considerable extent he shared them. But when the moment came security-oriented information providers – based in or linked to the Security Council – were in a privileged position, through the direct access to Putin of their bosses, to present them to a receptive audience.

Conclusion

Detail on how the decision to annex Crimea was made, including how important information was brought to bear, is sorely lacking. Nevertheless, the evidence suggests that as a security-related matter it was handled within a narrower range of participants and information than nonsecurity matters.

In terms of the actual decision, a small group of Putin's colleagues were involved, colleagues with expertise and experience in relevant areas to a degree that despite their personal links with Putin and the aggressive nature of their world view the word "crony" is perhaps inappropriate. That having been said, they were not the sort of people that one would expect to have exerted a moderating influence on Putin.

There is no strong evidence of discussion or decision-making within any formally constituted body, not even one of such narrow membership as the Security Council. Those who claim that there is no Russian equivalent to the Politburo appear to be correct, including with regard to security-related decision making. This has significant implications for the level of bureaucratic moderation that can be brought to bear. With regard specifically to the Security Council and Crimea, on the single occasion when there might have been discussion of substance in that forum the one "moderate" member was absent.

In terms of information input in the lead up to the decision, one should not exaggerate the narrowness of available information. Russia has a vibrant within- and without-system expert community and many of the key issues around the Crimean action had been widely debated. However, the expert community includes aggressively oriented analysts and information consolidators, both inside and outside state agencies, and it can be suggested that in security-related policy-making those specialists have a privileged position. That contributed to policy failure, particularly in the areas of the international reaction and Russia's response to it.

The issue is not just the ideological inclinations of Putin and his closest colleagues. There is an institutional element, of a constitutional and operational bifurcation of the state, its agencies, and organizations serving those agencies. The semi-presidential constitution might provide some protection from securitizing pressures in nonsecurity policy-making, concentrated as it is in the government. But it also sidelines moderating influences in security-related policy-making, as was evident in the case of the decision to annex Crimea.

Notes

1. This approach to analyzing Russia's policy behavior in security-related areas differs from the more common approach of security studies specialists, with their focus on whether or not Russia behaves according to a strategy. It could be argued that there is some concurrence between a "strategic" approach and a bureaucratic process, and between a lack of strategy and a crony-based decision-making system, although one would not want to push the comparison too hard. Monaghan (2013) discusses both the personalist and bureaucratic barriers to a strategic approach. See also Monaghan (2014) and Cooper (nd).
2. At a press conference on 4 March 2014, Putin denied that they were Russian soldiers. kremlin.ru/events/president/news/20366. The next month he admitted that Russian troops were indeed present. en.kremlin.ru/events/president/news/20796.
3. Zygar' (2016) claims that the first Russian troops were dispatched on 20 February. Reports of a Ministry of Defence campaign medal "For the return of Crimea" with the dates 20 February to 18 March might serve as confirmation (Kates 2014).
4. Bortnikov joined the Committee for State Security (KGB) in 1975 and served most of his career in Putin's home town of Leningrad/St Petersburg; Patrushev joined the KGB in 1974, was director of the FSB 1999–2008, and in 1998 worked with Putin in the presidential administration; Ivanov joined the KGB in 1975 and worked in the same department as Putin in Leningrad.
5. Monaghan states that Putin uses the Security Council to give direct instructions (2014, p. 5). In the case cited, in April 2014 Putin departed from the agenda to receive a report from Minister of Foreign Affairs Lavrov on the outcome of discussions with West European gas customers on issues arising from the situation in Ukraine. In response to the report, Putin asked Lavrov to provide additional information on Russia's gas contract with Ukraine to those customers. It is clear that the original policy action, a letter in Putin's name to customers, followed discussion in cabinet, and his rather vague instructions to Lavrov were also addressed to the government. It appears that generally Putin deals with or through the government regarding gas dealings with Europe. Indeed

Putin's performance at the Security Council reeks of a PR action – that it was published and released on video is unusual for Council meetings. There is not enough evidence from this case to suggest that as sensitive an issue as gas policy is the domain of the Security Council, or that Putin's instructions derived from a Security Council discussion (kremlin.ru/news/20763).

6. Naryshkin, a Leningrader, reputedly met Putin while studying at the KGB Academy in the late 1970s. Gryzlov went to school with Patrushev. He has a Soviet-era background in the defense industry and in the post-Soviet period worked in business before going into electoral politics. As a break from the Duma, he was brought into the Ministry of Internal Affairs as minister in 2001–2002 to shake things up, and in December 2015 was appointed Putin's representative at Donbas negotiations. Matvienko worked in the Leningrad komsomol in Soviet times, and then had a diplomatic career through the 1990s before entering politics.
7. Monaghan (2014, p. 10) notes the significance of the timing of this meeting.
8. In putting it this way Monaghan is referring to the entire membership of the Council. See also Ven Bruusgaard (2014, p. 88).
9. Allison (2014, p. 1271) sees it as possible that an annexation plan existed as early as autumn 2008, "for possible activation in the event that Kiev were to move close to accession to NATO in the near future." This is presumably based on Putin's reported threats at the Bucharest NATO summit, cited above.
10. The head of which, Anatolii Popov, has a very mixed background in business and state administration, including a brief appointment as finance director of Rosvooruzhenie. His work in charge of reconstruction work in Chechnya in 2001–2003 earned him a medal, "For comradeship in battle," from the FSB and a trophy gun from the Ministry of Internal Affairs.
11. It is perhaps instructive that in November 2015 there was a series of meetings chaired by Putin on security-related matters. No lists of participants were published, but from the photograph on the presidential website accompanying the report of the meeting on developments in space we can see that Siluanov attended (13 November 2015). If he attended the meeting on defence issues (12 November 2015), he cannot be seen in the photograph and was certainly not sitting where he had been at the 13 November meeting.
12. Zygar' (2016) claims that government liberals argued vigorously against the decision to proceed to annexation, rather than some form of Russian influence short of that, out of fear of the international reaction. He provides no detail on the forums in which they presented their arguments.

Bibliography

Allison, R. (2014). Russian "deniable' intervention in Ukraine: how and why Russia broke the rules. *International Affairs, 90*(6), 1255–1297.

Bjelakovic, N. (2008). Russian military procurement: Putin's impact on decision-making and budgeting. *Journal of Slavic Military Studies, 21*(3), 527–542.

Butrin, D. (2015, September 8). Sovet bezopasnosti i on. *Kommersant*. http://www.kommersant.ru/doc/2805251/. Accessed 8 September 2015.

Cooper, J. (nd). Reviewing Russian strategic planning: the emergence of Strategy 2020. NDC Research Review. NATO Defense College.

Dneprov, B. (2015, December 28). V kakikh "palatakh" formiruetsia antiukrainskaia strategiia Kremlia, *VectorNews*. vnews.agency/exclusive/24443-v-kakih-palatah-formiruetsya-antiukrainskaya-strategiya-kremlya.html. Accessed 4 January 2016.

Fortescue, S. (2006). Business-state negotiations and the reform of tax procedures in post-Yukos Russia. *Law in Context, 24*(2), 36–59.

Fortescue, S. (2009). The Russian law on subsurface resources: a policy marathon. *Post-Soviet Affairs, 25*(2), 160–184.

Fortescue, S. (2010a). Institutionalization and personalism in the policy-making process of the Soviet Union and post-Soviet Russia. In: S. Fortescue (Ed.), *Russian politics from Lenin to Putin*. Basingstoke: Palgrave.

Fortescue, S. (2010b). Russia's SWFs: controlled by a domestic agenda. In: X. Yi-Chong & G. Bahgat (Eds.), *The political economy of Sovereign wealth funds*. Basingstoke: Palgrave.

Fortescue, S. (2012). The policymaking process in Putin's prime ministership. In: L. Jonson & S. White (Eds.), *Waiting for reform under Putin and Medvedev*. Basingstoke: Palgrave.

Fortescue, S. (2014). The BRICS and Russia. In: V. Io Lo & M. Hiscock (Eds.), *The rise of the BRICS in the global political economy: changing paradigms?* Cheltenham: Edward Elgar.

Fortescue, S. (2015, June 15). Russia's "turn to the East": a study in policy making. *Post-Soviet Affairs*. doi: 10.1080/1060586X.2015.1051750.

Gaaze, K. (2014, September 1). Poker dlia odnogo. *Novoe vremia*. http://www.newtimes.ru/articles/print/86540/. Accessed 15 September 2014.

Gabuev, A., Mel'nikov, K., Surnacheva, E. (2013, December 23). Konfliktov net na samom del. *Kommersant*. http://www.kommersant.ru/doc/2370046. Accessed 23 December 2013.

Galeotii, M. (2015, October 12). Putin's spies and security men: his strongest allies, his greatest weakness. *Russian Analytical Digest*, No.173.

Hill, D. (2001, August 2). Russia: analyst ponders reasons for Luzhkov's Crimea comments, *Radio Free Europe/Radio Liberty*. rferl.org/content/article/1097079.html. Accessed 23 November 2015.

Jones, E., & Brusstar, J. H. (1993). Moscow's emerging security decisionmaking system: the role of the security council. *Journal of Slavic Military Studies, 6*(3), 345–374.

Kates, G. (2014, April 24). The online debate over a mysterious Russian "medal". *Radio Free Europe/Radio Liberty*. http://www.rferl.org/content/the-online-debate-over-a-mysterious-russian-medal/25361367.html. Accessed 4 February 2016.

Kondrashov, A. (2015, March 16). Crimea. Path to the Motherland (film). Announcement. *Ukraine Hot News*. youtube.com/watch?v=x_NQIUukfcI. Accessed 23 November 2015.

Kramer, M. (2014, March 19). Why did Russia give away Crimea sixty years ago? Cold War International History Project, e-dossier No.47. Washington, DC: Wilson Center. https://www.wilsoncenter.org/publication/why-did-russia-give-away-crimea-sixty-years-ago. Accessed 23 November 2015.

Kryshtanovskaya, O., & White, S. (2003). Putin's militocracy. *Post-Soviet Affairs, 19*(4), 289–306.

Levinson, A. (2015, July 28). Public opinion and propaganda in Russia, European Council on Foreign Relations. ecfr.eu/article/commentary_public_opinion_and_propaganda_in_russia3080. Accessed 4 January 2016.

Malloy, S. L. (2008). *Atomic tragedy: Henry L. Stimson and the decision to use the bomb against Japan*. Ithaca and New York: Cornell University Press.

Minchenko Consulting. (2014, October 22). "Politbiuro 2.0" i postkrymskaia Rossiia. minchenko.ru/netcat_files/File/Politburo%20October%202014.pdf. Accessed 13 April 2015.

Monaghan, A. (2013). Putin's Russia: shaping a grand strategy? *International Affairs, 89*(5), 1221–1236.

Monaghan, A. (2014). *Defibrillating the* Vertikal? *Putin and Russian grand strategy*. London: Chatham House Research Paper.

Polozhenie o Sovete Bezopasnosti Rossiiskoi Federatsii. (2011, May 6). Ukaz Prezidenta Rossiiskoi Federatsii, Voprosy Soveta Bezopasnosti Rossiiskoi Federatsii, No. 590, *Rossiiskaia gazeta*, 10 May.

Renz, B. (2012). The Russian power ministries and security services. In: G. Gill & J. Young (Eds.), *Routledge handbook of Russian politics and society*. London and New York: Routledge.

Sherr, J. (2015). The new East-West discord. Russian objectives, Western interests, Clingendael Report. Netherlands Institute of International Relations.

Shul'man, E. (2015, February 16). Verkhovenstvo prava: rol' lichnosti. *Vedomosti* http://www.vedomosti.ru/newspaper/article/844411/rol-lichnosti. Accessed 16 February 2015.

Stanovaia, T. (2016). Kak Sovet Bezopasnosti zamenil v Rossii pravitel'stvo. *Moskovskii tsentr Karnegi*. carnegie.ru/commentary/2016/01/28/ru-62605/it9z. Accessed 9 February 2016.

Surnacheva, E. (2014, May 10). Kak kovalas' pobeda v Krymu i pomogala li Rossiia provedeniiu. *Slon.ru*. slon.ru/Russia/kak_kovalas_pobeda_v_krymu-1095637.xhtml. Accessed 23 November 2015.

Putin, V. (2008, April 2). *Speech at NATO summit* (Bucharest, 2008). http://www.unian.info/world/111033-text-of-putins-speech-at-nato-summit-bucharest-april-2-2008.html. Accessed 23 November 2015.

Valenta, J. (1979). *Soviet intervention in Czechoslovakia, 1968. Anatomy of a decision*. Baltimore and London: Johns Hopkins University Press.

Vendil Pallin, C. (2007). The Russian power ministries: tool and insurance of power. *Journal of Slavic Military Studies, 20*(1), 1–25.

Vendil Pallin, C. (2009). *Russian military reform. A failed exercise in defence decision making*. London and New York: Routledge.

Ven Bruusgaard, K. (2014). Crimea and Russia's strategic overhaul. *Parameters, 44*(3), 81–90.

Williams, K. (1996). New sources on Soviet decision making during the 1968 Czechoslovak crisis. *Europe-Asia Studies, 48*(3), 457–470.

Zygar', M. (2016). *Vse kremlevskaia rat'. Kratkaia istoriia sovremennoi Rossii*. Moscow: Intellektual'naia literatura.

Stephen Fortescue has a PhD in Soviet Politics from the Australian National University (ANU) (1977). He is an Honorary Associate Professor at the University of New South Wales and a Visiting Fellow at the Centre for European Studies, ANU. His current research interests include the Russian policymaking process, Russian mining and metals, and the Russian Far East.

Chapter 12: Kazakhstan and the Eurasian Economic Union: The Dilemmas of Alliance-Making in the Post-Soviet Period

Kirill Nourzhanov

In January 2014, Kazakhstan adopted a new Foreign Policy Concept – a framework document outlining the principles, objectives and instruments of the country's engagement with the rest of the world. It contained many novel provisions reflecting the changing political, economic and security landscape regionally and internationally, yet its fundamental approach remained exactly the same as enunciated at independence: "Kazakhstan's foreign policy is based on the principles of multi-vector [*sic*], balance, pragmatism, mutual benefit and solid defense of its national interests" (Ministry of Foreign Affairs of the Republic of Kazakhstan 2014). In Kazakhstan, President Nursultan Nazarbaev's multi-vector diplomacy is widely regarded as a major achievement of his long tenure: "It has not only proved its usefulness but also demonstrated that it is the only correct method of survival in modern-day geopolitics" (Makasheva 2009, p. 117).

Until recently, this sentiment was widely shared by scholars and politicians in the West. In his comprehensive study of Kazakhstan's

K. Nourzhanov (✉)
Centre for Arab and Islamic Studies (The Middle East and Central Asia), Australian National University, Canberra, Australia
e-mail: kirill.nourzhanov@anu.edu.au

Fish, Gill, Petrovic (eds.), *A Quarter Century of Post-Communism Assessed*, DOI 10.1007/978-3-319-43437-7_13

foreign policy under Nazarbaev, Hanks defined "multi-vectorism" as a nonideological policy guided by two concerns – state security and economic development (Hanks 2009, p. 260). He highlighted its main achievements as follows: maintenance of internal societal peace and harmony; good working relations with Moscow, Washington and other major international players; active participation in a plethora of regional and global security organisations and extraction of concessions and favourable terms from foreign trade and investment partners. For two decades, Kazakhstan successfully avoided costly entanglements in geopolitical games simultaneously positioning itself as Russia's regional ally, supporting US military action in Afghanistan and Iraq, and working with Beijing on China's energy security. The republic's "exquisitely balanced response" (Eurasian Council on Foreign Affairs 2014, p. 5) to regional and international challenges won near-universal approbation among its partners. A visible symbol of this recognition was Kazakhstan's chairmanship of the Organisation for Security and Cooperation in Europe (OSCE) in 2010, for which role it was endorsed by Russia, the European Union (EU) and eventually the United States (Aitken 2009, pp. 209–211).

Since 2012, Kazakhstan's participation in Russia-led trading blocs culminating in the Eurasian Economic Union (EEU), which was officially launched on 1 January 2015, has been interpreted as a major deviation from the multi-vector policy by observers in the West. Nazarbaev's critics have posited that Kazakhstan's EEU membership is detrimental to its security and economic interests (Starr and Cornell 2014; International Crisis Group 2015), critically reduces the room for foreign policy manoeuvre (Clarke 2015) or, in the worst-case scenario, may lead to partial or complete loss of sovereignty at the hands of neo-imperialist Russia (De Haas 2015).

This chapter will argue that Kazakhstan's joining of the EEU should not be regarded as an act of submission, voluntary or otherwise, to the Kremlin's putative drive to re-establish an empire. It does not constitute a deviation from the multi-vector policy; on the contrary, it illustrates Astana's ability to maximise security and economic benefits without jeopardising the traditional balancing act. The chapter will provide a brief discussion on the EEU and then examine Kazakhstan's policy debate concerning the pros and contras of taking part in this bloc, with a particular emphasis on Nazarbaev's quest for legitimacy, dilemmas of economic development and sovereignty and relations with major international partners.

Interpreting the Eurasian Economic Union: Flawed Obsession with Geopolitics

The EEU came into existence on 1 January 2015 as an organisation for regional cooperation comprising Armenia, Belarus, Kazakhstan and Russia. Kyrgyzstan formally joined in August 2015. Foreshadowing the creation of the EEU in late 2011, Vladimir Putin characterised it as a "powerful supranational association capable of becoming one of the poles in the modern world and serving as an efficient bridge between Europe and the dynamic Asia-Pacific region". He was adamant that "none of this entails any kind of revival of the Soviet Union" and stressed its mission to work alongside China, the EU and the United States towards sustainable global development (Putin 2011).

This vision was quickly challenged by critics in the West who spoke about the project using idioms of Russian imperialism and the Kremlin's bid for continental or even global hegemony, thus casting it as primarily an adversarial geopolitical project. The US Secretary of State, Hillary Clinton, was unequivocal in passing judgement on the advancing Eurasian integration:

> There is a move to re-Sovietise the region . . . It's not going to be called that. It's going to be called a customs union, it will be called Eurasian Union and all of that . . . But let's make no mistake about it. We know what the goal is and we are trying to figure out effective ways to slow down or prevent it. (cited in Clover 2012)

There is now an impressive corpus of literature portraying the EEU as a sort of reservation established by the neo-imperialist Putin regime for neighbouring post-Soviet nations which they are intimidated or cajoled to join against their will (Blank 2014; Mankoff 2014; Orenstein 2015; Standish 2015). Even those authors who do not regard the Russian president as an aggressive thug tend to argue that the EEU is a defensive geopolitical project designed to secure Russia's hegemonic position in Eurasia, in the face of competing initiatives such as the European Neighbourhood Policy (Krickovic 2014).

The temptation to analyse the EEU through the lens of geopolitics – an ultimate form of realism – is understandable given the current tensions between Russia and the West, and the allure of a theory that explains alliance formation parsimoniously through the logic of balance of power. There are three problems inherent in this approach. First, as Chidley argued, the predominant concern of global security in any interstate alignment "need not preoccupy scholars to the extent that it obscures other motivators and accounts of state behaviour" (2014, p. 153). The EEU easily lends itself to the alternative analytical toolkit of new institutionalism, constructivism, policy network analysis, multilevel governance, regulatory politics, constitutionalism or the "politics like any other" approach (see Bulmer 2007, pp. 118–122). It is quite appropriate to tackle the EEU as a mechanism of cooperation divorced from the security field where participants pursue welfare through economies of scale, lower transaction costs and improved information flow (Rittberger et al. 2006 pp. 16–20; Cho 2014, p. 53). Far from constituting a political and military threat to the West, Eurasian integration may simply result in the emergence of yet another "economic region in the neo-liberal world system driven by global markets" (Lane 2014, pp. 4–6).

The second problem is the misrepresentation of the EEU's operational mode. It is often portrayed as a vehicle for Russian domination where supranational organs and regulations disproportionately benefit Moscow (Barbashin 2015). The EEU is implicitly measured against the old autarkic Council for Mutual Economic Assistance (COMECON) in such assessments. A closer look at the organisation's treaty and institutional setup actually evokes strong parallels with the process of European economic integration somewhere between the 1957 Treaty of Rome and the Single European Act of 1987 in terms of delegation of specific powers and competences from the national level and extent of policy coordination (Voronina 2013, p. 241).[1] Conflicts of interest in regional economic blocs are nothing new (Rittberger et al. 2006, pp. 145–146), and the EEU is yet to experience its equivalent of the EEC's "empty chair" crisis of 1965 when France boycotted Council meetings in an attempt to get its way on a range of issues.

The final and perhaps most egregious problem with the geopolitical mindset is its treatment of smaller countries as objects of international politics, the gormless pawns in various great games played by the superpowers. Although a lot of critical effort went into showing the remarkable resourcefulness of the former Soviet republics in engaging with, directing, harnessing and deflecting external agency (Cooley 2012; Kavalski 2010), the reductionist take on Eurasian integration that treats it as a function of power play by Moscow versus Washington (or Beijing, or Brussels) with little input from current and prospective EEU members continues to be widespread. At best, commentators insert brief caveats in their geopolitical narratives, for example, Krickovic (2014, p. 505): "This is not to argue that the region's smaller and weaker states are simply an object of Russia's power. These states will undoubtedly play an important role in the integration process and Russia will have to appeal to their interests and concerns".

The EEU at a Glance

According to the EEU's official portal, its history dates back to March 1994 when Kazakhstan's President Nursultan Nazarbaev delivered a public lecture at the Moscow State University calling for open borders, removal of customs barriers and the creation of a common economic space in the Commonwealth of Independent States (Eurasian Economic Union 2015). Nazarbaev's dream did not progress much beyond the proliferation of bilateral and multilateral free trade agreements until 1999, when Belarus, Kazakhstan, Kyrgyzstan, Russia and Tajikistan signed the Treaty on the Customs Union (CU) and Single Economic Space (SES). The CU became fully operational in 2010 among Belarus, Kazakhstan and Russia, and the SES came into effect in 2012 with the same membership.

Contrary to the caricature-like explanation that the CU was "suddenly declared" by Putin simply because he "wanted to prove his importance" having left the presidency shortly before (Aslund 2015); the quest for common tariff arrangements and an integrated internal market in the former USSR has a lengthy record of trials and errors and ferocious bargaining. The CU's normative base by 2012 comprised more than 70 international treaties signed since 1995 and 900 technical regulations. It also contained between 600 and 2000 exceptions and exclusions (Chufrin 2014, p. 11). The SES legislative framework consisted of 17 interstate agreements outlining the principles of achieving the "four freedoms", that is, the free movement of goods, capital, services and people. The EEU Treaty signed in May 2014, a bulky 1000-page document, represented an amalgamation, streamlining and deepening of the extant CU and SES instruments, and had two additional sections on the organisation's institutions and procedural matters, for example, admission of new members and termination of membership.

Article 4 of the treaty identifies the EEU's three central objectives: creating conditions for stable economic development; formation of a unified market of goods, services, capital and labour resources and modernisation and increased competitiveness of national economies within the global economy. It paved the way for the practical implementation of single markets in service provision (across 43 sectors) and labour in 2015, and set concrete benchmarks for single markets in pharmaceuticals and medical equipment (2016), electricity (2019) and hydrocarbons

(2025). It made provisions for a unified transport system and a joint financial regulator to coalesce by 2025.

The treaty's preamble and multiple articles contain numerous references to the norms, rules and principles of the World Trade Organisation (WTO). A separate agreement "on the functioning of the CU within a Multilateral Trade System" declares the priority of the WTO rules in the CU legal framework and obliges the CU to fulfil conditions undertaken by countries entering the WTO. The process of harmonisation between WTO and CU rules is ongoing, and has already led to the reduction of the CU Common Customs Tariff's weighted average rate from 10 % in 2012 to 8.7 % in 2014 (Eurasian Economic Commission 2014c). Further belying the perception that the CU is a protectionist entity (Aslund 2015) is the fact that it deploys few defensive trade measures against external partners – less than half the number of the EU or China, four times fewer than the United States and six times fewer than India (Slepnev 2014, p. 8).

The EEU's two peak bodies are the Supreme Eurasian Economic Council (SEEC), consisting of the heads of states, and the Intergovernmental Council comprising the heads of government. Both are convoked from time to time, and make decisions on a consensual basis. The organisation has only two permanently functioning supranational institutions inherited from the SES: the Eurasian Economic Commission (EEC) and the Eurasian Court (EC). The EEC, whose mandate is "to create an environment conducive to the smooth operation of the CU and the SES and to submit proposals that contribute to accelerating the integration process" (Eurasian Economic Commission 2014a, p. 26), draws top officials on a parity basis from all participating states, and each member on the council and board of the EEC has one vote. This is in contrast with the now defunct supranational organs of the CU where representatives of Russia used to enjoy 57 % of the vote.

The EEC, located in Moscow, has professional staff of about 1200 but its executive remit continues to be weak; it functions primarily as an expert, consultative and monitoring unit. Its directives, just like the rulings of the EC, are subject to multiple checks and often become mere recommendations to national actors. The EEC Board makes decisions by consensus and by qualified majority. Any issue resolved by the Board may be blocked by the EEC Council, where voting is by consensus only. All EEC resolutions may be revised or dumped by the Supreme and Intergovernmental Councils (Kalish 2014, p. 23).

The treaty refers to the parties' commitment to coordinated macroeconomic policies. In practice, the violation of guidelines concerning levels of government debt and the rate of inflation does not incur sanctions or penalties as is the case in the EU. Typically, in May 2014 the EEC noted that in Belarus "the inflation rate was exceeded considerably" (in fact overshooting the maximum critical value by 8 %), and meekly expressed hope that its authorities would continue taking steps to address the issue (Eurasian Economic Commission 2014b, p. 3). Article 118 of the treaty provides for an easy exit from the EEU: a member state should give a 12-month notice to its partners after which it ceases to be bound by the treaty and other legal instruments concluded under the union's aegis.

Although it is important to understand what the EEU stands for, it is also imperative to know what it does not do. Its statutory documents and institutions do not provide for the movement towards common foreign and security policy, citizenship, currency, and health, culture and legal systems. A supranational parliamentary body is not contemplated in the foreseeable future. The possibility of deeper integration in all these areas was included in the original proposals for the EEU Treaty tabled by the Russian Academy of Foreign Trade in February 2012. Over the course of five rounds of negotiations, 18 summits, and 247 meetings of expert groups (Eurasian Economic Commission 2014d, p. 20) the final version of the treaty adopted in May 2014 was completely devoid of the political dimension. This was a direct result of the position taken by Belarus and Kazakhstan (Netreba and Butrin 2013; Ionova 2014, pp. 10–11). As Kazakhstan's first deputy prime minister, who led his country's negotiating team, explained:

> The Eurasian Economic Union is not a political association. This is the most important thing. Economic cooperation is the exclusive subject of the Treaty. Our negotiating team has fully defended the line on the inadmissibility of the Union's politicisation and the debating of questions touching on national competencies and state sovereignty (cited in Mamaev 2014).

At present, the EEU appears to be a regional trading arrangement (RTA) that is rather common in world practice. On the scale of six levels of integration, ascending from preferential trading regime to "deep integration" where an RTA becomes indistinguishable from a nation state as a single unit in global economy (Pomfret 2006), it has just begun transition from a common market (Level 4; customs union + free movement of factors of production) to an economic union

(Level 5; common market + common economic policies). Whether the EEU will expand into new policy areas remains to be seen. What is clear however is that smaller countries such as Kazakhstan have been actively shaping the bloc's evolution. They are realistic about the challenges lying ahead including the problem of confrontation between Russia and the West over Ukraine, yet they remain optimistic about the EEU's long-term prospects. In April 2014, Nazarbaev criticised both those who wished the EEU to fail and the "maladroit impatience" of some experts in cobbling together a supranational union. His view of the EEU was not that of "a shiny white snowman" that would succumb easily to crisis situations in global and national economies or geopolitical turbulence (Nazarbaev 2014d).

Nazarbaev's Eurasianism

In his study of economic regionalism after the Cold War, Wunderlich (2007, p. 135) observed that leaders' preferences, personalities and agendas of political survival impact heavily on decisions regarding whom to cooperate with, what form cooperation should take and the extent to which it should be institutionalised. This argument applies fully to Nazarbaev: Kazakhstan's participation in the EEU owes much to its president's idiosyncratic beliefs and legitimation strategies.

Nazarbaev's nation-building project since independence has followed the notion of Eurasianism based on Kazakhstan's geographic position as a bridge between European and Asian civilisations. This places the country in an advantageous position, where it can adopt the best practices from all directions in its path of development and become an important connector for international markets in Asia, Europe and South Asia (Ambrosio and Lange 2014, p. 546). The original idea of the Eurasian Union floated in 1994 contained references to geopolitics in the mould of Lev Gumilev[2] as well as Kazakhstan's unique cultural identity (Nazarbaev 1997). Two decades after, one can still encounter echoes of this discourse extolling the exceptional virtues of Kazakhstanis who, unlike the calculating and essentially self-serving Russians and Belorussians, are able to weave the ideational fabric of the EEU through the loom of "spiritual unity, where the grounds for political and economic egotism and mercantilism are absent" (Avershin and Aubakirov 2014, p. 243–244). However, Nazarbaev himself has gradually purged the more esoteric content from the Eurasian Union concept in favour of economic substance. His updated vision was summarised in an article published in the Russian daily *Izvestiia* which appeared 3 weeks after Putin's programmatic piece in the same newspaper (Putin 2011), and was a polemical response to the latter. Kazakhstan's leader wrote:

> First, without denying the significance of cultural and civilizational factors, I have proposed that integration must be built on the basis of economic pragmatism first and foremost. Economic interests, and not abstract geopolitical ideas and slogans, are the main engine of integration processes...
>
> Second, I have always been and continue to be an advocate of the voluntary character of integration...
>
> Third, from the outset, I have envisaged the Eurasian Union as an association of states on the basis of equality, non-interference in the internal affairs of each other, respect for sovereignty and inviolability of state borders.
>
> Fourth, I have suggested creating the supranational organs of the Eurasian Union which would work on the basis of consensus, taking into account interests of each member state, and possess clear and real powers. This in no way implies the transfer of political sovereignty. It is an axiom. The successful experience of establishing the European Union was precisely about that (Nazarbaev 2011).

It is clear that the EEU as it emerged on 1 January 2015 carries more resemblance to Nazarbaev's agenda than Putin's idiom of a "powerful supranational association capable of becoming one of the poles in the modern world".

As the intellectual father of modern Eurasianism, Nazarbaev has a personal stake in its promotion and success. Moreover, being seen as the EEU leader is symbolically important for the President of Kazakhstan who, since 1991, has consistently aimed to bolster his legitimacy by broadcasting external recognition inward to domestic audiences (Schatz 2006, p. 270). Deferential references to Nazarbaev as the "patriarch of Eurasian integration" and "one of the brightest and most experienced heads of state in the Eurasian space with a firm grasp of global problems" (TASS 2015) coming thick and fast from the Russian political elite and mass media help construct the image of a wise father of the nation who "has compelled the entire world to accept our country as an equal partner" (Ergaliev 2015).

The EEU Debate in Kazakhstan: Issues of Economic Development and National Sovereignty

Nazarbaev's agency in pushing Kazakhstan towards the EEU is indisputable, yet it is only part of the story. There is a broad national consensus in the country on the advisability of this move based on rational cost–benefit analysis. The public debate on the EEU is quite robust, open and multi-faceted. Politicians, experts, journalists and civil society activists continuously analyse the pros and contras of Eurasian integration, with the three discursive threads of economic welfare, sovereignty and international relations being particularly prominent (Berkutova 2014).

The process of integration under the auspices of the CU and SES must have ticked the right boxes as the people of Kazakhstan have shown considerable enthusiasm towards it, leaving other member states behind (Table 12.1).

A survey conducted several months after the official launch of the EEU in 2015 found that 87.4 % of Kazakhstanis approved of it, and that they were rather well informed about the complex processes of economic integration (Sadvokasova 2015, pp. 7–8).

Nazarbaev's key message for his domestic audience has been that deepening economic integration is an objective necessity for the country's development. In his January 2014 state of the nation address, he identified Kazakhstan's participation in the EEU as an organic part of the country's ascent to the list of top 30 most developed nations in the world by 2050 (Nazarbaev 2014a). Shortly after, he even quantified the expected medium-term benefits of the EEU: "According to our estimates, by 2030 this integration will yield the three participants additional GDP growth of 25 percent and extra US$600 bn or more" (Nazarbaev 2014b). Later in the year, the president's Nur Otan political party, using analytical reports from

Table 12.1 Public attitude towards the common market (CU + SES) in Belarus, Kazakhstan and Russia

Country	*Positive (%)*	*Indifferent (%)*	*Negative (%)*	*Do not know (%)*
Kazakhstan	84	7	4	5
Russia	79	17	2	2
Belarus	68	24	6	2

Source: Poll conducted in May 2014. Adapted from Evraziiskii bank razvitiia (2014, p. 98).

government agencies and media surveys, published a handy booklet explaining in an accessible manner the economic gains the EEU will bring to Kazakhstan (Nur Otan 2014). According to its subtitle, the booklet provided answers to "twenty questions that Kazakhstanis most frequently ask". A summary of particularly salient benefits distilled from the FAQs is as follows:

1. Benefits for Kazakhstan's business: unfettered access to a giant market of 153 mn people; a share in the annual US$198 bn bonanza of state procurement in Russia and Belarus; colossal savings in using partners' transport infrastructure such as railways and pipelines (15 % of Kazakhstan's export transited through the Russian rail system in 2013).
2. Benefits for ordinary citizens: better consumer protection thanks to stringent technical regulations (e.g. the minimum content of meat in locally produced sausages will go up from 5 to 60 %); new jobs created via joint ventures; freedom to work anywhere with skills and qualifications fully recognised. There will be no influx of labour migrants into Kazakhstan as Russia with its 1.8 mn vacancies will continue to be the main destination country for them.
3. Benefits for industrialisation: Kazakhstan needs to industrialise, and a moderate (and temporary) rise in import tariffs within the CU has created appropriate conditions for import-substitution industrialisation. The flow of foreign direct investment from all sources has not suffered, but was redirected away from the resource sector towards manufacturing, with about half going to the latter now.
4. Better structure of trade: the share of manufactured and value-added goods in Kazakhstan's exports to the EEU states is much higher than in its external trade dominated by minerals. Eventually, Kazakhstani-manufactured goods will become competitive in the international market, too.

Other arguments proffered by pro-integration economists include references to Kazakhstan's receipts from the CU's consolidated customs revenue outpacing its actual value of imports (Dodonov 2012, p. 64); protection from predatory behaviour by transnational corporations (Berentaev 2012, p. 19); the exponential growth of Kazakhstani–Russian small and medium joint ventures, especially in the border areas, which generated employment and expanded the tax base (Ianovskaia 2015) and the dizzying prospect of a corporate alliance or even merger between

Kazakhstani and Russian hydrocarbon giants (KazMunaiGaz and Gazprom/Transneft) that will cause global competitors to tremble (Shabarova 2014, p. 94).

The official line on the issue of sovereignty is straightforward and unequivocal, and is broadcast daily to the point of saturation. In Nazarbaev's words, "we are not going to give away our hard-won freedom to anybody. If regional alliances start to inflict damage on our state interests, we will immediately leave such an organization. The union we are moving towards consists entirely of economic integration" (quoted in Sarmurzina 2013). His foreign minister also stayed on message: "There may be no associations whatsoever with our Soviet past. This is not a step backwards. We are reaching a new level of equal economic partnership whereas our independence remains unshakable . . . I can state for sure that the EEU politicization is not happening and there is no threat to Kazakhstan's sovereignty" (Idrisov 2014). Nazarbaev's routine statement in August 2014 that his country would withdraw from the organisation if the EEU Treaty's clauses are not properly implemented, and Kazakhstan's interests suffer as a result (Nazarbaev 2014c), looked like a sensational scoop only to the Western media galvanised into a fresh bout of Putinophobia by the events in Ukraine (Farchy 2014).

On the whole, there is little appetite among the public and expert communities for the rapid expansion of the EEU's supranational functions. Even ardent supporters of deeper economic integration believe that until all treaty objectives are fully implemented, the dilution of national sovereignty through such measures as the introduction of common currency is inadvisable. Dodonov (2013, p. 141) estimated that the process might take 20–30 years to reach the next stage.

The counter-narratives criticising Kazakhstan's participation in the EEU can be loosely divided into two categories. On the one hand, there are experts, politicians and activists who put emphasis on the "geopolitical hole" into which the country is being dragged. Using the idioms of "neo-colonialism" and "imperialism", they follow the logic and methodology of mainstream Western discourse (cf Kadyrzhanov 2014; Yesdauletova and Yesdauletov 2014; a good primer can be found in Daly 2014). A recent example of this discourse was supplied by the chairman of the opposition All-Nation Social-Democratic Party (OSDP), who published an open letter to the president warning him against closer cooperation with exploitative, nationalist and anti-Western Russia which could degenerate into the "integration of the oligarchies leading our countries to a historical dead end"

(Tuyakbai 2015). His proposed remedial action transcended the subject matter of the EEU: he called for the wholesale democratisation of Kazakhstan's political system, independence of courts, local self-government and respect for citizens' rights. This conflation of broader political issues and the specific cause of Eurasian integration may have undermined the opposition's ability to mount efficient collective action on the latter and rally mass support. The EEU critics are very good at publicising their views on various media platforms, but in 2013 they utterly failed in their attempt to collect signatures for a referendum on integration, and their PR stunts such as the "Stop the Eurasian Virus" flash mob in May 2014 petered out amidst public indifference and internal acrimony (Rahmetova 2014). Towards the end of 2015, even OSDP switched its rhetoric from wholesale denunciation of the EEU to the imperative of greater parliamentary oversight and public scrutiny of the "equivocal Eurasianist processes" (Makushina 2015). While not particularly challenging to Nazarbaev, these activities have certainly kept the government on its toes and compelled it to engage in the incessant public awareness campaign as discussed above.

The second group of critics has focused on the economic aftershocks of transition to a common market. Increased competition from Russian and Belarusian companies, currency volatility, inflationary pressures and general nervousness about the new rules of the game have caused great concern among the business community and public in general who have called on the government for extra protection (Syzdykova 2013, pp. 13–14). The authorities responded with a raft of measures including temporary subsidisation of critical goods, currency interventions and an ambitious programme of support for small and medium enterprises (Lis 2014). Most significantly, the government has assiduously pursued redress against unfair practices by EEU partners using the organisation's governing bodies and rules.

The outcomes have been impressive enough for one expert normally critical of Nazarbaev to concede that the authorities "have in fact taken the initiative from the hands of the opposition which had to weaken its anti-integrationist protestations for a while" (Chebotarev 2014, pp. 104–105). In late 2014, 78.7 % of Kazakhstanis believed that their country's interests were adequately protected and taken into account in policy decisions within the CU and SES, as opposed to 44.5 % the year before (Makanov 2015, p. 366). In 2015, the SEEC and EEC promptly resolved about a dozen trade disputes among member states, including a major complaint by Belarus about Kazakhstan's imminent accession to the WTO which required a compromise on more than a thousand tariff positions (Kirinitsiianov 2016).

Kazakhstan, whose hydrocarbon sector accounts for half of state budget revenue and 60 % of export income, was hit hard by the fall in oil prices starting in June 2014. Its GDP growth in 2015 was a paltry 1.2 %, down from 4.3 % in 2014. Recession in Russia and a slump in China's demand did not help the situation. The Kazakh tenge was floated in 2015 and lost 85 % of its value by the end of year. The government position was that these adverse developments were manifestations of a crisis in the global capitalist economy of which Kazakhstan was now a part. Nazarbaev made the point that economic downturn was a cyclical phenomenon that would not last forever and added: "This has nothing to do with the Eurasian Economic Union. The EEU is our strategic direction, and we won't digress from it" (quoted in Kasenova 2015). This sentiment appears to have been shared by the public, whose attitudes to the EEU did not register a catastrophic decline throughout 2015, and the business community in particular. A report published by Kazakhstan's top NGO representing national entrepreneurs argued that the country's participation in the EEU had proved beneficial to the economy's real sector under conditions of crisis (Konurov 2016). It pointed to the following dynamics: while Kazakhstan's overall foreign trade in 2015 fell by 37.1 %, its trade within the EEU contracted only by 28.6 %; the structure of Kazakhstani exports to the EEU was dominated by value-added goods rather than raw materials; privately owned small and medium companies successfully filled the consumer niches in Russia vacated by Western producers in areas such as poultry (annual growth of 141 %) and pharmaceuticals (annual growth of 93 %). The report concluded with an observation that without the EEU, Kazakhstan might continue indefinitely in its role as a "shabby petrol station" in the global division of capitalist labour.

Relations with Russia

Kazakhstan's closer economic cooperation with Russia has not compromised its multi-vector foreign policy. Astana has continued to maintain an independent line on principal issues of global and regional security. Gloomy predictions by Western pundits that the EEU would be "the first step in a drive by Mr. Putin to reunify, in one form or another, those former republics that contain significant numbers of ethnic Russians", including Kazakhstan (Bennets 2014), failed to materialise.

Commentary has now shifted to toned-down rhetoric that Kazakhstan is complying with the Kremlin's position due to "fear" of "a fading though still potentially dangerous empire" (Kuchins et al. 2015, p. 10). Such generalisations are not corroborated by empirical evidence. Public opinion surveys conducted in Kazakhstan during 2012–2015 demonstrated a stable and overwhelmingly high perception (82–84 % of those polled) of Russia as a friendly and nonthreatening nation (Eurasian Development Bank 2015, p. 25).[3]

The governing elite in Kazakhstan is not particularly concerned about the potential negative ramifications of the country's alliance with Russia. A prominent local political scientist who surveyed the evolution of Moscow's "pivoting to the East" during 2010–2015 agreed that "hypothetically, Astana might have been worried... about facing the risk of a shrinking space for manoeuvre in external affairs", but then concluded: "However, we can see that this is not happening" (Nursha 2015, p. 74). Part of the explanation is that Nazarbaev, unlike many leaders in the West, has an in-depth understanding of how the Kremlin operates and an appreciation of its legitimate security concerns as well as cognisance of the limits to Moscow's power. This awareness coupled with a dense plethora of institutions for mutual policy consultation has enabled what Laruelle (2015, pp. 9–10) described as Astana's "subtle and balanced policy... recognising Russia's key status for the country, and bolstering strategic cooperation in the framework of the Collective Security Treaty Organization (CSTO), all while seeking to preserve its strategic autonomy".

Kazakhstan's response to the Ukraine crisis, which erupted in February 2014 when the government of President Victor Yanukovich was overthrown, is illustrative of this autonomy. On the one hand, Astana treated the results of the March 2014 referendum in Crimea which supported the secession of the peninsula from Ukraine as broadly representative of the popular will. On the other hand, it refused to recognise Crimea's accession to the Russian Federation officially, claiming that under international law Ukraine's sovereignty and territorial integrity must remain intact (Baizakova and McDermott 2015, p. 4). Kazakhstan alone among Central Asian nations sent a high-level delegation to the inauguration ceremony of the newly elected President of Ukraine, Petro Poroshenko, in June 2014. It refrained from taking part in Russian economic sanctions imposed on Ukraine, and even cooperated with Azerbaijan and Georgia in devising the Trans-Caspian transport corridor which would allow Ukraine to bypass Russia in delivering up to 10 million tonnes of goods per year via rail and ferry to Central Asia and China (Platonova 2016).

Nazarbaev assumed the mantle of an avuncular statesman, "senior both in age and length of political career" (Baigarin 2014), calling on the presidents of Russia and Ukraine to find a political compromise. He opined that sanctions and counter-sanctions would not resolve the conflict, and offered to mediate between European, Russian and Ukrainian leaders: "Kazakhstan has the same attitude to Russia and Ukraine, we don't have a conflict of interest, I am what is called 'an honest broker' who supports neither side, a neutral person who could make a contribution" (quoted in Agimbetov 2014). Nazarbaev adopted a similarly conciliatory position in the crisis between Moscow and Ankara after a Russian military jet was downed by Turkey in November 2015. He declined to join the Russian economic embargo and promised to work hard to salvage friendly relations between Russia and Turkey, which he claimed he had spent many years nurturing (Panvilova 2015).

Kazakhstan has used the EEU as an instrument to increase its influence in the Central Asian region. It was a staunch supporter of Kyrgyzstan's membership in the bloc. In fact, Astana committed to providing US$177 mn out of the US$377 mn requested by Bishkek to implement its roadmap towards acceding to the organisation (Muminov 2014). Kazakhstani experts speak quite openly about building a Central Asian "economic system under the aegis of Kazakhstan" as a subset of the Russia-led EEU, whereby the water and other natural, production and labour resources of Kyrgyzstan and eventually Tajikistan will be locked into Kazakhstan's quest for development and prosperity (Muhamedzhanova 2015).

Recrudescent Multi-Vectorism

In December 2014, Nazarbaev reassured the citizens of Kazakhstan: "We are not abandoning the multi-vector nature of our [foreign] policy, there are no grounds for this . . . Every treaty we sign, including the one on the EEU, says that this does not impede our interaction with third countries" (2014e). The events of 2015 seemed to confirm the president's pledge. Kazakhstan finally joined the WTO after 19 years of painstaking negotiations. It avoided entanglement in the Ukraine imbroglio and stayed out of the sanctions and counter-sanctions game played by Russia, the West and Turkey. It signed an Enhanced Partnership and Cooperation

Agreement (EPCA) with the EU – the first Central Asian republic to have done so. According to Kazakhstan's Foreign Minister, Erlan Idrisov, the development of EPCA's trade section was helped by his country's experience in the CU and the EEU (Idrisov quoted in Turebekova 2015). Relations with the United States continued on an even keel, characterised by both sides as a "strategic partnership" (Nurbekov 2015).

While initially there was some apprehension in Kazakhstan's policy community about the compatibility of Eurasian economic integration with China's Silk Road Economic Belt (SREB) project (Amrebaev 2014), by the end of 2015 a substantial degree of harmonisation was achieved, at least on paper, among the interests of Kazakhstan, China and the EEU. The EEC's official documents began to refer to a "joint partnership" between Kazakhstan's Nurly Zhol programme of infrastructure development announced in November 2014, the EEU and the People's Republic of China (PRC) in the creation of a high-speed multimodal transport route connecting Western China and Western Europe – the Eurasian Transcontinental Corridor (Eurasian Economic Commission 2015, pp. 43–44).

Two salient themes in official policy discourse supporting the thesis about the EEU's neutral or even beneficial impact on Kazakhstan's independent foreign policy are worth noting here. The first addresses suspicions that Russia's economic preponderance in the EEU will inevitably translate into its political domination as well. The counterpoint to them is a simple comparison: a close analogue to the EEU in the family of RTAs is The North American Free Trade Agreement (NAFTA), where the largest economy (the USA) is nine and 13 times bigger, respectively, than Canada's and Mexico's – a (dis)proportion that is similar to the Russia–Kazakhstan–Belarus trio (Sultanov and Dodonov 2012, p. 6). The logbook of more than 300 trade disputes among NAFTA participants as of 2014 makes the track record of the EEU look rather good. The second theme centres on the openness of the EEU to trade deals with external partners. In May 2014, a Kazakhstani academic counted no less than 40 countries and RTAs interested in forming a free trade zone (FTZ) with the EEU (Baimanov 2014). The first FTZ with Vietnam went into effect in May 2015. Upon assuming the headship of SEEC for 2016, Nazarbaev reiterated his commitment to open regionalism and declared that his top priority in office would be the "deepening of economic relations of the Union with third countries and key integrationist entities" (Nazarbaev cited in Baimanov 2016). There is no reason to believe, as some have suggested (Nurgaliyeva 2016), that Astana's active search for foreign partners is a desperate attempt to balance Russian hegemony within the EEU: diversification of economic ties has been an essential feature of Kazakhstan's multi-vector policy since independence, and the EEU membership has actually given it extra vigour.

Foreign Minister Idrisov had every right to claim in December 2015 that Kazakhstan was a mature political actor and not a pawn in a fictional "great game", the concept of which he rejected out of hand. Instead, he identified Central Asia and Eurasia as a zone where "various big players have legitimate interests that can fortuitously cohere rather than conflict with each other" (Idrisov 2015). Nazarbaev clearly relished the role of peacemaker between Russia and the West when he called for the creation of the Eurasian Economic Space on the basis of the EU and EEU: "geopolitical games, mutual economic sanctions and other archaic atavisms should be forever left in the past. The creation of a peaceful, stable, prosperous and economically strong Eurasia will have a powerful multiplying effect on global growth and will be beneficial to all" (Nazarbaev 2016).

Conclusion

Kazakhstan has travelled a long way since gaining independence in 1991 to become a confident and self-assured middle power with a clear vision of its position in the world. The multi-vector foreign policy has enabled the government of Nazarbaev to uphold national interests in the international arena efficiently. Its membership in the EEU ought not to be regarded as a deviation from the pattern that has been carefully established over a quarter of a century.

Kazakhstan has entered into a deep economic alliance with Russia and three other post-Soviet nations voluntarily, and it has sought to be and thus far has succeeded in being treated as an equal in the EEU and averting its (geo)political mission creep. It is difficult to assess the organisation's prospects for success or failure in the future, and exactly how "powerful" and "supranational" it may become, but the important thing is that Kazakhstan has sufficient instruments and safeguards to protect its national interests within the EEU framework. The articulation and recalibration of these interests is an ongoing process based on a robust public debate. While Nazarbaev's personal agency is undeniable and hugely important in this context, there is a critical mass of support for Eurasian economic integration in Kazakhstan at the elite and popular level. There is an equally strong consensus that the country will not be party to any neo-imperialist venture or an ideological alliance under the conceptual veneer of Eurasianism. One can only agree with a prediction made by an astute observer from Russia: "Obviously, no matter who replaces Nazarbayev, Kazakhstan's stance on the Eurasian Union will remain pragmatic" (Malashenko 2013, p. 122).

Notes

1. Voronina suggests parallels with the European Economic Community (EEC) quite late in the period, between 1986 and 1992, but this is a stretch because many policy areas (environment, social cohesion, etc.) that were part of the European economic integration agenda circa 1986 are not in the sights of the EEU at present.
2. Gumilev (1912–1992), a prominent Soviet historian and ethnographer, advocated the existence of the Eurasian super-ethnos based on nomadic value systems which comprised, *inter alia*, Russians and Kazakhs (Shlapentokh 2012). Gumilev's ideas became popular among the intelligentsia of Soviet Turkic republics in the 1980s. Nazarbaev presided over the foundation of the Gumilev Eurasian National University in Astana in 1996.
3. In 2015, Kazakhstan was among the very few former Soviet republics that were relaxed about being threatened by other states. More than 51 % of the population believed that Kazakhstan had no enemies abroad; the United States topped the list of unfriendly/threatening nations, but only a low 24 % shared this view compared to 77 % in Russia (Eurasian Development Bank 2015, pp. 29–30).

Bibliography

Agimbetov, B. (2014, December 21). Nazarbaev gotov vystupit' 'chestnym menedzherom' v ukrainskom konflikte. *Kazakhstanskaia Pravda,* 1.

Aitken, J. (2009). *Nazarbayev and the making of Kazakhstan: from communism to capitalism.* London: Continuum.

Ambrosio, T., & Lange, W. A. (2014). Mapping Kazakhstan's geopolitical code: an analysis of Nazarbayev's presidential addresses, 1997–2014. *Eurasian Geography and Economics, 55*(5), 537–559.

Amrebaev, A. (2014). Ekonomicheskii poias Velikogo Shelkovogo puti: ot idei k realnosti. *Kazakhstan v globalnykh protsessakh, 3,* 30–39.

Aslund, A. (2015, January 5). The essence of the customs union is protectionism. *Emerging Europe News.* http://www.emerging-europe.com/slund-the-flawed-eurasian-economic-union,p1777505044. Accessed 2 February 2015.

Avershin, V. S., & Aubakirov, A. B. (2014). Evraziiskii soiuz v kontekste konstitutsionnykh prav cheloveka v Respublike Kazakshtan. In: V. G. Egorov (Ed.), *Politicheskie protsessy na postsovetskom prostranstve* (pp. 240–246). Moscow: MGOU.

Barbashin, A. (2015, January 15). The Eurasian illusion: the myth of Russia's Economic Union. *Foreign Affairs*. http://www.foreignaffairs.com/articles/142781/anton-barbashin/the-eurasian-illusion. Accessed 4 February 2015.

Baigarin, M. (2014, December 22). N. Nazarbaev predlozhil Rossii i Ukraine naiti kompromiss, chtoby sokhranit' territorialnuiu tselotnost' strany. *KazInform*. http://www.inform.kz/rus/article/2729804. Accessed 16 February 2015.

Baimanov, D. (2014, May 29). 40 stran khotiat prisoedinitsia k zone svobodnoi torgovli TS. *Kazinform*. http://www.inform.kz/rus/article/2662831. Accessed 4 January 2015.

Baimanov, D. (2016, February 11). N. Nazarbaev predlozhil ob'iavit' 2016 god 'Godom uglubleniia ekonomicheskikh otnoshenii EAES s tret'imi stranami'. *Kazinform*. http://kazinform.kz/rus/article/2869839. Accessed 25 February 2016.

Baizakova, Z., & McDermott, R. (2015, December 17). Threat perception in Central Asia in response to Russia-Ukraine: Kazakhstan will not be next research division – NATO Research College, Research Paper 119. http://www.ndc.nato.int/download/downloads.php?icode=462. Accessed 30 December 2015.

Bennets, M. (2014, September 4). Former Soviet Bloc nations fear Putin assembling new USSR. *Washington Times*. http://www.washingtontimes.com/news/2014/sep/4/former-soviet-bloc-nations-fear-vladimir-putin-ass/. Accessed 4 January 2016.

Berentaev, K. B. (2012). Nauchno-metodicheskie i institutsionalno-organizatsionnye problemy sozdaniia Evraziiskogo soiuza gosudarstv. In: B. K. Sultanov (Ed.), *Tamozhennyi soiuz i Edinoe ekonomicheskoe prostranstvo: problemy ekonomicheskoi integratsii* (pp. 13–48). Almaty: KISI.

Berkutova, E. (2014). *Sovremennoe vospriiatie integratsii v Respublike Kazakhstan (obzor kazakhoiazychnoi i russkoiazychnoi kazakhstanskoi pressy*. Almaty: IWEP.

Blank, S. (2014). From Eurasia with love. *American Foreign Policy Interests, 36*(3), 162–174.

Bulmer, S. (2007). Institutional and policy analysis in the European Union: from the treaty of Rome to the present. In: D. Phinnemore & A. Warleigh-Lack (Eds.), *Reflections on European integration: 50 years of the treaty of Rome* (pp. 109–126). Basingstoke: Palgrave Macmillan.

Chebotarev, A. E. (2014). Kazakhstanskoe izmerenie evraziiskoi integratsii: Pro&Contra. In: R. I. Murzagaleev (Ed.), *Obraz evraziiskoi integratsii v XXI v.: ogranichiteli i perspektivy* (pp. 96–107). Ufa: BashGU.

Chidley, C. (2014). Towards a framework of alignment in international relations. *Politikon, 41*(1), 141–157.

Cho, S. (2014). *The social foundations of world trade.* Cambridge: Cambridge University Press.

Chufrin, G. (2014). Etapnoe sobytie, *Rossiia i novye gosudarstva Evrazii, 3*(24), 9–22.

Clarke, M. E. (2015, April 9). Kazakhstan's multi-vector foreign policy: diminishing returns in an era of great power "pivots"? *The Asan Forum* http://www.theasanforum.org/kazakhstans-multi-vector-foreign-policy-diminishing-returns-in-an-era-of-great-power-pivots/. Accessed 6 June 2015.

Clover, C. (2012, December 6). Clinton vows to thwart new Soviet Union. *Financial Times.* http://www.ft.com/cms/s/0/a5b15b14-3fcf-11e2-9f71-00144feabdc0.html#axzz4KD0m9Hcc. Accessed 12 November 2014.

Cooley, A. (2012). *Great Games, local rules: the new great power contest in Central Asia.* Oxford: Oxford University Press.

Daly, J. C. K. (2014). Kazakhstan and Belarus: Buyer's Remorse? In: S. F. Starr & S. E. Cornell (Eds.), *Putin's grand strategy: the Eurasian union and its discontents* (pp. 82–97). Washington DC: CACI.

De Haas, M. (2015). Kazakhstan's security policy: steady as she goes? *Journal of Slavic Military Studies, 28*(4), 621–645.

Dodonov, V. I. (2012). Predvaritelnye makroekonomicheskie itogi uchstiia Kazakhstana v Tamozhennom soiuze. In: B. K. Sultanov (Ed.), *Tamozhennyi soiuz i Edinoe ekonomicheskoe prostranstvo: problemy ekonomicheskoi integratsii* (pp. 49–69). Almaty: KISI.

Dodonov, V. I. (2013). Integratsionnye protsessy v valiutno-finansovoi sfere: vozmozhnosti i ugrozy. In: B. K. Sultanov (Ed.), *Integratsionnye protsessy v Evraziiskom prostranstve i sovremennyi mir* (pp. 138–155). Almaty: KISI.

Ergaliev, Z. (2015, November 25). Priznannyi lider. *Kazakhstanskaia Pravda.* http://dknews.kz/bespretsedentnaya-podderzhka-malogo-i-srednego-biznesa/. Accessed 13 March 2015.

Eurasian Council on Foreign Affairs. (2014, June). *Foreign policy in Kazakhstan: looking outwards and moving forwards.* Occasional Paper. http://www.eurasiancouncilforeignaffairs.eu/wp-content/uploads/2014/02/Foreign-Policy-Paper-English.pdf. Accessed 18 April 2015.

Eurasian Development Bank. (2015). *Integratsionnyi barometr EABR – 2015.* St. Petersburg: Tsentr integratsionnykh issledovanii.

Eurasian Economic Commission. (2014a). *Eurasian economic integration: facts and figures.* Moscow: EEC.

Eurasian Economic Commission. (2014b, May 29). Key guidelines for macroeconomic policy in the member states of the Customs Union and the single economic space for 2014 – 2015. http://www.eurasiancommission.org/ru/act/integr_i_makroec/dep_makroec_pol/developDocs/Documents/The%20Key%20Guidelines%202014-2015.pdf. Accessed 6 June 2015.

Eurasian Economic Commission. (2014c, October 6). How the commitments of Russia regarding the accession to the WTO are fulfilled in the Customs Union. http://www.eurasiancommission.org/ru/act/trade/SiteAssets/Russias%20commitments%20in%20the%20WTO%20EN%20Nov2014%2006.10.2014.pdf. Accessed 2 January 2015.

Eurasian Economic Commission. (2014d). *Evraziiskii ekonomicheskii soiuz. Voprosy i otvety, tsifry i fakty*. Moscow: Evraziiskaia ekonomicheskaia komissiia.

Eurasian Economic Commission. (2015, December 23). *Transport*. http://www.eurasiancommission.org/ru/Documents/transport_eng.pdf. Accessed 15 January 2016.

Eurasian Economic Union. (2015). *President of Kazakhstan N. Nazarbayev at Lomonosov Moscow State University, Moscow, March 29, 1994*. http://www.eaeunion.org/upload/iblock/697/1994_1_1.jpg. Accessed 15 July 2015.

European Union. (2014, October 9). *Factsheet: EU-Kazakhstan enhanced partnership and cooperation agreement. European Union external action*. http://www.eeas.europa.eu/statements/docs/2014/141009_01_en.pdf. Accessed 3 March 2015.

Evraziiskii bank razvitiia. (2014). *Integratsionnyi barometr EABR 2014*. Saint Petersburg: Tsentr integratsionnykh issledovanii.

Farchy, J. (2014, September 2). Standoff with west reveals splinters in Putin's Eurasia project. *Financial Times*. http://www.ft.com/cms/s/0/0fd58e1c-32b7-11e4-b86e-00144feabdc0.html. Accessed 24 October 2014.

Hanks, R. R. (2009). "Multi-vector politics" and Kazakhstan's emerging role as a geo-strategic player in Central Asia. *Journal of Balkan and Near Eastern Studies, 11*(3), 257–267.

Ianovskaia, M. (2015, February 9). Ekonomist Elena Kuzmina – o EAES, sanktsiiakh, reitingakh i o tom, zachem vse eto nuzhno. *Fergana*. http://www.fergananews.com/article.php?id=8399. Accessed 20 February 2015.

Idrisov, E. (2014). With signed EEU treaty we get to principally new level of equal economic partnership. Here there should be no associations with Soviet past. *Interfax-Kazakhstan*. https://www.interfax.kz/?lang=eng&int_id=13&news_id=94. Accessed 20 February 2015.

Idrisov, E. (2015, December 23). Kazakhstan iavliaetsia zrelym politicheskim igrokom, a ne peshkoi ni v kakoi 'bolshoi igre'. *Novosti-Kazakhstan* http://newskaz.ru/politics/20151223/10576051.html. Accessed 6 January 2016.

International Crisis Group. (2015, May 13). *Stress Tests for Kazakhstan. Crisis Group Europe and Central Asia Briefing, 74*. http://www.crisisgroup.org/~/media/Files/asia/central-asia/kazakhstan/b074-stress-tests-for-kazakhstan.pdf. Accessed 24 August 2015.

Ionova, E. P. (2014). Novyi etap evraziiskoi integratsii. *Rossiia i novye gosudarstva Evrazii, 4*, 9–22.

Kadyrzhanov, D. (2014, May 29). Kazakhstanu otvedena rol' sub'ekta Federatsii? *Respublika*. http://www.respublika-kaz.info/news/politics/36781/ Accessed 3 February 2015.

Kalish, I. (2014) Dogovor o Evraziiskom ekonomicheskom soiuze. *Obozrevatel'*, *12*(299), 15–34.

Kasenova, A. (2015, February 11). Nazarbaev: v slozhivsheisia situatsii v Kazakhstane net viny EAES. *Tengri News*. http://tengrinews.kz/kazakhstan_news/v-slojivsheysya-situatsii-v-kazahstane-net-vinyi-eaes—nazarbaev-269888/ Accessed 25 February 2015.

Kavalski, E. (2010). Uncovering the 'new' Central Asia: the dynamics of external agency in a turbulent region. In: E. Kavalski (Ed.), *The new Central Asia: the regional impact of international actors* (pp. 1–23). Singapore: World Scientific Publishing.

Kirinitsiianov, Y. (2016, February 18). Razvoditsia nikto ne sobiraetsia. *Argumenty i fakty – Kazakhstan*. http://aif-kaz.kz/node/528. Accessed 12 March 2016.

Konurov, A. (2016, March 4). Bez EAES Kazakhstan vystupaet v roli 'nepri-gliadnoi benzokolonki'. *Atameken.info*. http://atameken.info/opinions/Bez-EAES-Kazahstan-vystupaet-v-roli-nepriglyadnoy-benzokolonki. Accessed 25 March 2016.

Khudaibergenova, A. (2014, December 31). Chem zapomnitsia kazakhstantsam 2014 god?, *Liter*. http://liter.kz/ru/articles/show/5992-chem_zapomnitsya_kazahstancam_2014_god. Accessed 25 July 2015.

Krickovic, A. (2014). Imperial nostalgia or prudent geopolitics? Russia's efforts to reintegrate the post-Soviet space in geopolitical perspective. *Post-Soviet Affairs, 30*(6), 503–528.

Kuchins, A. C., Mankoff, J., Kourmanova, A., Backes, O. (2015). *Central Asia in a reconnecting Eurasia: Kazakhstan's evolving foreign economic and security interests*. Lanham: Rowman & Littlefield.

Lane, D. (2014). Eurasian integration could offer a counterpoint to the EU and the United States, but only in close co-operation with states like India and China, http://blogs.lse.ac.uk/europpblog/2014/14/10/eurasian-integration-could-offer-a-counterpoint-to-the-eu-and-the-united-states-but-only-in-close-co-operation-with-states-like-india-and-china/ Accessed 6 March 2015.

Laruelle, M. (2015). Kazakhstan's posture in the Eurasian Union: in search of serene sovereignty. *Russian Analytical Digest, 165*, 7–10.

Lis, I. (2014, October 23). Programma podderzhki malogo i srednego biznesa (MSB). *Delovoi Kazakhstan*. http://dknews.kz/bespretsedentnaya-podderzhka-malogo-i-srednego-biznesa/. Accessed 13 March 2015.

Makanov, Z. K. (2015). Evraziiskaia integratsiia v vospriiatii naseleniia prigranichnykh regionov Respubliki Kazakhstan. *Mezhdunarodnyi zhurnal eksperimental'nogo obrazovaniia, 8*, 362–368.

Makasheva, K. N. (2009). Evoliutsiia vneshnepoliticheskikh prioritetotv Respubliki Kazakhstan v ezhegodnykh poslaniiakh prezidenta Nazarbaeva. *Vestnik KazNU, 4–5*(42–43), 117–121.

Makushina, O. (2015, October 20). Kto vedet Kazakhstan k destabilizatsii? *Respublika*. http://respublika-kaz.info/news/politics/44115/ Accessed 30 October 2015)

Malashenko, A. (2013). *The fight for influence: Russia in Central Asia*. Washington, DC: Carnegie Endowment for International Peace.

Mamaev, M. (2014, April 12). Integratsiia na postsovetskom prostranstve pozvolila Kazakhstanu diversifitsirovat' tovarooborot so stranami Tamozhennogo soiuza. *Liter*. http://liter.kz/ru/articles/show/4743-integraciya_na_postsovetskom_prostranstve_pozvolila_kazahstanu_diversificirovat_tovarooborot_so_stra. Accessed 12 July 2015.

Mankoff, J. (2014). Russia's latest land grab: how Putin won Crimea and lost Ukraine. *Foreign Affairs, 93*(3), 60–68.

Ministry of Foreign Affairs of the Republic of Kazakhstan. (2014). Foreign Policy Concept for 2014 – 2020 9 May. http://mfa.gov.kz/index.php/en/component/content/article/16-materials-english/1248-foreign-policy-concept-for-2014-2020-republic-of-kazakhstan. Accessed 3 February 2015.

Muminov, A. (2014, July 28). Bishkek khochet ot Astany $177 mln za vstuplenie v TS. *Kursiv*. http://www.kursiv.kz/news/vlast/bishkek_khochet_ot_astany_177_mln_za_vstuplenie_v_ts/. Accessed 10 March 2016.

Muhamedzhanova, D. S. (2015). Kyrgyzstan i perspektivy rasshireniia EAES dlia Kazakhstana. *Kazakhstan-Spektr, 4*(74), 57–73.

Nazarbaev, N. A. (1997). *Evraziiskii soiuz: idei, praktika, perspektivy, 1994–1997*. Moscow: Fond sodeistviia razvitiiu sotsialnykh i politicheskikh nauk.

Nazarbaev, N. (2011, October 25). Evraziiskii Soiuz: ot idei k istorii budushchego, *Izvestia*. http://izvestia.ru/news/504908. Accessed 4 October 2015.

Nazarbaev, N. (2014a, January 17). Kazakhstanskii put' – 2050. Edinaia tsel', edinye interesy, edinoe budushchee Kazakhstan – 2050. http://strategy2050.kz/ru/president/54/. Accessed 3 February 2015.

Nazarbaev, N. (2014b, February 8). Dlia Kazakhstana Evraziiskii ekonomicheskii soiuz – eto neobkhodimost'. Kazakhstan – 2050. http://strategy2050.kz/ru/news/5935. Accessed 3 February 2015.

Nazarbaev, N. (2014c, August 25). Iskliuchit' liubuiu diskriminatsiiu po iazykovomu priznaku, *KTK TV*. http://www.ktk.kz/ru/news/video/2014/8/25/29387. Accessed 4 February 2015.

Nazarbaev, N. (2014d, April 28). Ot idei Evraziiskogo soiuza – k novym perspektivam evraziiskoi integratsii. *Akorda*. http://www.akorda.kz/ru/speeches/external_political_affairs/ext_speeches_and_addresses/page_216601_vystuplenie-prezidenta-respubliki-kazakhstan-n-a-nazarbaeva-v-moskovskom-gosudarstvennom-universit. Accessed 4 February 2015.

Nazarbaev, N. (2014e, December 22). Vstrecha s predstaviteliami vedushchikh otechestvennykh telekanalov. *Akorda*. http://www.akorda.kz/ru/events/akorda_news/press_conferences/page_218761_vstrecha-s-predstavitelyami-vedushchikh-otechestvennykh-telekanalov. Accessed 4 February 2015.

Nazarbaev, N. (2016, March 2). Sanktsii i geopoliticheskie igry dolzhny navsegda uiti v proshloe. *Tengri News*. http://tengrinews.kz/kazakhstan_news/sanktsii-geopoliticheskie-igryi-doljnyi-navsegda-uyti-290025/ Accessed 15 March 2016.

Netreba, P., & Butrin, D. (2013, December 25). Pered Soiuzom staviat znaki prepinaniia. *Kommersant*.

Nurbekov, A. (2015, October 5). Nazarbayev, Obama reaffirm strategic partnership during New York meeting. *The Astana Times*, A3.

Nurgaliyeva, L. (2016). Kazakhstan's economic soft balancing policy vis-à-vis Russia: from the Eurasian Union to the economic cooperation with Turkey. *Journal of Eurasian Studies, 7*(1), 92–105.

Nur Otan. (2014). *Evraziiskaia ekonomicheskaia integratsiia: 20 naibolee chasto zadavaemykh kazakhstantsami voprosov*. Astana: Qoghamdyq sayasat instituty.

Nursha, A. (2015). *Novaia vostochnaia politika Rossii na sovremennom etape*. Almaty: IWEP.

Orenstein, M. A. (2015). Geopolitics of a divided Europe. *East European Politics and Societies, 29*(2), 531–540.

Panvilova, V. (2015, December 1). Rossiisko-turetskii krizis mozhet skazatsia na Evraziiskom ekonomicheskom soiuze, *Nezavisimaia gazeta*.

Platonova, E. (2016, January 16). Ukraina edet na vostok. *Gazeta.ru*. http://www.gazeta.ru/business/2016/01/15/8023517.shtml. Accessed 3 March 2016.

Pomfret, R. (2006). Regional trade agreements. In: M. Fratianni (ed.), *Regional economic integration* (pp. 39–54). USA: Elsevier JAI.

Pomfret, R. (2014). The economics of the Customs Union and Eurasian Union. In: S. Frederick Starr & S. E. Cornell (Eds.), *Putin's grand strategy: the Eurasian Union and its discontents* (pp. 49–58). Washington, DC: CACI.

Putin, V. (2011, October 3). Novyi integratsionnyi proekt dlia Evrazii – budushchee, kotoroe rozhdaetsia segodnia. *Izvestiia*.

Rahmetova, A. (2014, May 20). Maska vyzvala spory sredi natsionalistov. *Zona.kz*. http://zonakz.net/view-maska-vyzvala-spory-sredi-nacionalistov.html. Accessed 15 June 2015.

Rittberger, V., Zangl, B., Staisch, M. (2006). *International organisation. Polity, politics and policies*. Basingstoke: Palgrave Macmillan.

Sadvokasova, A. K. (2015). Otnoshenie naseleniia Kazakhstana k integratsionnym proektam. *Evraziiskaia ekonomicheskaia integratsiia, 3*(28), 5–12.

Sarmurzina, S. (2013, May 2). Evraziiskaia integratsiia: punkty i punktiki. *Vremia*.

Schatz, E. (2006). Access by accident: legitimacy claims and democracy promotion in authoritarian Central Asia. *International Political Science Review, 27*(3), 263–284.

Shabarova, A. K. (2014). Energeticheskaia integratsiia Kazakhstana i Rossii. In: S. V. Zhukov (Ed.), *Tsentralnaia Aziia: rol' v perestroika mirovykh rynkov nefti i gaza* (pp. 88–94). Moscow: IMEMO RAN.

Shlapentokh, D. (2012). Lev Gumilev: the ideologist of the Soviet Empire. *History of European Ideas, 38*(3), 483–492.

Slepnev, A. (2014). Eurasian integration: linking economies for future growth. *Russia Direct Monthly Memo, 8*, 8–11.

Standish, R. (2015, January 6). Putin's Eurasian dream is over before it began. *Foreign Policy*. https://foreignpolicy.com/2015/01/06/putins-eurasian-dream-is-over-before-it-began/. Accessed 24 June 2015.

Starr, S. F., & Cornell, S. E. (Eds.) (2014). *Putin's grand strategy: the Eurasian Union and its discontents*. Washington, DC: Johns Hopkins University-SAIS.

Sultanov, B. K., Dodonov, V. I. (2012). Tamozhennyi soiuz, Edinoe ekonomicheskoe prostranstvo: mify i deistvitelnost'. In: B. K. Sultanov (Ed.), *Tamozhennyi soiuz i Edinoe ekonomicheskoe prostranstvo: problemy ekonomicheskoi integratsii* (pp. 5–13). Almaty: KISI.

Syzdykova, E. S. (2013). Evraziiskaia integratsiia v otsenkakh nauchno-issledovatlskogo i ekspertno-analiticheskogo soobshchestva stran TS-EEP. *Kazakhstan-Spektr, 3*(65), 5–29.

TASS. (2015, March 20). Putin podderzhal kandidaturu Nazarbaeva na vyborakh prezidenta Kazakhstana. http://tass.ru/politika/1843212. Accessed 16 May 2015.

Turebekova, A. (2015, December 22). Kazakhstan, EU sign landmark agreement. *The Astana Times*, A3.

Tuyakbai, Z. (2015, February 12). Otkrytoe pis'mo Predsedatelia OSDP Prezidentu RK. *OSDP*. http://www.osdp.info/otkryitoe-pismo-predsedate lya-osdp-prezidentu-rk/ Accessed 16 June 2015.

Voronina, T. V. (2013). *Mezhdunarodnaia ekonomicheskaia integratsiia: teoriia, protivorechiia, tendentsii razvitiia v mire i na Evropeisko-Evraziiskom prostranstve*. Moscow: Vuzovskaia kniga.

Wunderlich, J.-U. (2007). *Regionalism, globalisation and international order: Europe and Southeast Asia*. Aldershot: Ashgate.

Yesdauletova, A., & Yesdauletov, A. (2014). The Eurasian Union: dynamics and difficulties of the post-Soviet integration. *Trames, 18*(1), 3–17.

Dr Kirill Nourzhanov is a senior lecturer at the Centre for Arab and Islamic Studies (the Middle East and Central Asia) at the ANU. He has an MA from Moscow State University and a PhD from ANU. His most recent book is *Afghanistan and Its Neighbors after the NATO Withdrawal* (Lanham: Lexington Books, 2016) co-edited with Amin Saikal.

Index

A

Abkhazia, 90, 284, 285
Accession to the EU, *see* EU enlargement
Acquis chapters/communautaire, 48, 53, 63, 66, 129, 205
See also EU accession/enlargement conditions
Agency/agent (driven actions/explanations), 3, 4, 42, 77, 79–85, 129, 248, 263, 311, 322, 328
Agenda 2000, 109
Ahtisaari plan, 189–190
Akaev, Askar, 92, 95, 96
Akhmetov, Rinat, 256
Aksenov, Sergei Valer'evich, 298, 300
al-Assad, Bashar, 273, 274, 288
Albania, 20, 30, 33, 35, 44, 46, 51, 54, 56, 64, 65, 66, 68, 193
Albanian minority, 58, 68
Albanians, 56, 191
Aliev, Heidar, 88
Andijan massacre, 94
Angola, 21
Anti-communism, 43–44
Anti-Russian(ism) sentiment, 43, 236, 287, 298, 299
Anti-Soviet sentiment, 43
Argentina, 35
Armenia, 18, 31, 33, 34, 35, 45, 46, 51, 76, 81, 84, 85, 88, 90, 91, 94, 95, 96, 316
Ashdown, Paddy, 205
Ashton, Catherine, 191
Asia, 24, 25, 89, 142, 321, 326, 334
Assembly of the Republic of Kosovo, *see* Kosovo, Parliament
Association Agreements/association (process) with the EU, 47, 121, 141, 260, 263, 286, 288, 297, 299
See also Europe Agreements
Austria, 149–150, 179
Austro-Hungarian Monarchy, 179
Authoritarianism/authoritarian, 1–4, 5, 6, 11, 13, 20, 21, 25, 26, 29–31, 35–36, 56–57, 66, 76, 77–85, 87–97, 114, 117, 176, 217, 220, 249, 262, 265, 272, 279, 281–283
Authority, 29, 35, 77, 78, 89, 180, 188, 189, 196, 199, 255, 281, 301
Automotive/automotive industry (ies), 135, 139, 142, 144

Fish, Gill, Petrovic (eds.), *A Quarter Century of Post-Communism Assessed*, DOI 10.1007/978-3-319-43437-7

Azerbaijan, 18, 19, 23, 33, 45, 46, 51, 76, 81, 86, 88, 90, 93, 95, 97, 333
Azeri Popular Front, 88

B

Bakiev, Kurmanbek, 96
Balkans/Balkan, 2–3, 6, 41–70, 104, 111, 115, 142, 188, 279, 282
  political elites, *see* Elite
  Western, *see* Western Balkans/ Western Balkan states/countries
Baltic states/Baltics, 3, 5, 26, 41–70, 86, 87, 96, 217–240, 285, 286
  ethno-nationalist identity and relations, 218–224, 232, 234
  post-Soviet intra-ethnic relations, 224–231, 233–239
Bamieh, Maria, 196
Ban Ki-moon, 190
Băsescu, Traian, 116
Barons, Krišjanis, 218
BEEPS (Business Environment and Economic) survey, *see* Surveys
Belarus, 18, 23, 26, 31, 33–36, 46, 51, 76, 81, 84–86, 88–89, 93, 95, 223–224, 226, 228, 259, 321, 323, 325, 328, 329, 331, 335
Belaventsev, Oleg Evgen'evich, 298
Belgrade, 275, 288
Belgrade-Pristina dialogue, 58–60, 69, 197, 209
Benin, 21
Bertelsmann Stiftung Transformation Index, 250
Black Sea Fleet, 287
Borisov, Boiko, 112
Bortnikov, Aleksandr Vasil'evich, 300, 304, 314
Bosnia and Herzegovina (also Bosnia-Herzegovina, Bosnia B-H and BiH and Bosnia), 4, 26, 30, 34, 69, 187
  constitutional order/status, 56
  civil/ethnic war, 45, 56, 67, 68, 272
  democratization of, 26, 30, 34, 51, 56–57
  ethnic relations, 56–58, 62
  EUPM mission in B-H. *see* EUPM
  no-fly zone, 274, 276, 277, 278
  progress in SAP and EU accession, 54, 58, 61–63
  safe areas, 274, 275, 279
Bosniak/Croat Federation, 57, 67, 69
Bosniaks/Bosnian Muslims, 14–16, 28, 30–31
Bosnian Croats, 58, 62
Bosnian Serbs, 57, 58, 62, 271, 273, 275
Bribery, 101–103, 106, 108–109, 112, 119–120, 196
BRICS (Brazil, Russia, India, China and South Africa), 290, 310, 312
Britain, *see* United Kingdom (UK)
Brussels agreement, 197
Buddhism, 14, 38
Bulgaria, 52, 58, 66, 68, 144, 151, 173
  accession to the EU, 3, 4, 47, 56, 61, 67, 100, 139
  corruption in, 4, 50, 102–112, 114–115, 117–118, 120
  democratization of, 4, 31–34, 38, 50, 55, 60, 117
Bulgarian Orthodox Church, 31–32
Bush, George H., 249, 276, 284
Byrnes, Joseph, 306

C

Cardinal law, 164
Case-studies
  critical, 100
  crucial, 100, 117–118
  deviant, 119

negative, 100
theory-infirming, 119
Catholic Church, *see* Church
Catholic/s/ism, 13, 16, 27, 29, 31, 32
Central Asia, 30, 89, 334, 335, 336
Central Bank (Russia), 311
Charisma/charismatic, 173, 175
See also Hungary; Orbán
Charter 77, 43
Chechnya, 45, 282–283, 285, 286, 309, 315
Chemical Weapons Convention, 273
China/Chinese, 24, 133, 141, 142, 258, 277, 280, 310, 312, 316, 317, 321, 324, 332, 334
Christian/ity/ians, 163
Orthodox (Eastern), 14, 15, 27, 28, 29, 31, 32, 38
Western, 13, 14–16, 27, 29, 31
Church, 165
Catholic, 29, 43
Orthodox, 31, 32
Protestant, 13, 27, 29
Churkin, Vitalii, 273
Civil liberties, 66, 75, 116, 249, 250–251
Civil society, 3, 19, 66, 80, 82, 88, 89, 92, 93, 94, 116–117, 164, 174, 230, 233, 247, 249, 250–251, 253, 257, 264, 283, 328
Civil war, 26, 45, 53, 88, 94, 203, 252, 273, 274, 275
Clinton, Hillary, 317
Coal, 13, 21
Čobutas, Medardas, 240
Coercion/coercive, 23, 83, 84
Cold War, 175, 178, 248, 271–272, 284, 286, 290, 326
Collective Security Treaty Organization (CSTO), 333
Colour revolutions, 2, 81, 93, 94, 95, 249, 254, 258
COMECON (Council for Mutual Economic Cooperation), 322
Commonwealth of Independent States (CIS), 99, 323
Communist industrialization and urbanization, 3
See also Industrialization/industrialized countries
Communist legacies, *see* Legacies
Communist nomenklatura, 178
Communist Party(ies), 21, 31, 37, 43, 44, 86, 88, 89, 91
Communist party rule, 43–45
Communist regimes/communist systems, 1, 3, 43, 44, 130, 133, 141, 145, 148, 173, 179
Community acquis, *see* Acquis chapters/communautaire
Comparative advantage, 135, 153, 155, 173
Congo-Brazzaville, 21
Constitution/constitutional, 56, 58, 59, 62, 68, 69, 92, 120, 161–181, 235–236, 250, 259, 265, 295, 313–314, 318
arrangements, 34–35, 37, 38
Consumer electronics, 134, 135–136, 155
Copenhagen conditions/criteria, 48, 64, 263
accession conditions, 56, 59, 60, 64
See also EU accession/enlargement conditions
Corruption, 2, 4, 38, 50, 55, 56, 66, 70, 154, 173, 177, 188, 189, 192, 194–196, 199, 200, 201, 202, 204, 205, 206, 208, 247, 249, 250, 251, 252, 255, 256, 257, 259
border guards, 111

Corruption (*cont.*)
customs officers, 111
economic, 101
effect, 23
grand, 103, 113
measurement of, 109, 113
petty, 113
in police, 113
political, 103, 104, 115
social, 100
Corruption Perceptions Index (CPI), *see* Transparency International's Corruption Perception Index
Council of Europe (CE), 180, 225, 231
Crime
organised, 50, 109, 110, 112, 188–189, 192, 195, 197, 199–206, 208
petty, 207
serious, 189, 193, 194–195, 196, 197, 198, 201, 208, 272
war, 195, 197
Crimea
annexation of, 238, 252, 301, 302, 304, 311, 312
decision to annex, 5, 288, 295–315
integration into Russia, 297–299, 300
polling of residents, 298–299, 305
referendum on annexation, 298, 300, 305
transfer to Ukraine in 1954, 288
Criminal justice system, 200, 202, 205–206, 207
Croatia, 2, 46, 64, 65, 67, 273
civil/ethnic war, 26, 45, 52, 53
democratization of, 4, 26, 32, 33, 51, 52–53, 55, 81, 118
CSDP (Common Security and Defence Policy), 187–188, 191, 202, 203, 206–209
civilian missions, 188, 203, 206
Cultural
memories, 222, 226, 232, 238
tradition, 235
Culture
managerial, 49
political, 27, 77–78, 97, 116, 172–174, 178–179
Customs Union (CU), 287, 317, 323, 325
CVM (Cooperation and Verification Mechanism), 110
Czech Republic/lands (also Czechia), 4, 33, 118, 132, 145–146, 148, 154
EU15 relations with/impact/ influence of, 133, 142, 149, 151–152
FDI inflow, 46, 132, 135, 141–143
foreign trade, *see* V4 countries
labour migration, *see* V4 countries
Czechoslovakia, 43, 44, 47, 306

D

Daukantas, Simonas, 219
Dayton Peace Agreement/Accords, 57, 62, 67, 68, 199
De-communization, 175
Diaspora, 174, 228
Democracy/democratization
and post-communist elections, 26, 34, 44, 66, 80–83, 93, 249
consolidation of, 5, 35, 47, 56
factors of *see* Agency/agent driven actions/factors, Structural factors *and* Legacy argument
Illiberal *see* Illiberal democracy
liberal *see* Liberal democracy
Democracy Index
Electoral (V-Dem project), 12, 17–20, 25, 27–30, 32

Economist Intelligence Unit's, 116–117, 120
Democracy score *see* NIT democracy score
Democratic Party of Socialists of Montenegro, 69
Denmark, 149
dictators/dictatorships, 1, 25, 26, 35, 41, 43, 51, 67, 68, 173, 220
Djukanovic,Milo, 69
Donbas, 252, 253, 256, 310, 315
Donetsk, 288
Dugin, Aleksandr Gel'evich, 297

E

East Germany, 43, 44
Elections, first post-communist (muti-party), 44, 66
Electoral Democracy Index, 12, 17, 18, 20, 25, 27, 28
Electrical engineering, 135–136
Elite, 3, 84, 177, 206, 218, 226, 234, 236, 248, 253, 261, 264
  communist, 43, 44, 66, 179
  oppositionist, 89, 219
  political, 24, 26, 35, 42, 62, 65, 86, 87, 88, 91, 92–93, 94, 96, 238, 253, 254–255, 258, 262, 327
  regime/ruling, 43, 79, 80, 82, 83, 85, 86, 89, 92–93, 95, 96, 97, 162, 220, 257
El Salvador, 38
Emigration, 149, 153, 227
Energy resources, 22, 32, 38
  See also Natural resources
Enlargement, *see* EU enlargement
Equatorial Guinea, 21
Estonia, 11, 29, 33, 36, 37, 46, 54, 76, 85, 86, 87, 95, 118, 217–231, 237, 239
Ethnic nationalism, 228, 235
  See also Ethnic relations/conflicts; Nationalism/nationalist
Ethnic/national minority(ies)
  in Baltic states, 217–240
  in Hungary, 163, 177
  in Kosovo, 56, 58, 281
  in Macedonia, 56
  See also Ethnic relations/conflicts
Ethnic relations/conflicts, 5, 26, 44, 56, 198, 217, 220, 221–222, 224, 230, 234, 236, 239
  See also Ethnic nationalism
Ethno-symbolism, 181
EU accession, *see* EU enlargement
EU accession/enlargement conditions, 26, 41–42, 47–48, 49, 52, 53, 56, 59, 60, 61, 63–64, 110, 262
  See also Copenhagen conditions and SAP
EU Council, 53
EU enlargement/accession
  fatigue, 42, 53, 64
  impact/leverage, 42, 49–65, 100, 117–119, 130, 145–146, 148–152, 262–264
  requirements/conditions, *see* EU accession/enlargement conditions
EU15 (fifteen EU Member States before 2004), 130, 133, 134, 142, 143, 144, 147, 148, 149, 150, 151, 152
EUFOR (European Union Force) Althea, 68, 199, 200
EULEX (European Union Rule of Law mission in Kosovo), 4, 187–209
EUPM (European Union Policy Mission in Bosnia and Herzegovina), 4, 68, 187–209

Eurasian Economic Union (EEU)
EEU Treaty, 323, 325, 330
Eurasian Court (EC), 324
Eurasian Economic Commission (EEC), 322, 324, 325, 335
Supreme Eurasian Economic Council (SEEC), 324, 331, 335
tariffs, 323, 329, 332
trade disputes, 331, 335
See also Customs Union (CU); Single Economic Space (SES)
Eurasianism, 326–327, 337
Eurasian Transcontinental Corridor, 335
Euromaidan (movement), 256, 257, 262, 297, 299
Europe Agreements, 47, 54, 66, 133, 139
See also Association agreements/ association (process) with the EU
European Commission, 50, 53, 61, 62, 63, 68, 69, 109, 110, 111, 120, 143, 146, 148, 153, 188, 194, 195, 196, 198, 205, 225, 259
European Community (EC)/ European Economic Community (EEC), 60, 61, 62, 145, 335
European Council, 48, 53, 59, 64
European Neighbourhood Policy, 66, 259, 317
European Union, *see* EU
Europe/European states
Central and East(ern), 55, 99, 219–240
East(ern), 1, 3, 6, 11, 26, 29, 37, 44, 45–47, 55, 81, 99, 139, 248, 253, 259
East Central, 3, 41–70, 179, 228, 238–239
Western, 13, 24, 26, 133, 139, 151, 335

F
Fascism, 225, 298
FDI (Foreign Direct Investment), 46, 49–51, 65, 66, 130, 132, 133, 134, 135, 138, 139–144, 152–153, 329
FIDESZ (Fiatal Demokraták Szövetsége-Alliance of Young Democrats – Hungary), 164, 165, 168, 176, 178, 179
Financial Intelligence Unit (FIU), 195
Finland, 111, 148
First post-communist/multi-party elections, *see* Elections, first post-communist (muti-party
First World War, 219, 220
Firtash, Dmitry, 256
Foreign trade, 133–138, 139, 143, 152, 154, 316, 332
Fossil fuels production, 13, 16, 19–24
Fradkov, Mikhail Efimovich, 303
France, 111, 139, 149, 220, 264, 298, 318
Freedom House (FH), 6, 50, 51, 56, 75, 116, 165, 217, 250
FSB (Federal'naia sluzhba bezopasnosti - Russian Federal Security Service), 283, 300, 303, 314, 315
FTZ (Free trade zone), 288, 335
Fujimori, Alberto, 24

G
Gabon, 21
Gaddafi, Muammar, 277
Gagauz, 89

Gamsakhurdia, Zviad, 90, 95, 97
Gazprom, 330
GDR (German Democratic Republic), *see* East Germany
Geographical location/position, 12, 16, 24, 25, 32, 37, 83, 139
Georgia/Georgians, 2, 4, 27, 31, 33, 35, 45, 46, 51, 76, 81, 84, 85, 90, 91, 94, 95, 96, 97, 100, 101–108, 113–115, 117, 119, 120, 121, 232, 271, 283, 284, 285, 287, 291, 309, 333
  corruption in, 101–108, 113–115, 117–119
Germany/Germans, 43, 44, 47, 111, 135, 139, 149, 150, 154, 220, 264, 298
Ghana, 18, 22, 38
Global Competitiveness Report (GCR), 103, 104, 106, 119
Global Corruption Barometer (GCB), 102, 103, 109
Global value chains, 134, 136, 138
Gorbachev, Mikhail, 44, 236
  reforms, *see* Perestroika
Grand Duchy of Lithuania, 218, 219, 231, 235
Great Britain, *see* United Kingdom (UK)
Greece/Greek, 4, 29–30, 31, 58, 60–61, 68–69, 133, 135, 137, 139, 142, 143, 145, 146, 148, 151, 152, 190, 264
Greek Cypriots, 31
Gross expenditure on research and development (GERD), 145, 147
Gross fixed capital formation, 130, 131
Gruevski, Nikola, 56–57, 68
Gryzlov, Boris Viacheslavovich, 303, 315
Gumilev, Lev, 326, 337

H

Hahn, Johannes, 68
Helsinki Final Act, 275–276
Highly-skilled jobs, 152
High-tech exports, 135
High-tech industries, 153
Hungarians, 144, 151, 152, 168, 172–175, 178–179
Hungary, 4, 43, 118, 130, 132, 264
  democracy/democratization, 6, 29, 32, 33, 36, 44, 47, 55
  EU15 relations with/impact/influence, 132, 135, 142, 149, 151–152
  FDI inflow, 46, 51, 132, 134, 141–143
  foreign trade, *see* V4 countries
  illiberalism/illiberal, 4, 161–181, 265
  labour migration, *see* V4 countries
  1956 Revolution of, 176
  Orbán's strategy, *see* Orbán, Viktor
Hybrid regime(s)/system(s), 76, 94, 117, 120, 265
Hybrid war, 309
Hydrocarbons, 12, 20, 21, 22, 23, 24, 32, 323, 330, 332

I

Illiberal democracy, 4, 44, 161–181, 247, 249, 261, 265
Illiberal multipartism, 173
IMF (International Monetary Fund), 47, 49, 67, 180
Indonesia, 18, 29, 35, 38, 100
Industrialization/industrialized countries, 3, 19, 22, 23, 44, 78, 140, 329
International Criminal Tribunal for the former Yugoslavia, 274
International Crisis Group, 197, 316
International law
  sovereignty, 275, 278, 333

International law
  humanitarian intervention, 275, 277, 278
International organizations, 66, 180, 221, 224, 225, 230
IPTF (International Police Task Force), 199, 201
Iraq, 271, 276, 279, 283, 316
Ireland, 148, 149, 150
Islamic fundamentalism, 274, 276, 282, 289
Islam/Islamism, 11, 13, 23, 27, 28, 30, 162
ISPA (The Instrument for Structural Policies for Pre-Accession), 65
Italy, 4, 145, 148, 149, 150, 264
Ivanov, Sergei Borisovich, 115, 300, 304, 314

J

Jacovskis, Eusėjus, 240
Jacqué, Jean-Paul, 192, 193, 194, 196
Jahjaga, Atifete, 191
Jakobson, Robert, 219

K

Kadyrov, Ramzan, 283
Kaliningrad, 286
Karadžić, Radovan, 273
Karimov, Islam, 23
Kasatkina, Natalija, 240
Kazakhstan
  democratization of, 19, 21, 31, 33, 76, 86–87, 330–331
  economic development (and relations) and EEU, 23, 321–332
  See also EEU
  multi-vector foreign policy, 319–320, 332, 334–336
  relations with Russia, 332–334
Kenya, 35
KGB (Komitet gosudarstvennoy bezopasnosti - Committee for State Security)
Khrushchev, Nikita Sergeevich, 288, 297
Knowledge economy, 129, 138, 144
Knowledge transfer, 141, 148
Kobeckaitė, Halina, 232, 240
Koler, Johan, 219
Kolokol'tsev, Vladimir Aleksandrovich, 303, 304
Kosovo
  Correction Service, 194
  crisis (1999), 275
  Customs, 194, 197–198
  independence of, 59, 67, 69, 190, 275–276, 285
  democratization of, 33, 56, 58
  Kosovars, *see* Kosovo Albanians
  Ministry of Economics, 195
  Ministry of Security, 204
  National Coordinator on Economic Crime, 195
  Parliament, 191
  progress in SAP and EU accession, 54, 58, 59
  Prosecutorial Council, 194
Kosovo Albanians, 56, 191
Kosovo Police Crowd and Riot Control Unit, 198
Kosovo Police Quick Response Team, 198
Kosovo Police Witness Protection Directorate, 197
Kosovo Property Claims Commission (KPCC), 194
Kosovo Serbs, 191, 198
Krasts, Guntars, 225

Kravchuk, Leonid, 91, 97, 248, 249, 254
Kremlin, 257, 260, 264, 298, 299, 304, 316, 317, 333
Kuchma, Leonid, 92, 96, 249, 255, 256
Kudrin, Aleksei Leonidovich, 311, 312
Kuwait, 23
Kyrgyzstan, 2, 30, 32, 33, 76, 81, 84, 86, 92, 93, 94, 95, 96, 316, 320, 334

L
Laar, Mart, 36
Labour migration, 133, 148–152
Labour productivity, 153
Landsbergis, Vytautus, 95
Laos, 100
Latin America, 11–12, 24–25, 29, 80, 141, 142
Latvia, 4, 29, 33, 46, 50, 54, 76, 85, 86, 95, 118, 217–231, 239
Lavrov, Sergei Viktorovich, 273
Leadership, 35–38, 57, 60, 96, 115–117, 119, 187, 196, 205, 208, 262, 301
Legacy/ies, 3, 23, 96
  argument, 77–79
  See also Structural explanations
  communist, 42, 99
  pre-communist, 15, 42
Leverage (international influence), 82, 83, 84, 260
Levitsky, Steven, 76, 82, 83, 84, 162
Liberal democracy, 43, 247, 248, 253, 257, 262, 264, 276, 283
Liberal-democratic opposition, 176
  See also Anti-communism
Libya, 23, 276, 277, 278, 279
Lidington, David, 192
Linkage (international influence), 82–83
Lipset, Seymour Martin, 13, 29
Lithuania, 33, 46, 50, 54, 76, 85, 86, 95, 118, 217–240
'Little green men', 294, 300
Litvinenko, Alexander, 283
Living standards, 45, 173
Livonia, 218
Livonian Confederation, 218
Lugansk, 288
Lukashenka, Aleksandr, 23, 26–27, 36, 88
Lutherans, 29
Luzhkov, Yurii Mikhailovich, 297

M
Macedonia and Former Yugoslav Republic of Macedonia (FYRM), 57, 193
  democratization, 31, 33, 35, 51, 53, 58, 59
  inter-ethnic relations, 56, 58, 68
  name-issue, 60, 61, 68
  progress in SAP and EU accession, 54, 55, 59–61, 62, 63, 64, 65
Macedonian Orthodox Church, 31
Macedonians, 59, 60
Makhkamov, Kahar, 87
Mali, 35
Malta, 145
Marcos, Ferdinand, 25
Market economy, 41, 45, 48, 51, 130, 140, 152, 172, 177, 179, 217
Marketization, 2, 42, 44, 51, 52, 66
  and economic reforms, 45
Mass movements/protests, 44, 249, 287–288, 297–298, 300
Matvienko, Valentina Ivanovna, 303, 304, 315

Mečiar, Vladimir, 130, 262
Media, 24, 66, 110, 116, 117, 165, 174, 227, 239, 247, 250, 254, 259, 327, 329, 330, 331
Medvedev, Dmitry, 102, 104, 112, 113, 115, 116, 120, 302–303, 304, 312
MENA (Middle East and North Africa), 12, 21, 30, 281
Mexico, 29, 35, 335
Michniova, Tatjana, 240
Middle East, 12, 24, 279, 281, 282, 283, 288–289
Milošević, Slobodan, 23, 33–34, 66, 273, 291
Mitrofanova, Eleonora, 230
MMA (Monitoring, Mentoring, and Advising), 188, 189, 192, 193, 197, 200, 206, 208
Modernization effect, 22, 23
Moldova, 31, 33, 35, 45, 46, 51, 76, 79, 84, 85, 89, 90, 91, 94, 95, 173, 259
Moldovan Popular Front, 89
Money laundering, 113, 203
Mongolia, 14, 17–22, 26, 33, 35, 37–38, 41
Montenegrins, 69
Montenegro
  democratization, 31, 33, 51, 52, 53, 55, 69
  progress in SAP and EU accession, 53, 54, 63
Moscow, 17, 86, 91, 282, 288, 297, 301, 304, 308, 309, 311, 316, 318, 322, 323, 333, 334
Multinational companies, 133, 134
Munich Security Conference (2007), 281
Muslim/s, 14, 15, 16, 28, 30, 31
Mutalibov, Ayaz, 88

N

Nabiev, Rakhmon, 87, 97
Nagorno-Karabakh, 45, 88, 90
Naryshkin, Sergei Evgen'evich, 303, 315
Năstase, Adrian, 111
National-ethnic relations, *see* Ethnic relations/conflicts
Nationalism/nationalist, 44–45, 86, 92, 146, 169, 171, 172, 218–219, 228, 231, 232, 234, 235–239, 272, 287, 291, 297, 330
  See also Ethnic nationalism; Ethnic relations/conflicts
NATO (North Atlantic Treaty Organization), 57, 61, 67, 220, 225, 226, 229, 239, 271–287, 297, 299, 315
  bombing of Serbia and Montenegro (1999), 68
  See also Operation "Allied Force"
  Bucharest summit 2008, 297, 315
  Operation "Allied Force", 275, 276
  Operation "Deliberate Force", 275
Natural gas, 13, 21
Natural resources, 22
  See also Energy resources
Nazarbaev, Nursultan, 315, 316, 320, 326–336
  legitimacy, 316, 326, 327
  Nurly Zhol program of infrastructure development, 335
  Nur Otan party, 328
Neighborhood diffusion effects, 13, 25
Neighborhood effects, 24
Neoconservative, 162, 171
Neoliberal
  consensus, 172
  model of transition, 139
  policy(ies), 171
Netherlands, The, 111

New Zealand, 114
NGOs (non-governmental organizations), 84, 115, 165–166, 172, 174, 258, 259, 283, 332
Nigeria, 21–22
NIT (Nations in Transit), 50, 51, 55, 56, 66
NIT democracy score, 50, 51, 55, 56, 66
North Africa, 12, 281
Norway, 21, 22, 115
Nurgaliev, Rashid Gumarovich, 303

O

Obama, Barrack, 274, 280
Odessa, 120
Ohrid Agreement (2001), 68
Oil dependence, 16, 20
Okinčicas, Česlovas, 240
Oligarchs/Oligarchization of power, 5, 24, 248, 253–257, 261, 262, 264, 287, 330
Olympics, Sochi, 310
Opposition in/to communism, *see* Anti-communism
Orange divorce, 256
Orange Revolution, external involvement in, 5, 257–261
Orange rule (2005-10), 250, 256
Orbán, Viktor
  illiberalism, 161, 166–172
  strategy, 174–180
  See also Hungary
Orthodox Christian(s)/ity/, *see* Christian/ity/ians
Orthodox church(es), *see* Church
OSCE (Organization for Security and Co-operation in Europe), 225, 238, 250, 285, 316

P

Pan Armenian National Movement, 90
Paris, 67, 112
Parliamentary/ism, 2, 34–35, 68, 86, 88, 89, 90, 91, 95, 112, 113, 114, 115, 164, 165, 168, 170, 176, 227, 250, 251–252, 303, 325, 331
Partocracy, 174
Path dependence, 77, 79, 129
Patronal polity/cs/regime(s), 96, 254
Patrushev, Nikolai Platonovich, 300, 303, 304, 314, 315
Perestroika, 86–87, 88, 236
Peru, 24
PHARE (Poland, Hungary, Assistance to the Restructuring of the Economy), 47, 65
Philippines, 29, 35, 81
Placebo, 172
Poland, 4, 47, 54, 65, 118, 237, 264, 286, 298
  church in communism, 31, 43
  democratization of, 31, 33, 35, 37, 43, 44, 46, 51
  EU15 relations with/impact/influence, 133, 134, 142, 149, 151–152
  FDI inflow, 46, 51, 132, 141–143
  foreign trade, *see* V4 countries
  labour migration, *see* V4 countries
Poles, 151, 152, 224, 232, 237, 239, 317, 327
Police
  accountability of, 200, 204
  apparatus(es), 23
  corruption in, 113
  reform of, 187–209
Polish Catholic Church, *see under* Poland
Polish-Lithuanian Commonwealth, 218, 234, 237, 238

Polish minority in Lithuania, 234, 237
Politburo (Communist Party of), 88, 89, 301–302, 306, 313
Political capacity, 116
Political choices/options, 44, 45, 52
Political will, 61–62, 100, 115, 116, 119, 195
Politkovskaia, Anna, 283
Polittekhnologi, 309
Ponta, Victor, 111, 112
Popov, Anatolii Aleksandrovich, 315
Popular Front movement, 86
Popular Front of Belarus, 88
Popular mobilization, 94, 254, 262
  See also Mass movements/protests
Poroshenko, Petro, 252, 256, 257, 262, 333
Portugal, 4, 29, 130, 133, 136, 137, 139, 142, 143, 145–146, 148, 151, 152–153
Post-communism/post-communist
  authoritarian leaders, *see* Authoritarianism/authoritarian
  choices, *see* political choices/options
  countries/states, 1, 2, 4, 26, 41, 44–45, 47, 49, 53, 55, 64, 67, 70, 99–100, 109, 112, 119, 174, 258, 263
  pathways/trajectory(ies), 1, 3, 5, 11, 16, 35, 42, 44–45, 59, 60, 67, 75–97, 129, 256, 261–264
  reform(s), 41–70
  regime change, *see* Regime, change
  region, 11–38, 42
  space, *see* region
  transition, 41–70, 217–240
Post-Soviet
  autocracy, 31
  democratization, 83, 88–90, 93
  non-Baltic states and non-Baltic post-Soviet states, 2–3, 43, 44, 50–51
  political life, 77, 96
  post-communist (Central) Asian states, 30, 89, 336
  reform(s), 41–70
  states, 75–97
  transition, 41–70, 217–240
Presidential administration, *see* Russia
Presidential/ism, 34–35, 38, 90, 91, 115, 249, 250, 251, 256, 259
Primakov, Evgenii, 289
Pristina, 58, 59, 60, 69, 197, 209, 271
Protestant churches, *see* Church
Protestant/s/ism, 13, 27, 29
Prussia, 218
Public order, 188, 189, 199, 206
Putin, Vladimir
  cronies, 295, 296, 303, 306, 307, 310, 313, 314
  personal links to, 301, 313
  poll ratings, 300
  world view, 313
Putinophobia, 330

Q

Qatar, 22

R

Rakhmon, Emomali, 87
RAND Corporation, 120
R&D (Research and Development), 133, 143, 144–148, 152, 308
Refugees, 112
Regime (political)
  capacity, 81
  change, 3, 11, 13, 16, 19, 21, 22, 24, 35, 43, 44, 45, 47, 80, 81–82, 85–96,

258, 275, 276, 279, 281, 282, 283, 284, 287
religion, 11–13, 27–32
trajectories of regime change, *see* Post-communist, trajectories
Rentier effect, 22, 23
Repression effect, 22–23, 24
Republika Srpska, 67, 288
'Revolution from above', 85
Romania, 66, 139, 144, 145, 151, 190
accession to the EU, 2, 4, 53, 58, 100
corruption in, 4, 102–112, 114–118
democratization of, 31, 33, 50, 51, 52, 55, 60, 67
Romanians, 27, 109–112, 115–116
Rome, 31, 318
Roundtable talks, 177
RTA (regional trading arrangement), 325, 335
Rule of law, 4, 48, 53, 66, 162, 164, 168, 169, 187–209, 247, 250, 251, 252, 257, 259, 264, 277
Russia, 133, 139, 189, 217
and the Baltic states, 217–240
and Crimea, 295–315
and Kazakhstan, 332–334
and the West, 271–291
and Ukraine, 248, 252, 253, 256, 257–261, 264, 271, 272, 282, 284, 286–289, 297–299, 303–305, 307, 314
democratization of, 17, 18, 19, 20, 23, 26, 31, 33, 35, 36, 38, 46, 51, 76, 77–79, 84–87, 89, 91, 92, 94, 95
corruption in, 4, 24, 101–108, 112–113, 115–117
Duma, 278, 283, 288, 303, 315
Federal Assembly, 112, 113, 284
Finance Ministry, 311
Foreign Affairs Ministry, 303, 311, 314
foreign policy, 296, 311, 312
industry policy, 311–313
peacekeepers, 278, 336
presidential administration, 300–306, 309, 310, 314
presidential power, 295–296, 302
Security Council, 300, 301–306, 307, 308, 309, 310, 311, 312, 313, 314, 315
See also anti-Russianism
Russian Federation, *see* Russia
Russian Orthodox Church, 31
Russians, 25, 77, 112, 218, 223, 224, 225, 226, 229, 232, 237, 238, 239, 284, 286, 287, 322, 329, 336

S

SAA (Stabilization and Association Agreement), 54, 61, 63, 66
Saakashvili, Mikheil, 4, 96, 114, 115, 116, 120–121, 284
Saint-Petersburg/St. Petersburg, 17, 218–219, 314
Sanctions (against Russia), 274, 307, 310, 312, 333–334, 336
SAP (Stabilization and Association Process), 50, 52, 59, 60, 64, 66, 68
SAPARD (Special Accession Programme for Agriculture and Rural Development), 65
SAP conditions, 59, 60, 64
Sarajevo, 272, 273, 275
Saudi Arabia, 18–19, 23
SBS (State Border Service), 204
Scandinavia, 218
Schengen Area, 111, 112, 115

SDSM (Socijaldemokratski sojuz na Makedonija - Social Democratic Union of Macedonia), 68
Second World War, 29, 31
Secular/ism, 27, 30, 31
Security agencies in policy making (Russia), 113, 296, 301, 307
Security Council (Russia), 279, 290, 300–302, 303–315
  apparatus, 312
  coordinating role, 301–306, 307
  interdepartmental committees, 308, 312
  meetings, 304, 315, 318
  membership, 304, 305
  Scientific Council, 308, 312
Sejdić-Finci ruling, 69
Serbia, 23, 46, 67, 69, 81, 198, 207, 273, 274, 275, 279, 285, 288, 291
  democratization, 26, 31, 32, 33, 34, 35, 51, 52, 53
  and Montenegro, 3, 46, 68
  progress in SAP and EU accession, 54, 55, 58, 59–60, 62, 63, 64
Serbian Orthodox Church, 31
Serbs, 57, 62, 190, 191, 195, 197, 198, 271, 273, 274
Sevastopol, 287–288, 297, 298, 299
Shevardnadze, Eduard, 90, 96, 114
Shoigu, Sergei Kuzhugetovich, 298, 300–301, 303
Shushkevich, StanislauSikorski, Radek, 88
Siloviki, 296, 302, 311
Siluanov, Anton Germanovich, 311, 315
Singapore, 18, 114, 120
Single Economic Space (SES), 323, 324, 328, 331
Single European Act (EC/EU), 318
SIPA (State Investigation and Protection Agency), 204
Slovakia, 2, 4, 6, 12, 33, 46, 50, 54, 55, 81, 118, 190, 262
  EU15 relations with/impact/ influence, 135, 142, 149, 151–152
  FDI inflow, 46, 130, 141–143, 144
  foreign trade, *see* V4 countries
  labour migration, *see* V4 countries
Slovaks, 149, 151, 152
Slovenia, 33, 44, 46, 54, 118, 139, 173
Smetona, Antanas, 220
Snegur, Mircea, 89
Social
  changes, 22
  composition/system/structures, 27, 32, 223
  conflicts, 224, 227
  corruption, 100
  movements, 86, 92, 95
  practices, 30, 224
  security, 308, 312
  services, 22, 23, 153
  status, 219, 220, 238
  tensions, *see* conflicts
  values, 78
Soft power, 227, 263
Solana, Javier, 68, 188
South Korea, 25
South Ossetia, 90, 284, 285
  Tskhinvali, 291
Soviet bloc, 44, 47
  See also COMECON; Warsaw Pact
Soviet economic model, 23, 50
Soviet Union/USSR, 26, 51, 75, 78, 79, 85, 86, 91, 92, 93, 95, 96, 97, 222, 224, 226, 232, 239, 254, 284, 288,

289, 290, 291, 297, 301, 317, 321
Spain, 4, 29, 34, 130, 133, 135, 136, 137, 139, 142, 143, 144, 145, 146, 148, 149, 150, 151, 152, 190
Special Accession Programme for Agriculture and Rural Development, 110
Stalin, Josef, 176
State socialism, *see* Communist regimes/communist systems
Structural explanations/factors/capacities/conditions, 3, 12–34, 42, 80, 129, *see also* Legacy argument
Supreme Court for Kosovo Property Agency, 194
Supreme Court of Hungary, 164, 181
Supreme Court of Kosovo, 194
Surveys
  attitudinal, 78, 101
  Business Environment and Economic Performance, 108, 119, 120
  experiential, 103, 108
  Perceptual, 101, 103, 108
  value, 77–79
Sweden, 148, 218, 264
Switzerland, 115
Syria, 5, 112, 271, 272–282, 286–289, 291, 292, 304
  Ghouta Chemical attack, 273

T

Taiwan, 35
Tajikistan, 33, 76, 86, 87, 93, 94, 95, 323, 334
Tartus, 279
Tavares-report, 164
Technology transfer, 143, 153
Ter-Petrossian, Levon, 90, 95, 96
Territorial reorientation, 133
Terrorism, 112, 282–283, 289, 308
Thessaloniki Agenda, 66
Trajectory/ieas (political), *see* post-communism/post-communist
Transparency International's Corruption Perception Index (TICPI), 4, 50, 51, 101, 102, 103, 112, 118, 119, 255
Treaty of Rome (EC/EU), 318
Treaty of Trianon, 174
Truman, Harry, 306
Tudjman, Franjo, 66
Turkey, 334
Turkmenistan, 20, 23, 33, 35, 37, 76, 86, 87, 93, 95

U

Ukraine, 2, 5, 25, 31, 33, 46, 51, 76, 81, 84, 86, 91-93, 94, 95, 96, 238
  Association Agreement *also* Deep and Comprehensive Free Trade Agreement (with EU), 260, 263, 286, 288, 297
  relations with EU, 248, 253, 256, 257–261, 262, 263, 264
  relations with Russia, *see* Russia
  Russian troops in, 298–300, 314
UN (United Nations)
  General Assembly, 278
  High Representative (for B-H), 26, 68, 205
  Mission in Kosovo, 189–190
  peace-keeping forces, 279
  Security Council, 70, 189–190, 273–279, 281
  Security Council Resolution, 189–190, 273, 274, 275, 276, 279

United Kingdom (UK), 115, 148, 149, 150, 192, 220, 273–274, 286
United States (US/USA)
  exceptionalism, 280–281
  State Department, 280, 287
  Washington, 280, 316, 318
  White House, 280
USSR, *see* Soviet Union
Uzbekistan, 11, 23, 33, 37, 76, 86, 87, 93, 94

V
Valančius, Motiejus, 219
Valdemars, Kritjanis, 218
Valiukov, Valentin Vladimirovich, 308
V-Dem (Varieties of Democracy) project, 12, 15, 65
V4 (Visegrád Four) countries (Czech Republic, Hungary, Slovakia, Poland), 4
  economic transition, development and trends, 129–155
  foreign trade, 133–138
  labour migration, 148–152
  R&D (Research and Development), 133, 143, 144–148, 152, 308
Venezuela, 21
Victimization, 174
Vienna, 13, 14, 15, 24, 25, 32
Vilnius Summit, 260
Voting booth revolution, 168, 179

W
Wages, 84, 139, 140, 149, 153
Warsaw, 31
Warsaw Pact, 276
Waves of democratic change, 2
Wealth, 13, 14, 16–19, 22–24, 120, 177, 255, 256
West (the)
  assistance for (post-communist) reforms, 45–52, 65, 66
  civilization, 220
  hegemony, 290, 291
  norms/values, 248, 310
  political and economic concepts, 42
  proximity to, 14, 16, 24–27
  relations with, 271–291, 334
  technology and expertise, 49, 144, 192, 197, 202, 206, 207, 296, 303, 311, 312, 313
  unilateralism, 272, 275, 281
West Africa, 21
Western Balkans/Western Balkan states/countries, 6, 187, 263
  post-communist reforms, 47, 50–52, 55–57, 59, 60, 61, 62, 65, 66
  relations with the EU, 2, 42, 50, 52–55, 57–65, 263
  status of the multi-national States in, 56, 57, 58, 59, 60, 61, 62, 63, 64, 65
Western Europe
  neighbours, 24, 26
  relations with, 151, 335
Work-based society, 167
World Bank, 47, 49, 67, 99, 103, 108, 119, 120, 131, 154, 179, 180

Y
Yanukovych, Viktor Fedorovich, 96, 248, 249, 251–252, 256, 259, 260–261, 284, 287
Yatsenyuk, Arseniy, 287
Yeltsin, Boris, 24, 36, 91, 95, 272, 291
Yugoslavia (former), 44, 57, 58, 67, 272, 273, 274, 275, 276, 279, 285, 287, 288
  Federal Republic of (Serbia and Montenegro), 69
Yushchenko, Viktor, 249, 251, 255, 256, 259–260

The manufacturer's authorised representative in the EU is Springer Nature Customer Service Centre GmbH, Europaplatz 3, 69115 Heidelberg, Germany. If you have any concerns regarding our products, please contact ProductSafety@springernature.com

Printed and bound by CPI Group (UK) Ltd, Croydon, CR0 4YY
30/09/2026
02225195-0009